8/95

COMSTOCK LODE

COMSTOCK LODE

LOUIS L'AMOUR

BANTAM BOOKS
TORONTO · NEW YORK · LONDON · SYDNEY · AUCKLAND

COMSTOCK LODE
A Bantam Book / March 1981
Louis L'Amour Hardcover Collection / August 1986

If you would be interested in receiving bookends for The Louis L'Amour Collection, please write to this address for information:

The Louis L'Amour Collection
Bantam Books
P.O. Box 956
Hicksville, NY 11801

ISBN 0-553-06290-5

Published simultaneously in the United States and Canada

Bantam Books are published by Bantam Books, a division of Bantam Doubleday Dell Publishing Group, Inc. Its trademark, consisting of the words "Bantam Books" and the portrayal of a rooster, is Registerd in U.S. Patent and Trademark Office and in other countries, Marca Registrada, Bantam Books, 666 Fifth Avenue, New York, New York 10103.

PRINTED IN THE UNITED STATES OF AMERICA

10   9   8   7   6   5   4   3   3   2

To Joseph
and Shirley Wershba

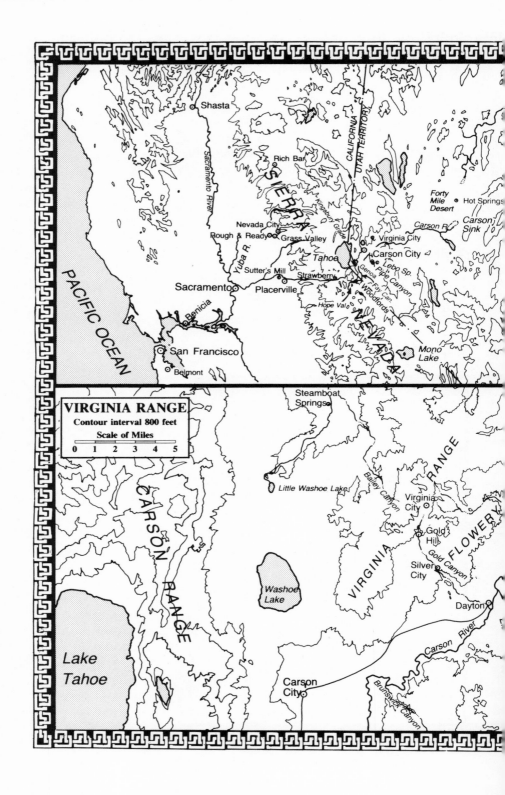

Shasta

Rich Bar

SIERRA

CALIFORNIA
UTAH TERRITORY

Sacramento River

Forty
Mile
Desert

Hot Springs

Carson R.

Carson
Sink

Nevada City
Rough & Ready
Grass Valley

Virginia City

Yuba R.

Kingsbury Grade

L. Tahoe

Carson City

Lebo Sp.

Sutter's Mill

Strawberry

Genoa

Pipe Canyon

Fay Can.

Sacramento

Placerville

Woodfords

Hope Val.

NEVADA

Benicia

PACIFIC OCEAN

San Francisco

Mono
Lake

Belmont

VIRGINIA RANGE
Contour interval 800 feet
Scale of Miles
0 1 2 3 4 5

Steamboat
Springs

RANGE

CARSON

Little Washoe Lake

Bailey Canyon

Virginia
City

VIRGINIA

Gold
Hill

FLOWERY

Gold Canyon

Silver
City

RANGE

Washoe
Lake

Dayton

Lake
Tahoe

Carson River

Carson
City

Brunswick Canyon

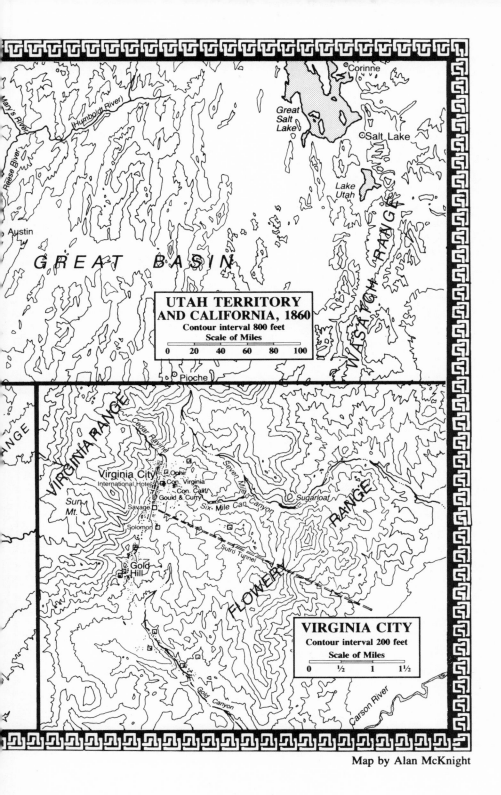

**UTAH TERRITORY
AND CALIFORNIA, 1860**
Contour interval 800 feet
Scale of Miles
0   20   40   60   80   100

VIRGINIA CITY
Contour interval 200 feet
Scale of Miles
0   ½   1   1½

Corinne

Great
Salt
Lake

Salt Lake

Lake
Utah

WASATCH RANGE

(Humboldt River)

Mary's River

Reese River

Austin

G R E A T   B A S I N

Pioche

RANGE

VIRGINIA RANGE

Cedar Ravine

Virginia City

Ophir

International Hotel

Con. Virginia

Con. Calif.

Gould & Curry

Savage

Sun
Mt.

Six- Mile Can.

Seven Mile Canyon

Sugarloaf

RANGE

Solomon

Sutro Tunnel

FLOWERY RANGE

Gold
Hill

Gold Canyon

Carson River

Map by Alan McKnight

PART ONE

ONE

It began with a dream, a dream that ended in horror.

It began in a thatched cottage with wind around it and rain beating on the shutters, with a flagstone floor and the smell of fish frying, and his mother putting blue plates on the table and his father sitting by the fire. It began in Cornwall, in England, in 1849.

It began with listening to the storm blowing in from the sea and the fire hissing from occasional drops that fell down the chimney.

It began with Val Trevallion's father saying, "Mary, we are going to America."

His mother stopped, holding a blue plate in her two hands, staring at his father.

"We are going to California, to the goldfields. There will be no more mines for our son, and this day I have decided."

Tom Trevallion leaned over and knocked his pipe empty of ash on the edge of the hearth. "Tomorrow we will go to Gunwalloe."

"But aren't there mines in the goldfields?"

"It is placer-mining like we tinners used to do before the deep mines began. A man need not go underground there, nor a lad, either.

"Look at him! He has been a year in the mines now and the color is gone from him. He was a fine lad with a fine brown color to him when he worked with the fishing. I'll not have it, Mary. He shall not live hidden from the sun as I have."

"But how can we, Tom?"

"I've put by a little . . . not enough, but something. And we shall go to Gunwalloe by the sea for a few days."

"To Gunwalloe? Oh!" She realized her husband was speaking of the treasure. "But it is useless. So many have tried, and some of them for years."

"Aye. Yet I have been told a thing or two. I have spent days and nights with old Tregor. The man's dying now and well he knows it. He's always liked me, Mary—"

"Your grandfather was shipmates with him. They went through it together, those two."

3

"He's whispered a thing to me, the old man has, and nothing about the money-ship, she from whom the coins wash ashore from time to time. 'Tis another vessel entirely, their own vessel. When she was sinking off the Lizard some of the men escaped overside, each with his own keeping, the share each man had for himself. They tried to run up the coast to Gunwalloe where they had friends, but it was a bloody beast of a gale, and they went on the rocks off there, and only grandfather and old Tregor reached the shore.

"Most of what they had, and those with them, still lies yonder, off the rocks. No great treasure, mind you, but enough for California, I'm thinking."

"But if you start diving off the rocks you'll have half the village around you!"

"At night, Mary, only at night. On the last days of fishing . . . 'twas then I found the wreck.

"We've but one son, Mary, and he must have his chance. In the old days of tinners it was not a bad thing, working along the streams and such. We were out in the air and working for ourselves only. Now it is the big companies who have it all, and they do not like me, Mary. We tinners were a different breed, too free to suit them.

"It's for America we are, a bit of land and a cow, some chickens for eggs, and a horse or two for riding or driving to a cart."

His father was dark of visage, as Val would be, a man square-shouldered and powerful from hard work and the lifting. A man who talked little but was listened to because of the manner he had. Those in charge at the mines liked his father little because of his straight back and the way he looked right at them when he spoke. Yet they kept him on because he was the best of them.

Val himself had gone into the mines at the age of twelve, as did most boys, but it was the change in him that led his father to move. That and some drive within himself that asked for better things.

The day the Trevallions left for Gunwalloe was a memorable one. Jenkins, the owner himself, had come around to the house to ask his father back, a thing unheard of, with all the village watching from behind doors and curtains.

"Leave now, man, and you canna come back. I will not have my men coming and going."

"I shall not come back," Tom Trevallion said. "There are mines over the sea, and I shall have one of my own."

"Fool's talk! What do you know of gold? You're a tinner and a copper man, maybe, but gold? 'Tis another thing."

"I can learn."

"Have you money enough then?"

"We've put some by, and I'll sell the house."

Val stood beside his father, a proud lad to see it, for never before had the owner come down to a miner's cottage to ask after any man.

His father looked the owner in the eye and said, "Why don't you come yourself, then? Sell this and come out to California. This—" he waved a hand, "is but a teapot operation to what you will find there."

This made the owner angry. "A teapot opera—"

"You're a canny man," his father said, "you would do well, yon."

Jenkins grunted his disdain. "You dare to advise me? You'll starve over there, if you manage to leave at all. You will starve or drown or be killed by savages."

He started to turn away, his back stiff with offense. "You have been given your chance to forget such nonsense but now I'll not have you. Go, then! Go!"

Jenkins strode away down the street, anger and damaged pride in every step. His father had turned to see his mother smiling. "Ah, Tom, if starve it is to be I shall starve a proud woman! Who would think to hear the owner told so completely. You are a bold man, Tom."

"I shall needs be bold. Do not think I go lightly from here, Mary. We shall face trouble. But now we will go to Gunwalloe."

"You will sell the cottage?"

"I have spoken to Edward Bayne, the new man who keeps the shop, and he would be having it from me, and a fair price, too."

Val had looked up at his father then and asked, "Is it far to California?"

"It is far . . . very far, I am told."

"Will we go upon a ship?"

"A very small ship, I am afraid, with very many other people. Then, when we get to America, I must find work and when we know what we are about, we must buy a wagon—"

"A wagon?"

"Aye. One is needed for the crossing of the great plains. We will need cattle for the drawing of it, and a horse for riding. And a rifle-gun for shooting game."

"But what of the wardens?" Mary protested.

"There are no wardens. The game run wild for any to hunt who will."

"Have you shot a rifle?"

"I have not. Nor have I so much as held one in my hands. Here in England only the great landowners may hunt, so the only guns I have seen were in the hands of soldiers. But I shall learn. We all must learn."

"Father? What are 'plains'?"

"It is like a moor. It is grassland, miles upon miles of it, with no trees but those along the streams, and there are few streams."

"Tom? Is it as far as London? To cross the plains, I mean?"

He looked at her, smiling. "Will Holder, you know? He who returned to Helston for his family? He said it would be five months in the crossing . . . perhaps six."

He paused. "It is very far. We must carry with us all we will need. It will cost us dear to go to California, Mary, but it will be worth it.

"Do you remember Will Holder? He left here with nothing, and when he came back he wore fine clothes, had new boots, and with money to spend."

They went down the road in the morning to Gunwalloe by the sea, and they went to the house where Mary Trevallion was born and where her brother Tony still lived. "You still have the boat?" his father asked.

"Aye." Tony was a stocky man with a blue kerchief at his throat and a leather coat. "You have need of a boat?"

"There are fish in the sea, yonder. If you will help you may have a bit of what I catch."

"You will catch nothing if you seek more than fish. John Knill searched long for the King of Portugal's ship but found nothing. You will find nothing, too."

"Have you a memory for old Tregor?"

"Who does not, who lives in Gunwalloe? He was of this place, but always away upon the sea, and when at last he came back, he came walking up from the sea, all dripping and soaked. I remember it well. He staggered from the waves like a man drunken. And then away he went to live out his years in Mullion."

"Did he not come back to Gunwalloe at all?"

"He did. A time or two he returned for the fishing and to share a pint or two in the tavern."

"All those years? What did he live on then?"

Tony shrugged. "It is said he cared for horses for the Godolphins."

"What he lived on," his father had said, "was what he brought back from the seas. Old Tregor is dying now, and he left to me what is out there, and when I have had what I need, the rest is for you. When Old Tregor went out fishing he was actually diving, at a place he knew. There's no enormous treasure, just some packets of it, and rich enough for the likes of you and me.

"When I have had mine there will be a bit left. Use it sparingly, and let no man or woman know what you have, and there will always be a loaf in the cupboard and a pint on the table."

When the morning came they went down the coast for the fishing, and when dark was coming on, they crept back up the coast and dropped anchor off the rocks. While Tony sat with a line out, Tom Trevallion dove down, and when he came up he held a small box, and in it were a few gold coins and a piece or two of jewelry. Then, while he rested, Tony went down and came up with a canvas sack, small but with gold coins also, a silver buckle, and some odds and ends.

It was not much, for it was what each man had for himself before the big treasure was divided, that stormy night long ago. But each man brought the share he had at hand when they fled the boat, before it broke up and sank off Gunwalloe. Tregor had lived his life away on what remained of one or two of the shares.

Tony kept only one gold coin for himself, but came away with the knowledge of where the boat lay. At least two more packets were down there, and possibly a third.

The morning after, Tony drove the Trevallions in his cart to Falmouth, a far piece. The ship lay there, small, dirty, and over-crowded, but a ship.

Only hours later they were at sea. Val loved the great sails, the creak of the bumpkins, and the rush of water along the hull. The storms frightened him, yet "I could be a sailor," he told his father.

" 'Tis a dog's life, that. Work by day and by night, and naught but poor food and much abuse with small payment at the end."

"But they are out in the air!" Val protested.

"Aye," his father agreed, "there is that."

"When we reach America we will not go to California at once?"

"Will Holder advised against it. First, he said, we should come to know the people and the climate of things. A newcomer can make mistakes."

"Have we enough, then?" Mary asked.

"With care we've what is needed for California and to hold us a bit until I can earn."

"It seems a lot . . . the gold, I mean."

"Not much when we think of all that must be bought. A wagon, oxen, a horse, a rifle, and much food. Will says a poor man cannot go west, it is too expensive by far."

Val's father and mother talked of little else but California and what they would do there and how they should live. It seemed a far off, magnificent dream, but all aboard the ship were dreaming, some of one thing and some of another.

Gold was everywhere, people said, they had simply to pick it off the bottom of streams, or wash it from the earth. Tom Trevallion smiled at that.

"They will sing another tune when they have worked at it for a few hours. We tinners grew up panning for tin before the big mines took over everything. It is hard, hard work."

A Yorkshireman who slept near them spoke up. "You may have your gold and your California. I am for Oregon. I want no gold, just the good earth. Let me dip my hands in good black loam and feel the richness of it in my fingers.

"Treat the earth kindly, my friends, and it will give you comfort, security, and all a man may need. If you plant a flake of gold in the earth, will anything come of it? But plant a seed and it will repay you many times over."

Their ship took them to New Orleans, and a river steamer to Westport. In New Orleans they all bought new clothes. "We will need them," his father advised, "they will be cheaper here than in St. Louis or Westport."

At Westport suddenly their plans changed. Mary Trevallion saw a woman crying. She was seated in the lobby of the small tavern where they had taken a room until they found a wagon in which to live and travel.

"Tom," Mary said suddenly, "this woman's husband has died. She is left with two small children and a wagon and stock she cannot use."

"She will have no trouble selling them here."

"Why not to us?"

The woman looked up. "If you will buy today I will sell cheap. I want to go home. I want to go back to my folks."

The wagon was strongly built and painted blue. Tom Trevallion, who knew much of such things, examined it carefully.

"You can have the oxen—there are eight head—for two hundred dollars. The wagon should be worth fifty."

Val's father had squatted on his heels to study the underpinning. There was a spare wagon-tongue lashed there and a sheet of canvas, suspended by its corners and almost the length of the wagon. It sagged a little.

"What's that for?"

"Buffalo chips," a bystander said. "The womenfolks walk behind the wagon and pick up buffalo chips and toss them onto that canvas. They're the only fuel you are likely to find."

"Buffalo chips?" Mary Trevallion's distaste was obvious. "But aren't they—"

The man grinned. "They are, lady, but they're very dry . . . old ones. They make quite a good fire. Ask any plainsman."

They bought the wagon and the animals. A man in a store-bought suit, a pale man with hollows at his temples, stood by and watched the purchase completed. He was neatly dressed but he did not smile, merely watched through pale eyes. His beard was sparse but carefully trimmed.

A farmer standing by lighted his pipe and glanced at Tom Trevallion. "You made you a good deal. Mighty lucky to have that much. Two hundred dollars is about a year's income for a farmer, these days. I'd like to go west, m'self, if I could afford it."

The woman took the coins Tom Trevallion paid her, and the man with the pale eyes stepped quickly forward, reaching for one of the coins. "May I see that?" He looked at the woman. "I'll give it back. It is a rare coin, I think."

The coin was gold, quite heavy. "A doubloon," the man said. "One sees very few of them." He looked around at Tom Trevallion. "Where did you get it?"

"Something my father brought from the wars. Had it for years," he added.

The man with the pale eyes handed back the coin. "Interesting," he said. "Have you more of them?"

"No," Val's father spoke stiffly, and turned away. The man lingered, watching them.

It took the Trevallions another week to prepare, to buy what was needed in tools, ammunition, and food supplies.

The woman from whom they bought the wagon had a prepared list. Her husband had talked to several wagonmasters and frontiersmen before compiling the list and it was, she assured them, as complete as they were apt to find.

For each adult 200 lbs of flour, 75 lbs of bacon, 30 lbs of pilot bread, 10 lbs of rice, 25 lbs of sugar, ½ bushel to a bushel of dried beans, 1 bushel of dried fruit, 2 lbs of saleratus, 10 lbs of salt, ½ bushel of cornmeal, 5 lbs of coffee, 2 lbs of tea, ½ bushel of corn, parched and ground, a keg of vinegar, and assorted medicines. They also bought a cast-iron Dutch oven and skillet as well as a small sheet-iron stove and boiler that could be used inside the wagon when rain or strong winds made outside cooking impractical. Added to that was a pair of ten-gallon kegs for water, to be fastened one on each side of the wagon, a churn, cups and plates of tinware, and tools.

"I will sell you my husband's rifle," the woman said. "It is of a calibre that uses about thirty-two to the pound. There is also a pistol."

"We had thought of staying in the States until June," Mary said. "We have so much to learn."

"It is too late," the woman told them. "Not earlier than April fifteenth as there is no grass to feed your stock, and if you leave after May fifteenth you won't make it through the Sierra passes because of snow."

There wasn't much to Westport, just a cluster of log and frame buildings on the bank of the river. Tom Trevallion moved his family into the wagon to save money. Beside the fire that night he put his hand on his son's shoulder. "It is a different life, this. The people are different. We've got to learn to do things right the first time, because where we are going there isn't much room for mistakes. Keep your eyes open, Val, and you will learn fast."

"That man who asked you about the gold, he was in the store when you bought things."

"I saw him."

"He started talking to me," Mary Trevallion said, "asked when we were going." She looked up at her husband. "I told him we had not decided, that we might decide to stay here and farm."

Tom Trevallion smiled. "Good girl. No reason to let anybody know our business."

"That man bothers me. I don't like him."

Val's father shrugged. "Just nosy . . . lots of people are."

Val helped load the wagon. He learned to build a fire, to grease the axles, to care for the oxen. As was his way, he said little. When two or three of the wagonmasters and trail guides got together, Val managed to sit close.

On the day after they bought the wagon, Val went into the street to pick up a coil of rope his father had bought. The man with the pale eyes was seated against the side of the store-building eating a piece of bread. He seemed to have nothing else.

Walking back there were several young men from fifteen to twenty-five years standing in a group, talking. ". . . says he pays for everything in gold."

"Damned furriner!" another said. "How's he have so much when we're down to our last?"

Were they talking of his father? Val hurried to the wagon. "Papa? I heard some men—"

His father listened. "They could have been speaking of many a man here, Val. But I have no choice. It is gold that I have, although little enough of it, so it is gold I must spend."

Later his father came to him. "Do you watch over the little Redaway girl. Her father and I must go up to town on business. Your mother is resting and Mrs. Redaway will be bathing in her wagon. We shall be back soon."

"But, pa!" Val protested.

"Do as you are told. She is a fine little girl and you can play—"

"*Play!*" he scoffed. "She's only *eight!*"

"No matter. Each must do his bit and that is for you. Be kind, now."

Her name was Marguerita, she told him politely, but her papa called her Grita.

Val started by telling Grita stories, and what followed was horror.

TWO

Never before had Val talked to a strange girl. Those he had known at Redruth or St. Just-In-Penwith knew all the stories he knew, and it was not much different at Gunwalloe, although he had known almost nobody there. This was different.

Grita Redaway was a very thin girl with large eyes that seemed dark in the darkness. She listened wide-eyed as he told her of working deep underground, of the tommy-knockers who haunted the mines, and then of shipwrecks and storms along the rocky coast of Cornwall.

The two wagons stood isolated, the next closest wagon was at least two hundred yards away, beyond a roll of the hill and some trees. Their camp-fire had burned low. Val could hear the water splashing in the tin tub where Grita's mother was bathing.

Val and Grita were seated back at the very edge of the brush inside the circle of darkness. Trevallion's voice was low, so as not to disturb his mother who rested in their wagon. He was in the midst of a shipwreck off the Lizard when he became aware of a mutter of voices, drunken voices.

"We've got to move fast," somebody was saying, a voice not at all drunken. "The wagons will be empty and that gold is hidden—" The sound trailed away, and several men came into the circle of light. Instinctively, Val put a hand over Grita's mouth and pulled her back under the brush.

One of the men took a pull at a bottle, and another grabbed it from him. "Hey! Gimme that! Share an' share—"

"George?" It was Grita's mother. "Is that you?"

One of the drunken men lurched toward the wagon and jerked back the canvas. "No, this here ain't George, this here's—" His voice broke off sharply and then . . . a scream.

Holding Grita tightly, keeping her face against his chest, young Val watched in horror. The first man leaped into the wagon and others scrambled after him.

There was a stifled scream and the sounds of men brawling and angry.

At least four of them were in the wagon and others were struggling to get in. Suddenly Val's mother thrust her head from the rear of their wagon. "Edith? *Edith?* What is it? What—"

The men outside the wagon turned and rushed at Mary Trevallion. All but one. That one drew back in the brush opposite the children and seemed to be waiting.

Several men came from the wagons, almost falling over each other, and suddenly, into the glare of light came Grita's father. He came striding into the circle of light totally unaware. Stopping suddenly he looked around wildly. "Wha—"

"Kill him," somebody said, and suddenly they rushed at Redaway, striking and clubbing.

He struck out wildly, landing a grazing blow. He struck again, and then a club drove him to his knees. Redaway tried to rise, his head streaming with blood, and he was beaten down again.

Frozen in fear the boy clutched Grita to him, knowing if he released her she would run to her mother and be killed.

Suddenly someone shouted. "Look out! *Run!* Here they come!"

The violators scattered. One man toppled from a wagon, falling full length, then getting up, looking around, obviously frightened. There were bloody scratches on the side of his face. For an instant he was staring hard right at them, and Val recognized him as the man who had spoken of those "damned furriners" only that afternoon.

As quickly as they had come, they were gone. And then the lone man came quickly from the shadows and scrambled into the wagon. There was a shuffling around and then a muffled scream and a thud. The canvas curtains parted and the man came out, holding his father's money-box in his hands.

The thief took a quick look around and started away when George Redaway groaned. The man stopped, then turned slowly. Drawing a pistol, he stood astride the fallen man. Holding the money-box under his arm, he held the pistol in two hands and shot Grita's father between the eyes. Then he thrust the pistol behind his belt and walked away.

Grita tugged at Val. "Please! You're hurting me."

He released her slowly. "Don't look," Val said sternly. He took her by the hand. "We've got to go get papa."

Afterward Val could never remember the days that followed. They had found his father, loaded with a few last-minute purchases, and somehow he had blurted out his story of what had happened. His father dropped his purchases and ran. The storekeeper folded his apron, caught up a pistol, and ran after him.

The storekeeper's wife caught him as he started to leave. "You . . . you two stay here with me. It's for the men to do now. There's nothing you can do. It's *awful!*" she said. "Just *awful!*"

During all those days he stayed close to Grita. She was younger, he told himself, and she had lost both her parents. She clung to him, and he comforted her as best he could.

"Boy," one man advised him, "you be careful who you tell that you recognized one of those men. If they find that out, they'll try to kill you."

"Not much we can do." The man who spoke wore a badge. "Drifters, more than likely, scattered to the four corners by now. Him with the scratched face that the boy saw coming out of the wagon, he won't be showing himself until it's healed.

"Anyway," he added, "that crowd trampled out any footprints."

"I'll find them," Tom Trevallion said.

"Be careful when you do," the man with the badge said, "there's some rough men in that lot."

The storekeeper's name was Kirby. He reached into a drawer and drew out a pistol. "Tom, you take this. You may meet them close up where a rifle won't be much use. You take this—it's a gift from me—and good luck to you."

The bodies of Grita's mother and father and Mary Trevallion were buried side by side on a little hill not far out of Westport. Val clung to his father's hand, his other arm around Grita. Numbly he stared at the casket being lowered into the grave, and he could associate none of it with his mother. She was gone . . . that was all.

When it was over he asked, "What will we do now?"

"We'll go west," his father said. "Mary would wish for it to be that way."

"What about Grita?"

"We will take her with us. She is one of us now."

The minister spoke up. "She may have kinfolk who would take her in. Did they ever speak of anybody else?"

His father frowned. "Come to think of it, George did speak of his wife having a sister. We shall go through her things. In fact, Marguerita may know where she lives."

Slowly, Val walked back to where Grita stood alone. She looked up at him, her eyes wide and frightened. She was alone now, all alone. "You will be one of us," he said. "My father has said it. Although," he added, "he says you have an aunt."

"Yes. Aunt Ellen. She lives in New Orleans."

"We'll have to go through your folks' things to find her address." Val hesitated, hanging his thumbs in his pants pockets. "Wish you could stay with us, though. I never had no girl around before." He flushed. "You're kinda nice."

His father wrote a letter, and it went down the river on a steamboat, and then they waited.

Kirby came around to see them. "Tom," he said, "if you're figuring on going west, you'd best go. Time's short if you want to make it through the passes."

"I'll wait until I hear from her aunt," he said.

Kirby studied him. He had grown thinner, the bones in his face seemed sharper. "You've got a fine boy, there," he said. "He's going to miss his mother."

"Aye." Tom Trevallion stood quiet for a minute or so, and then he said, "I miss her, too. God, how I miss her!"

Ellen Devereaux arrived on the next boat from New Orleans, and she was not at all what Tom Trevallion expected. She was slim and very lovely, with cool eyes and an easy, gracious manner. "Thank you, Mr. Trevallion, for taking care of my niece. She tells me you have both been wonderful." Ellen Devereaux looked down at Val, smiling. "She has quite a case on you, young man, and I can see why. You're a handsome lad."

She turned to his father. "They got away? The men who did this?"

"They did. The boy here, he saw some of them, but nobody recognized any of them from his descriptions. We didn't talk about that much," he added, "being fearful they might come back and kill the boy."

"That sort of thing is rare. They were a bunch of drifting scum, but even so, they were drunk."

"My brother-in-law? He was killed outright?"

"They beat him down," Val said. "With clubs and fists. There were eight or nine of them. Then later one man stood over them and shot him right between the eyes."

"Afraid of a witness," Tom suggested. He frowned. "From what the lad says there was something peculiar about that. The man who did the killing had stood aside during most of it, but he was the one who got our money and he was the one killed George."

"They should be punished!" Ellen Devereaux's eyes were no longer cool. "Every one of them!"

"There's no law out there. No way to reach them."

Val spoke suddenly. "I will kill them. I will kill every one of them. I will kill them or die trying."

Startled, they looked at him. Grita clutched his hand suddenly, and Ellen said quietly, "I know how you feel, Val. I could kill them, too, but you must not let it ruin your life. You're young. You've much to live for. Someday you will have a nice home, you will get married—"

"I want to marry Grita."

She laughed. "Now, there, Grita! You have your first proposal! If you could call it that."

The next morning they joined a wagon train for California.

Overhead was a vast blue dome of the sky, around them an ocean of grass, rippling away in endless waves when touched by the wind. Day after day the oxen plodded on. At night there were camp-fires, the circle of wagons, and wolves howling. Several times they saw Indians, but they were not molested.

Then the rains came, and the prairies became muddy; they made slower time. Once they camped within sight of the previous night's camp.

Val drove the oxen at times. He took them to water, built the fires. His father had become morose and silent, speaking rarely and then in anger. Val learned to keep silent and to keep his distance. Sometimes at night, watching the camp-fire from near their own wagon, his father would start to talk, and for hours he would ramble on about mines and mining, about drilling, breaking rock, using explosives. Long afterward Val would remember those times and realize that his father was trying, in the only way he knew how, to pass on what knowledge he had, and he would understand how inadequate his father felt at suddenly becoming an only parent, trying to fill the roles of both father and mother.

He had ever been a solitary man, totally involved with his wife and child but depending on his wife to offer their son the gentleness and warmth that he somehow could not impart.

Val had always understood that his father loved him, but somehow that feeling had always come to him through his mother.

Westward they went, day after plodding day, moving at a pace that never exceeded about two and a half miles per hour. Over the long flatlands, up the low hills, down steep declivities, gathering buffalo chips as they went against the fires of the night, and ever alert for the Indians that never came.

Never until one morning they awakened to find some of the saddle-stock driven off. Because of Val's affection for their mare, it had been kept inside the wagon circle and so was safe.

Nobody saw an Indian, nobody heard an Indian, only the horses were missing and there were unshod pony tracks. Several of the men were for pursuing them and trying to recover their stock. The guide advised against it.

"That there was a war party headin' for home," he said. "Several of them was afoot and they needed mounts. You ain't about to catch them, and if you did, somebody would lose his hair . . . maybe all of you.

"There was," he added, "about twenty warriors in that party. That's enough to work all kinds of mischief. You just be glad they taken your horses an' kep' goin'."

Later, the scout rode out when it was Val's turn to watch the horses. He drew up beside Val and cut off a chew. He offered the plug to the boy, who shook his head. "That pa o' yourn seems a right solid man," the scout commented, "but quiet. Heard he lost his woman, your ma."

"Yes, sir."

"It's a hard thing to lose somebody you set store by, a mighty hard thing. There's men who find another right off, there's others never get over it. I reckon that's the kind your pa is. He's a mighty lonely man, your pa. You got to think of that, boy, you got to understand him.

"Had a couple of horses one time, always ran together, stayed together. If I rode off on one without the other, the one left behind he sulked until I got back. One got hisself killed by a b'ar . . .'t other one was never much good after.

"Your pa's a one-woman man. It's like he's lost part of hisself. You think of that, boy, an' if he's hard or angry, you make allowances, y' hear me? You make allowances."

The scout got to his feet. "Come to think of it, that's how we all live with each other, by makin' allowances."

A few days later, with the mountains showing snow-topped crests against the sky, he stopped by again. "You an' your pa take my advice. These here are just the first mountains, and they already got snow. You take my advice an' stop this side of the Sierras an' wait for spring. A man can die in those passes of a winter."

The scout said, "Name's Hiram Ward, son. Don't know we ever met, really." Ward glanced at him. "I hear tell you saw those men who kilt your ma."

"I saw them. I'd know some of them."

"Can you describe them to me?"

Slowly, carefully, he described those he had seen clearly. Some of the faces had never been turned his way, some had been in shadow. One he would never forget. It was the one who had stood over George and shot him. He did not describe him.

"That one with the scratched face. The way you tell it, that sounds like Obie Skinner. He's a bad one. I don't even think that's his right name, but he's been robbin' and murderin' along the Mississippi.

"Runs with a mean crowd. You tell your pa to fight shy of them. Kill him soon's look at him."

They sat silent for a few minutes and then the boy said, "I will not forget them."

Ward glanced at him, struck by something in his tone. "What is it, boy? What are you thinkin' of?"

"I am going to kill them. I am going to kill every one of them."

Ward was silent for a few minutes. "Know how you feel, boy, but remember what the Good Book says? 'Vengeance is mine saith the Lord.' The evil men do catches up with them, boy. You leave it to time, and the Lord."

Val said nothing. Within him there was a resolution, a hard core of something that no words could touch. He could only remember his mother and how his father had been while she lived. His mother and Grita's mother had been brutally murdered, and the men who had done it were free.

"You got your life to live, boy. You get taken up with thoughts of killin' those men . . . A man can lose sight of everything else when he's bent on revenge, and it ain't worth it.

"Suppose you find them and kill them all? Half your life will be gone and what's left? I mean, something like that becomes an obsession that rules out everything else, and when it's done, a man's left empty. I ain't got much in the way of book learnin', boy, but I seen a sight of men.

"Your pa's going to need help, these comin' years. You got your life ahead of you. You build you a life and forget those men."

"I think," Val said slowly, "one man caused it all. They were all drinking but him."

Ward turned sharply. "What's that?"

"The man who stood over Grita's father and killed him was not drunk. He waited until the others had . . . had done what they were doing, and then he called out that somebody was coming, and when they scattered, he went into the wagon and took the money. When he came out, Grita's father groaned, and that man came back and shot him. I saw it."

Ward stared at him. "Boy, are you sure of that? Would you know that man?"

"I . . . I think so. I didn't *really* see his face, but I think I know who it was."

"Be careful, son. Many a man's been hung on no more than that. You don't want to hang the wrong man."

"No, sir."

The grass grew shorter, the trail more sandy, and to right and left

were sand-hills. The oxen made slow time of it. Once they saw a
herd of over a hundred elk drifting along a hillside perhaps a mile
away.

The cattle grew leaner, people talked less, and many a worried
glance went to the snow on the high ridges. It was early for snow,
yet it was there. Only a little as yet, but frightening in its implications.

"We waited too late," his father said, "but we couldn't leave that
girl."

"Hiram Ward said we should not try to go to California this year.
That we should wait until spring."

His father was silent for a long time. They were seated together on
the wagon seat, one of the few times they had ridden so. The wheels
rocked and rolled over rocks and rough places in the trail. It was
steadily uphill now. He had not realized how much they were
climbing until he turned to look back and could see the end of the
wagon train a half-mile back and much lower.

"Might be best," his father said at last, "if our supplies last. We
need some meat."

Ward drifted back from the head of the train and rode beside their
wagon for a few minutes. "Tomorrow we cross the Divide. Mostly
downhill until we reach the Sierras."

They saw no game. The herds of buffalo seemed to be behind
them. Far off, they glimpsed antelope.

It was almost sundown when they made camp, and his father got
down his rifle. Val looked at it in awe. His father rarely handled the
gun, and there had been too little chance for hunting.

"Can I come?"

His father was about to refuse, then said, "Yes."

They started out from camp and Ward rode after them. "Huntin'
meat?" he asked.

"We are."

"Easy to get lost. Injuns out yonder, too."

"We will not go far. If we see nothing we will return."

"Yonder," Ward pointed, "there's a crick. Some years the deer
come down to drink there. You go easy and you might find game. Be
careful, there's Injuns about."

They walked on, down a slope of sparse gray-green grass, around
an outcropping of rock, through some trees. They saw a glint of
water and stopped, looking carefully about.

Val looked up at his father, but said nothing. They moved through
the trees, trying to walk softly. They glimpsed the water again,
dipped through a low place, and came up a grassy slope to look down
along the creek where five buffalo were standing.

Val looked quickly at his father, whose face was white. Slowly, carefully, he lifted the rifle, and laying it over a low branch, he took careful aim at the nearest cow buffalo. He aimed, then stopped and straightened up, wiping his eyes. Val looked at him again but his father was intent upon the buffalo.

There was something moving over there. "Pa?"

"Ssh!"

His father took aim again and slowly squeezed off his shot. The cow lunged, then slumped to her knees and rolled over. Excited, Tom Trevallion burst from the brush and then pulled up short.

Still quivering in the flank of the buffalo was an arrow!

There was a pound of hoofs. The boy and the man looked up to see five Indians sitting their ponies.

One Indian pointed to the buffalo. "He belong me," he said.

Tom Trevallion shook his head and touched his rifle. "I killed it."

The Indian lifted his bow and then pointed at the arrow. Then he indicated Trevallion's rifle. "You gun gone. He empty." He held up the bow with an arrow ready. "Bow no empty. You go." He pointed at the buffalo. "Mine."

"No." Tom Trevallion stood his ground. "My bullet killed him. You see."

The Indian looked at his companions. "Five mans. You one mans. We take meat."

There was a sharp click and the Indian turned his head sharply to Val. The boy saw his father look around, too. He held his father's pistol with the hammer eared back.

Val took one hand from the gun and spread five fingers toward the Indians. "Five," he said, "five balls, five mans."

Without turning his eyes from the Indians he said to his father, "Fifty-fifty?"

Tom Trevallion looked at his son as if he had seen him for the first time. Then he said to the Indians, "Fifty-fifty? You take half, we take half?"

Suddenly something like a smile came into the Indian's face. "Hifty-hifty," he agreed.

Carefully, Val lowered the hammer on his six-shooter and put it back behind his belt.

The Indians went quickly to the buffalo and began skinning it, carefully dividing the meat.

Tom Trevallion looked at his son. "Who gave you permission to bring that pistol?"

"Nobody."

"After this, you ask me first."

When the Indians had finished skinning and cutting up the meat, one of them indicated the hide. "Hifty-hifty?"

Tom Trevallion smiled. "You take it. You will use it better than I could."

They started off, then one of them turned and looked back. He waved a hand. "Hifty-hifty!" he shouted, and away they went.

Tom Trevallion watched them go, then loaded his rifle. "All right," he said, "let's go back. We've got some meat."

THREE

They camped one night on a branch of Mary's River, and Hiram
Ward stopped by their wagon. "Fill up your kegs and anything
else that will carry water. Then cut some grass for hay. You'll find
neither water nor feed this side of the Carson River."

"What's the problem?"

"Desert . . . two days of it."

"We've seen a lot of desert, Ward."

"You ain't seen the Forty-Mile. This here's the worst of all, and
none of the stock is in good shape. There'll be no water at all, and no
grass. There'll be a dead animal for every fifty yards and a ruined
wagon for every hundred. There's one spring, boiling hot water.

"It's about twenty-four hours of travel. We'll not set out until
afternoon; it's too hot. Every few hours we'll stop, feed a little hay
and give them water, and then we'll go on. Fill everything you've
got with water . . . you'll need it all."

With hand sickles they went to cutting grass in a meadow close by.
They carried it in their arms to the back of the wagon. Much of the
weight they had when they started was now gone, for they had used
their spare wagon-tongue, and they had eaten most of the food. There
was more left than expected, because they were feeding one less
than planned.

Val walked into the meadow and, crouching down, began cutting
the grass off short. It was not very tall, and they needed every bit.
The morning was hot and his back ached. From time to time, he
would gather the hay and carry it to the side of the meadow. He
looked at the river and thought of swimming in the ocean at Gunwalloe.
Would he ever see Gunwalloe again?

His father went by, leading the oxen to water. He glanced over.
"Get on with it, boy. There's no time for idleness."

He went back to work, cutting another armful, and still another.

His father returned with the oxen and left them to graze. A bee
buzzed near Val in the warm, lazy day. He was hungry, but there
was nothing to eat except at the wagon, and he dared not go back

while his father was around, and there was little enough. He might get a piece of jerky.

They had food, but there wouldn't be enough if they had to stay the winter on this side of the mountains. He went back to work and cut grass. He was still cutting grass when the sun went down, and then slowly he tied up bundles of it and carried them to the wagon.

Ward came by their fire and drank coffee with them.

"Nineteen wagons left," he said, "and we started with twenty-four. Buried five people along the way."

"Is that a lot for the trip?" his father asked.

"Can't rightly say it is. Hansen's wife died of fever the second week, Burnside shot hisself pulling his rifle out of the wagon, muzzle first, and then there was the Hansen baby, and McCrane who wandered off."

"Who was the fifth? I don't recall anybody else?"

"John Helder. He died last night." Ward glanced at Tom Trevallion. "You two take care of yourselves. I think you can make it out here, and we need good men." He stood up, swallowed the last of his coffee and placed the cup on the ground near them. "We'll lose some more before we see the Carson. Folks are in bad shape. Some of the womenfolks are ailin' and there's Thorsby. He's coiled his rope too tight. One of these days she's goin' to come unwound, sudden-like."

They slept the night, at least Val slept part of it. His father seemed to be wide awake whenever Val opened his eyes, staring up at the underside of the wagon.

The day dawned hot and still. Not a breath stirred. At noon they led the oxen to the wagon and hooked up. The horse they tied behind the wagon.

Slowly, without fanfare or confusion, the wagons moved out. Puffs of alkali dust arose from the rolling wheels and the hoofs of the animals. Nobody talked, and there was little yelling at the animals. The oxen, heads low, plodded steadily in an almost hypnotic trance. As the day wore on, the sun grew hotter. Val longed for a drink but dared not ask for one, nor take it.

He glimpsed the rib cage of a mule, half-buried in sand, and a little further along the ruins of a broken wagon, gray and splintery from long exposure. He plodded on, walking beside the lead team. The wagons rumbled along, and they mounted a low rise to look over the land ahead, and there . . . a miracle of miracles, a shimmering blue lake!

"Pa! *Look!*"

Others had stopped, staring. "Water! My God, it's water and they told us—"

"Mirage," Ward said. "It just looks like water."

One man turned hotly. "Are you trying to tell me that isn't a lake yonder?"

"You'll be seein' that every day. It's only mirage. Caused by heat waves or such. Can't say I understand it myself, but it's a reg'lar thing out here. Wonder you ain't seen it before."

Several of the men gathered together, staring at it. Finally Tom Trevallion turned away. "Maybe it is a lake," he said, "but it's off the trail."

He took up his ox goad and started his team. Reluctantly the others turned back to their teams, and one by one they started.

Suddenly, one of them shouted, "The hell you say!" Deliberately he turned his team and started out toward the shimmering blue water. Ward shouted at him, shouted again, then rode after him, but the man would not listen. "I don't know what reason you got for lyin'," he shouted, "but that there's *water!*"

Hiram Ward swore bitterly. "He wouldn't listen. He just wouldn't listen at all! And he's got a wife and two youngsters with him!"

"Maybe he's right," one man muttered. "Maybe we're the fools."

"He's not right," Ward said. "There's a mirage out here some-where most of the time when the sun's high. He'll kill himself. Worst of all, he'll kill those youngsters."

"If he's wrong," a man said, "he can always come back to the trail and follow on."

Ward shot him an angry glance. "Did you look at his oxen? When they get into that basin they'll never have strength enough to come out. His only chance will be to leave the wagon and mount his wife and youngsters on the oxen and try to get back. Not one chance in a hundred he'll have sense enough to try it."

Slowly they moved on, the heavy wagons rocking and swaying over the desert. After sundown Ward signaled a stop, and they pulled up right where they were, unyoked the oxen and carried to each one a small bundle of hay. It was not enough by far, but it was something. When they had finished, each one was given a hatful of water to drink.

"We'll rest two hours," Ward told them. "Then we'll move on until after midnight. We'll pull ahead for a few hours after a rest and take another rest just before daybreak or right after."

"And then?"

"The Carson River by noon, if we're lucky. Then we'll rest."

Val lay down in the wagon, desperately weary. He heard his father fumbling about and then no sound. The movement of the wagon startled him, and he awakened, and for a time he lay still. Had his father forgotten him? Why was he not awakened? He crawled back to the end of the wagon and got down over the tailgate.

His father was plodding along near the oxen, and as Val sighted him, he saw him stagger. For a moment, trembling with fear, he was afraid his father would fall, but he recovered, and plodded on.

Catching up to him, Val said, "Pa? Why don't you get in the wagon? Why don't you rest?"

"Don't be a fool, boy. They're having all they can do to pull the wagon now, let alone with me in it."

It was after midnight when they stopped again. The night was very clear and the stars seemed close. There was nothing but the stench of dead animals and dust, ever and always, the dust.

His father sank to the ground and rested his head in his hands, and Val slowly took what remained of the hay to each of the animals, and once more filled his father's hat with water and gave each animal just that much.

Ward stopped by. "You all right, son?"

"Yes, sir."

"Boy, I'm gonna ride back a ways, see if I can see anything of the Thompsons. If they got back to the road they'll need help."

Tom Trevallion looked up. "And if they didn't?"

"Their funeral. I can't go killin' a good horse an' maybe myself to find 'em. They were warned, but he wouldn't listen."

He turned his horse, then stopped. "Tom? If I shouldn't make it back, you take charge. You take them on to California."

"Me?"

"You. You're the steadiest man on the train, and folks listen to you. You just use your own good sense and take them on in." He chuckled without humor. "But don't count me out. I aim to come back."

He walked his horse off into the night. Much later, a long way off, they heard him calling. They heard no answer.

It was daybreak before he returned, walking and leading his horse. "Get 'em moving, Tom," he said, his voice husky with weariness, "get 'em moving or we'll lose some more."

"You didn't find them?"

"No, only their tracks, and them almost wiped out by drifting dust." He accepted the coffee Val handed him. "You see the mirage is always ahead of you. You never catch up. Toward the end . . . as far as I went, their wagon wheels were cutting deep, oxen were making hard work of it. They'll mire down in the playa, an'—"

"Playa?"

"Dry lake. Only it ain't really dry. The crust breaks through, and it's muck, bad as quicksand. Once you get in there, it would take two or three fresh teams to haul a wagon out. They ain't going to get out no way."

"What can they do?"

"Mount their oxen an' try to walk out. Can't carry much water, and he didn't have much hay. If he's smart, he'll start back. Trouble is, he ain't smart, or he'd have listened and not gone off like that."

"Maybe if we got a bunch together—"

"Nothing doing. I'll not stand for it. He took this on hisself, and I'm not going to lose good men trying to save a damn' fool. It's tough on his family, but the men who'd go after him have families, too."

Wearily, Ward got to his feet, staggering a little. "It's up to them now. If they get back to the trail, they may catch a ride with somebody. Trouble is, Thompson had gear in that wagon he set store by. I don't think he'll leave it. He'll keep fighting to get it out until there's no more time.

"I give him two days if he tried to get out, and in two days he can make it afoot. If he stays there struggling to get that wagon out, he won't last that long."

Tom Trevallion walked along the line of wagons stirring people to move. With a jolt and a rumble they started again.

Wagon after wagon started, and at last Hiram Ward came up, leading his horse. The wind began to blow, irritating, fitful gusts that filled the eyes and ears with gray-white alkali dust that made the eyes smart and the lips crack. Time and again the oxen stopped; after a few minutes of rest, they started on again. Only a few wisps of hay were left, and almost no water. The slosh of it in the kegs was an agonizing sound.

Val walked, urging the oxen when he could, his throat sore from dryness and dust. His father, walking ahead of him, stumbled and fell. Slowly, heavily, he got to his feet.

The wagon ahead of them had stopped, and one of its oxen was down. With Tom Trevallion's help the ox was unyoked and left to lie. A few minutes later they passed the lead wagon, circling around it as it stood in the trail.

"Trevallion? Can you take some of my gear? I can't leave it here. It's all I've got. It's my clothes, my tools . . . I need 'em."

"Make packs," Ward advised, "put 'em on your oxen. Just let the wagon set. No use to overload another wagon and do him in, too."

Beside the trail some books lay in the sand, a six-volume set of Rollin's *Ancient History*. Just beyond it there was a rocking chair, an old trunk, all left behind by overloaded wagons.

All the night through they had been seeing the stark white bones of long-dead animals as well as others, not long dead, but stripped by buzzard and coyote until only bones remained.

They stopped again in the gray hours of the morning. His father dipped out enough water for coffee and took the rest to the oxen. There was less than a half-hatful for each.

"How far?"

Ward shrugged. "Ten mile, maybe more. They'll smell water about midmorning, and you'll have to hold 'em, if you can. They'll stampede for it."

Parkins, now driving the wagon ahead of them, shook his head. "They haven't strength enough, Hiram. If my stock tries to run, they'll fall down."

"When they smell water, it gives them strength. You mark my words. If they start to run, just pile in the wagon and hang on!"

Red-eyed with weariness, their faces, their hair, and their clothing gray with dust, they started on. Now each step was an ordeal, each step a victory. Twice Val fell, and each time he crawled to his feet in time to avoid being walked over by the following team.

From beside the wagon, he looked back. The once long train of wagons was pitifully short now. Where had they all gone? How many had dropped off during the night that he had not even seen?

Midmorning came and passed, and still the oxen plodded steadily, hypnotically onward, heads low, leaning dumbly into their yokes.

All about them was gray desolation littered with dead animals, parched and shriveled hides clinging to stark white bones, broken wagons, blankets, tools, odd bits of furniture, and the stuff of people's lives now abandoned.

Suddenly there was a sharp gust of wind, a brief spatter of rain that vanished as soon as it came, and then the wind. . . .

Val had only time to see a vast billowing cloud, black and ugly, rolling down upon them, and then it hit. Sharp particles of sand stung his face. He glimpsed his father struggling to pull his kerchief up over his mouth and nose, and he did likewise. In the midst of it, he heard a weird sound, a low moan from the nearest ox, a moan that swept through them, and all back down the line. Their pace quickened, suddenly they began to trot. He lunged for the tailgate of the wagon and pulled himself over it, and then they were running.

Rolling, rumbling, bouncing off occasional rocks. He clung to the wagon-bow and prayed the wagon would not break up. Around him other wagons were rumbling and bouncing, banging into each other. Dust filled the wagon, choking dust that had him coughing and gagging. Everything inside the wagon was thrown together. The shotgun fell into the bedding, and the stove door slammed open, and it was with difficulty he got it closed, while ashes spilled over everything. Fortunately the stove had been for days unused, so no fire remained.

From the right Val heard a splintering crash and a scream of pain, and he caught one wild, fleeting glimpse out of the back of the wagon of another, turned on its side, wheels spinning, the oxen gone.

They raced on, and he clung to the wagon in an agony of fear. Would it never stop? Would it never end? Where was pa?

Suddenly, it did stop. Val felt a delicious coolness coming into the wagon, and crawling to the back, he peered out. The oxen were knee-deep in water, their heads plunged into it. Slipping over the tailgate, he crouched down into the water himself, scooping great handfuls into his mouth, throwing it over him, dipping his head into it.

To left and right were other wagons. A few yards away Dottie Parkins stood in the water, her dress sopping, clinging to her figure in every shocking detail. Amazed, he stared at her, and seeing him, she laughed, smoothing the dress over her breasts. Val turned his head quickly away and she laughed again. Dottie Parkins was sixteen, and he was three, almost four years younger. She had always seemed serene, quiet, and very much the prim young lady.

He got up from the water, and, rescuing his ox-goad from the wagon, he went around to the lead team to get them out of the water.

His father was nowhere around.

He heard a sharp gasp from Dottie Parkins and looked around to see a rider had pulled up on the bank of the river and was staring at her.

"Got quite a figger there, missy," the rider said.

"It's none of your business!" she flared.

Val reached into the back of his wagon and handed her a blanket which she hastily wrapped around herself.

The man looked from her to Val, and Val felt a queer, sharp pang of recognition.

He *knew* him! One of the men who attacked and killed his mother!

Turning, Val lunged at the wagon and grabbed for the shotgun. It came free of the wagon and he turned with it in his hands. Seeing it, the man touched a spur to his horse and was gone.

Dottie stared at him, her eyes wide. "Why! Why, you were going to fight for me!" she said. "Well, I never! Val Trevallion, I never thought— Why, you were *wonderful*! Just *wonderful*!"

Embarrassed, he put the shotgun back into the wagon, unwilling to spoil her appreciation by telling her who the man was and why he acted as he had.

Parkins came splashing around his wagon and looked at them. Dottie splashed over to him and began telling what had happened.

Val's father suddenly loomed on the riverbank. "I'll be damned!"

Parkins shouted. "You've got a spunky lad there, Tom! A spunky lad! He'd have fought for my daughter."

Later when they were alone, Val said, "Pa, she took it wrong. I went for the shotgun because that man was one of those who killed mother."

"What? What kind of horse was he riding? What did he look like?"

"A medium-tall man, dark, thin, straggly beard. He was riding a chestnut with three white stockings and a blaze face."

They got the wagon out of the water and turned the cattle loose on a meadow near the stream. Other cattle and some horses were there.

"Son, you keep an eye on the wagon and the stock. There's a trading post over there. I shall ride over."

"Pa? Don't tell her about him, that man, I mean. Don't tell Parkins or Dottie. She thinks I done . . . did it for her."

His father nodded, then walked his horse away.

Hours later he returned, undressed, and went to bathe in the river. When he came back Val asked, "Did you find him?"

"No. He rode out before I got there, but they know him. His name is Skinner. The man at the trading post says he is a hard character."

Tom Trevallion went about fixing a meal, and Hiram Ward joined them, bringing a chunk of fresh meat. "Mind company?"

"No."

After a bit Ward asked, "That feller you run off? Did you know him?"

"I know his face. I remembered him. He was one of those who killed my mother."

Ward looked across the fire at Tom. "They told me over at Spafford's that you were askin' after him. You be careful, Tom, that's a mighty mean man and he runs with a bad outfit. If he gets an idea you're hunting him, he'll kill you."

"He will have to shoot first, then."

"Tom, you don't understand. Skinner will guess it was the boy who told you, so he'll kill the boy, too. And I believe he knows who you are. He was down at the post asking folks from the train who you were, if you were married. Somebody told him your wife had been murdered back in Missouri."

"So he knows, then?"

"He knows."

FOUR

Tom Trevallion moved his wagon higher up the river and away from Spafford's. Hiram Ward came to him on the last day. "You stayin', Tom?"

"I am."

"You're wiser than them, but I'm the guide, and I have to take them through, somehow." He paused, lighting his pipe. "Keep an eye out, you and the boy. That's a bad outfit."

"All right."

"Ever kill a man, Tom?"

"No."

"With their kind, you kill. Don't talk, don't tell them what you think of them, just kill. They understand nothing else. They're worse than wolves, Tom. You can bet time is holding a rope noosed just for them. Don't go hunting them, Tom."

They watched the wagons go. Val felt a pang as of something lost. He knew few of them well, but for months now they had been together. The wagons slowly rumbled past, and only a few waved. Their eyes were on the trail, their hearts and heads were in the magic land across the mountains.

"It will be cold this winter," his father said, "and we must gather wood. There's a deserted cabin here where we can stay the winter through, and when the snows melt, we will cross over."

They cleaned out the old cabin, and his father repaired the roof. Val gathered wood along the slope; there were many fallen trees and branches, great slabs of bark, enough wood for many winters, just lying about. He stacked it against the house to help keep out the cold and where it would be close to hand when needed.

"No need to worry about snakes," Ward had told him. "Not in this cold weather. First sign of frost they hole up for the winter in caves and the like. But there's bears . . . keep an eye out."

He saw no bears, but he did see tracks. His father killed a deer the second day they were there, an easy shot, not thirty yards away.

Val was up on the slope when the men came. His father was near the wagon and heard them coming and he reached in the back for the shotgun.

30

The mountain air was clear and Val could hear it all.

"Is that the wagon?"

"Same one, painted just that shade of blue. It's them, all right."

"But how could he *know*? He wasn't there!"

"He knows; it was that kid told him. We didn't see the kid, but he must have been there."

They rounded the rocks and trees within sight of his father.

One of them was carrying a rifle, another had drawn a six-shooter, and Tom Trevallion lifted his shotgun and blew a man out of the saddle. His second shot killed the man with the pistol, and he dropped the shotgun and reached for the six-shooter, and Val saw his father's body jerk with the impact of the bullets. He went to his knees, got the pistol out and fired again and again, some of the shots going wild as he was himself hit.

As suddenly as the shooting began it was over, and in the silence they heard the rattle of approaching hoofs. Somebody swore, and another said, "Let's get out of here!"

They wheeled their horses, and Val got up from where he had been hiding. Rushing down he grabbed up his father's pistol and fired just as they vanished into the brush.

From the direction of the Carson, a party of horsemen came rushing up. A lean, bearded man swung his horse around and looked at Val, then at his father.

"Who did it, boy?"

Val told them, then ran to his father. Dropping to his knees beside him, he stared down, shocked and sick. His father's skull and shirt were bloody. "Val . . . Val, I . . . ." Then, more softly, he whispered, "Be a good boy, your mother—" His voice trailed away, and he was gone.

The bearded man put a hand on his shoulder. "Your pa was a good man, son. He died game."

They buried his father there, on a low knoll under the trees, and Val carved the marker himself, a slab of sandstone on which he laboriously chipped out the words with a hammer and chisel.

He lived on in the cabin all that winter. Spafford let him clean up around the store for twenty-five cents a week. With only one mouth to feed, there was enough food to last, and they had already cut most of the wood needed. He had warm blankets, a rifle, a shotgun, and a pistol. Later, walking up the trail the murderers had taken when they fled, he found a second pistol. The name A.X. Elder was carved on the butt; evidently the pistol had been dropped in flight, perhaps by a wounded man.

During the winter he went through what his parents had left, their clothing, their small chest of keepsakes, some old letters. Among his mother's things he found five gold coins, hidden away against some emergency. He hid them again, and when spring came, he yoked up the oxen and took the wagon over the mountains to California with the first wagon train that went through. He was thirteen then, already man-grown and strong for his years.

In Sacramento he sold the oxen and the wagon but kept the mare, and the firearms. The pistol with the name on the butt he packed away. He now knew two names, Skinner and A.X. Elder.

That summer he tended cattle, helped dig an irrigation ditch, and built a flume. In the fall he helped construct a log barn and cut and squared timber for a cabin.

A stoop-shouldered, lantern-jawed man from Missouri squared timbers with a broadax right beside him. He was a talker, a loose-tongued man who talked sunup to last light, with many a frontier story of hunting, fighting, rafting on the rivers.

Toward sundown one day he said, "Pirates! Boy, they was on the river them days! Steal the hat off your head! Mostly they laid in wait for rafters or boaters, come aboard in the night, murder folks and steal what all they had!

"My ma, she was a God-fearing woman. Raised us right. She was a Methodist. Swore by that there John Wesley, and never a Sunday but we'd go to the preaching. I never paid much mind, but it was a time to see the gals whose folks brought them to the preaching. We'd make eyes at one another, and one time I got to hold hands with that Sawyer girl, right in church, too!

"Had me a fight over her, knuckle-an'-skull with another boy, but then Obie come along, an'—"

"Who?"

"Obie, Obie Skinner. Him who lived over nigh Bald Knob. He—"

"Tell me about him."

"Obie? He was no-account. Year or two younger than me, but mean as all get-out right then. I mean he was a knowed boy, stealin' an' all that. I was winnin' that fight, but Obie he come along and hit that other boy with a club. It wa'n't fair. I'd of whupped him anyway, but Obie he come from my fork of the crick, and he just fetched that boy a clout.

"Laid that boy out stone cold. I rizz up and cussed Obie, told him I would handle my own fightin', but he just laughed at me.

"That was the year he taken out an' joined up with river pirates. He stole a mule and got ketched with it, and then he wormed his way out of jail somehow and taken to the river."

"You tell me about Obie Skinner," Val said. "Who did he run with?"

PART TWO

FIVE

Eighteen fifty-nine. Ten years gone . . . ten years during which Val Trevallion was a driven man. Filled with hatred for the men who had killed his mother and father, he had worked from job to job, saving a little money, doing the jobs given him with a single-minded purpose.

He had helped around a trading post, clerked in the store, had worked for a printer who had a small newspaper, had been a packer with a mule train, prospected, fought Indians, worked as a deckhand on a Sacramento riverboat, and had covered the country from Sonora to the upper Frazier River country in British Columbia. He had worked in mines, been a shift-boss when he was eighteen, superintendent of a mine at twenty.

Trevallion came to be known as a man who could get things done. He could handle men and he knew ore. Several times he had taken over mines that were failing, had turned them into producers and then left, nor would any amount of money get him to stay on.

For ten years Trevallion had lived with no other thought than to find and kill the murderers of his father and mother, to see them punished for what they had done. His father had killed two, Trevallion had been able to find and kill two more, and he was still determined to search out the others. Which led him now, ten hard years later, on his way back over the mountains.

It was hot and stuffy in the small shack where they awaited the horses and mules that would take them over the Sierras. Glancing around at the others he felt a sharp impatience . . . fools, wild-eyed with dreams of gold. He had seen their kind before, men and women hungry for wealth and most of them totally unwilling to do the work it required.

He went to the door and stepped out into the bitter cold. There was snow upon the mountains, but in town the earth was bare and frozen. Humping his shoulders against the wind, he walked to the end of the freight platform and was turning back when his eyes caught a flicker of movement.

Pausing, Trevallion fumbled in his pockets as if searching for something and, without turning his head, saw from the corner of his eye a man in a heavy overcoat come out of the trees on the hill opposite. Hesitating only an instant, the man started down the slope in a stumbling run.

At that hour it was unlikely the man would be headed for any place but here, for day had just broken and the sky was scarcely gray.

Nine people waited inside for the mules that would carry them over the mountains to Washoe, but the only one who had seemed apprehensive was the frail blonde girl with the flashy young man.

Whatever it was she feared had drawn only scoffing replies from him, and Trevallion had turned away mildly irritated at the two. Young love—he had seen it all before.

Why did all these youngsters believe they had discovered something new? Why did so many repeat the same mistakes and blunders? Maybe life wanted it that way.

Trevallion had been over too many rough trails with too many men not to recognize the young man for what he was. He had the flashy good looks that appealed to some women and a shallow mind tied to a glib tongue, but he was strictly lightweight and would quit when the going got rough.

For the girl Trevallion had only compassion. Young she certainly was, and quite pretty, but there was a shading of character there, too. Time and trial had not yet demanded that character to surface, but surface it surely would.

He was turning back to the door when the scuff of boots on the frozen road turned him around.

It was the man he had seen on the hill opposite, a dirty, unshaved man, inclining toward fat. Despite the intense cold his coat hung open. No doubt to permit access to a gun.

Brushing by him without a glance, the man went to the window and peered in. His fingers fumbled under the coat again.

Trevallion had known too much of trouble not to recognize the signs. Any minute now the mules would be brought around for mounting, and the people would be emerging. Trevallion did not like the man peering in the window, nor did he want anything to interfere with their leaving. A shooting might do just that.

His tone was casual. "Remember what they used to call this place?"

His concentration broken, the man looked around, seeming to notice Trevallion for the first time. "Wha—? What did you say? You speakin' to me?"

"Just wondering if you knew what they used to call this town?"

Irritated by the interruption, and impatient, the man straightened up. He had round, flabby cheeks and small eyes. He peered at Trevallion. "Ol' Dry Diggin's, wasn't it? Now it's called Placerville. What's it matter?"

"There was a time it was called *Hang*town. Folks around here had a short way with murderers. They never discussed it, they just hanged them."

"What's that got to do with me? Who're you, anyway?"

Trevallion smiled. It was a good question. It was a very good question. Just who *was* he?

Hoofs rattled on the frozen mud and stones as a man on muleback rounded the corner, leading a string of saddled mules and pack animals. Trevallion recognized the rider, Jim Ledbetter.

"How are you, Jim?"

The rider in the buffalo coat pulled up sharply, peered, then spat. "Val? Well, I'll be damned! Last I heard the Modocs had killed you somewhere over back of Shasta."

"It was close. They got some lead into me and one arrow. Seemed like a good time to leave out of there so I did."

"Heard they found blood all over the rocks, so the boys figured you'd been scalped and your body dropped into a hole in the lava beds."

"They had it in mind."

Ledbetter swung down. "You headed for Washoe?"

"Isn't everybody?" Trevallion indicated a black Spanish mule. "How about that one for me?"

"He's yours. Be good to have you along."

"Expecting trouble?"

"No more'n usual. The trail's god-awful. Mud's knee-deep when it ain't froze. There's a solid line of travel both ways so the road is all chewed up. Most of them are pilgrims who don't know which end is up. Wouldn't know a color if they saw one."

"How's things in Washoe?"

"Virginia town, they're callin' it now. At least some do. Nothin' but scattered shacks an' dugouts, with here and there a rock-house. God knows there's rock enough to build a city, just lyin' there."

"Are they finding any ore?"

"Aplenty." Ledbetter hitched his pants and spat. "You could go to work tomorrow, Val. The Washoe started as placer, and there's still a good bit of it being done, but the big thing is going to be quartz-mining and there's nobody around knows how to work in hard rock. Nobody but a few of you Cousin Jacks."

"Jim, I left Cornwall when I was a youngster. All I know about mining is what I learned here." He paused. "Of course, my pa tried to teach me something. He grew up in tin and copper mines. I did work in them a little, but only as a youngster."

"You forgot more than most of them will ever know, Val. Once they find out you're a Cousin Jack you will have a job . . . if you want it."

The door opened suddenly behind him and Trevallion heard the people coming to mount their mules. He thought suddenly of the fat man to whom he had spoken. Trevallion caught Jim's eye and jerked his head to indicate the man. "Watch it, Jim. This is trouble."

The blonde girl and her flashy young man were the first to emerge.

"You, there!" The fat man drew back his coat.

The two stopped in midstride. The girl's eyes went wide with fright. Her mouth opened but no sound came.

Suddenly all the young man's flash and style were gone. He tried to bluster. "You got no say over her! We're agonna be married!"

"Like hell you are!" The fat man produced a pistol. Trevallion was startled to see it was an old-fashioned dueling pistol.

The young man broke and ran, the pistol exploding just as he ducked around the corner. Shouting, the man ran after him, waving the now empty pistol. At the corner of the building he turned and walked back to the girl, grabbing her arm. "You! You git for home! By the Lord, I'll—"

Fear was gone from her eyes. She braced herself against his grip. "I'll not! You leave go of me!"

Her eyes turned to Trevallion. "Please, mister! I don't want to go with him!"

"Is he your father?"

"He is *not*! He married my mother after pa died, an' ever since ma died he's been after me. I . . . . I *hate* him!"

"Damn you! You come with—"

"Let her alone."

Trevallion's tone was low, but there was a quality in it that stopped the man. "If she doesn't wish to go with you, she doesn't have to."

"You stay out of this!" The man clung to her arm with his left hand, holding the dueling pistol in his right. "This here's none of your business."

"Mister, in this country we don't abuse women. Take your hand off the lady."

The man let go but he lifted his gun and pointed it at Trevallion.

"Don't be a damned fool!" Trevallion said irritably. "Your gun's empty. When you go hunting meat, my friend, you'd better be better armed than that."

Ignoring him, he glanced at the girl. "Do you want to go with this man?"

"No, I don't! I want to get away. He, Alfie, he was going to help me."

"You're well rid of him. Have you any money?"

"A . . . a little."

Jim Ledbetter spoke up. "Her ride's paid for. So's his. I can sell that ride and give her the money." A little wryly, he added, "It doesn't look like Alfie's going to show up."

Trevallion glanced back at the girl. "It will be rough up there. Maybe you should try Sacramento?"

"No. I want to go to Washoe. To Virginia City."

"Mount up, then."

The others had started getting into their saddles, some clumsily, others with expert ease. The fat man started forward but Trevallion blocked his way.

"Damn you! You've no right to interfere!"

"You've no claim on her. If I had my way they'd run you out of town. Your kind aren't wanted anywhere. When you pointed that gun at me, I could have killed you, and probably should have."

The man backed off, but his plump cheeks shook with fury. "Damn you! You'll see! I'll get even! I'll get both of you! *Both* of you!"

The agent came from the door. "Jim? Here's a packet of mail. Most of it is for Hesketh."

"Hesketh? Isn't he that bookkeeper for the Solomon?"

"That's him. He gets more mail than his boss, seems like."

Ledbetter tucked the letters into a saddlebag, then swung to the saddle and led off, the others following. Trevallion fell in behind the girl. She had a nice straight back and sat her saddle well.

"I'm Trevallion," he offered.

She smiled. "I am Melissa Turney." The smile left her face. "His name was Mousel. He's a placer-miner sometimes, sometimes a trapper."

She offered no comment on Alfie and Trevallion decided it was no time to ask questions.

The morning was cold and overcast. The wind from off the ranges was chilling, and as they mounted steadily they could catch glimpses of snow under the pines.

The Spanish mule had an easy gait and, like most mules, a no-nonsense attitude. The mule knew exactly where he was going to step and was not about to be guided by some casual pilgrim who might or might not be trail-wise. He had his own way, and Trevallion let him have his head.

The trail was badly rutted, and here and there run-off water had cut deep trenches across the way, and the ruts had frozen into a maze of rocklike ridges, making every step a hazard.

Even at this hour the trail was already crowded with a winding, snakelike procession of men, animals, and occasional wagons. Mule trains forged ahead with that complete indifference to the life and limb of others typical of pack mules the world over. Nobody in his right mind disputed the right-of-way with a pack mule who brushed people aside like so many trailside branches or clumps of brush.

Jim Ledbetter was as single-minded as any mule. His sole responsibility was to those who paid to ride his mules, and to their packs, and he forged ahead like the others.

Nobody wished to stop or even pause for fear someone would pass them by in the rush for Washoe. Wrecked wagons were thrust rudely aside, some of them leaning perilously over cliffs, others already toppled into canyons.

At one point a keg of whiskey fell off the back of a wagon and was immediately seized by a passerby who helped himself to the contents. As if by magic, tin cups appeared, and by the time the teamster, whip in hand, came striding back, the situation was too far out of hand to permit interference. With a shrug he accepted the cup of whiskey extended as a peace offering, drank it, and returned to his team.

Slowly they worked their way up the steep, winding trail bordered by pines. It was a brutal road, horses, mules, and men scrambling over rocks, slipping on ice, plunging and buck-jumping through occasional drifts, turning out to avoid rock falls or small slides. Despite the trail they made good time.

Occasionally they were passed by pack trains of ore returning from the mines.

At the ridge's crest they drew up to let the mules catch their breath and to drink the clear, cold water of a rivulet that fell from the bank in a miniature cascade, and crossed the trail to pitch off into the canyon.

Ledbetter walked back to Trevallion. "It's like every boom camp in the world, Val. Everybody hopes to strike it rich, many of them believe they have, others are con men just looking for a gullible newcomer to whom they can sell their claim or a piece of one. Everybody has 'feet' to sell, and most of it ain't worth the price of a Digger Injun's breakfast."

He paused, gesturing toward the east. "There's forty or fifty pieces of good ground up there and several dozen others where a man can dig a living. That's about it. Why, I know of some claims that have been sold time and again without anybody seeing a color."

Ledbetter bit off a chew and offered the plug. Trevallion declined.
Ledbetter glanced sharply at him. "Didn't you an' your pa come this
way?"

"We did."

"Man, I'll never forget that Forty-Mile Desert ifen I live to be a
hundred. Dead animals ever' few feet and busted down wagons
scattered all over."

Later, at a widening of the trail, Melissa rode up beside Ledbetter.
"You all right?" he asked her.

"Yes, sir."

"You got a pair o' man's pants? Be a sight easier if you rode astride
on these steep slopes. I know it ain't what's considered ladylike, but
you'll see most womenfolks usin' them on the road."

"I'll be all right." A few steps further along she asked, "Who is
he?"

"Trevallion? He's a Cousin Jack. That means he's from Cornwall,
over in England. They're about the only ones around who know
anything about hard-rock mining."

"I mean . . . *who* is he?"

"He's a loner, ma'am, a hard, tough, dangerous man. He rides
alone, walks alone, lives alone. There's nothing to him that ain't
rawhide and iron, but if a body's in any kind of trouble, he's the man
you want beside you.

"If you've got ore, he will get it out. If you lose a lead, he'll find it
for you quicker than anybody I know. He knows *ground*, ma'am,
mining ground. He knows how to load his holes so the ground breaks
fine, and he's one of the best men with a single-jack I ever did see."

"What's a single-jack?"

"It's a small sledgehammer, ma'am. That's about the easiest way to
explain it. Used with one hand, for drillin' into rock. A double-jack is
used with two hands and is a reg'lar sledgehammer. Mostly one man
turns the drill, the other strikes it. Trevallion is *good*. The best I
ever did see. He's got more power in those shoulders and arms . . .
well, that's one way to build power, swinging a double-jack.

"He come over from the old country with his folks. Beyond that
nobody knows much about him. A few years back when he was only
about sixteen he hired out to deliver twenty thousand dollars in gold
to a bank in Sacramento. There were outlaws after that gold and
Injun trouble, too. When he didn't show up folks figured him for
dead. Three months later he come down out of the woods lookin' like
the wrath of God. He had two festerin' arrow wounds and was wore
down to skin an' bone, but he brought in the gold, ever' pinch of it."
Ledbetter paused. "Such things get talked about, so he become a
known man."

"How old is he?"

Ledbetter shrugged. "Who knows? Or really cares? Most men out here are young, even the ones who look old. Country does that to a man, that an' hard work. I know he could have been superintendent of a big mine in Grass Valley, and he wouldn't take it. Somethin's eatin' on him, I reckon."

The trail narrowed, and Ledbetter rode on ahead, glancing back from time to time at the winding black snake of men, animals, and wagons that followed.

Melissa shivered at the cold wind off the mountain. What would she do in Virginia City? Her whole thought was to escape, to get away, by whatever means. How she would exist after that was something to which she had given no thought aside from supposing she would be married. She flushed with shame, remembering the way Alfie had fled.

There would be something, there had to be something! Her mother had hoarded a little money Mousel had never known she possessed. She had married him when left alone and desperate, with a young daughter to bring up. He had proved a cruel, parsimonious man, vindictive and petty.

Alfie—she did not want to think about Alfie. She had half persuaded herself she was in love with him, but when she warned him of Mousel, he had laughed, skeptical of her fears. She saw him now for the shoddy, third-rate sort of man he was. She had been in a fair way to make as serious a mistake as her mother, marrying to escape.

Later, she asked Trevallion, "Why do they call Cornishmen 'Cousin Jacks'?"

"They say if you hire one Cornishman he will immediately tell you about his Cousin Jack, who is a good miner and hunting a job, and soon the Cousin Jacks have all the jobs."

"They must be good miners."

"Generally speaking they don't know much else. When I was six, I was working in a tin mine picking waste rock out of the ore. Then pa took me out, and I worked with fishermen until I was eleven, then back to the mines."

Melissa glanced at him slyly. "My grandfather used to say the people of Cornwall were wreckers. That they used to display lights to lure ships on the rocks so they could loot the ships."

"It might have happened," Trevallion said, "long, long ago. Usually they just claimed what was washed ashore. In fact, there's a story in the family that that was how my great-grandfather got his wife. He helped her ashore from a wreck and claimed her for his own."

"And she stayed with him?"

"By all accounts they were a happy pair. He was a fine, upstanding young man, considered very handsome. When I was a child, there were still things in the house that had been hers, things saved from the wreck."

Ledbetter turned in his saddle. "We'll stop at Dirty Mike's. We've made good time, and Mike serves the best grub. Only trouble is the people come and go so fast he never takes time to wash the dishes. Complain about them and you'll go hungry."

A rider on a fine bay horse was overtaking them. He was a tall, strikingly handsome man with a blond mustache, and as he came abreast he glanced sharply at Trevallion, then looked a second time, frowning a little. He spoke to his horse then, and rode rapidly away.

"That man knew you," Melissa said.

"Aye," Trevallion agreed. "I believe he did."

SIX

Dirty Mike's was a ramshackle place of stained canvas and poles. The few tables with benches were already crowded, and men were scattered over the grass, eating from tin plates, dishes of chipped enamel, or heavy crockery.

"Must be three or four hundred," Ledbetter said, "about average for this time of day, and this season."

He pointed. "Look at 'em." His disgust was evident. "Ain't one in ten knows what he's after or would know a color if they saw it. They'll spend all they bring with them, and here or there a few will make a little. Most of them will jump at the chance to move on to any other boom camp, always ready to believe the pot of gold is right over yonder, but they want to stumble over it, not work for it. Most of them are looking for something easy, something to find or steal, or what's offered on a platter."

"There's good men among them," Trevallion said.

"Aye. That there is."

"And there are some women over there," Melissa said.

"They aren't your kind," Trevallion replied. "Fight shy of them. If you're seen with them, you're likely to be taken for one of them. Just stay away from them."

"Do you think that's fair?"

"We're not talking about what's fair or unfair. We're talking realities. Some of those women would lend you their last dollar or nurse you if you were sick, but there's others would steal the fillings from your teeth or give you a knife in the ribs for what's in your pockets."

The area was incredibly dirty. Horses and mules were tied to brush or trees, others were picketed. Here and there a wagon was drawn up and all the spaces between were crowded with men in every possible costume. Coonskin caps, Mexican sombreros, old Army hats or caps, silk hats, beaver hats, and battered woolen hats . . . men in frock coats, sailor's jackets, fringed buckskin, and homespun.

There were men from all the world, sailors who had deserted their ships, adventurers, drifters, ne'er-do-wells, and mining men. Men

44

who had worked the Mother Lode or were rebounding from the disaster on the Frazier River.

A crude bar, a plank laid across barrel-tops, was lined three deep with men practicing for the saloons of Washoe. Several monte games were going, and at one of them somebody asked, "What's Washoe?"

"It's a place, a place where the mines are. It's a lake, too, named for a tribe of Indians."

"Indians? You mean there's real *Indians*?"

"Aplenty. Take your hair, too, given a chance."

"Naw," somebody interrupted. "Rob you, maybe. Even kill you, but these Injuns don't take hair."

A burly man with unshaven cheeks and a ragged beard as well as foodstains on his checkered vest pushed up to Trevallion. "Mister, I've got a claim I can let you have for the right price." With a glance to left and right he leaned closer, his breath smelling of whiskey. "This here's a steal for the right man. I won't sell to just anybody, but you look the right sort." He coughed effectively. "I'm a sick man. Located the best claim on the lode but can't stand the weather. Got to get back to the coast. Like leavin' my own private mint, it is. I've been lookin' for just the right man—"

"Keep looking," Trevallion said, brushing by.

The man swore bitterly, then reached for Melissa. "Ma'am, I tell you this here—"

"Leave her alone," Trevallion said.

The man's eyes turned mean. "Listen, mister—"

"The lady is with me," Trevallion said.

" 'Lady'!" The man sneered. "Why, she ain't no more a—"

Trevallion knocked him down. It was a backhanded blow, almost casual, but the man's heels flew up and he landed on his back in the mud, lips broken and bloody.

He started to get up but someone hissed, "Stay down, you fool! That's *Trevallion!*"

Trevallion took Melissa's elbow and guided her through the crowd. "There's always somebody who hasn't learned how to behave."

He took her to the counter and men, seeing a woman, crowded back and made a place for her.

"Mike?"

The rough-looking man standing over the fire with a long spoon in his hand turned impatiently. When he saw Trevallion he smiled. "Oh, it's you, Mr. Trevallion." He glanced at Melissa. "What can I do for you?"

"Some grub. Whatever you've got. And Mike? Two clean plates."

Mike chuckled. "Wouldn't do it for anybody but you, Mr. Trevallion.

Why, I've fed five, maybe six hundred so far today, and if the pack train doesn't get here, folks are goin' hungry tomorrow."

Taking two plates he sloshed them around in what appeared to be relatively clean water, then polished them with a dry cloth he took from under the counter.

"Beef an' beans, and there's some dried apples left." He glanced at Trevallion. "You two travelin' alone?"

"We're with Jim Ledbetter."

"One o' the best, Jim is." Mike heaped the plates. "You prospectin' or hirin' out?"

"There's a place up there I want to look at again, if somebody hasn't beaten me to it. I thought I'd placer awhile until I can look the situation over."

Mike glanced around, then in a lower tone. "You be careful. There's been a man or two askin' after you. I didn't much like their looks."

"Thanks, Mike."

Mike glanced at Melissa. "Not much up there for a decent woman, nor any place to live." He filled two mugs with coffee and took them to a table inside his cooking tent. "Sit here," he said. He looked at Melissa again. "Ma'am? Can you bake? Pies, doughnuts an' such?"

"I can."

"That's it, then. These men can't get enough of such truck. I'd hire you on m'self but you'd do better on the Washoe. You bake pies an' you can get whatever you ask for 'em. They're hungry for home cookin', sweets, an' such."

"All right."

"You'll be rich, ma'am. You'll make more money than if you had some feet in the richest claim on the Comstock."

"The Comstock?"

"That's what they call the lode. Named for Ol' Pancake Comstock who was one of the first on the ground, and a four-flusher if I ever seen one. Claims ever' thing in sight, but he's a bluffer an' a liar to boot.

"The man who knows most about that place and the leads is Ol' Virginny—when he's sober. He knows more about minin' in a minute than all the rest in a year."

"The Grosch brothers gone?" Trevallion asked.

"You knew them? Well, they're gone, all right. Dead. One of them drove a pick into his foot, and when blood pizenin' set in, he wouldn't let them take it off. He died, and his brother stayed too long nursin' him and got caught in the Sierra snows. He made it over but was in such bad shape he failed. He died, too."

"They were good men."

"That they were. When they were gone, ol' Comstock busted into their cabin. Claimed they left him in charge and maybe they done so.

"Anyway, he found maps and such, and he crawled all over Gold Canyon an' Sun Mountain tryin' to figure out what they meant.

"Trouble was, he didn't understand any of it. He didn't know what they'd found or what to do with the maps he had and was scared to take anybody in with him.

"He never did find anything, but any time a newcomer found something, the ol' buzzard would swoop in an' lay claim to part of it. I don't know whether the Grosch brothers found anything or not, but they sure thought they had."

As Trevallion ate his eyes scanned the crowd. The faces were mostly strange but like faces in all the gold camps. Most of them were the type who crowded in with the first rush, and for a few days they were in all the saloons and brothels, and then somehow they just melted away, disappearing so gradually nobody realized they were gone.

Rumpled and mud-stained, most of them armed, they gulped down their food and headed back for the trail.

"You've been here before?" Melissa asked.

"A couple of times. Boom camps are all much the same. The first time I was just a youngster, and after the deserts the Carson River looked like paradise."

He emptied his cup, glanced at it, and Mike walked over with the pot and filled both their cups. "Ain't many I'd do that for," he told Melissa, "but if you're ever in trouble, Trevallion's your man."

He walked away, boots sucking at the mud. Melissa glanced at Trevallion. "He likes you."

"Known him awhile. Pulled a man off him, once. Another time I staked him when he was on his uppers."

"I think you're nice."

He shook his head. "No, I am not. I think I'm a fair man, but not many take to me, and I'm a loner. I'd seen Mike around, always working, always trying, so when I heard he was broke, I staked him. Mike's not very smart, and he has no education to speak of, and he's failed a dozen times, but he always comes up trying. One of these days he'll make it."

His eyes strayed to the mules. Ledbetter was tightening cinches, talking to a lean, hard-bitten Arkansawyer, a man dressed far too lightly for the country, but who carried a rifle like it was an extension of himself. He was one of their party.

"Finish up," Trevallion said. "Jim's ready to move out."

They went to the mules, and the Arkansawyer thrust out a bony hand.

"Name's Tapley, Mr. Trevallion. Christian Tapley. Folks call me Tap."

"They call me Trevallion, no mister. This is Melissa Turney."

"I reckon."

Mounting up, Ledbetter took off at a good pace, and glancing back, Trevallion saw Tapley fall in at the rear. He had known the kind before. Probably Tap had grown up in a backwoods cabin listening to gospel-shouting preachers. A lean, stoop-shouldered man who had lived his life along the ragged edge of poverty, asking nothing of God or man but freedom to make his own way. He would always be where he was most needed because he was that kind of man, and he could probably shoot the head off a turkey at two hundred yards with that old rifle.

Ledbetter pushed into the first gap in the line, despite the cursing of those who followed. Coolly, he blocked the way until all his train were on the trail, then, oblivious to the curses, waved at them and rode on to the head of the line.

Several times in the next few hours Trevallion saw men stumble and fall, get clumsily to their feet, and keep on. A broken-down wagon was rudely shoved out of the way and left hanging over the lip of the cliff, despite the loud complaints of the teamster.

A ragged returner shouted angrily at them. "You're wastin' your time! Nothin' up there but rocks an' wind! Everything worth havin' has already been taken!"

Nobody paid any attention and he glowered at them, muttering. Then he shouted, "You're a pack o' fools! I *been* there!"

A more sober-seeming man agreed, pausing in his downhill trek. "He's right, you know. It's a cold, windy, altogether miserable place. Nothing decent to eat and no shelter unless you build for yourself."

Other passersby merely stared sullenly and continued their way down the slope, heading back for the placer streams of the California Mother Lode.

Melissa turned in her saddle. "Mr. Trevallion? What is it really like?"

The air was growing colder, the sky was bleak. It was coming on to snow. "Probably much like they say," he commented, at last. "When I was there, no Virginia City existed and nobody had heard of a Comstock Lode, if there is such a thing. There were some raw, ragged hills, some sagebrush, stunted cedar, and winds that didn't blow dust, they blew *rocks*!

"If it's like other such places we'll have to build places for ourselves, or hire somebody to build. I'm not talking about houses, just shelters, anything away from the wind."

He thought back to that remembered time when they had come

out of the Forty-Mile into the minor paradise of the Carson River. One of the older men had tried a pan in one of the small streams that came down from the mountains to flow into the Carson. He found gold.

The others laughed at him. "That little bit? Throw it away! That's *nothing*! Just wait until we get to California!"

"But this here's gold!" the man protested. "My very first pan!"

"Forget it! Ain't more'n a couple of dollars there, an' in California your pan would be covered with it! Not just those few flakes!"

That was what they believed, that was the dream that led them on.

His father had said nothing, but he was the only miner among them. He knew little about gold, but he knew something of ores and how they occurred. He looked up at the small cluster of mountains from which the gold had to come. "Maybe if California doesn't pan out we will come back here."

At that time he had no idea that his father would never live to see California and that, having lost his mother, he was soon to lose his father to the same men.

SEVEN

Trevallion hunched his shoulders against the increasing chill. A slow rain began that turned almost at once to snow, and the icy trail grew more icy still. Men slipped on the steep path, scrambling up only to fall again. The mules, wise in the ways of trails, plodded on, ignoring the cursing of the men around them. At the trail's end there would be feed, and there would be water to drink, and they walked for that.

Trevallion tugged his hat brim lower and watched the girl ahead. She was taking it well, with no words of complaint. He had known few women well, but he could read human sign as well as that found on trails, and this girl had iron in her system which, in a few years, would turn to steel. She was strong and would grow stronger, yet he believed he had detected a fatal flaw that he had discovered in women before this.

There were women with a penchant for picking up stray cats and dogs, which was all very well. There were others who had the same tendency to pick up superficially attractive but empty men. Judging by Alfie, Melissa might be such a one.

His thoughts reverted to his own situation. The blond man who had passed them, forging on ahead, had recognized him, but who was he?

Not one of the men he still sought, he was too young, not much older than Trevallion himself.

Yet they would be coming here. The chances that any of them were still together was slight, but thieves and murderers were attracted to the boom camps, and it was a certainty one or more of them would come to the Comstock.

Riding along hour after hour, with nothing to think of but the trail, gave a man time to consider, and lately he had been doing a lot of thinking. Possibly it was because he was growing older, and perhaps wiser, but he had detected a slackening of purpose in himself and it angered him.

For years the horror of what he had seen and heard that night had obsessed him. The murderers had gotten off scot-free and then had

50

killed his father. There had been no convenient law to pursue and punish. Even before his father's death, his father had become a changed man, from a quiet but easygoing man he had become a sullen, morose shadow of himself.

As for himself, there had been years when he had awakened, crying out in fear, the horror of his mother's last hour indelibly imprinted on his mind.

Trevallion's thoughts turned to the night he saw a man playing cards, and it was a face he remembered.

To the bartender he spoke casually. "Who is he? The one in the blue-checked shirt?"

"Drifter, name of Rory. I've seen him around." The bartender poured the beer Trevallion ordered. "I'd steer clear of him. He's a bad one . . . cheats, I think. One of these days somebody will catch him at it."

There was no doubt. A little older, a little harder, but a face he remembered. Trevallion finished his beer, then crossed the room, and when there was an opening, sat in the game.

At Trevallion's deal Rory pushed the cards toward him and palmed one or more cards in the process. The man beside Trevallion made an involuntary start, so he must also have seen it, but Trevallion said nothing. It would happen again.

When it was Rory's deal again, the man swept in the cards and gathered them up, and Trevallion said, "What ever became of Skinner?"

Carefully, Rory shuffled the cards into a packet and said, "Skinner? I don't know any Skinner."

"Thought you might have," Trevallion said, "back in Missouri."

Rory said nothing. He put down the cards and got out a cigar. "Everybody's been in Missouri," he said finally.

"You're right. Some of them come west in wagons, starting from there, only some of them never get started."

Rory lit the cigar and took up the cards. "You talkin' or playin' cards?"

"Just thought you might remember Skinner," Trevallion said.

Rory rolled his cigar into the corner of his mouth and began to deal.

They played silently, yet Rory kept glancing at him, growing increasingly nervous. Trevallion met his eyes and smiled and Rory's jaw set; he started to speak, then changed his mind and ordered a drink.

A man seated near him put down his cards and quietly withdrew from the game.

Rory was winning and the winning seemed to give him confidence. His staring at Trevallion grew belligerent, but Trevallion seemed unaware. Again it was Rory's turn to deal, and as he picked up the cards, Trevallion commented, "That was an ugly night."

Rory's hands dropped to the table. His right hand slid back toward the edge of the table.

Trevallion gestured toward the deck. "Come on, man, deal!"

Rory took up the cards and dealt them, avoiding Trevallion's eyes. They played the hand in silence and then another. Rory won several small pots and had another drink. He stared at Trevallion, frowning a little. Finally he said, "Do I know you?"

Trevallion shrugged. "You've never seen me before tonight."

Rory dropped his hands to the discards and gave them a casual thrust toward Trevallion.

Trevallion said, "But I've seen you before. One night back in Missouri—*what's that in your left hand, Rory?*"

Rory went for his gun, and Trevallion shot him.

His left hand opened slowly and dropped two slightly crimped cards on the table.

Rory's eyes were on Trevallion's with sudden attention. The hand that had reached the gun in his waistband fell away into his lap. There was a growing red stain on his shirt front. Men pulled slowly back from the table.

"You . . . you . . ." Rory's lips struggled for the words that would not come.

"I was a boy then, Rory, but I was there. I saw it all."

There was dead silence in the room. Rory started to rise then slumped back in his chair.

"You saw it," Trevallion said. "He was cheating."

"I seen it before!" The speaker was the man who quit the game. "I saw him steal some cards from the discards!"

"But," a portly man with a heavy gold watch chain interrupted, "there was something else. What was all that talk?"

Trevallion's eyes were cold. "A private matter," he said.

He holstered his pistol, picked up the money from beside his cards, and walked from the room.

That had been three years ago.

He was jolted from his reverie by Ledbetter. "We'll spend the night at Strawberry. I got my own corner there if somebody hasn't beat me to it."

It was almost dark when they came up to Strawberry, and the fresh snow had already been churned into slush. From the building there was a sound of loud voices and a rattle of dishes.

Ledbetter rode by and up into the trees on the slope. Not more than three minutes further on, he led them into an open place among the trees. At one side a row of trees had been pushed half over by an avalanche of snow in some bygone winter. A dozen or more of them leaned at a sharp angle, and behind them debris and fallen logs had reared a wall, offering shelter from the wind. Beneath it there was almost no snow.

"Don't cotton to crowds," Ledbetter said, "so I found me this place."

"I'll start a fire," Trevallion offered.

Melissa followed him and stood by. "If I can help?" she asked.

He broke suckers from low on the trunks of the trees, gathered some dead, broken branches and chunks of bark. From a pocket he took a bit of tinder, part of an old bird's nest.

"Do you always carry something like that?"

Without looking up, he nodded. "Can't be sure of finding something dry."

When Trevallion had a fire started he led his mule to water, stripped off the gear, and located a place under the trees for his bed. It was back away from the crowd. Nearer the fire he prepared some boughs and grass for Melissa's bed.

"You mustn't blame Alfie," she said suddenly. "Mousel was armed. He might have killed him."

"Alfie had a gun. He had a pocket-pistol and it was double-barreled. He had two shots to Mousel's one; he ran like a rabbit."

He glanced around at her. "Learn to judge men. His kind will always run."

"Wouldn't you ever?"

"Nobody knows what he will do. I never have, except from Indians, when outnumbered. But I might. It all depends on the situation. All Alfie needed was nerve. If he'd have pulled that gun, Mousel would have quit cold, although he might try to shoot him in the back, later."

Ledbetter fried bacon. Several of the men went down to Strawberry to eat. Trevallion brought a loaf of bread from his pack. The three ate without much talk.

Suddenly Trevallion looked around. Tapley was back under the trees, nearly out of sight. "Pull up a chair," Trevallion suggested. "There's plenty."

"I got nothing to offer."

"You're company. Come on."

Slowly he walked down and squatted on his heels. He accepted some bread and bacon and ate, obviously hungry. "Thank you," he said when finished. "I'm beholden."

"You can put your feet under my table any time," Ledbetter said.

"Goes for me," Trevallion added.

The Arkansawyer squatted again and took up a burning twig to light his pipe. "Lost my outfit." He puffed a moment. "Caught in a flash flood away down yonder in the desert. Had us two cows. Injuns got 'em."

" 'Us'?"

"Had me a wife." He dropped his eyes to the fire. "She was a good woman. Died out yonder . . . fever. My girl, she's goin' to school. She's in Benecia."

"Hard," Ledbetter muttered. "A man comes on hard times."

"I seen no others," Tapley replied. "Worked hard all my years but can't seem to come up winners. Grasshoppers ate me out of two crops back in the States, hail done for another. Injuns burned me out a couple of times. I worked Rich Bar, come up empty. Made the rush to the Frazier," he turned to glance at Trevallion, "you know how that was."

"A bust. Gold too fine and too little of it."

"Aye." He added sticks to the fire. "Got to make it this time. I got that girl," he looked up proudly, "and she's beautiful. I don't know how come it, me bein' a homely sort of man and her ma just passin' pretty, but she's *beautiful*. A girl like that, with nothing, she'll have only trouble."

The morning dawned clear and cold, but there was no wind. The pines edged themselves black against the sullen sky, and the mules were restless when they saddled up.

Nobody talked. Once in the saddle, Ledbetter started off at a good pace. Only a few were on the trail when they reached it, and Ledbetter forged right into the column. Some drew aside, others cursed him, but he ignored the curses, lifting a hand to those who stepped aside and broke into a trot.

There was an odd feeling to the wind. Melissa caught up with Trevallion as today she had fallen behind him. "What's wrong?"

"Snow. There's snow on that wind."

"But it's clear!"

"You'll see. Jim wants to get us off the mountain before it strikes. Woodford's is next, but it's down off the hill."

Clouds piled up over the peaks and ridges behind them. A small wind fiddled among the pines. The mules quickened their step. Ledbetter glanced back at the sky.

The trail dipped down into a thicker stand of pines, and the sky was no longer visible except directly overhead. Occasionally, through the trees ahead and much lower, they caught glimpses of a valley and some grassland.

Trevallion knew where he was and what was coming and did not think of it. He was thinking of himself now. He was changing. The

sullen fury that had burned within him for so long was gone or
seemed to be gone, dissipated by time and the killing of Rory and
Skinner.

There was time now to think of the future, if he was to have any
future. He remembered only too well the words of the man long ago,
who had told him revenge could steal a man's life until there was
nothing left but emptiness.

They were nearing Genoa when Ledbetter fell back beside him.
"I'm riding back with some ore, Val. Will you keep an eye on her?"

"As much as I can."

"Just if she needs a hand. Hate to see a young girl up here alone."

"You know how they are, Jim. They talk rough and some of them
are rough, but nobody will see a decent woman bothered."

"Maybe. This ain't like it was in the States. Men coming in from
everywhere. Ain't got the same upbringing or ideas."

"They'll learn."

For a time they rode in silence, then Trevallion said, "Jim, I know
how hard they are to come by, but I'd like to buy this mule . . . and
hers, too."

"All right," Ledbetter agreed. "I'll sell you the black one, and you
can use hers until I come over on my next trip. She can ride it to
Virginia town."

"Fair enough."

They drew up at a hitching-rail, and both men dismounted.
Trevallion looked up at the mountain. *Maybe*, his brain said, *just
maybe this is it*.

He glanced at Melissa Turney's blanket-roll. It was pitifully thin.
"You'll need a better groundsheet," he said, "and more blankets. It's
cold up there."

"It will be summer soon," she protested.

"Aye, that it will, but there'll be cold nights aplenty before then."

"I can't afford it."

"No problem. I'll stake you that far." He hesitated then suggested,
"If you're that serious about the baking, we might go partners for a
bit."

Ledbetter agreed. "I've fifty dollars I'll venture. If you can bake,
you'll have all the money you'll need in no time at all."

"We'd better get what she needs now," Trevallion said. "No need
making another trip back down the mountain."

He held the door for her as she entered, Ledbetter following.
Trevallion was the last one through the door, and the first person he
saw was Ramos Kitt.

EIGHT

For an instant Trevallion had an impulse to turn around and walk out, but if Kitt was in the area, they must one day meet. He was halfway across the room when Kitt turned and saw him.

Startled, Kitt froze in position, his right hand holding a pair of pants he was examining. Carefully, he put them down.

"How are you, Ramos? You're looking well."

Slowly, Ramos Kitt relaxed. "I'm doing all right. I wasn't expecting you."

Trevallion smiled. "So I noticed. I wasn't expecting you, either."

Ramos took the makings from his pocket and began to build a cigarette. As he touched the paper to his tongue, he looked over it at Trevallion. "I hear Skinner is dead."

"Last time I saw him, he was."

"He was a friend of mine."

"What was between us was no business of yours. You met him at Sutter's Mill, after Marshall's find. What was between us goes back before that."

"I met him in '54. Sutter's was finished by then."

Trevallion stepped to the bar. "I'll buy a drink, Ramos." Ledbetter and Melissa were watching, puzzled. "There need be no trouble between you and me."

"He was my friend."

"Skinner was a friend to no man. A riding partner, maybe. An associate, maybe. But not a friend. Anyway, he's gone. He had a fair shake and he lost."

"He was good with a gun."

"But not good enough. Will you have that drink?"

Ramos hesitated. He was a slim, wiry man who had easy, catlike movements. He wore sideburns and a mustache. "All right."

They moved to the bar and were served, the man behind the bar large-eyed with awareness.

"Prospecting?" Kitt asked.

"In a way."

"What was it between you an' Obie?"

56

Trevallion did not want to talk about it. Neither did he want to kill this man. "He was one of them who killed my mother and father. That was ten years ago."

"Do I know any of the others?"

"You might. Maybe you knew Rory?"

"I knew him. A no-good card—" he broke off suddenly. "Rory's dead?"

"He is. He was killed when caught cheating."

Ramos looked at him out of the corners of his eyes, then gulped half the whiskey. "There is gold here," he said then, "but not much. I've been thinking of leaving."

"Have you heard about the silver, then?"

"Silver?"

"The blue stuff. The stuff they've been mucking out of the sluices and cursing for a nuisance. There's been an assay, and it runs strong with silver."

"The hell you say!" He paused, then asked, "Do you think it's worth staying for?"

"I do." Trevallion finished his drink. "Ramos, I've some friends to help here, and a young lady who wishes to start a bakeshop. I'll be going then. But, Ramos?"

"Yes?"

"There's going to be money to be made here. A great lot of it, and there's a lot of no-nonsense sort of men coming in who will be making it and not wanting trouble. You're not a miner, but you'd make a guard for gold shipments, other things."

Ramos smiled, showing even, white teeth. "A *guard*? Me?"

"I'd trust you, Ramos." Trevallion looked into the suddenly unsmiling eyes. "I'd trust you with any amount, and know that if it didn't get to Sacramento it would only be because you were dead or out of ammunition."

"Maybe you trust too easily, my friend. There are those who say I ride the other trail."

"There are many trails and if one doesn't suit, we can try another." He gestured a hand. "I smell money, Ramos. You can be rich here, honestly, and end your days on a ranch over in the valley with a lot of fat Kitts running about. You've been riding a bad horse, Ramos, and so have I, but it's time to switch saddles."

"Maybe."

Trevallion turned away, then added, "Carry plenty of ammunition, Ramos."

Trevallion rode with Melissa up through Gold Canyon. Their mules' hoofs clattered on the rock under the thin soil. It was bleak and barren, marked with clumps of short, sad grass mingled with the sagebrush and cedar.

They drew up within sight of the settlement, if such it could be called. Scattered stone huts, some ramshackle shacks of dirty canvas and planks, further along a frame building or two, and a log house built of cedar cut on the mountainside.

A dog barked, and a woman in a faded blue dress stood in the door of the log cabin and shaded her eyes at them.

"Is . . . is this *it*?"

"It is."

Wind stirred her pale blonde hair as she turned to look at him. "I expected more."

"They are all the same. Boom camps start like this. If there's rich ore, they grow."

"Will there be stores? Places like that?"

"Saloons first, then boarding houses, and what will be called hotels. Many of those will be in tents. Usually two or three mines pan out and the rest come to nothing. The discoverers will sell out, take their money, spend it, and when broke they will go out looking for another strike.

"Those who don't sell out will be tricked or forced out. Then they will drift on and be forgotten. Then will come the men who know how to develop and manage properties, the ones who know how to make their money work for them. I saw one of them on the trail, a man named George Hearst. He was at Sheep Camp and Grass Valley."

"What will become of me?"

"If you stick to what you are planning, you will do well. Stay away from mines and do not invest in mining stocks. Just bake, sell, and save. And steer clear of Alfies."

"He was all right. He just—"

"He ran like a rabbit. Ma'am, I will help you build your own place and get started, but let me warn you.

"You're a good woman. You will work hard and you will do well, and you will find a good man if you will wait.

"Probably you'll not wait. There will be another Alfie. He will be good-looking and empty, and he will spend your money and come back for more and more, and finally he will leave. Another will come along who might have different hair and eyes, but he will be Alfie all over again."

"You don't think much of me."

"On the contrary, I do. Just don't mistake loneliness for love."

"I'm afraid of this place. It frightens me." She hesitated. "Mr. Trevallion, I don't have much money. I don't have a place to live. I wanted to come but now that I am here—"

"You will start by sleeping on the ground. We all will, and we all have. As for a place, I will help you build one. As of today, I shall buy into your business. I will help you build, and I'll buy what you need for the first month. I want twenty percent of the profits."

"That's a lot."

"As of now, it is nothing."

"I have two hundred dollars. My mother saved it and· hid it from—from him. There's a little more than that, actually, but not much more."

"You've made another mistake. Never tell anybody what you have. Especially the Alfies."

"I'll never see him again."

Trevallion smiled. "Want to bet? He knew you had some money, didn't he? No doubt he believes you have more than you do, so he will be here in a few days with a very smooth story to tell. Later, after you've talked a bit, he will tell you of this great chance he's got, if he only had a little more money. He will need a stake, just for a start."

"You don't like him."

"I know his kind. I'll tell you what to do. In the first place, don't lend him even one dollar, but tell him you need help building your place of business, and you will pay him just what you pay the others."

"He will not come. Not now. Anyway, he was nice and he wanted to help."

"Forget him. Stay away from the Alfies and you will become a rich woman."

"And lonely."

"We are all lonely. Be lonely, but plan for security. The winds blow very cold for a poor man. Know all the Alfies you wish, ma'am, but when they ask for money, no matter how little, tell them no. If it does nothing else, it will help to find the ones who really care."

"You're hard, Trevallion."

He pointed suddenly. "There! That's a likely spot! Right beside the road and not too much work to clear the ground . . . if somebody hasn't claimed it."

The place was fairly level and scattered with rock, with a fair-sized cedar a few yards back from it. Melissa looked around, dismayed. "Isn't there a better place? It's so rough, and all those rocks!"

"Building material. But take a good look around. There isn't much choice."

He glanced up along the narrow strip of trail. Here and there men were working, sinking holes, building their own shelters, or simply talking. "Stay here," he advised, "and start moving those rocks. Pile them yonder."

"Move the rocks?" She dismounted and looked around. "I guess I can, all but those real heavy ones."

"I know you can. Just you get started, keep busy, and let me handle the rest of it."

He walked his horse along to where three men were sinking a shaft. They were down about five feet. He drew up and watched them work for a minute or two. When one of them straightened up from his work, he asked, "You boys have been here a spell. See that piece up yonder where the lady is working? Has anybody filed on that?"

"Lady?" As one man they turned to look. Melissa had removed her hat and her blonde hair caught the feeble sun. "No, not that I know of. What's she doin'? Does she aim to work that claim?"

"Says she's going to build a bakery. Of course, it will take awhile, her being all alone like that, but she figures to bake pies, doughnuts, and such."

"Can she really bake?"

"Damned if I know, but Jim Ledbetter, she came up with one of his pack trains, he says she makes the best doughnuts a man ever ate."

A slim red-haired man leaned on his shovel. "Makes a man's mouth water. I ain't had a doughnut since I left Ohio, an' that's three years this comin' spring."

"Lone woman like that," the speaker was a chunky, solidly built man with a bald spot, "it'll be too much for her. Her chimney, f'r instance, buildin' a chimney that will draw well—that's an art!"

"I'm no hand at chimneys," Trevallion said, "but I am sure enough hungry for doughnuts. I figured to help her a little, just to hurry it up."

"Hell!" The third man dropped his pick. "Let's all go! With three or four working, it will take no time at all, an' this talk of pies, doughnuts an' such, it fairly makes my mouth water."

Red agreed. "Eilley makes a fair dried-apple pie, but doughnuts . . . ?"

They started down the trail with their tools. Seeing them, a man on the next claim called over, "Hey! What's goin' on?"

"He'p a lady with her house! She figures to open a bakery!"

The man shouldered his shovel. "Come along, John. If they can help, so can we."

"A bakery, is it?" John said. "She'll be needing ovens then."

"Three rooms," another commented, "one for the baking, one for the selling, and one for sleeping. Three should do it."

Trevallion rode on ahead. "Melissa," he said, "you've got help. They will have your house up before sundown. Smile a lot, now, and let them advise you. There's men in that group who could build anything, and will."

The man who knew how to build fireplaces immediately took charge, laying out the foundations and walls. Trevallion helped for some time, then mounted his mule and rode back down the canyon. As he rode he scanned the hills. He should be finding a claim for himself, but he avoided crowds, and the bottom of the canyon was filling rapidly.

He was riding through the settlement at Gold Hill when he saw a man he remembered from the Frazier. "Tom?" he called.

The lean, narrow-shouldered man looked up, squinting. "Val? I'll be damned! Heard you were dead!"

Trevallion gestured at the hole. "How's it look?"

"Too soon to tell. But the canyon looks good. I think this is the big one, Val. I really do." He looked up at Trevallion. "We're all used to hunting gold. We've seen strikes come an' go, but it was gold we hunted. Most of us never knew anything else.

"All the time we were panning for gold or working the sluices, that damn blue stuff kept clogging things up. I must've mucked out fifty tons of the stuff, an' maybe more. Then somebody got smart and took some over to Grass Valley.

"Atwood—d' you remember him? He ran the assay. Silver! Pure-dee silver! That was when the boom started."

He gestured toward a canvas-roofed shed nearby that had a bar running its full length and men standing three and four deep in front of it. "There they are! The workers and the talkers! You just go over an' listen. You never heard so much damn' nonsense in your life! Men bragging about their mines! Talking about ore, leads, offshoots, shafts, and winzes and most of them never held a muckstick in their hands, let alone a single-jack or a drill. To hear them tell it you'd think the camp was full of mining engineers!"

Tom took a plug of tobacco from his pocket, offered it to Trevallion, who refused, then bit off a corner and returned the plug to his pocket. "By the way, there's been a man asking for you. A couple of days back."

"Asking for me?"

"Wanted to know if you'd come into camp yet. When I asked if he was a friend of yours he said not exactly, but he'd heard of you. Big man. I found out later his name was Waggoner."

The name was unfamiliar.

"Staked a claim yet?" Tom asked.

"Not yet." Trevallion gestured back the way he had come. "Young lady back yonder plans to open a bakery. Some of us have been helping her build a place."

"We could use one. Eilley's all right, but she's so busy she doesn't know which end is up."

"Tom? That young lady, she's a good girl. Her name is Melissa Turney. Jim Ledbetter and me, we're sort of keeping an eye on her. You could do the same when you're up that way."

"Sure as shootin'. Got a girl of my own back east, and I hope to bring her out soon's I have a stake. Sure, I'll go up there now and again, just to pass the time of day."

Waggoner? Trevallion considered the name. He knew no one of that name, and his memory for names was usually good. Nor was he a man apt to be asked for. Trevallion was a loner and known to be such. He traveled alone, worked alone, and so he had no old chums or partners who might be looking for him.

Tom Lasho he had known for years. Tom had been on Rich Bar, he had worked in Grass Valley, and he had done his first mining at Rough an' Ready. Lasho had done well on Rich Bar, but then he had gone back to the States and spent it all.

Trevallion was in no hurry. He took several days to scout around, talking little, listening a lot, but most of the time he simply spent studying the country. The best ground had been taken and old "Pancake" Comstock claimed everything in sight, bullying, threatening, or arguing what he called his "rights."

On the fourth day, at Spafford Hall's Station, he encountered a square-set, bearded man with a quick smile. "You're Trevallion?"

"I am."

"I'm Will Crockett. I own the Solomon." He paused. "Can I buy you a drink?"

"No. Just tell me what you want."

"They say you're a first-class miner, a hard-rock miner. I've a job for you, a good job."

"Sorry."

"Working for someone else?"

"For myself, when I locate a claim."

"The good stuff is taken. I'll pay top wages and start you at shift boss."

"Thank you, no."

"I need a good man, a man who knows ground and who knows how to sink a shaft and get the ore out."

"Sorry."

"You won't even talk about it? Damn it, man, I've a good claim!

One of the best! But I'm no miner. I'm working ten men over there, and we're getting out some ore, but it isn't paying off like it should. I need a mining man."

"Sorry." Then, liking the man, he said, "I may not even stay. I'm a drifter, Crockett. If I do stay I'd rather have a place of my own that I can work when I wish." He permitted himself a slight smile. "You see, Crockett, I am probably the only man on the lode who doesn't want to get rich."

"Then what are you here for? No man lives in this godforsaken place unless he wants to be rich!"

When Crockett had gone Trevallion stood outside Spafford's, trying to remember where he had heard of the Solomon. Then it came to him. That batch of mail Ledbetter had brought over from Placerville was for the Solomon, most of it for Hesketh, the bookkeeper.

He watched the line of wagons, horseback riders, and walkers heading up Gold Canyon. Occasionally one would come over to Spafford Hall's, but Trevallion avoided them, and avoided their questions. He was restless and irritable, and he knew he should locate a claim and get to work, for instinctively he felt that was what he needed.

He needed hard work, yet it was more than that. He was changing.

Crockett's question irritated him. What had he come for? Why was he here?

The answer was plain. He had come to find a man . . . or men. He had come to kill.

Four of the men who had killed his father and mother were dead. The others still lived, unpunished for their crimes, but they would come here, lured to the honeypot of gold and silver. They were not miners, they were wolves, and they would flock to this place.

And he would be waiting.

The trouble was, he no longer wanted to kill.

NINE

In the gray light of a windy morning Trevallion rode up Gold Canyon to Melissa's bakeshop. Leaving his mule in the lee of the stone building, he went inside to complete the shelves he had begun.

"I'm glad you stopped." Her face was flushed from the heat of the stove and her hands covered with flour. "Today I am baking for the first time in this house, and I have made a pie, just for you!"

"Thanks." He dropped into a chair made from a barrel. "Is everything all right?"

"All right? Yes, of course, only I'm scared. I have never baked for anybody but homefolks and maybe a few picnics before we came west. I guess I can do it."

"Of course you can."

"Have you filed on a claim?"

He glanced out the window. Wherever he looked somebody was digging or building. "No," he said, at last, "I haven't. There's one away up the canyon I want to look at. Long ago I wandered up there with my father, and he fancied one piece of ground. Said it wasn't much but would make a man a good living."

"You don't want to be rich?"

"You know? I've thought about that and I really don't know. Once I thought I did. Now I am not sure."

Suddenly curious, she asked, "What *do* you want, Mr. Trevallion?"

He accepted the coffee she poured for him. For a moment he was silent, shying away from the question. After all, what *did* he want?

Once he could have said he wanted to find and kill the men who killed his parents. Now he was no longer sure, and his good sense told him that was a negative goal. What did he want? Did he want anything? Had he become an empty man, drifting just to find and kill when he no longer wished it?

"An awfully nice man came by yesterday. He had coffee with me. His name was Will Crockett."

"I know him. He offered me a job."

"He seemed nice. What does he do?"

64

"Owns a mine, a pretty good one, from what I hear. He has the reputation of being an honest man."

"He told me if I wanted a partner he had capital to invest, but I told him I already had a partner."

The room was warm with the smell of freshly made coffee and baking. Looking out the window he could see a half-dozen buildings going up, some of stone like the bakery, some frame. "If the boom holds," he said, "there will be ten thousand people here in another year."

"So many?"

"Aye. Just look at them. You've only to keep baking and you'll be rich." He glanced around. "Keep your eyes open for an older man or woman, a strong one. You're going to need help."

"That reminds me. I met a woman I like. She runs a boarding house."

"Eilley Orrum?"

"Yes. She's a Scot, isn't she?"

"Highland, and proud of it. She's been married a time or two—Mormons, I understand—and she's ambitious."

"Have you seen her 'peep-stone' as she calls it? It's a crystal ball."

"I've heard of it." He finished his coffee and got up. "I'll be back for the pie."

He rode up the canyon and staked his claim.

Trevallion had first come to the place with his father. A trickle of water ran in the streambed, and they tried a few pans and found color. Then they sat down and shared some biscuits and jerky.

"There's mineral," his father said, "if we don't find what we want in California, we may come back here."

Now Trevallion was back, alone. Ten years later and a thousand years older, or so it seemed.

On the site where he and his father had first tried the stream, he made camp. Several gnarled and ancient cedars had grouped to offer shelter behind their thick trunks and twisted branches. The mountain lifted steeply behind him and there was no way he could be taken from the rear.

He built his fire back under the edge of the trees and set up a large, flat rock for a reflector. After he started his coffee, he got out the gold pan he bought at Spafford Hall's, his own having been lost swimming the Yuba.

As it was a new pan, he heated it over the fire until it took on a dull red glow to give it a proper burn. Then he dunked it into the creek. This removed the oily film but also gave the pan a dark blue shade that enabled the gold particles to show up much better.

When the coffee was ready, he sat back under the trees, chewed on some jerked meat, and listened to the sound of the creek and the stirring of wind in the cedars. He had never been much of a camp cook, rarely taking time to prepare a meal. When he had finished eating he left the coffeepot on a rock amid the coals and went back to the stream.

Filling the pan nearly full of gravel, he held it just beneath the surface of the water, and holding the pan with one hand, he broke up the few lumps of clay with the other, meanwhile throwing out the larger rocks.

Then, holding the pan just beneath the surface he proceeded to swirl the water about, first in one direction, then in the other, to settle the larger pieces. Lifting the pan clear of the water, he tipped it slightly to allow the sand and dirt that was in suspension to trickle over the edge of the pan. A few sharp blows on the edge of the pan helped to settle the gold particles.

By repeating the process he soon had left only the heavy sands and gold. With tweezers he picked out the more obvious fragments, then put the material aside to dry and started again.

He worked the afternoon through, and in four hours of hard work, handling six to seven pans an hour, he netted approximately four dollars, which was good for the time and the place.

At Spafford Hall's he had bought a half sack of barley, and he fed a little to the mule, frying some bacon for himself. Adding water, he heated up the coffee.

With his cup of coffee in his hand, he left the fire and walked out to study the rock formations and drift along the stream. That stream, he surmised, would run only part of the year, and possibly only until the snow melted off. He walked back to his fire, convinced he had best use it while he could.

He went back to the fire and poked sticks into the flames. Suddenly irritated, he put down his cup. What was he doing here, anyway? He could pan out a living on this creek, but was that what he wanted? Why not take the job Crockett offered? That was a living, too, and if prospects looked good, he might ask for a piece of the operation for his services would be in demand.

He poked more sticks in the fire, then sat down under the cedars and refilled his cup. He told himself he no longer wished to kill anyone, not even those who so richly deserved it; yet here he was, like an old hound on the scent, following a haphazard trail because he knew nothing else.

He had done just what he had been warned against. He had allowed the hunt, the thirst for revenge, to take up his whole life. What he should do was to leave here, to go back east, somewhere far from all this, and drive it from his mind.

For days now he had been obsessed with a growing feeling of discontent that left him depressed and restless. Moreover, he had been warned on several occasions that men were inquiring for him. He was a man with many acquaintances and no close friends, and the possibility of anybody asking about him was slight.

Unless the hunted had now become the hunters.

If so, why? Who would know about him? Who could? True, two of that crowd had been killed, but everyone who knew Rory had known that sooner or later he would be killed. He was not only a card-cheat but a clumsy one. He was also a quarrelsome man.

As for Skinner, he had come west with Rory, and they had been associated in various crimes along the river and the way west. Skinner had known that his old companion had been killed.

Trevallion recalled the day they met on the trail. Skinner had been riding toward him and Trevallion had recognized him at once. Trevallion drew up, waiting.

Skinner pulled up, warily.

"Hello, Skinner."

"You know me?"

"You were a friend to Rory. You came from Missouri together."

Skinner steadied his horse. Every instinct told him this was trouble, but he had no idea why.

"Who are you?"

"You wouldn't remember. I was only a youngster, Skinner, and I didn't have a gun. Also, I was too scared."

Skinner let his right hand fall to his thigh, within inches of his gun. "I don't know what you're talkin' about."

"It was a camp by the river, Skinner. There were two wagons."

Skinner's mouth was dry and he felt sick inside. A thief and occasional murderer, he had shied from crimes against women, but that night, with that whiskey they'd been drinking—

"What d' you want?" His voice was hoarse. He was not worried. He was too good with a gun. Nevertheless, that night had haunted him, and for some reason it had kept him looking over his shoulder for years.

"I killed Rory, Skinner. He was caught cheating but that wasn't the reason."

Skinner was poised for it. He was ready. He had chosen his target, right over the belt buckle.

"Where'd the whiskey come from, Skinner?"

The sudden, unexpected question disconcerted him. "Why . . . ! Why, I'm damned if I know," he said honestly. "All of us were short. We were holding nothing."

"How much did you get out of it, Skinner?"

Skinner spat angrily. "Not a damn thing! Somebody yelled an' . . . well, we taken out."

"I know you did, Skinner. I was there. I saw you run, and I saw a man climb into the wagon. He killed my mother, Skinner, whatever was left to kill. And he got the money-box. I want his name, Skinner."

So that was how it was? Skinner had suspected as much. They'd been tricked, the lot of them, they'd been used. "If I knew," he said, "I'd kill the—"

"He fed you whiskey, got you all drunk, got you to do the dirty work, and then he got away with everything." He paused just a moment. "But you were there, Skinner. You were one of them."

"Look," Skinner protested, "I—" He went for his gun.

Trevallion shot him.

Skinner completed the draw, but the strength was suddenly gone from his hand, and the gun slipped from his fingers.

"Damn you!" Skinner said. "I'm goin'! I'll get—"

"Skinner? I know where I put that bullet. You aren't going anywhere, Skinner."

Deliberately, Trevallion rode around him and started up the trail. At the crest of the low hill, he turned in his saddle and looked back.

Skinner was lying face down on the ground, and his horse had walked off a few steps.

Nobody had associated him with the killing of Skinner. The body had been found, he later learned, several days after. It lay on the grass, a drawn pistol lying at hand. Skinner was known. It was decided he had been killed in a gunfight or by some intended victim.

Trevallion had felt no elation. There was no satisfaction, only a dull heaviness within him.

Long ago, as a boy, he had told himself he would kill them all, but now he no longer wanted to. . . . Yet he was here, and he was here because sooner or later he knew the prospects for loot would bring them to the Comstock. They were among the vultures who followed booms to prey on the unwary, the unguarded, and the innocent.

Darkness had settled over the canyon. Trevallion banked his fire and spread his bed under the cedars.

For a long time he lay looking up at the few stars he could see through the cedars.

That little girl, the one he'd held so tight, stifling her cries so they might not be murdered, too, she lost both her parents that night. It was bad enough for a boy, but much worse for a girl.

Grita, that was her name. Marguerita Redaway, called Grita for short.

He had said he was going to marry her.

He smiled up into the cedars, thinking of it. What had become of her? Where was she now? Probably dead. . . .

Anyway, marrying him would have been a poor bargain.

TEN

The man in the gray suit leaned back in his chair and placed the fingertips of his two hands together. "Mademoiselle Redaway, you do not seem to understand. You have nothing, or next to nothing. Your aunt was in debt, very heavily in debt. The chateau must be sold, the horses as well.

"You will have one thousand American dollars, and some worthless mining stock. Of course, you will have whatever personal effects she left. That is all."

"I shall need no more."

"You do not seem to understand. No doubt the money seems a great sum to you, but living as you have it will last no time at all, and you will be penniless.

"It could be invested, and you could realize a small sum from it each year, but I think—"

"Uncle André, you worry too much. Please don't. I shall be all right. I have made my decision."

"And that is?"

"I shall be an actress."

André dropped his hands to the arms of his chair and sat forward. "An actress! But that is impossible. You have no training. And it isn't quite the life I should choose—"

She laughed. "But you are not choosing, Uncle André. I am!"

"Need I remind you that you are under age?"

The smile left her face. "You know that, I know that, but need anyone else? You are not my guardian. You are not a blood relative. You were and have been a very good friend. I had hoped you would help me."

"I? I know few people in the theater, mademoiselle."

"But you do know some? Rachel, for instance, Rachel Felix?"

He flushed, and she was amused. "Ah, then you *did* know her!"

"Slightly, mademoiselle, and that was years ago. Many years ago."

"But if you went to see her? She would know your name?"

He hesitated. "Well, we were both very young. . . . It was a long time ago."

He gave a gesture of dismissal. "It does not matter. You are not an actress. Do you think a professional company, performing every night, could afford some inexperienced girl?"

She sat down opposite him. "Uncle André, it is confession time. When my aunt married the count it was her second marriage. He knew this, but no one else did. Not on this side of the Atlantic."

"So?"

"My aunt was for many years an actress. She toured on the American stage, and I with her."

"You?"

"My parents were killed when I was eight. I went to live with another aunt, then when I was ten I went to live with Claire and began to appear here and there, always in plays with her. I played children's parts, both boys and girls, and then maids, and finally some quite good roles.

"When Claire married the count he insisted I drop all that and return to school. It was very easy for me, that school was, so I studied music and the dance as well. Rachel is soon to do a play I know very well, and there is a part, a very small part, that I could do easily."

"She does not cast her plays, I am sure."

"She does not—officially. Unofficially I am quite sure she has very much to say."

"Perhaps, perhaps." He looked around at her as she moved across the room. "Mademoiselle? Did you know Rachel is considering an American tour?"

"I did."

"You would go?"

"Of course. After all, I was born there. And you say I have all that mining stock. Perhaps I should see to my investments."

"They are nothing, nothing! Most of the mines are unknown, unheard of! Your aunt bought foolishly, just as she loaned money. Why, among those papers there must be fifty notes! Long overdue and uncollectable now."

"No matter. If I ever get out west again I shall collect them, or try."

He stood up. "Mademoiselle? There is another thing. You are very young, very fresh. You are also beautiful. I have heard it said that older actresses do not always like to have younger, more beautiful actresses in their plays."

She shrugged her shoulders. "I have heard Rachel Felix is a very shrewd woman, a good businesswoman. I do not think she will mind if the play is successful."

When she was home, she took the faded carpetbag he had brought and opened it. Packets of papers! Old letters, notes of money loaned and never repaid, old lists of mining shares for mines no doubt long forgotten, some of them her aunt's possessions, some her own that had been left with her aunt when she went off to school.

Suddenly among the papers she saw a familiar corner, and spreading the packet of envelopes she extracted it. The date was 1850, almost ten years ago.

> *Dear Grita,*
>
> *I am in Sacramento, working. It is not very good work but all I could find. My father, too, is killed. Killed by the same men, although he shot two of them before dying.*
>
> *When I sold the wagon and the things from it I found a packet of letters belonging to your father and mother. Some were from a man your father had helped start in business. He is doing very well now. When he found I knew you he asked what he should do with the money and I said to invest it. He said if I would accept part of the responsibility he would do so. This has been done.*
>
> *I remain your obed. svt.,*
>
> *Trevallion*

Had that been his name? She remembered him only as a boy named Val, who was very strong and very kind and how she had been terribly frightened and he had held her.

As to the money, she knew nothing of that, and it could not have been much.

Trevallion—odd, that. No other name, simply Trevallion.

Had she replied? She could not remember, yet oddly enough she could remember him. He had been a very serious boy, and for his age, very strong. He had helped her father load some things into the wagon, and her father had commented upon it.

Later, when she was in the company and they were working, she asked an actress who was applying her makeup at the same table, "Aren't you the one who has been to America?"

"I have been. They are hungry for theater there."

"Do you know a town called Sacramento? I believe it is in California."

"It is near San Francisco, I think. There are no large cities but they have found gold there. Have you not heard? Everyone is going. It is said if they like what you do or how you look they shower you with gold nuggets."

"Better than flowers," another actress commented. "All I ever get is flowers and suggestions."

"Someday," Grita said thoughtfully, "I shall go there."

Several times each night Trevallion would awaken and listen. It was a habit he had begun to develop on the way west. At daybreak in the canyon, he was up and panning for gold. The water supply he had was mostly from melting snow, and there would soon be an end to that, so whatever he could find to supplement his small stake would have to be found quickly.

On the third day he found a pocket under a boulder where the water spilling over created a natural riffle and he netted sixty-six dollars in four pans. As his supplies had run low, he saddled the mule, leaving most of his gear where it was. He rode down the canyon to its junction at Seven Mile and then down Gold Canyon, going by a roundabout route that brought him into town from the north. He had no desire to advertise the location of his camp or his direction of travel.

At least a dozen new buildings were going up, and he guessed there would be three or four hundred men in the area. Probably more, for Gold Hill and Silver City had become communities.

Melissa met him at the door. "I saw you coming," she said. "Jim's here."

Ledbetter was seated at the table with a cup of coffee and some doughnuts. "Sit down," he said. "I've been wishful of seeing you."

Trevallion dropped into a chair and accepted the coffee and doughnuts Melissa put before him. He glanced up at her. "How are you doing?"

Ledbetter chuckled. "You should do so well! She can't bake them fast enough! My guess is she's staked a better claim than anybody on the lode." He put down his cup and looked at Trevallion. "How about you?"

"I've been washing a little dust."

"A pan won't do it. You need a rocker, or better still, a sluice."

"Maybe. I may not stay long."

Ledbetter glanced at him thoughtfully but offered no comment. After a moment he said, "Before the summer is over, there will be three or four thousand men here."

He sipped his coffee, then dunked a doughnut. "Val," he said, "you be careful."

Trevallion's expression did not change. Ledbetter was puzzled by him, having known many men. Trevallion was a slim, dark-featured man with the broad, powerful shoulders common among men who used a double-jack for hours at a time. When he smiled, which was rarely, Trevallion was, he reflected, a remarkably handsome man.

"Somebody's interested in you," he commented. "Asking around here and there. Have you got enemies?"

"Who hasn't?"

"With your savvy you could become a rich man," Ledbetter commented. "Atwood over to Grass Valley assayed some of that blue stuff they been throwing out. Runs three thousand to the ton, I hear."

"There's always rumors. I've heard five different stories on how rich it is."

"Surprised they haven't tried to hire you over at the Solomon. They're sinking a shaft."

"I was asked."

"If you go over there—Crockett is all right, a solid man. Hesketh, well, I don't know. He's a man I'd watch. He's in touch with some of those high-flyers in San Francisco."

"A bookkeeper, isn't he?"

"Aye, a bookkeeper. Knows every ounce of ore that comes from any claim on the Comstock, and he's bought a few claims himself. Some of them don't make sense. He's bought cheap, too."

Trevallion glanced at Melissa. She was filling out a little, eating better, no doubt. She had two men and a woman working for her now.

"Jim? This man who has been asking for me?"

"Big, slow-moving man. Takes his time, I mean. Handlebar mustache and a bad scar over one eye. He's no miner, I'll bank on that. I never heard his name, but he seems to have money enough to live and get around."

Ledbetter finished his coffee and stood up. "Got to get back over to Mormon Station—Genoa, I mean. I'm meeting a Mexican over there with some mules to sell."

"Branching out?"

"Uh-huh. But one day I'm going to pack it all in and go back to Kentucky. I'll buy me a place there and settle down to raise horses."

He left, and Trevallion refilled his cup. Ledbetter at least had a plan, an idea of what he wanted. He might never really do what he said, but at least he had it in mind. He had somewhere to go.

Trevallion gulped a mouthful of coffee, then suddenly angry with himself, he started to rise. Slowly he sat down again.

There was a man riding by on a rawboned paint gelding, a big man with a handlebar mustache. As he drew abreast of the bakeshop he squinted his eyes to stare within. Where Trevallion sat it was dark and shadowy, and there was not one chance in a hundred the rider could make him out, but Trevallion noticed something.

The rider had a deep scar over one eye.

ELEVEN

Trevallion had no memory of the man. Watching from where he sat, he saw him dismount in front of Eilley's and tie his horse there.

His first impulse was to walk down, sit opposite him and give him a chance to open the ball. Yet there was no use inviting trouble.

His memory for the night of his mother's murder was stark and clear, yet he had seen only a few of the men's faces, and those only half-seen in the flickering light from the campfires. Yet this man could be one of them.

But why hunt *him*? Had the deaths of Rory and Skinner alerted them?

The chances of the group still being together were slight. Such men had a way of drifting, taking up with anyone who was available to do whatever they had in mind.

Suppose, however, the man who came from the shadows, the unknown men, knew what was going on? He was the only one who had come out of it with any money and somehow he did not fit the pattern of the others. All of them had the look and manner of typical border ruffians but him. There had been something cold and calculating about him.

Melissa returned to the table with a cup and filled it from the pot, then his. "Mr. Trevallion? There's a lot of talk going on about Secession. The men who come here for coffee argue about it and sometimes they get very angry. I don't even know what they are talking about."

"It's a matter of States' rights," he said, "and the slavery question is involved. With most of the men who come in here I believe the slavery question is secondary to the right of a state to do as it pleases. You must remember that better than half of the men in camp are from the South, and whether a state is to be admitted to the Union as Slave or Free is very important to them."

"I wish they'd take their arguments somewhere else! That's about all they talk about except for how dangerous Langford Peel is or who will win when Heenan and Sayers fight."

"Just listen," he advised, "and stay out of it. They won't expect a woman to know anything about politics, so you don't have to take sides. Keep your own conscience and let them debate the issues. Nobody is ever convinced by argument, anyway. They just think up new reasons for maintaining old positions and become more defensive. The thing for you to remember is that no matter what they believe they all drink coffee, eat doughnuts and pies."

"But there are so many new names to keep straight. Who are Heenan and Sayers?"

"Prizefighters. Heenan is an American, Sayers an Englishman, and they are both good. Heenan is the better of the two, I believe, and he is also somewhat larger."

"And Langford Peel?"

"Sometimes a gambler. He's a very good man with a gun—used to be a soldier, in the Cavalry."

"Do you know a man they call Ol' Virginny?" she asked.

"I do. If he ever advises you on anything pertaining to mining, pay attention. He knows what he's talking about, drunk or sober."

"What about Mr. Comstock? The one the lode is named for?"

"He's a four-flusher, Melissa. He got hold of some maps and estimates left by the Grosch brothers, and on the strength of that, he's laid claim to everything around."

"I know. He convinced O'Riley and McLaughlin that they were on his ground and they took him in as a partner. Mr. Penrod is a partner, too."

"There's nothing wrong with Penrod except the company he keeps."

The bakery had become a clearing house for information for Trevallion, as sooner or later everyone stopped by, and the men talked freely among themselves or to her. Most of the miners had worked ground that was soon played out in other places and this, they felt, would be the same.

From where he sat, he could look out the door or the windows and see the entire side of the mountain was scattered with prospect holes and beginning mine shafts. Penrod had told him they were down over fifteen feet and expected to reach thirty before long. Several others were down as far and most of them were finding ore.

Trevallion finished his coffee. The paint horse was still tied at Eilley's.

He looked into his coffee cup with disgust. What in God's world was he doing with his life when all he could think of was that killing ten years ago? All around him things were growing, expanding, becoming, and now was the time to do . . . whatever he intended or wished to do. Was he to be driven always by hatred? Had it become so much a part of him that he was an empty man?

Ten years in the mountains and wild country of the west, and what did he have to show for it but two dead men, neither of whom was worth the pinch of powder it required to kill.

He was twenty-two, but he knew men of his age who owned mines or ranches, who had become or were in the process of becoming wealthy, or achieving something for their country or themselves.

It was a time when no man asked another his age. A good half the men on the Comstock were his age or younger. It was what a man could *do* that mattered. Several, no older or wiser than himself, had staked good claims here.

Of course, if this place followed the pattern, these men would sell out and move on, driven more by the urge to discover than to develop. In fact, few of them had the knowledge or the business skill needed to develop a mine. They were the seekers and finders, the men who knew placer mining and surface indications. Few had any knowledge of hard-rock mining or what it entailed.

The discoverers lacked the mental and emotional attitude needed to develop and improve a mine. It would be a long process, and much money would be needed to open up a mine such as these would be.

Until now he had been a finder—a finder and a mover. If he was to become anything here, he must become involved in development.

He made a decision then. He would forget that night ten years ago, as he knew his mother would wish him to forget, and his father also. He would look about, stake a likely claim, and work it. He would, if possible, acquire a working interest in another mine, perhaps with Crockett.

When he looked again, the horse was gone. Irritated, he got up and went to the door. Neither horse nor rider was anywhere in sight.

He walked into the street and went to Eilley's. Eilley had been washing clothes and cooking for miners for some time. She was a hearty, easygoing, friendly woman who stood for no foolishness and treated all the miners as so many unruly boys, and they loved her for it.

"Howdy," she glanced at him sharply. "Hadn't heard you was in camp today."

"You had a visitor just now, a big man with a scar and a mustache."

"I did. He's a good eater, too."

"Know him?"

"Waggoner, and he's a bad one. Leave him alone. I mean even you, leave him alone."

Trevallion dropped on a bench. The place was empty, and Eilley was cleaning up around. "Get yourself a claim, Eilley. This is it."

"It?"

"The big one. I've got a feeling."

"I'll believe that when you get a claim. What is it with you, Trevallion? You've more savvy about mining than any man in the fields, but you just drift. Why don't you find yourself a woman and settle down?"

He grinned at her. "I'm waiting for you, Eilley."

She laughed. "Now ain't that likely? No, I ain't your type, and I spotted it the moment I first seen you. I look 'em over, Trevallion. After all, I've been married twice, and I ain't agin tryin' on another one, but not you.

"Even if you were my type I'd fight shy of you. You wear that gun too loose, Trevallion. I don't want my husband brought home on a shutter or hangin' at the end of a rope."

He glanced at her. "Ever know me to hunt trouble, Eilley?"

"No, I never. That's what worries me. I can understand a trouble-hunter like that Eldorado Johnny from down the country. He's a nice boy but he sure does fancy himself as a bold, bad man. What makes me uneasy are these quiet, easy ones like you."

"I'm just a prospector and a miner, Eilley."

"Aye, but I wonder what you're prospectin' for. Wasn't it you who killed Rory?"

"I caught him cheating."

"So you did. And had some talk with him, too, a lot of talk nobody could make any sense out of. Seemed like there was something between you."

Trevallion got up. "What do you know about Waggoner?"

"He's always got money. Doesn't flash it around, but he doesn't count it, either. And he's not prospectin' and he ain't lookin' for work. I'd say he's the kind to fight shy of."

"Eilley? We're old friends. Keep your eyes open."

"To what?"

"Oh, I'm just curious. I'd like to know who his friends are—if he has any."

"What's between you?"

Trevallion stopped in the door. "That's just it. I don't know, but he's been asking around about me."

He went back, tightened his cinches, and rode down the canyon toward Silver City and Dayton.

Trevallion did not hear the voices behind him. He did not see the miner who had come in just after he left. "Who is he, Eilley? He has a look about him."

"Aye, he's a Cousin Jack. As good a miner as lives they do be saying, but a lonely man and a man to leave alone."

"A trouble-hunter?"

"Trevallion? I should say not. But he has a way about him that makes men just back off, but not women."

"So that's Trevallion? I've heard about him." The miner was about five foot ten, with a quiet, easy way. He had a certain hesitancy in his speech. "It pays to know the good ones," he added, "the ones a man can trust."

"There's no better." Eilley paused then looked up from the dishes she was washing. "There's a black thing riding him, I don't know what. He killed Rory, you know?"

"Rory had been asking it for years."

"So he had, so he had! Nonetheless there are some who say Trevallion pushed him into it." She dried a cup and placed it on the table. "There was a friend of Rory's. A man named Skinner. He's dead, too, found with a gun beside him but shot dead."

"This man Trevallion, who are his friends?"

She brushed a wisp of hair back over her brow. "He has none, and seems to want none. He's helped the lass down at the bakery some, but she knows nothing more than the rest of us."

"A drinker?"

"Not him. A drink now and again maybe, but a drinker? No. Watch him, John. He's a man who is completely in control of himself, and he seems to want nothing from anyone, anywhere."

"Would he work for someone else?"

"If he liked him, he might. Usually he washes a little dust here and there, keeps to himself. He brings shirts for me, and when I take them down to the hot springs to wash, the pockets are always empty. I have to watch the others, they leave things. I save them and return . . . nothing ever in his pockets and no ragged, worn clothes. Neat, patched sometimes, but neat."

At the office of the Solomon, Crockett closed the door behind him and went to the table that served as his desk. Albert Hesketh, who worked at a long table opposite, did not look up.

Crockett seated himself and cocked his feet up on the table and looked thoughtfully at his bookkeeper. "How's everything?" he asked, finally.

Hesketh looked up. "Fine, Mr. Crockett. I think we could use two more men and we'll need a shift-boss."

"Tried to hire one." Crockett got out his pipe. "A Cornishman named Trevallion."

Hesketh continued to make entries in the ledger.

"They tell me he's a top miner."

Hesketh blotted the line. "And did you get him?"

"Turned me down," Crockett said, "and they say he's the best." He took his feet down from the table. "We need him. I want to open up a cross-cut between our east and west drifts to improve the air circulation down there. Better for the miners," he added, "and I want to sink the shaft deeper."

"We are getting out good ore." Hesketh made the simple statement, but it sounded like an objection. "We can show a profit without further expenditure."

"Damn it, Hesk!" Crockett said. "I'm not interested in just showing a profit! There's a big ore body down there somewhere and I want it!

"Oh, I know! We have to spend more than we're making to do it, but I'll be damned if I'll go against my hunch! There's silver down there! Tons of it! And I want to get it out. Trevallion's our man. I know he is, and I'll be damned if I take no for an answer. I'll see him again."

He stoked his pipe. "Or you can."

"No. I'd rather you did, Mr. Crockett. You are the one who believes in that ore body, and you are the boss." He hesitated. "If you think Trevallion's the man, hire him. Personally, I believe there are several around town who would serve us better.

"I hear," Hesketh added, "that he's a sullen, unresponsive sort of man."

Crockett lit his pipe and threw the match on the floor, and Hesketh's lips tightened a little.

Trevallion here? Well, why not? He might indeed find that ore body, and if he did the stock . . .

Why not, after all?

TWELVE

Trevallion studied the gold in his pan under a small glass. It was not a good grade of gold, and during these past years he had handled a lot of gold dust. This was impregnated with silver, and he doubted it would go for more than ten dollars to the ounce.

So far he had made a living and edged ahead a little, yet that was not what he wanted. What was happening in Virginia town and Gold Hill was getting to him. Men were coming and going. Not a few gave up in the first few days, others lasted for weeks, some for months. The water was bad, food was expensive, and powder was also. Everything had to be brought over the Sierras from California.

Jim Ledbetter was running six trains of mules now, and couldn't keep up with the business.

"Val," he said seriously, "quit the mining and come in with me. I need help, and we can be rich—rich, I tell you! The money in these camps is in supplying what they need.

"No matter whether they find silver, they still have to eat, they have to wear clothes, they have to sleep! Eilley's getting rich just washing clothes! She rinses them out really good and pans out the dirt and she's doing better than some of the placer miners are."

Trevallion computed the small stake he was holding. He was a careful man, never a gambler. Uneasily, he shifted in his chair, looking out the window at the crowded street. It was his first time in Gold Hill or Virginia in over a month.

He'd had the feeling he was being stalked, hunted. As a result he had simply pulled out, had left his claim in the canyon, and had wandered over east and staked another claim in a canyon above Pipe Spring. On the certain theory that a man who makes no tracks leaves no tracks, he stayed where he was, killing an occasional deer, living sparsely and working hard.

He found gold, accumulated a little dust and a few nuggets until finally the longing for a good cup of coffee and some decent food drew him down from the mountains. He took a roundabout route and suddenly appeared at the bakery just as Ledbetter was also arriving.

"In the spring," Ledbetter said, "this place is going to bust wide open. The Ophir has ten men working and so does the Central. Plato's got a few over at his mine, and they're getting out ore.

"Come in with me now, and we can be ready to move men and goods by spring."

On the trail, fully exposed, handling regularly scheduled mule caravans, he would be an easy target for anyone out there who wanted his scalp.

"I can't do it, Jim," he said, finally, "but I've a little put by. What are mules going for?"

Ledbetter hesitated. "Val, I've just got in touch with a Mexican who packed into Sacramento and wants to sell out and stay. I can get his mules, twenty of them for one hundred dollars each, and they're worth it. Big, strong mules and horses are going for god-awful prices, the demand is terrific! I've agreed to take them, but every dime I have is tied up."

Two thousand dollars, and they would need pack-saddles, halters.

He thought of the dust he carried and of the cache up in the canyon. He'd left another cache back near Pipe Spring. "I'll buy in," he said, "but I can't work the trail."

"All right. How much?"

"Twenty-five hundred." He took a poke of dust from his pocket. "There's about two hundred there, and here," he took five gold coins from his pocket, "is a hundred more." He put the gold on the table and pushed it toward Ledbetter. "I'll have the rest for you tomorrow."

"This is the best buy you ever made, Val." Ledbetter picked up the gold, glancing up as a man went past him out the door, a man with fringed knee-high leggings and a ragged coat. "Here tomorrow, then?"

"Tomorrow." Trevallion got to his feet and looked along the line of buildings. Unbelievable, but there it was, a town.

Melissa came toward him. "Mr. Trevallion! We haven't had time for even a word!"

"I'll be back."

"Wait, I've somebody I want you to meet."

She gestured to a man seated at her table near the back of the bakery. The man got up and strolled over. He was a few years older than Trevallion, a slim, Spanish-looking man, who was not Spanish, with neatly polished boots into which his gray pants were tucked, and a black frock coat. A gold chain, heavy with nuggets, crossed the front of a checkered vest.

He flashed a smile, revealing even white teeth.

"Vern Kelby," he said, holding out a hand.

Trevallion took it, and the man gave a quick, hearty squeeze with just a shade too much strength in it, like a man trying for effect.

"How do you 'do?" The man wore a gun seated for a cross-draw. Both gun and holster looked very new. So did the boots.

"I'm a mining man," he explained, "but I've been helping Melissa a bit."

"Helping her?" Trevallion's tone was mild. "Well, that's very nice. I wasn't aware she needed help. She seems to be doing very well all by herself."

Kelby smiled. "Of course. But a man, well, a man can do some things better than a woman."

"That's right," Trevallion agreed, "there must be a lot of lifting around here you could do, and Jake's a bit old for it."

"I wasn't exactly thinking of that," Kelby replied.

"He's been helping me set up the books," Melissa interposed, "so I can keep track of expenditures better and know where I stand at all times."

"I suspect that's something we all should know," he agreed. "I'm sure Alfie can—oh, pardon me! Sorry, Mr. Kelby, I was thinking of somebody else."

"Well," Melissa said sharply, "you needn't!"

Ledbetter finished his coffee and got up. His face was expressionless. "See you tomorrow, Val."

Trevallion went to the door, glanced around, and went around the building to his mule. He mounted up and rode out. There was at least five hundred in dust in the cache up the canyon where he had first filed his claim.

He took a trail east out of Gold Hill, rode about a half mile and turned north, then wound around through the prospect holes and shacks into the rough country again and reached Six Mile Canyon. Several times he checked his back trail, and he was not followed. At Six Mile he turned east and rode up the canyon at a rapid trot and did not slow his pace until he was nearing his claim.

The late afternoon sun was dipping down beyond the far mountains and there were shadows in the canyons but no darkness as yet. He tied his mule with a slipknot as usual and went to the cedars where he usually made camp.

He was jumpy and uneasy. Yet the camp showed no sign that anyone had been there since he had gone. He broke sticks as if for a fire, laid the sticks in order and then, rising, went to where his cache was. He was squatting to dig out his cache when he saw the round white rock from the stream placed atop the rock near his cache. Right below it, barely visible in the vague light except for the sharp whiteness of the scar, a deep scratch as if made by a glancing bullet.

He threw himself to the right, heard the vicious whip of the bullet and the snapping sound as it clicked off the rock, and then he was firing from his drawn Colt. Firing at the flash of a rifle, and then he was up and running. There was another shot, a hasty shot fired by an angry man who had missed a perfect setup, and then he was among the rocks.

For a few minutes he waited but heard no sound at all, and he expected none.

This was a careful man, a most careful man. He had located Trevallion's cache, had set the rock up as an easily seen target, and had checked the distance and range with at least one shot. And then he had waited.

That man with the fringed leggings, the one who left the bakery. He would have been the one who went to the hunter to report what he had heard. Trevallion was buying mules, he would need money, he would go to his cache.

For an hour, Trevallion waited. By then it was totally dark, and he went down to his cache and dug into the sand, into the hollow under the rock.

His gold was gone.

Five hundred dollars—much hard work, and all for nothing.

Moreover, there was simply no way in which he could get to Pipe Spring and back in time for the meeting tomorrow. He rode up the canyon and away from town then circled back to Spafford's.

The station was open and Spafford was sweeping out when he rode up. Hall glanced at him and then at his mule. "Put some grain in the bin after you rub him down," he said. "You've had a hard ride."

"Spaff," Trevallion said, "I need five hundred dollars."

Hall stopped sweeping. "If you need it, you need it," he said. "I always liked your father. He was a good man."

"I'm buying a piece of Ledbetter's business," Trevallion explained. "He needs it by noon today, and I can't make it in time. With what I've given him he can swing the deal and I'll pay him, and you, the next time he comes over the trail."

"All right." Hall went back inside and Trevallion led the mule around to the stable, where he rubbed him down and fed him grain. At the stable door he paused and glanced up and down the road, then went into the store by the back door.

Hall had the money ready. "You're making a good buy," he commented. "Ledbetter's coining money."

"Aye." Trevallion took the money and pocketed it. "If anybody asks for me, you haven't seen me."

"Trouble?"

"That old trouble."

"You saw it, didn't you? When they killed your ma?"

"I did."

"Somebody's scared, Trevallion, and that's odd. A bunch of renegades like that. They'd probably killed a lot of people, one time or another."

He struck a match and lit his pipe. "Looks to me like somebody has something to lose. Ever think of that?"

"I've thought of it. I've never talked of this, Spaff, but I've always believed one man engineered that affair. That man knew my father and his friend Redaway had money. He wanted the money. He had probably spied on them and saw the two men go into town and knew the women were there alone.

"Somehow that bunch got some whiskey—they didn't have any money, but the whiskey came from somewhere. I've done a lot of nosing around these past years and have picked up with a few men who knew Skinner."

"He was one of them?"

"Aye. A voice called out that somebody was coming and they all took out. Killing a woman was a hanging offense, and they wouldn't have had a chance. So they ran. Then one man came out of the woods, got the money, killed Redaway and I think my mother, and then left."

"Do you know who he was?"

"I'm not sure. I think so. I didn't really see the face of the man, but there was one around town whom I think I'd know."

"Ten years is a while."

Trevallion nodded. "That thing last night was set up for killing. When I squatted down to dig out a little cache I had, I saw that small rock placed atop the one that marked the cache. That small rock was no larger than my fist, nice and round and very white.

"I saw that scratch on the rock and instantly knew somebody had shot at it to test the range. So I hit the dirt rolling just as he shot."

"Close."

"Too damned close."

"He'd been watching you then, saw you cache the stuff."

Neither man talked for awhile and Trevallion watched the road. Finally he said, "Spaff, it's going to be a big camp. They've cut trenches exposing the ore body for a couple of hundred feet through the Ophir and the Mexican. Some of that ore is rich enough to be taken out and sorted by hand. A lot of men are going to get rich here."

"It's hell here in the winter," Hall said. "You staying or riding out?"

"Staying, I think. I've seen a lot of hard winters."

Hall chuckled. "Wait until you see one of those Washoe zephyrs!"

"Nobody on the road yet. Come and have breakfast with me."

An hour later Trevallion, his Winchester in his hands, started up the Gold Canyon trail.

THIRTEEN

Trevallion wanted trouble with no man, but when he rode back up the canyon to Gold Hill it was with mounting irritation. He wished for nothing so much as to settle down to mining, whether on his own or for someone else, and he wanted no trouble. At the same time he was perfectly aware that having missed once was no reason the unknown marksman would quit and go elsewhere. He was not only here but he had taken five hundred hard-earned dollars.

Ledbetter was at the bakery to meet him, and he paid over the borrowed five hundred, adding that on the next trip he would have the rest. He said nothing to Ledbetter about the shot fired at him. He did say his cache had been robbed.

"There's more of that. There was a man murdered on the trail only last week, struck over the head from behind and then robbed, probably by a man who was traveling with him."

"There'll be vigilantes if they keep that up," another man suggested.

"Any idea who got your gold?" Ledbetter asked.

"An idea. But I couldn't prove a thing, and I don't actually know."

Ledbetter put the money away and said, "Do you know Sam Brown?"

"No."

"Be careful of him. He's a big, uncombed man, a brute, and utterly vicious. He's killed several men and doesn't care how he does it. I heard that he has beaten one man to death with a club, and I know he has stabbed several. You're in less danger than most, but you can't be sure, not even you."

"Why not 'even' me?"

"You've a reputation, Val, whether you know it or not. You've been in a few Indian fights, you brought back that gold when you were given up for dead, and you killed Rory. Somebody asked Farmer Peel who was the most dangerous man around, and he did not even hesitate. He named you."

"That's nonsense. I mind my own affairs, that's all. And I fight my own battles."

The street was crowded, and a dozen new buildings were going up. The double row of structures facing each other across the street was now a quarter of a mile long and growing with each day. The gambling houses were open all night long.

There was talk of trouble with the Indians.

"There needn't be trouble," Trevallion said. "Talk to old Chief Winnemucca. He's a reasonable man."

George Hearst came into town and made an offer for McLaughlin's one-sixth, taking an option on it when McLaughlin agreed. He rode out of town for Nevada City to borrow the money.

McLaughlin chuckled. "Those damn' Californians don't know nothin'! I sold Hearst a hole in the ground for three thousand dollars!"

"What are you going to say when it turns out to be a rich one?"

McLaughlin shrugged and filled his glass. "I'll say fine! Good for him! Look, I've taken a couple of thousand out of that hole and worked awful hard to do it. From here on the work will get harder, not easier. If anybody's going to make money there, he'd better have money to spend, that's all I've got to say!"

"Wait until spring," Kelby suggested. "When the snow goes off the ground in the spring the pigeons will come aflying! They'll come in here with all that fresh California money, just what we want!"

The bakery was becoming more and more of a meeting place, and he moved back to Melissa's table. She was rarely there, for she now had three bakers working shifts around the clock.

Trevallion, his Winchester under his arm, walked the street from end to end, looking for Waggoner.

There was no sign of him.

Instead, he met Crockett. "When are you going to work for me, Trevallion?"

"When you offer me a share of the mine instead of wages."

Crockett's smile vanished. "A share? You've got to be crazy!"

"Why? You think the ore is there but you don't know how to get it out. I do. So why shouldn't I have a share?"

He walked away up the street, but when Crockett called after him, he did not stop.

At the next saloon he saw Ol' Virginny, and lifted a hand in greeting.

"Buy me a drink?" Virginny suggested. "I spent my last or was rolled for it."

Trevallion stepped to the bar. "Two whiskeys." As the glasses were filled, Trevallion turned to face Virginny. "Tell me something, have you worked in the Solomon?"

"Don't need to." Virginny picked up his glass and his hand trembled. "They've got nothing in sight. An' maybe," he paused and looked at Trevallion out of wise old eyes, "they aren't lookin' too hard!"

He downed his liquor. "The way I see, that ground there should be ore, rich ore. Well, there isn't. They're getting out enough rock to mill, but when all's said an' done, it's mighty poor stuff."

"Crockett believes in it."

"He does that. What he needs," Virginny glanced at him out of the corners of his eyes, "is a good mining man."

"Crockett run the mine himself?"

"Well, sort of. He's too good-natured to hold the men to their jobs, so he leaves that to Al Hesketh, who's a hard man."

"This Hesketh? Is he a mining man?"

Ol' Virginny shrugged. "Some might call him that, but I would not. But he's canny, canny."

"What's that mean?"

Ol' Virginny downed another drink. "Like I said, maybe they ain't lookin' too hard. If a strike comes at the right time, when the price of the stock is down, a man who knows that strike is coming can do himself proud, mighty proud."

"Has Hesketh been buying stock?"

"All I said was, he's canny. What he does I don't know, but there's no Solomon stock been bought for some time. Folks figure she's played out an' the stock's way down."

"But they are shipping ore?"

"Some, low-grade stuff. Crockett's workin' eight, maybe ten men. Varies some with the quittin' that goes on. Miners in a boom camp are a restless lot.

"Anyway, if Crockett is payin' those miners, payin' Hesketh and buyin' powder an' such, he's not makin' ends meet. Or that would be my guess."

Trevallion bought another drink for Ol' Virginny. They talked mines and mining, then Ol' Virginny began to ramble on about the Comstock. "I ain't no gee—no geologist," he said, "but this here's a mighty broken, twisted country. That lode, she doesn't always lie where you figger, an' sometimes you strike a rich pocket and then she plays out, with a big 'horse' or block of no-good ground thrust up betwixt that ore body and one next to it. Folks strike that horse of no-pay ground and they think she's played out, sometimes it is.

"Often as not there's more lies beyond, which they never find. That Solomon now—they started runnin' a drift, tunnel, whatever you want to call it, and all of a sudden they quit. Decided they were wasting money, an' maybe they were. Anyway, they quit and took off on another tangent."

"What do you think?"

"I think they should've kept on the way they were goin', but who am I to say? They were on the ground, takin' samples all along. They know what they were wantin' to do."

Taking the bottle, they went to one of the few tables and seated themselves. Ol' Virginny was in a mellow but talkative mood. "I worked in Grass Valley when you was there," he said, "and folks from Rich Bar have spoke of you. They tell me you're a top man with a single-jack. Like to work with you sometime."

He gestured at the busy mountainside. "You watch. Come winter they'll disappear. Most of 'em. They'll just take out for Califorńy an' try to beat the winter over the mountains. You have any cash you hang to it, sure as shootin' come the first cold spell you can buy cheap. I seen it before.

"You an' me, Trev, we got to take us a walk. Show you a thing or two about this here layout." He gestured widely at the hillside. "Them Grosch boys, they knowed! But ol' Pancake, he knows nothing! Nothing atall!

"You mind what I say. Come spring the moneyboys from Frisco will be comin' in, buyin' everything in sight. That Ralston, he already knows a good bit, and he's a mighty shrewd man. You take my word for it and buy with ever' dime you can get before winter shuts down."

"What about you?"

Virginny shot him a shrewd look from under his brows. "Never you mind about me. I done taken steps, but it'll do me no good. Drink it up, that's what I'll do. Young man like you, you should have a wife, youngsters. You should build you a home."

When night came he rode up the canyon, as if returning to his original claim near the Sugarloaf, and circling back, he camped in some low willows near the Carson River. At an hour before daybreak and without breakfast, he mounted and headed back for his claim near Pipe Spring.

For a week he worked hard and, making a few small discoveries, he located a claim about a mile northwest of Pipe Spring. He made the discoveries while scouting around to see if there had been any visitors. He found no tracks but those of animals, and even they were few. Saturday morning when he started to make coffee he found a thin coating of ice in the bucket.

The week just ending had been his best by far, with several neat little pockets of alluvial gold found in natural riffles and a clean-up on the bedrock of a trench he had dug along an old streambed.

The gold found here was of better quality than that found in Gold Canyon and would run about sixteen dollars to the ounce. Yet he was not deceived. Well as he had done, he knew he had found only pockets, and the chances of any major discovery were nil.

Yet he persisted through another week, working from daylight to dark. By the end of the second week since his return, the water had almost ceased to run, and there was no chance of working further. At that, only the fact that the mountains lifted abruptly around had given him as much water as he had, and most of the intermittent streams had long ceased to flow.

Saddling the black mule and taking what gold he had, he avoided the route by which he had come into the area and rode east to Lebo Spring, then cut across to the head of Eldorado Canyon.

About an hour after starting, he paused to water the mule at some springs beneath a steep bluff, then after a brief rest started on down the canyon. There was a settlement of miners along there some-where, but he had never visited the place. When he found it, there were but three shacks and a somewhat larger structure that doubled as a store and saloon.

Leaving the mule at the hitching rail he went into the saloon.

A bald-headed man with a red fringe of hair glanced around at him. "Howdy! We got whiskey and we got some cold beer."

"I'll have the beer. How do you keep it cold?"

The man chuckled. "Got me a lil ol' cave back yonder, and the air that comes out o' there is cold, and I mean really cold! I set my beer in the opening, and you couldn't want it better."

"Are you Trevallion?"

He looked around at the speaker. He was a slim, handsome young man with a wave in his hair and a quick, friendly smile. "I'm Eldorado Johnny," the speaker said.

"Heard of you. Yes, I'm Trevallion."

"Hear you're mighty good with a gun."

Trevallion looked at him coolly. "When I have to be."

Johnny laughed. "So am I good," he said. "I'm probably the best there is. That's why I am going into Virginia City. I want to see that Farmer Peel, Langford Peel. Is he as good as they say?"

"He's always been good enough."

"I wonder if he's as good as me?"

Trevallion was irritated. Yet Johnny was nothing if not charming. There was something warm and friendly about him one could scarcely avoid liking. "Leave him alone," he advised.

"He's good, is he?"

"He's very good, and he minds his own business and doesn't go hunting trouble." And then he added, "The only trouble-hunters I ever knew were young."

"Yeah? I wonder why that is?"

"Because they don't live long enough to get old."

Eldorado Johnny laughed. "Well, maybe you're right. But don't you ever wonder if you're better than him? Or me?"

Trevallion finished his beer and then he said, "No, I don't wonder about it. I just don't give a damn. If a man needed killing, I'd kill him. I've never seen the Farmer be anything but a gentleman."

"Tell him I'm coming up to see him."

"I'll do no such thing. You bring your own message, Johnny, but when you do, buy yourself whatever you want to be buried in."

He put down his glass and went to the door. He stepped into the saddle and looked back at Johnny, who had walked to the edge of the porch. Trevallion lifted a hand and Johnny replied, then he walked back inside.

For a moment he was silent, then he looked across the bar at the bald man. "He's got it all, hasn't he? Damn him, he's so sure! I wish—"

"He's been through it, Johnny. He's been up the river and over the mountain. He's the kind you leave alone, Johnny."

FOURTEEN

A bitter wind was blowing off Sun Mountain when he dismounted at the bakery. He led his mule to the stable, and then, bowing his head against the wind, he went around to the front door of the bakery.

Melissa was there with Vern Kelby and two other men. She got up quickly. "Trevallion! Of all people! Sit down and I'll get a cup!"

"Come far?" Kelby asked.

"Eldorado," he said.

Melissa put a cup of hot coffee before him and began fixing a plate. The bakery smelled good, and it was warm and snug.

"Many pulling out?" he asked.

Kelby nodded. "Here and there. We catch them coming and going here, but nobody in his right mind would spend a winter here."

"Weather doesn't interfere with mining. Not when you're underground."

"But a man has to come up once in a while. The placer miners are pulling out, most of them." Kelby turned his head to look at him. "How about you?"

"I'll stay."

"You must do all right." There was a question there and Trevallion did not like it. "I understand yours is a placer operation."

"It's hard work."

Even in his brief absence, the town had grown. More buildings, and at least two of them for business. The others were residences, if such they could be called. As he looked up the street, watching the men struggling against the hard-blowing wind, he decided he did not like Kelby, but it was probably prejudice. Actually, he knew nothing about the man, one way or the other.

"Are you staying?" he asked then.

Kelby hesitated. "I am not certain." He glanced up at Melissa as she returned with a plate of food for Trevallion. "Melissa certainly does not wish to leave."

"Leave? This is all I have! This is my business, my life, really. I am independent for the first time in my life."

Kelby smiled. "Independence may not always be the best thing. Especially," he added, "for a woman."

"A woman can be independent as well as a man," Trevallion said. "Gives her a choice. A woman alone, with nobody, and with no income can have a bleak future. I would say Melissa has done well here, and with the coming of spring she will do better, much better."

"You believe this place will boom?" Kelby was skeptical.

"I do."

Kelby gestured up the street toward Lyman Jones's hotel, a canvas and frame structure where an old sluice-box doubled for a bar and whiskey was served in tin cups and drawn from a barrel. "Lyman's staying, and so are some others, but the smart ones are getting out. I've been advising Melissa to sell out and go back to California. With what she has she could open a business out there."

"You don't understand, Vern," Melissa protested. "I am doing well here because there are a lot of men and very little to eat but bacon and beans. Down there baked goods is no novelty."

"With what this would bring you," he said, "we could—"

" 'We'?" Trevallion said.

"Well, I'd be glad to help her get started. With a little capital one can do a lot."

Trevallion put down his knife and fork and took up the coffeepot and refilled the cup. "Mr. Kelby," he said, "Melissa has a going business in a boom mining camp. If she stays with it, she can become rich. Operating a business up here is quite simple, and down there in California it is quite otherwise.

"True, she is barely going to make expenses this winter, but she will be on the ground when the crowds come in next spring. She has worked hard, very hard, to build this business. She built the business not for what she has done but for what she will do."

"That's what I have been telling him," Melissa said.

"But the winter will be hard for a woman," Kelby protested. "I am only thinking of her."

"Of course," Trevallion said.

"After we are married I shall be helping her with the business," Kelby said. "I am sure with a bit of assistance in the management she can do much better."

Melissa flushed. "Now, Vern, we had not decided anything of the kind," she protested.

"I think—" Trevallion started to say, when Kelby interrupted.

His irritation was obvious. "Look," he said, "I realize you are a friend of Melissa's but that doesn't give you reason to run her life.

She will do what she wishes. When you finish your coffee, I would suggest you leave."

Trevallion put down his cup. His face showed nothing. "Melissa," he spoke quietly, "suppose you tell him."

"Vern," she said hastily, "you don't understand! Trevallion is my partner. He put up some of the money to get me started, he and Jim Ledbetter. Without them I would have had no business."

He flushed angrily. "You did not tell me!"

"No reason why she should," Trevallion replied. "Her business affairs are confidential. They are her own business and hers alone.

"As of this moment, if she sold out she would have almost nothing. If she stays on here she can become very well off. It is a business she has built by hard work and her skill at baking. Furthermore, I am afraid that Jim Ledbetter and I did not have any plans for taking on a manager. If you two get married, that is your affair and none of ours. How the business is conducted is another thing."

"I see." He got up. "I am afraid I did not understand."

"Vern, please! There's no need to be angry."

"You could have told me before I made a fool of myself."

"Mr. Kelby," Trevallion said, "in the course of a week there are several hundred men come in here. All of them are friendly. I venture to say that Melissa has had at least fifty proposals since she has been in town. Naturally, she could not tell her business affairs to every one of them.

"Melissa has done all the hard work. The business is moving, growing, but it is the future that holds promise. She has handled her business very, very well. I would suggest to you, sir, that Melissa is an uncommonly practical young lady, with a good business sense."

"The winters here are cruel," he protested. "She's not strong enough. I simply do not want her to have to go through all that."

Trevallion smiled. "Mr. Kelby, you are right. The winters are tough, but I think you underestimate Melissa. When spring comes she will be here, and all the stronger for it. I know very little about women, but I have observed that there's often a lot of steel in some of those fragile-seeming girls."

Kelby glanced at her. "I doubt if I shall stay. I want to be where there are lights and music and some sunshine."

Kelby left, and Trevallion turned to Melissa. "Have you heard from Jim?"

"No, I haven't. The weather has been bad over the mountains, and I guess he's waiting for a break."

Trevallion finished his coffee and went up the street to Lyman Jones's saloon. There was a sheet-iron stove inside, and men were clustered about it, almost as many as were at the bar.

Trevallion ordered a beer and listened, for this was the surest way to pick up the news. Jones himself brought him his beer, and Trevallion asked, "Seen Jim Ledbetter around?"

Jones shook his head. "No, can't say I have."

Tapley came in and he beckoned to the Arkansawyer. "Seen Jim?"

"No, I ain't, and that there is a worrisome thing. Knowin' Jim, I'd say he'd push to get at least one more trip in before the passes closed. He's got good stock, and if anybody could make it, he could. Besides, he'd have plenty of folks to take back with him."

A big man in a red blanket coat turned around, asking, "You fellers stayin'?"

"I reckon," Tapley replied.

"Got me a good claim I'd sell cheap," Trevallion noticed the calluses on the man's hands, "and this here's no pipe dream."

"Why don't you work it your own self, then?" Tapley asked.

"Wife's sick. Got to get her outside to a doctor. I been minin' ten year, and this here's the best I've seen. Silver, with a showin' of gold. It ain't showin' much right now, but she's there, I know it is."

"Where's it lie?" Trevallion asked.

"Up the hill a way. If you're interested, I'll show you." He gestured around. "This bunch is on their uppers as much as I am. I'll need cash on the barrelhead, no deals."

"Let's have a look," Trevallion suggested.

As they went out into the cold, the man said, "My name's MacNeale. You're Trevallion, aren't you? Seen you over to Rough an' Ready a time or two, and on the Yuba.

"Remember John Mackay? Quiet sort, an Irishman with a mite of a stutter? He's here, he and O'Brien have a place on the mountain above the Ophir."

"I remember him. A good, steady man."

The claim was at the top of Union Street, and the location did not look too good. MacNeale had put a shaft down fifteen feet and started a drift following a lead that looked promising.

MacNeale showed him several samples from a sack near the shaft. Samples were, of course, usually carefully chosen from the best ore.

"Look," MacNeale said, "I'm in a bind. This here's all I've got, and all the men with cash money have gone out to California. I've got to get my wife out of here right now, and I don't have more'n twenty bucks to my name. You name it and I'll take it."

"I haven't much, myself," Trevallion said, "and there's a long winter ahead. I'll give you two hundred in gold."

"I'll take it."

MacNeale held out his hand and they shook hands. Trevallion stood for a moment, looking around him, studying the lay of the land. The ore bodies on the Ophir, Central, and Mexican claims had been exposed for some three hundred odd feet and the indications were good. Something in excess of thirty tons had just been shipped to the coast for refining.

Descending into the shaft again, he walked along the drift. He held his lamp so the light could shine to the best effect, and he studied the vein. It was very thin but seemed to widen toward the tunnel's face.

What lay beyond? It was anybody's guess, but he had a good feeling about it.

"Come on, we'll weigh out the gold." He paused for a moment and said, "MacNeale, I think you're right. I think the claim is a good one, and I'm not one to take advantage. I'm paying you the two hundred, but I'm going to give you five percent on top of that."

MacNeale flushed. "Now that's mighty straight, but I—"

"It was your discovery. You get five percent of whatever we get, which may be nothing at all."

When he had paid out the gold, his sack was somewhat lighter. He hefted it thoughtfully. He might have enough for another buy, and now was the time. In the spring the Californians would be coming in with money and know-how, and they would start things moving. He tucked away the bill of sale in his pocket and said, "Now, Tap, we'll go see what happened to Jim."

"I'll be goin' west m'self," MacNeale said, "and I'll have a look about."

"We will go now," Trevallion said. "You will have no time for looking about, and you with a sick wife."

"Nonetheless, I'll have my eyes open," MacNeale said, "but you'd better look alive yourselves. There's those about who would kill a man for a two-bit piece."

They rode down the trail in the evening with a gray sky overhead and a wind behind them. They rode down to the trading post first, but they saw no mules nor had they word of a pack train.

"Woodford's," Tapley said. "Might be he stopped there, with the wind and all."

The hoofs of their mules clattered on the frozen road. There was a sifting of snow in the air.

"If he's caught in the passes—"

"He's a canny man, Jim is. He knows that trail better than either of us, and he knows places to hole up that we do not."

"There will be tracks then," Tapley said.

They pushed on into the growing storm, with snow falling thick about them.

Darkness came and the thick snow falling. "Tap," Trevallion said, "we'd best camp or there'll be somebody out looking for us. We'll find nothing in this."

"Aye," Tapley drew up, peering about.

Trevallion started to turn from the trail, but the mule would have none of it. He tugged at the bit, wanting to go on.

"Tap," Trevallion loosened the rein, "the mule knows something. I'm going to let him have his head."

"First time I ever heard of a mule wanting to go on," Tapley grumbled, "but he may. They're uncanny smart, mules are."

The black mule broke into a trot, plunging ahead into the thick snow. For several minutes he forged ahead. Finally Tapley called out, "Trev, I think that mule's crazy! We're getting nowhere, nowhere at all!"

Suddenly the mules drew up, hee-hawing into the storm. From somewhere ahead and off in the woods, there came an answering call.

"I'll be damned!" Tapley said.

The wind whipped snow in their faces, catching their breath. The mule pushed on, buck-jumping through drifts, and suddenly they came upon the body of a mule, beyond it a dozen others huddled together.

"Jim?" Trevallion called.

"Over here," the voice was faint. "For God's sake, hurry!"

FIFTEEN

He was lying in the snow behind a log, half-sheltered by brush, his face twisted by pain.

"Bust a leg?" Tapley asked.

"Like hell! I was shot! Shot, damn it, by a bunch of murdering scum! Get me out of here, will you?"

Trevallion wasted no time. He made a hasty bed of boughs and covered it with Jim's slicker. Then he helped Tapley lift the injured man over the log to the makeshift bed.

Quickly he crumpled bark in his fists, gathered twigs and, in a matter of minutes, had a small fire going. "When did it happen?" he asked.

"Been lyin' here two days," Ledbetter grumbled. "They was lyin' in wait when I come around the bend just below here, and they shot me out of the saddle, killed my mule.

"Fallin', I grabbed my rifle and got off a couple of shots. One of them started for the mules, and I dusted his scalp. You'll find his hat lying yonder, unless they sneaked back to get it.

"After a bit they gave up on me and drove off six or seven of my mules. I'd hunkered down behind this log because they might come back, and sure enough, they did.

"They knew they had lead into me and figured I'd be dead, but I taught 'em otherwise. I put one of them down—gut-shot him—and they pulled out again."

"Know who they were?"

"I caught a glimpse of one of them. Take a look for that hat, might tell us something."

Tapley had rounded up the mules and got their packs off. Moving out at that hour was beyond question, so they banked snow around to keep out the wind and visibility for any interlopers.

Trevallion cut away the pant-leg and examined the leg. It was broken below the knee, and there was a bad gash where the bullet had torn through the flesh. Evidently a ricochet from the nature of the wound.

"Killed a good mule," Ledbetter grumbled. "Lucky I wasn't riding

Emma. She's my best. She was feeling poorly, so I left her behind this trip."

"How many were there?"

"Six, maybe seven. That one I gut-shot, he just isn't going to make it. I'd bet on it. I scratched another one or two."

"What did they get?"

"Flour, sugar, coffee, some canned goods, and two mule-loads of blankets. I'll have to take a look to make sure. Most of the mules just stood. They know my voice, and also they don't stampede worth a damn. Those men yelled and threw rocks, but it was no use. The mules they got were some of the newer ones."

Trevallion bathed the wound with hot water, finding no evidence of infection, probably due to the cold. How the man had survived was a miracle, but he had seen too many such things to be surprised.

When he had bound the wound as best he could, he covered Ledbetter warmly and built up the fire.

"I'll get some sleep, Tap," he said. "You take first watch."

"Think they'll try it again?"

"Likely. This load of stuff is worth thousands of dollars in any mining camp in the country. In Virginia or Gold Hill this winter, it will be worth its weight in gold, and they know it."

"Well, I hope they come. I got me a good eye for skunks."

Trevallion made a bed for himself and stretched out. "If there's enough of 'em to make it interesting, wake me up."

Tapley grinned. "I cut loose with the old piece here, you'll wake up, believe me! She speaks loud, real loud."

Wind moaned in the pines and a little snow skittered along the ground. The hungry mules, pawing at the snow to get at the little browse, made occasional sounds. Trevallion closed his eyes, slowly relaxing. It was cold, but slowly his body warmed the blankets and he slept. He slept and the dreams returned, the dreams—and the faces. The real faces? Or only faces concocted from crowding memories of other days and other places?

Tapley shook him awake an hour after midnight. "Fear I'm gettin' sleepy. Can you handle the watch for a couple of hours?"

Trevallion sat up, shook out his boots from long habit, even though in this cold nothing would be crawling about. "Quiet?" he asked.

"Mules been a mite restless in this last half hour. Maybe just my imagination, or theirs."

"Mules don't have much imagination," Trevallion replied. "How's Ledbetter?"

"Sleepin'. Do him more good than all the medicines. He's got him a little fever, I think, but no more than a body could expect, him gun-shot and all."

Trevallion rolled his bed and tied it securely. He went to the black mule and stood beside it, stroking it gently while he whispered a few words. The black mule turned his head toward him, then suddenly swung his head back and up.

Trevallion dropped to a knee and moved away, listening. Something was out there. At this time of night and in this weather it might be a wolf but was more likely to be a man.

Did they know he and Tapley were there? It was unlikely they had kept that close a watch. Probably they were huddling around a warm fire somewhere, waiting for Ledbetter to die.

Thieves were not much given to patience. Not highwaymen, at least, or the kind these were. They would want to get the loot and get out, and they had lingered too long in the cold already.

He was crouching near a dead-fall close to the mules when he heard a hoarse whisper. "Frank? There's *two* of them! Somebody's come in!"

"Ssh!" Another movement. Dimly he could see two figures looming through the slowly falling snow.

Trevallion lifted his rifle. "All right," his voice was low, almost conversational, "you can drop your guns and step forward."

Of course, they would do nothing of the kind, and he knew it. Both men turned and fired.

Trevallion was ready and he shot first. His first bullet caught the nearest man in the middle of his move. He dropped his gun, staggering back into the second, who snapped off a hurried shot that missed by several feet. It was no more than fifteen feet, and Trevallion had a rifle. The second man fell across the body of the first.

Christian Tapley was up and ready, but as the echo of the shots faded there was no further sound.

"Hard for a man to git any rest around here," Tapley complained, "what with all that shootin' and all."

"There'll be another night tomorrow," Trevallion said. "Let's load up for an early start. I'm getting a little tired of this place."

With a toe he rolled the top man off the other, and the man on the snow groaned. "Well, don't that beat all!" Tapley commented. "He's still alive."

"Help me," the man pleaded.

"The way you helped Ledbetter?" Trevallion reached over and threw the wounded man's coat back, taking a gun from his belt. The man was hit bad, and no amount of help would be of any use.

Trevallion had no sympathy for the man. When one man takes a gun and sets out to rob another, maybe to kill in the process, he should expect no sympathy.

"Who's he?" he gestured toward the dead man.

"Got no idea."

"And the others? The one we got last night? I mean that Ledbetter got?"

"No idea."

He was a strongly built man with sandy hair and a few freckles, his face very pale now. Due to the shock and the cold, the pain had not yet reached him. That would come soon.

"You goin' to let me lie here?"

"Tough, isn't it? We've got to get Jim Ledbetter, the man you shot from ambush, to some help. Maybe if we get him cared for we can come back."

"Hell, that's liable to be a week!"

"Maybe. And maybe you can't last that long."

The man stared at him. "You're a hard man, Trevallion."

"Ledbetter's my friend. My very good friend. He is also my partner."

Trevallion had been working, brushing snow off the backs of the mules, hoisting the packs into place and tying them on. "Where's the rest of our goods?"

Whatever his answer might have been it did not come. Instead, he doubled up with a shuddering groan, eyes wild with agony.

"Damn you, Treval—" His voice broke off in mid-sentence and slowly, carefully, he stretched out. The last action was purely reflex. He was dead.

Tapley called. "Can you help me with Jim?"

Together they lifted him into the saddle, a crude splint protecting the broken leg.

"Can you make it, Jim?"

Ledbetter's eyes were bright with fever and pain, but he nodded. "Just try me," he whispered. "Try me."

He was still sitting in the saddle when they rode up to the bakery.

Tapley's dug-out cabin was only a few hundred yards away, and after a few days they carried Jim to Tapley's place on a makeshift stretcher.

It was a snug two-room cabin, with the bedroom built back into the side of the mountain, actually carved from rock, one side showing a substantial lacing of silver ore.

"Started to mine," Tapley said, "and then decided I needed shelter for the winter more than ore, so I just smoothed out the walls and floor of this one and built on the front room." He indicated a door in the back wall. "There's sixty feet of tunnel back of that with a vein about an inch wide, silver sulphurets. That ain't much, but I think she'll widen as she goes deeper."

Ledbetter looked over at Trevallion. "Hate to ask it, Trev, but can you find somebody to care for my stock? All I've got is tied up in those mules, and you've a stake in them, too."

"We'll manage. What about those in California?"

"We've got a good man yonder. No need to worry. I figured to have these back there to winter on good grass."

"Spafford sold out awhile back," Trevallion said, "even though he's stayed around. He's got two stacks of good hay back there, and I think we can make a deal. He's also got some fenced pasture along the Carson and an old corral."

"I'll leave it up to you. We lost some good mules."

"You haven't lost them."

"What's that mean?"

"Look," Trevallion said, "those mules are worth more on this side of the Sierras than the other. So's the stuff they got. Across the mountains, even if they could get over, they'd be a drug on the market. With goods piling up against the spring thaw, they couldn't get much for them, but over here, where everything is in short supply, they could do well."

"So?"

"I'm going to pass the word around, and I'm going to go scouting. They've got to hold those mules somewhere not too far off, and they've got to have a cache for their goods, unless they make a quick sale.

"If they've sold them, I'll find them. If they have not sold them, I'll find them and the thieves."

"How many were there, do you think?"

"Six, at least. Maybe seven or more. Three are dead. I'd say we're talking of four or five men."

He cleaned his rifle, checked his pistol, and then, leaving the rifle, went out into the cold wind and walked down to Lyman Jones's.

The place was full. Langford Peel was at the end of the bar, and he pushed through to his side, for there was a good bit of space around him.

"Hello, Trev," Peel said. "Heard you did some shooting down the trail."

"Nothing much, Lang. Jim Ledbetter lost some good mules and their packs, though, and I'd take it as a favor if you'd keep your eyes and ears open."

"I will do that."

Trevallion bought a drink and then said, "Sam Brown in town?"

"He is." Peel considered the question and then said, "There are about eight or ten really tough men hanging around with him. Back-shooters, though, and knife-men, so be careful. And Sam will kill anybody he takes a notion to, so don't turn your back."

Trevallion finished his drink, drew his coat tight, and stepped outside. For a moment he waited in the lee of the building, sheltered from the icy wind. There was a light in the bakery and he considered going there, then bending into the blast, he started up the hill toward Tapley's place.

Then he turned abruptly and stepped under the overhang in front of a store, looking up the hill. To reach Tap's place he would have to pass in front of several lighted windows, and suddenly he did not like the thought. Experience had taught him to play his hunches, and he did so now.

Keeping under the awning, he ran along for twenty feet, then stepped into the deep shadow alongside a cabin. MacNeale had a dug-out shack on the claim Trevallion had bought.

He went up Union Street, keeping as much to the shadows as he could, and when he reached the cabin, he lifted the latch. The door resisted, and just as he started to lunge against it with his shoulder, something clicked in his mind, and he stepped back quickly, drawing his gun. Then he kicked the door, hard.

It swung inward, then hung there, half-open.

"If you're friendly," he said, "come out with your hands up. If you're not, come shooting."

SIXTEEN

Take it easy, mister! I was just looking for a place to sleep!"
"Then step out here with your hands up."

The man stepped out, nobody Trevallion had ever seen before. Of about medium height, well set-up, and wearing a white shirt with sleeve-garters. Trevallion could see little of his face beyond the fact that he wore a mustache and sideburns.

"All right, turn around and face the wall."

Trevallion gave the man a quick frisk. He was unarmed, smelled faintly of cologne, and his boots had been polished, although dusty now. "Get inside and light a light," he said, and followed him in.

A match flared and the man lifted the globe on a lantern and lighted it, then let the globe back into place.

The room was bare and simple. Two bunk beds on either side, a table, a sheet-iron stove, a black coat hung over a chair back, and at one side a carpetbag.

Seen in the light the man was clean-cut and not unattractive. No weapons were visible in the room.

"Who are you? And what are you doing here?"

"I am Dane Clyde. I am an actor hunting a job, and I'm empty, haven't a farthing. Down at the saloon I heard somebody say Mr. MacNeale had left town with his wife, so I assumed this place would be empty."

"I bought it from MacNeale."

"I am sorry." He reached for his coat. "I will get out of your way at once."

"Don't be a damned fool. Where will you go? You can't get a bed in this town without putting money on the counter." He indicated a bunk across the room. "You can sleep there if you aren't gun-shy."

"What's that mean?"

"My name is Trevallion, and there are some thieves around who don't like me. They might come hunting for me."

Dane Clyde shrugged. "Wake me up when the shooting starts," he said cheerfully. "I'm so tired it would take a war to wake me up once I hit the mattress."

106

Trevallion barred the door and shielded the light, then hung his coat on a peg. "Had anything to eat?"

"Not much, lately."

Trevallion made coffee and hunted through the cupboard. It was very neat, as he would have expected, for until she became too ill, MacNeale had lived here with his wife. He found a slab of bacon from which some slices had been cut and in the breadbox some baking-powder biscuits that were several days old.

"It isn't much," he said, "but we'll get along." Then, turning to look at Clyde, he said, "What's an actor doing in Virginia City?"

"I heard there was a boom, or about to be one. I figured the town could do with some entertainment."

"You could be right. What can you do?"

"Act, sing, impersonations, play almost anything there is in the way of an instrument." He removed his tie and collar, carefully placing the collar button on the table where it could be immediately found. "Actually, it's the only thing I wish to do. My father insisted on an education. He was a scholar of the old school."

"Where you from?"

"Dublin, Ireland. My people were transplanted English, and like many of them, we became more Irish than the Irish themselves."

Trevallion put a twenty-dollar gold piece on the table. "That's a loan. You can sleep here."

"Say, that's decent of you! I am obliged."

"Forget it, and pay me when you can. You say you can sing? Tell Lyman Jones, you might sing down there and let them put money in the pot. There's not much entertainment here, as you guessed."

"There will be in the spring. I know of two or three companies who are thinking of coming up here to play. Is there a theater?"

"No, they'll have to play in a corral or an inn-yard, like Shake-speare did."

Clyde glanced at him. "You know about that, do you?"

Trevallion was sitting over coffee in the bakery the following morning when Will Crockett came in.

"When are you going to work for me, Trevallion?"

"I'm not. When are we going to be partners, Crockett?"

Crockett laughed. "I don't need a partner. There's scarcely enough for one."

"Maybe that's why you need a partner."

"What? What's that mean?" Crockett's good humor was gone. "I am doing all right."

"No doubt, but is 'all right' good enough? I've seen some of your ore, and it's just what you said. It is all right. Who manages your operation, Crockett?"

"I do, why?"

"How many tons are you getting out? Right now, for example?"

"Now? We're closed down. Al Hesketh had to go to the coast on business, and as some of our miners pulled out, we decided to close down for the winter."

"If you've got the capital to pay miners, you should be working, piling up ore to ship when spring opens the trail. At least, that's my feeling."

Will Crockett stared out of the window, obviously irritated, less by what Trevallion had said than by thoughts developed from it.

"I need a mining man over there. Al's against it, says we are doing well enough and he has plans, but he doesn't know much more about mining than I do, although he's a top businessman. Knows exactly what he's doing all the time."

"Maybe you should listen to him."

"Why don't you come over and have a look? Tell me what you think?"

"I will do that, but it will cost you fifty dollars."

"Fifty dol—" Crockett's face flushed. "You want fifty dollars just for walking through a mine? Take you no more than thirty minutes?"

Trevallion finished his coffee. He got up. "See you later, Melissa."

When he was gone, Crockett slammed down his cup. "Confound the man! Fifty dollars? That's preposterous!"

"You asked him, Will. He did not come to you. He never comes to anyone . . . at least not to ask for anything. He will go out of his way to help someone. He helped me get started here, and when Jim Ledbetter did not come in on time, he went looking for him."

"Damn it, the man's a miner! I've had a dozen people tell me that Trevallion knows more about mining and about getting the ore out than anybody they know. I need him."

Melissa smiled. "Will, if you need him, you'd better make up your mind to pay him. One thing you have to understand, Trevallion doesn't seem to *want* anything. If he really cares for anything or anybody, I don't know what it is."

Crockett sat quietly for a few minutes. "Melissa, you're a good woman. You're also a calming influence. Whenever I come here, I feel better when I leave."

She smiled. "It's the coffee, Will. I make a good cup of coffee."

They were silent for a few minutes, and then she said, "Will? If you do have Trevallion look at your mine, don't tell Al Hesketh."

He stared at her. "Don't tell Al? Why not? Why, I never make a move without Al! He's my right hand!"

"Did you ever suggest having Trevallion look at the mine?"

"I suggested hiring him. As near as I can recall Al didn't think it was necessary."

"Will, if I were you I'd pay Trevallion to look at the mine, and I'd listen to what he had to say, and I wouldn't even mention it to Al Hesketh."

Crockett took out a cigar and bit off the end. He stared at it for a minute, then lighted it. Melissa refilled his cup. "A lot of men are going to get rich here, Will. You could be one of them. You're in on the ground floor like George Hearst, and you can do well, but you're too trusting, Will, much too trusting . . . of me, of Al Hesketh, of everybody."

"Maybe," he muttered, "maybe."

Trevallion went to work on the MacNeale claim, mucking out rock that had already been shot down and sorting it for that worth shipping. He crushed some of the richest-looking fragments and panned out what gold he could find. It was a piddling operation, but it added a little to his supply of ready money as well as giving him an idea of the ore's potential.

The lode seemed to dip to the west, but he distrusted it and spent a good bit of time wandering over the side of the mountain or sitting on the slope below the town, just studying the roll of the hill and the convolutions of what exposed strata he could see. Several times he encountered others doing the same thing, but none seemed to have any idea what they were looking for. Probably they hoped to find an outcropping of gold ore thrusting itself up at them.

There was no sign of Waggoner.

Two weeks after the return with Ledbetter, he got his first lead. It came from Langford Peel.

He was having coffee at the bakery when Peel entered. He crossed the room and sat down, and Melissa brought them coffee. "I was in Genoa a few days ago," he commented, "and there was a man in there with some blankets for sale. A bundle of them. Now there hasn't been a pack train over the mountain in a couple of months, and I just thought you'd be interested."

"Know the man?"

"I do. As I once suggested, he trails around with Sam Brown. The name he's using is Kip Hauser, but when he was around Corinne awhile back, he was using another name."

"I think I'll go see him."

Peel nodded. "Want me to come along?"

Trevallion smiled. "Now that's kindly of you, Lang, it really is, but I think we feel just alike on that score. That every man should saddle his own horses and fight his own battles."

"But this is Jim Ledbetter's fight. I like Jim, and he's laid up."

"I'll handle it. But, thanks."

Peel finished his coffee and glanced over at Melissa. "Thanks, ma'am. That was right good coffee."

When he had gone Melissa looked after him. "So that's the fabled Farmer Peel, the Chief of the Comstock! He seems such a nice man."

"He is. He was a fine soldier, too. He was a bugler at first, survived many Indian battles and was noted even then for his skill with weapons. He's not a man who looks for trouble.

"As a matter of fact, few of the men who are noted as gunfighters are trouble-hunters. It's been the custom from the beginning of time for men to settle their difficulties with weapons. It's not a policy I advocate, Melissa, but that's the way it is, and the way it has been.

"By the time a man has won two or three such arguments, he has a reputation. If a man is drawing a gun on you, there's not much choice but to shoot him, if you can."

He sat over his coffee, thinking it out. If Hauser was peddling blankets, they were almost certainly some of those stolen from Ledbetter's mules. Every available blanket in town had been sold long ago, and as Peel said, no mule trains had come in.

He remembered Hauser somewhat vaguely as a man seen around Gold Hill. He was a lean, tired-looking man with watchful black eyes, but his tired looks were deceptive. Trevallion had seen him win considerable money in a jumping contest when he had seemed the least likely jumper in the lot.

Hauser knew him by sight, and as Clyde entered the bakery the solution became obvious. "Sit down." He gestured to Melissa. "I want you to meet Dane Clyde. He's an actor, and a friend of mine."

Later, he described Hauser. "You can do something for me, but I don't want you in trouble. At the first sign that he has recognized you as someone he has seen before, quit. He's a dangerous man."

"What do you want to know?"

"Who he hangs out with, and if possible, where he goes."

"He doesn't know you, and I want you to keep away from me until this is over." He explained about the robbed pack train and what he suspected. He also described Sam Brown. "Avoid him, he's deadly. He needs no excuse to kill."

"I'll be careful."

Clyde was a pleasant man, easy to talk to and a good listener. "My last job was in Frisco," he explained. "I'd come out with a company from New York. Came around the Horn. Before that I played in Dublin, London, Paris—wherever there was a good role." He smiled. "And often enough where there was any kind of a role!

"But I worked a season with Rachel Felix, and then went on tour with Miss Redaway in *Ticket Of Leave Man*."

"Who did you say?"

"Miss Redaway, Grita Redaway. You wouldn't have heard of her. She's new, but very good. She was with Felix for a season or two as an ingenue, but she's just been coming up this past year or so. Good notices, very professional."

"Unusual name."

"It is, you know? She's a Yank, too. American, I mean. Played some through the South when very young."

"Attractive?"

"More than that. She's beautiful, a very rare beauty. That was why she and Rachel parted ways. No hard feelings you understand, Rachel just told her she was too beautiful and was drawing attention from her, from Rachel, that is.

"I heard it, myself. Rachel just told her, 'Honey, you've got it, use it.' But they're good friends."

"How old would she be? This Miss Redaway?"

"Young, just a girl, actually. I doubt if she's twenty. In fact, I am sure she isn't."

Dane Clyde drifted away and Trevallion finished his coffee. An uncommon name, certainly, but unlikely, very unlikely.

He remembered that night all too well, remembered holding the trembling child in his arms, frightened himself but braver because he was needed, because she needed him. Her need had made him stronger, helped to bring him through what followed.

It was, he reflected sourly, the only time anybody had ever needed him, the only time he had ever felt that need to protect, to shield. Grita had given him, in those few moments, something priceless, something he had been a long time recognizing.

His father had had his mother; whom did *he* have?

SEVENTEEN

When the winter came he stayed in the cabin, warm against the threat of wind and snow. The fires in the sheet-metal stove blushed its sides with heat, and the rooms were snug against the storm. Trevallion heard the wind and remembered old rocks upon the Cornwall coast and the sea against them, and the cold rain falling.

He read a little from the few books MacNeale had left, and by day he worked in the drift, deepening it, and finding a little more width to the vein. He took the gold from the best rock and put the silver ore to one side.

From his hillside he could look down upon much of the town and see it scattered along the streets, if such they could be called. Snow turned white the hills, and the Washoe zephyrs filled the air with it, moaning about the eaves of the cabin and prying with ghostly fingers to find a way to the warmth inside.

On a Monday night when the snow fell, Dane Clyde came up the hill and tapped on the door. Trevallion opened for him with a gun tucked behind his belt, and Clyde went to the stove, slipping off his mittens and extending stiff fingers to the heat.

"I found where the blankets are kept, and all the rest too, aside from what they've eaten."

Trevallion waited, and he said, "It's a cabin, not where we thought, but in a canyon about a mile above Cedar. There's a trail. Do you know it?"

"I do."

"The cabin's about two hundred yards up. Nobody lives there, but there's a corral and a shed. The cabin's mostly dug-out."

"Anybody there?"

"No. They come and go. Mostly it's empty."

"Good." He turned to the coffeepot. "Sit down. It's almighty cold out there." He filled his cup. "Did they see you?"

He shrugged. "Maybe. I started the story that I was getting over an illness, and the doctor had told me I must walk. I started walking

112

each evening a different direction, and finally, I think, they got used to me and paid no attention."

"I hear you've been singing a bit down at Lyman's."

"I have. But elsewhere too. It's the old Irish songs they like best, but I've a lot of amusing ones from the music halls. It's a living."

He was quiet for a moment. "You've not been down for a few days?"

"No."

"Sam Brown killed a man. Cut him with a bowie knife, ripped him wide open, then shoved the body under a table and went to sleep on it, his hands still bloody."

"That's the way he is."

"I could stand the murdering brute if he'd just take a bath sometimes. He's about the foulest thing I've ever seen on two feet."

Clyde sipped his coffee. "I've seen Hauser with Brown, and I've seen him with several others."

"With a man named Waggoner?" Trevallion described him.

"No, there's no such man around now. If he was here, he must have gone out with the crowd for California."

For a while they were silent, sipping their coffee. Clyde glanced at the books on the makeshift shelf. "Yours?"

"They came with the house. He picked them up, here and there, in abandoned camps. Some of them he found in the Forty-Mile Desert, thrown out to lighten the load."

"Read much?"

"Now and again. A man alone gets hungry for some kind of communication, even if he's not a reader. I knew one who was snowed in one year, and when he came out with the spring thaw, he'd come so close to memorizing the Bible that he became a preacher."

Trevallion got up. "If you want to you can wait here, but I'd guess the bakery would be a better place."

Clyde looked up, startled. "You aren't going over there *alone*?"

"I think that's the best way. I can come in the back way. I won't ride through town. With any luck I'll find what I'm looking for and get back here before they know what happened."

"I'll come with you."

"Thanks, but no." He glanced at Clyde. "Have you ever used a gun?"

"No, no, I haven't. I guess I could if it came to that."

"Better leave them alone, although it might pay you to learn how to handle one. This is rough country, and a gun is handy in many ways."

He needed help to do what he wished to do, and the first man who came to mind was Tapley. Clyde, despite his willingness, was not the man for what he had in mind.

He found Tapley in his dug-out, nursing a cup of coffee. "You sure picked a night," he commented. "What's up?"

Trevallion explained, then concluded, "We'll need about four pack mules, I guess, and a lot of luck."

"None of that outfit likely to be out tonight," Tapley said. "Hauser was down to Lyman's, and he was about half-drunk."

Icy wind slammed into their faces and bodies as they rode out, the mules fighting to return to the reasonably warm barns. Trevallion led off, the wind sucking the breath from his throat as he tried to hide his chin behind his coat collar.

There were many lights visible from the town, and farther along, from Gold Hill and Silver City, but they could see no movement.

The cabin was where Clyde had said it would be, and Trevallion was in no mood for waiting about. He rode right up to it, half expecting the door to burst open and a man with a gun to appear. Yet when he reached the door it was closed with a hasp and a lock.

It was a solid door, but the hasp itself did not look strong. On the third kick the hasp tore free, and the door opened.

It was all there, everything but the mules. There were bales of blankets, sacks of flour, sugar, and coffee. Wasting no time they loaded the mules, overloaded them, actually. Some of the supplies listed as stolen were already gone, either used by the thieves themselves or peddled here and there. Even so it needed two trips to empty the cabin, and it was almost daylight when the job was completed. All the goods were stored in Ledbetter's own storeroom.

Over coffee back in his cabin he looked over at Tapley. "The mules, we've got to find those mules."

"They'll be down along the river, more'n likely. Has to be a place where they can be hidden and where there is water and feed—feed means hay or else browse."

"First, I move we catch some sleep," Trevallion said, "and then we hunt mules."

"You reckon that stuff will be safe?"

"It's right in the middle of town. Cash money is scarce. I'll find two or three tough miners to keep an eye on it."

Tapley rode beside him into the quiet morning, this the third morning of their search and no mules yet. The blown snow was gone, except for threads of white in the shadow of boulders or places where long dead streams had cut banks and then abandoned them to wind and sun.

"You need a woman," Tapley said again. "It's no life for a man alone."

"You're alone."

"I have my daughter. It's a comfort to think of her and plan for her. Maybe the plans will come to nothing, but it is something to think on, and she's someone to love."

"Maybe, someday."

"You're young. When you're young there's always a tomorrow, or so the young believe. There isn't, of course. As many of the young die as the old. In this land it is an accomplishment to grow old, and mighty few will ever make it."

"Man back at the store said he saw some tracks up here, paid·them no mind."

"We'll find them."

They rode a winding trail westward along the canyon of the Carson. Trevallion looked up at the canyon wall, haggard with years, its hard shoulders worn by the sand-blowing wind. "Good place for a man to get himself killed," he commented.

"Aye, that's an easy thing to do, anyway. You thought of what Sam Brown will do when he finds that shack?"

"I don't like him," Trevallion replied. "I don't care what he does."

"Somebody will be guarding the mules," Tapley said. "Come spring, they'll be worth a fortune. Jim's brand can be changed. That JED brand of his, saw a man in a bar the other night with a pencil. He was showing Hauser how it could be changed to three 8s or a 3 and two 8s."

"Ledbetter knows those mules like a man knows his own youngsters."

"Aye," Tapley agreed, "but can he prove it? We've got lawyers in town now."

"That's the beginning of trouble."

Ancient cedars reached for them with twisted, gnarled arms. Trevallion broke off some cedar leaves and rubbed them in his fingers. "I like the smell," he commented.

"You better shuck your rifle," Tapley said, "look at your mule's ears."

The ears were pricked forward, and the black mule was about to bray. Trevallion kicked it lightly in the ribs to distract its attention and took out his rifle.

They came around a slight bend in the canyon and saw there at the junction of Carson and Brunswick Canyon a small meadow with some brown grass struggling to become green.

The mules were there, all of them, and a fire was burning in front of a tent.

At that moment a man backed out of the tent with a frying pan in his hand. He put it down on a flat rock and began slicing bacon into it. When he had finished, he turned and walked to the fire.

Something must have caught the tail of his eye, for he suddenly looked sharply around and saw them sitting quiet on their mules. "Wha— Who the devil are you?"

He was wearing a gun, and there was a rifle standing against a rock near the tent door.

Neither of them spoke. Slowly, very carefully, he put the bacon and the frying pan down on the flat rock. Then he wiped his hands on his pants, and it was in his mind to reach for his gun, but both rifles covered him. Neither man had made a move, each had his rifle across his saddle, each muzzle was pointed at him, but there was no threat, no gesture.

"You fellers lookin' for something?"

"We found it," Trevallion said.

The man's tongue fumbled at his lips. He dearly wished to draw, but the rifle muzzles were there, right on him.

"I was fixin' bacon," the man said.

Neither responded, they just looked at him. Tapley rolled his chewing tobacco in his jaws and spat.

Trevallion said, "That cedar yonder?"

"Ain't hardly tall enough. Got to be six foot, anyway, maybe eight. Eight's better," Tapley added. "Got to have clearance." He gestured at a coil of rope on the man's saddle. "Brung his own rope."

"Now see here!" The man's hands were still on his thighs where he had started to dry them. "Who are you fellers? What d' you want?"

"Did we say we wanted anything?" Trevallion said. "We just found Ledbetter's mules. That's what we came for."

"You're huntin' trouble. These here mules—"

"Were stolen. And we find you in possession. How far's the nearest court, Tap?"

"Placerville, I expect. Maybe Salt Lake, as this here's Utah Territory."

"Too far. We take him there for trial we got to stay there to testify. We'd be tied up half the summer. No sense to that. And when we got through they'd just hang him."

"Don't make sense," Tapley said, "takin' him all that way for such a little job. We got us a tree, an' he's got a rope."

"He's also got a gun," Trevallion said. "Shall we just shoot him a little first?"

"Look, you fellers! Now, see here. I didn't know these mules was stole! I swear I didn't!"

"Who put you to watchin' them?"

"Some fellers offered to grub-stake me if I'd see to them. I hadn't no idea—"

"I've seen him with Hauser up to Gold Hill," Tapley said, "an' that feller with the dirty beard, Sam Brown."

"Can you write?" Trevallion asked.

"What kind of a question is that?" the man demanded indignantly. "Of course, I can!"

"Good!" With his left hand Trevallion reached into his coat pocket and took out a notebook such as miners used for claim notices or to tally loads taken out. "You just write on that top page, *Sam Brown, Kip Hauser, and some others stole these mules and shot Jim Ledbetter.*"

"Are you crazy? I couldn't do that! They'd kill me!"

"And we'll hang you."

The man was trembling, and for a moment Trevallion thought he would draw, then the resolution left him and he lowered his hands helplessly. Before he could speak, Trevallion said quietly, "Seems to me you've got two ways to die, and one to live."

"What's that mean?"

"You can write that paper and then get on your horse and ride out of here for Salt Lake."

Hope brightened his eyes. "You'd let me do that?"

"I wouldn't waste around about writing that note. I ain't hung a man this week," Tapley said.

The man wrote, and when he had finished, Trevallion glanced at it. "You've got ten minutes," he said.

EIGHTEEN

A harsh winter blended almost unrealized into an even harsher
spring. The booming Washoe Zephyrs swept down the mountain, flattening shacks, tent-huts, and saloons. Scarce fuel had become even scarcer, and most of the squatters were cooking with
sagebrush for fuel.

Snow sifted in through the cracks in the poorly built cabins,
melting on the scarcely warm stoves and sifting in a shadowy white
blanket over the sleeping men.

The spring of 1860 came, and the cold withdrew into the higher
peaks. Only the wind remained, blowing rocks rather than sand,
battering at walls, rattling against the few intact windows, but by
March a few daring men were already pushing through the snow-
drifted passes.

Trevallion came down the hill in the morning. John Moore had
arrived with a stock of liquor and goods, and was already setting up a
makeshift saloon while men hung around waiting. The winter's supply of whiskey had run short, the nearest thing to a disaster that the
new camp had experienced.

Jim Ledbetter was at the bakery before him, helping Melissa
prepare breakfast.

"My cook skipped," she explained. "He bought an outfit and went
prospecting."

"He'd do better right here," Will Crockett spoke from the door,
closing it behind him.

Trevallion poured a cup for himself and one for Crockett. "Ready
to look over the Solomon?"

Trevallion shrugged. "Are you ready with the money? Fifty dollars
for a walk through and a working interest if I work there."

"You're a hard man."

Trevallion sat down, sipping his coffee. "I've got a claim of my
own. It looks good."

"Bah! I've seen that MacNeale claim! Only a showing of ore! Not
worth bothering with!"

"It might be we don't see the same things when we look," Trevallion replied. "I've been looking at ore and at rock formations all my life. You were a merchant or something of the kind, weren't you?"

"A man can learn," Crockett said.

"Thank God for that." Ledbetter came over and joined them. "Jim, when you go out, I've got a dozen mule loads of ore I want to send."

"All right!" Crockett said irritably. "Fifty dollars! I hope you're worth it."

Trevallion nodded. "In the morning then."

Melissa added, "Whatever he tells you, Will, keep it to yourself."

Irritated, he glanced at her. "Look, have I ever asked you—"

"No, Will, you haven't, but do you ever show your poker hand to the other players?"

"Of course not. This isn't the same. How can he operate the mine if he doesn't know the facts?"

"All I ask is that you not show your cards. Not all of them, anyway."

After she had gone into the kitchen, Crockett said, "Melissa's a fine girl, but sometimes she seems to think I'm a child."

Ledbetter shook his head. "Not so, Will. Melissa hears a lot of talk. Miners, businessmen, they all sit here and talk over their coffee. You're a good man, Will, but a trusting one, too trusting."

"The trouble is," Trevallion suggested, "that when a man gets a very capable assistant, he tends to leave more and more of his work to that assistant, until soon he's really running the show."

"Not my show," Crockett said. He got up. "See you in the morning, Trevallion."

After he had gone, Trevallion asked, "Who is this Hesketh, anyhow? I hear his name mentioned but never see him around."

"He doesn't come around," Melissa replied. "I don't know him, and he is probably a perfectly trustworthy man. I just don't believe in trusting anyone too far."

"Good thing to know," Trevallion commented.

Melissa flushed, then she went on. "He keeps very much to himself when he's here. He's got a cabin up the hill a ways, and he spends his time either there or with his books down at the office."

"Minds his own affairs," Ledbetter said, "doesn't drink, doesn't chew tobacco, and he seems to have no interest except in that mine."

"Is he a miner?"

"Not so's you'd notice. First I heard of him was six or eight years ago over in Sacramento. He was buying ore from miners, mostly from those who needed money quick, so he bought cheap."

Trevallion came down the hill in the morning and walked over to the Solomon.

He already knew most of the basic facts. Will Crockett had claimed 150 feet along the Comstock Lode, and had sunk a shaft that was now sixty feet deep. From that they had run a drift at right angles to the shaft with a fair showing of ore. At that point work was stopped, and another drift was started at right angles to the first. In this second drift there was a fair showing of ore, and the width of the vein increased as they went deeper.

The showings were good, and they had shipped several pack trains of ore for milling. All that was commonly known about town, where miners talked freely and there were few, if any, secrets.

Crockett was waiting at the collar of the shaft. There was no talk. They lighted their lamps and descended into the mine. Trevallion was no geologist and made no pretense at so being. He was simply a man with practical mining experience who automatically studied every rock formation he encountered.

What they were beginning to call the Comstock Lode lay along a fault where there were also a number of lesser faults, or which seemed to be so, trending toward the northeast or northwest. Trevallion knew little about the ground, but surmised much, which might or might not prove to be true. The richest ores he had seen thus far were in quartz mixed with calcite, galena, and pyrite. In all of this, there was gold and argentite.

The major thrust of the Comstock seemed to be northeast from the Solomon. He walked along the drift, studying the rock formations. The timber work, such as it was, seemed well done, and the mining seemed thoroughly professional.

In Number Two drift the ore was low-grade quartz with some galena, a little argentite, and a good deal more of sphalerite. No silver was visible, although the ore had a fair showing of it when milled.

He started back. "I'll check Number One next," he suggested.

"Scarcely worth the bother," Crockett assured him, "but I want it all studied."

The Number One drift, where work had been abandoned, showed nothing of interest until right at the face of the drift. At the face he stood for a moment or two, puzzled. There was no rocky debris, chipped or broken rock lying at the foot of the face. Still more puzzled, he walked back a few feet and studied the wall again, while Will Crockett waited with some impatience.

After a bit he walked back down the drift and began to examine the scattered rock with care.

Several times he squatted to pick up small fragments of ore or rock, and some he discarded, others he pocketed. Finally he stood up and walked back to the face.

"Why did you stop work here?"

"It wasn't showing any pay dirt. We decided to pull out and try drifting another direction." He flashed his light around. "You can see for yourself. There's nothing in sight."

Trevallion turned around. "Let's go on top," he said. "I've seen enough."

When they were back in the air, the afternoon was cool. Noon had just passed, and a wind was blowing down the slopes of Sun Mountain.

"Let's go have a cup of coffee," Trevallion suggested, "we've got some talking to do."

"Seems to me all you do is drink coffee," Will complained, "or is it Melissa?"

"It isn't Melissa. She's a fine girl, and I've helped her get started, as did Jim Ledbetter, but we're only friends."

Seated inside the bakery, Trevallion sipped a taste of coffee and then said, "Crockett, there's somebody in that mine who has plans of his own."

"What's that mean?"

"You're drifting the wrong way, and there's somebody who is working there who knows it. Maybe there's more than one."

"You got that bee in your bonnet, too?" Will said impatiently. "You trying to tell me Al Hesketh is a crook? Well, I'm not buying it. Not one bit."

"I mentioned no names, and I do not know your Mr. Hesketh. I only know that you were touted into drifting in the wrong direction by somebody who knew better."

From his pocket he took some of the ore fragments he had selected from the floor of the drift. "Look, and look closely."

Crockett took the fragments, glanced at them impatiently, and then looked again. "I don't know what you're after, mister, but these didn't come from my mine!"

"I took them off the floor right before your eyes. You were watching."

"You must have switched them. Why, I've no ore anywhere near this good!"

"Crockett? Did you see me examine the face of the drift? I'll tell you what happened. This ore is very spotty, all of it. Comes in great hunks, sometimes running to tons and tons of ore, then breaks off into nothing, then more bonanza stuff.

"Whoever was working down there put in a round of shots that shot down some very good stuff. Then he stopped work, cleaned up very carefully, and pulled out. What he failed to recall is that when

the holes blow, fragments of rock are sometimes thirty or forty feet
down the tunnel. That's what happened here. He, or they, cleaned
up close along the face but forgot what might have been blown back
down the drift."

"Nonsense! If there was any good ore there, there'd be signs of it
on the face!"

"Usually, yes, but the way the pay dirt has been showing in some
of the mines here, it could happen. Somebody had several tons of
ore or rock moved out of the mine and hidden somewhere."

"Wouldn't be enough in it to pay," Crockett protested.

"In the few tons of ore they got, there wouldn't be, but what if
they were playing for higher stakes? Your mine, for example?"

"What are you getting at?"

"Simply this. It looks to me as if someone discovered a small
pocket of good ore, which made him suspect there might be more of
it; so he removed the ore, stopped work on the drift, and started
somewhere else."

"The vein's wider in the other tunnel. We gave up down there in
Number One because we didn't find anything."

"Have you had any offers for the mine?"

"Of course not."

"The Solomon is a stock operation, is it not?"

"Of course it is! I had to sell stock to get the money to carry on.
Nearly every mine on the Comstock operates that way.

"We need capital, so we incorporate and sell stock. We've done
well, too."

"Who controls the stock? I mean, who has a controlling interest?"

"I do, of course. I own forty-two percent of the stock, and Hesketh
owns ten percent. That leaves us in control."

Trevallion glanced out the window. A dust devil skipped along the
narrow street, and two miners walked by with their lunch-pails.
Work was starting again in some of the mines that had been closed
down.

"Crockett," he said quietly, "you paid me to check your mine. I
did just that. My advice is to start now, today. Put some miners in
there and get out some ore.

"I would also send a man you can trust to California to buy up any
loose stock that's lying around. My guess is that you're not more than
thirty feet from something very good."

"Your *guess*?"

"That's what it is. No man knows what lies beyond that face, so it
has to be a guess. I think what blew down in that last round of shots
was an outcropping of what lies beyond, and I think that ore was

fair-to-middling stuff, not rich enough for anyone to high-grade, but an indication."

"You think I should start mining now?"

"I do, and I don't see why you ever stopped. I've worked off and on all winter and got out quite a bit of ore in what's a piddling operation compared to yours. You could have had tons of ore waiting for shipment."

"Well, I wondered about that, but Al said—"

"Of course, if the mine wasn't being worked, nobody could accidentally come onto a discovery that might change things."

The door opened and George Hearst came in. "How's the coffee? Oh, hello, Will! Trevallion, how about a refill?"

"George, Trevallion here has been telling me I should send somebody out to the coast and buy up all my stock. He thinks we're on the verge of—"

"You'd be too late, Will." There was sympathy in Hearst's eyes. "Every bit of Solomon stock has been snapped up. It went for two to three dollars a share."

"Are you serious?" He stared blankly. "Well, what do you know about that?"

"Well," he added after a minute, "we still have control, Al and I."

"Will?" Hearst spoke gently. "Will, it was Al who bought the stock. Every dollar of it!"

NINETEEN

Will Crockett had gotten up, now he sank back into his chair. He fumbled for the handle of his cup, glancing at Hearst. "George? Are you sure?"

"When I first reached San Francisco, there was talk of an assessment on Solomon stock to finance further exploration.

"Then I was shown several pieces of Solomon ore, all pretty poor stuff. Naturally, with all that talk going around the price of stock fell.

"Two different people asked me if it was true that Hesketh was pulling out, planning on some mining venture of his own.

"By then the passes were all snowed in and nobody was coming through, but you know how rumors are. People began coming forward with Solomon stock for sale, and I heard one loudmouth, a big man I've seen around here, scoffing at Solomon stock." Hearst paused. "He was saying they should save the stock to paper their walls. That was all it was good for."

Melissa filled Will's cup. "The Solomon isn't the only mine, Will," she said gently, "and you still own a large piece of it."

"He had control, Will," Hearst said quietly, "he told me so. He told me he had forty-eight percent of the stock."

"I—I can't believe it," Crockett muttered. "Why, the Solomon is mine! I discovered it. I opened it up, dug the first shaft with my own hands, started a drift. . . . I took out some good ore, too. I never would have sold any stock, but I needed a grub-stake, and Hesketh had some cash. He had gold.

"I sold him some shares, then he advised me to sell more to get working capital. Him and me, we had control, and with the extra cash we could . . ."

He stopped talking, rubbing a hand over his face. His hand trembled. He looked around suddenly. "Well, what the hell? Wait until Al gets back. He will have some explanation. He just saw a chance to pick up that stock for us and did it. A mighty smart move, I'd say."

Trevallion got to his feet. "It's a long day tomorrow, Will. I think I'll say good-night."

He went out and walked back up the hill to the MacNeale claim.

There was a cold wind from off Sun Mountain, and the streets were empty. Trevallion stood in the darkness near the door and listened, studying the shadows. He had cut right across Sam Brown's trail, and the man was vicious.

He took a roundabout route up the mountain, circling some mine dumps and crawling over others.

Dane Clyde was reading a San Francisco paper when he came in. He pointed to the paper. "Half the items are about the Comstock," he said. "If a man wants to be rich, this is the place."

"If he can stay alive."

"Are you talking about Brown?"

Trevallion was bathing his hands in the basin. He shook the water from them, then dried them on the hand-towel. "Brown is only part of it. They've got to find a new way of timbering the mines. Scares me to death to see what they're doing down there.

"We need water, decent drinking water, as well as water to work the mines. We need a local government, and we need some representation in Washington."

"Do you think there will be a war?"

"I do. Some of it may be right here in camp. Terry is a blood-in-the-eye Southerner. Tom Paisley and his firefighters are strong Union men. So is Bill Stewart. The South seems to be having things all their own way at the moment, but that won't last."

The town was booming. Silver was being extracted from the mines at an unbelievable rate. Trading in mining stocks on the San Francisco market had become a form of madness that rarely had any connection with true values. Trevallion worked on his claim, keeping out of sight, working with the simplest tools.

Frame hotels were going up, and there were plans for a large brick hotel with an elegant dining room. A theater was being built, and there were plans to bring in some traveling stock companies. Of a sudden, Virginia City was no longer a squalid cluster of stone huts and dug-outs but a city.

There came the night when Trevallion walked into Lyman Jones's place with Ledbetter. "Look out," Ledbetter said softly, "there's Brown."

"I see him. If it is to happen, the sooner the better."

Trevallion's eyes met Brown's across the heads of two dozen gambling, drinking men. Trevallion walked to the bar. The bartender glanced up, saw who it was, and his face went a shade whiter.

"You heeled?" Ledbetter asked.

"Always," Trevallion said.

Brown glanced at him again. He was a big, shaggy man with small, mean eyes. Yet he was also a cautious man.

Kip Hauser's eyes followed Brown's. "Don't do it, Sam," he whispered.

"Why not?"

"Just take my advice. Leave him alone. He's good with fists or gun and he won't back up, not even a little. He won't be bluffed and he won't scare. If you brace him, you've got to be ready to go all the way."

"He's that good?"

"The best. Langford Peel isn't in the same class, take it from me."

Suddenly there was a stirring in the crowd near him. He looked around and Trevallion was there. "Hello, Sam." Trevallion looked into the cold little eyes and smiled. "Want a drink, Sam?"

"Don't mind if I do."

Trevallion leaned one elbow on the bar. Was Trevallion right- or left-handed? Sam couldn't remember. When they had their drinks, Trevallion said, "I heard there was trouble between us, Sam. I can't think of anything, can you?"

"Trouble? No, I don't know of nothin'."

"Of course not. I said the same thing. I knew you had nothing to do with Ledbetter's mules, Sam. If you did I would have hung you."

"You would have—" Sam stared, starting to get angry, but a little worried, too. "What do you mean, hung me?"

"Why not, Sam? Isn't that what they do with horse thieves? But that's foolish talk. I told them to forget it. We've no trouble, Sam. You just remember that." He indicated the drink. "Go ahead! Drink up!"

He paused. "If we ever do have any trouble, Sam, you just tell me, and you can choose the weapons. Man to man, that's the way we like it, isn't it?"

He downed his drink, then with a slap on the back he turned and walked away. Ledbetter lingered just a moment, finished his own drink, and then followed.

Sam Brown stood at the bar, scowling. He had a feeling he had somehow been tricked, but he couldn't see how. Nonetheless, he was irritated.

"Damn it!" he muttered. "I think I'll—"

"Don't," Kip Hauser advised. "Leave him alone. He's poison, Sam. He's real trouble. He's got too many friends around and Ledbetter probably has more. Anyway, all the time we were talkin', that Tapley was over against the wall behind us, just settin' there, watchin'. My advice is forget him. There's easier pigeons around.

"Anyway," he added, "the word's around that somebody else wants to kill him. Let them do it."

Trevallion went outside with Ledbetter, and a few minutes later they were joined by Tapley. "First time I ever saw Sam buffaloed," Ledbetter commented. "He just didn't know what to make of you. An' Tap here, he had Kip Hauser worried. Kep' turnin' his head to look at him, an' there you sat, Tap, with that six-shooter in your belt, watching them."

They went up the hill to the MacNeale claim, and Trevallion stoked up the fire. "Still cold," he said. "That wind makes a man wonder what he did with his summer's wages."

"They've started building a theater," Clyde commented, "and the Westwoods are going to play here."

"I was counting up," Ledbetter said, "and there's thirty-eight general stores now, nine restaurants, and twenty-five saloons."

"Four butcher shops," Tapley commented, "and there's nine or ten livery stables, a couple of barber shops, and there's plenty of laundries and such. The town's growin', boys. She's gettin' to be a reg'lar metropolis."

"I'm worried about Will Crockett," Ledbetter said suddenly. "Has anybody seen him?"

"He's get nothing to worry about," Tap said, "with forty-two percent of the Solomon. No matter who controls, he stands to make money."

"He's a trusting man," Ledbetter said, "and he trusted Hesketh. That's more than I ever did."

"Never met him," Trevallion said.

"He's a cold man," Ledbetter replied, "and no mixer. Keeps to himself. He's shrewd, though, but I'd not trust him across the street."

"Word is he's on his way back from the coast."

Ledbetter turned to Trevallion. "You looked his mine over. Have they got anything?"

"There's some good-looking rock in that old drift. I was advising Will to start it up again and then the word came through."

The fire was warm and pleasant. Trevallion filled his cup and put it down on the oilcloth-covered table. Below the sound of their voices he listened for sounds from the outside, but there was no sound but the wind.

A theater, they said. He had not seen a play in years, but he had always loved the theater. He said as much. "Will Crockett, too," Ledbetter said. "Will raised some of his first money from theatrical people. He bought back most of the shares he sold them as soon as he raised the money, but they were always the ones he went to when he needed cash."

Trevallion stood up and put on his coat and stepped out into the night. It was cold. The sky was very clear, and the stars were bright and sharp against the night. He walked away from the mine and looked down the hill at the town. There were lights everywhere. They were right, of course; Virginia City was growing. A few months ago the town had been numbered in hundreds, and now it could be counted in thousands, and more coming all the time.

Waggoner . . . where was he? Had he given up? Who was he, anyway? One of them, certainly, although there was still a chance he was just a thief.

He was sure it had been Waggoner who stole his gold. And the man would be back.

He thought again of the men who murdered his mother and killed his father. Nine of them, he believed, and not less than eight. His father had killed two in that final fight, and he had killed two since.

Four or five left, at least two of them he would remember.

What about the man who instigated the affair? He was the one Trevallion wanted.

Or did he? He thought about it less and less all the time, and blamed himself for it. Those men deserved to die, and there had been no law to punish them or even to seek them out.

He seated himself on a large rock and looked thoughtfully at the town. In a booming town like this, a man could get rich. He was here, with a couple of good claims, and he knew what to do with them. He owned a small part of Ledbetter's operation and a small piece of the bakery. Both of these were making money.

He turned his thinking to the lode itself. Several of the mines looked very good. The Ophir, the Mexican, and others were showing large ore bodies, and the ore was the richest he had seen. The vein in the Ophir was sixty-five feet wide.

Nobody had ever worked a vein that wide, and nobody knew how. The earth was crumbly and unstable. There were constant rock falls. Some method must be found to handle the unstable ground and enable the miners to get out the ore in quantity. That such a method would be found he had no doubt.

Trevallion realized he had been so concerned with his own immediate problems that he had not taken the long view. Apparently the affair of Ledbetter's mules was over. He could, for the time, leave Brown out of his thinking and concentrate on the larger issues.

First, he would let Melissa know he was in the market for a claim or two, if the price was right. Her bakery was the best listening post on the Comstock, as miners and mining men talked freely and often confided in her.

Ledbetter was another source of information, as he was constantly moving ore. Most of it was being milled locally now, however. Very little ore was shipped to the coast. Milling had become a big business in Washoe.

The road over the Sierras had been improved and Ledbetter had already begun to shift from pack mules to wagons. Times were changing, and changing fast.

Trevallion went back inside, and on a sheet of tablet paper he drew a rough diagram of the Comstock and Sun Mountain. He drew in the mines, so far as he could remember them, and began to study the situation. There were a few outlying claims that showed no promise. He would look them over, and if the price was right, buy them.

He looked again at the Solomon. Will Crockett was still a major stockholder but no longer in control. He owned forty-two percent and Hesketh now had forty-eight percent, and—

He looked at the figures again. Forty-two and forty-eight figured to only ninety percent.

Who owned the remaining shares? The shares that could represent the controlling interest?

TWENTY

Albert Hesketh disliked riding, and he distrusted horses, but it was the best method of travel, and he was returning to the Comstock in triumph. From his first arrival on the west coast, he had planned for this moment, yet this was only a beginning.

He had known exactly what he wished to do and exactly how to go about it. He had begun by getting a job as bookkeeper for the Solomon and gradually had taken more and more detail off the hands of Will Crockett, until within a year he was virtually in control.

Each evening he had gone into the mine and taken samples from the faces of the workings, and he had paid occasional bottles of whiskey to workers in other mines for news of developments. Gradually, he had accumulated considerable data as to the situation on the Comstock.

Hoarding the small amount of gold he had brought with him, he added to it what he could save by frugal living and from discreet skimming of high-grade from the Solomon.

At the first indication of increased values, he had stopped work in the main drift and begun exploration elsewhere. He had gone himself into the mine each night to see the results of the blasting before the morning shift came to work. He had himself mucked out some good-looking ore and hidden it in a cross-cut, and cleaned up along the face of the drift. The following morning the new exploration began.

Will Crockett rarely came into the mine, spending more time buying supplies and cutting timber, and Hesketh had carefully nurtured the idea that Crockett was of greater value on the surface than below. Hesketh made a practice of reporting carefully all the developments below ground so Crockett would seem to have a grasp of what was going on.

Purposely, Hesketh had hired miners who loafed on the job or were just putting in their time, as they would be less likely to wonder at the orders they received.

From the beginning he had known he would not have money enough to bring off the coup he intended, so on his winter in San

130

Francisco, with the mine closed down, he located the man he wanted.

Marcus Zetsev was a ship chandler who also dealt in mining supplies. A short, stocky, somewhat corpulent man with slightly protruding eyes, he operated a small business on the waterfront, a business that suddenly began to prosper.

Albert Hesketh was inquisitive. He was suspicious, also. His first lead to the character of Marcus Zetsev came in a small restaurant where he overheard a conversation at an adjoining table.

"Buy it from Marcus," a man was saying, low-voiced, "you can get it cheaper. A lot cheaper."

"But how can he afford to sell that much cheaper?"

"Don't ask me. And don't ask him. Just make your deal and keep your mouth shut."

A few days later he bought drills, cable, and powder from Zetsev, paying less than the market price. "I appreciate the favor," he commented to Zetsev. "I am operating on the Comstock and can bring quite a bit of business your way."

"You do that. Treat you right." He glanced left and right. "If the word gets out, I'd have to raise prices. Other dealers don't take to price-cutting. Live and let live, I say."

A few days later Hesketh dropped around, and after a bit of desultory conversation, he asked, "Buy you a drink?"

Zetsev glanced at him, looked out the door, then nodded, "Don't mind if I do."

After some conversation in a nearby saloon, Hesketh said, "There's money to be made in the mining business if you have inside information. Or if you can pick up good properties at a low cost."

A few minutes later, he said, "There's a deal coming up—it will be a few months—but it needs more capital than I have."

"Lay it out for me."

"Later," Hesketh said. "But it could mean millions. And that's only one deal."

"I've got some Solomon stock."

"Sell it."

"What if it goes up?"

"It won't. Not for a while, at least, and then you can buy it back at a lower price."

Marcus accepted the advice and sold, and through a broker, Hesketh bought the stock himself. A few days later when the stock went down, Marcus was pleased. "A good tip. I appreciate that."

"Wait," Hesketh said, "and save your money."

Marcus Zetsev was, he suspected, buying stolen goods. There were several large gangs, including the Sydney Ducks, operating along the waterfront, and they constantly slipped aboard ships in the harbor and stole cargo from them or from the warehouses.

Later, Marcus said, in a confidential mood, "I never buy stolen goods. Take a strong stand on it. Only," he smiled widely, "I just don't ask questions. Man comes to me with something to sell, and the price is right, I buy it. I got no reason to think he's not an honest man, now do I?"

A few weeks later when the price of Solomon stock was right, Zetsev loaned Hesketh the money with which to buy.

He bought discreetly, seeking out owners whose names he had taken from the Solomon files, first talking to them about a coming stock assessment, then suggesting the alternative. He had been careful enough so most of the stock was in his possession before even such an astute mining man as George Hearst was aware of what was happening. Hearst was in no way involved with the Solomon, but it was important to know what was going on, and then, he considered Will Crockett a friend, as did nearly everyone on the lode.

Hesketh rode into Virginia City after dark. Purposely he had waited until the saloons were crowded and most of the miners off the streets. He had chosen the less traveled ways, and he rode right to the office of the Solomon.

A few minutes later he posted a sign on the outside of the office and another on the headframe at the shaft-collar. Walking down the trail to the point where entry was made to mine property, he put up a third sign. All denied entry without a pass signed by the superintendent.

At daybreak the following morning an armed guard was stationed at the first sign, and the first man up the trail was Will Crockett.

The guard stopped him. "You got business here?"

"I'm Will Crockett!"

The guard shrugged. "I don't give a damn who you are. If you've got a pass you can go ahead, no pass—no pass."

"What the hell is this? I *own* this mine!"

"My orders are you got to have a pass. Those orders come right from Superintendent Hesketh, and he—"

"Super *who*?"

The guard was a large man who carried a club. He also wore a six-shooter. "Mister, if you want a pass, you ask for it in writing. You give me a letter to Mr. Hesketh and I'll see it is delivered."

He waved a hand at the mine-workings behind him. "There's blasting going on. We wouldn't want you to get hurt."

Will stared at him, looked past him at the office, then turned and walked back down the trail.

"I'll be damned if I'll write a letter!" he said at the bakery. "The nerve of him!"

"He owns a controlling interest," somebody said. "So I guess he makes the rules."

Trevallion heard the news at the mine. He had just loaded a round of holes and had spit the fuses, then come on top. He listened but offered no comment. Will had always been a straightforward man.

Other than mining there were only two topics of conversation in the camp, the Heenan-Sayers fight and the coming election. Seward was favored for the nomination. The South was threatening Secession.

When asked, he shrugged. "I don't know much about politics here. I've never been east. All I know is the west coast."

Yet it irritated him that he knew so little. He felt inadequate. He was a citizen now, had become one more than a year ago, and a man should know. He had always been a loner, avoiding talk of politics, reading a little about it from the occasional newspapers he found, usually newspapers long out of date.

Somebody had mentioned Lincoln to him. "What about Lincoln?" he asked.

"Who?" They looked at him.

"Abe Lincoln. He's from Illinois."

"Never heard of him."

Ledbetter spoke up. "Sure you have! Remember? He's the one had those debates with Douglas."

"Oh, him? I was west then. Never did get the hang of what they were talking about."

When he went back into the hole after his last round of shots, the powder smoke had cleared. He picked his way over the broken rock to the face.

He looked at it, then sat down on the pile of muck, picked up a piece of ore and studied it, then looked at the face again. The vein had taken a downward dip, but it was wider—wider and richer. He swore softly and went back into the air.

He went back, mucked out his ore, then sorted it with care. Never a talkative man, he preferred nobody know his business. The ore was rich, but crumbly. It would be hard ground to work.

Fortunately, nobody believed he had anything here, and the longer they believed that the better off he would be.

After he had washed up and taken off his digging clothes, he got into a clean outfit and put on his coffee, then he walked out front. Evening was coming on, and some work had ceased. The big stamp mills continued to pound, but he rarely heard them any more. His mind had learned to blot out the sound.

He strolled down the slope and sat down on a rock, looking back up the mountain. Of course, there was no telling which way that vein would go. That was one thing the Comstock had taught them. He glanced at the claim adjoining his on the north. It belonged to an Irishman named Lydon, and the one east of him belonged to a Dutchman who kept a store and sometimes cut hair as a sideline.

He dropped around to the store. "How's for a haircut?"

"Set over there. In the cane chair."

Trevallion dropped into the chair, studying himself in the mirror. It was time he had a haircut. "If you find any dust in my hair," he commented, "don't bother to pan it out."

"What's the matter? Not paying off?"

"I've got a claim up on Seven Mile. If I work I can make a living."

"Don't you have the old MacNeale place?"

"Uh-huh. I live there."

"But you're working that a little, aren't you?"

"Tried. It doesn't show much so I'm widening out the hole. Make a basement of it."

"A basement?"

"I'm going to build myself a house. I'm tired of sleeping in that bunk of MacNeale's. I want to build a six-room house, something really nice. Trouble is, I don't have quite room enough. I'm going to see who owns that place north of me. If I could pick it up cheap I'd—"

"I own the one to the east."

"You do? Well, I'll be damned. If it was to the north we could make a deal."

When the Dutchman had finished cutting his hair he put up his scissors and said, "You'd not be interested in my place then?"

"Well, no." He paused, as if thinking. "Still, if the price was right—"

He picked up his coat and put it on. "I'll want a garden, of course. I can bring in some earth from the valley. I might plant east of the house."

"Of course," the Dutchman said, "there might be mineral on it."

"Could be. No use taking my place as an example. You might strike it rich up there. Of course, all the best ores are deep here, and it will cost you some money to develop it."

He changed the subject, talking of the failure of the Pony to arrive. The situation in the east was growing daily more serious, and the lack of news was a disturbing thing.

"I'm for the Union," the Dutchman said. "If the South secedes there will be a war, that much is certain."

A miner had come in from outside, and heard the comment.

"Aye," he said grimly, "and Terry expects to seize the Comstock for the South!"

"How do you know that?" Trevallion asked.

The miner glanced at him, started to speak, then shrugged. "There's talk," he muttered. Suddenly, as if sorry for having spoken, he turned and walked out.

"He spoke as if he knew something," Trevallion commented.

"He probably does. He just realized he didn't know us and stopped talking." The Dutchman sat down, brushing the hair from his sleeves. "Terry's done a lot of talking, and there are many who think as he does. They leave me alone because they think of me as a foreigner." He glanced at Trevallion. "You're a Cornishman, aren't you?"

"I was. I'm an American now." He gestured widely. "I was born overseas, but I make my living here. I vote here, when I stay any place long enough to vote."

"It will be well," the Dutchman spoke quietly, "to know where one stands. I am Dutch, but I went to American schools." He paused a minute. "The Southerners talk the most for they feel very strongly about it all, the Unionists don't talk so much, but they are here."

Trevallion started for the door, but the Dutchman spoke. "Trevallion? If you want that claim of mine east of you, I'll let you have it for five hundred dollars." He hesitated. "Take it or leave it."

"I'll take it," Trevallion said.

They shook hands.

"Although you'd be wise to leave," the Dutchman said. "I hear things, and there's going to be trouble."

"Trouble?"

"Serious trouble. I'm going to pull out, now."

TWENTY-ONE

Trevallion was lonely and restless. The old pattern of his life no longer would do. He sensed that Ledbetter felt much the same way, but they saw little of each other as even now, with growing affluence, Ledbetter was much on the trail.

Will Crockett was no longer around. There were rumors that he had gone to San Francisco, others that he was prospecting. Hesketh, a rumor said, had offered Crockett three dollars a share for his forty-two percent of the stock. Crockett had refused and Hesketh had replied, "All right, my offer is now two dollars per share, and not a cent more."

Trevallion worked alone on his claim. He got out more ore, sorted out the best stuff, and had it milled where Tapley had found work. From time to time he thought of moving on, of going to some other area, to Austin, on the Reese River, but his good sense told him things would be no better there than here. To keep moving was to try to escape from a problem he carried with him.

At night, lying in his bunk alone, he thought of what some of his friends had said, that he needed to find a woman, get married and settle down, but there was no woman. Yet he considered his situation honestly and found it not bad. He had some mining claims, his as long as he did at least one hundred dollars work per year, and they were good claims. He now owned the adjoining claim on the east, in the direction he believed his own lead to be taking.

He sat up suddenly, swinging his feet to the floor. What was he thinking about? He could be *rich*! True, riches had never been one of the things he wanted, but it was here, at hand, and he thought of John Mackay, and something he had said during one of their idle moments of conversation. "Sometimes I think it is not the money, but the game. It isn't the winning so much as it is to play the cards right."

Trevallion got out his plat of Virginia City and Gold Hill and studied them. Most of the mines had now passed from the hands of the discoverers into those of developers, and they were rapidly going deeper and deeper. The Ophir was into bonanza ore, others were going deeper and richer. Down C Street the International Hotel was going up, destined to be a haven of elegance, if plans matured.

He looked at the plat again. If his drawing was correct, and he was sure it was, there remained a corner near the Solomon on which nobody had filed. Surrounded by mines that were already into bonanza, it was idle. Did no one realize it was there?

Trevallion studied the plat carefully, rechecked his figures, and looked again. When the first filings had begun on claims on the Comstock, the record book had been kept in a saloon, and anyone had access to it. The entries had often been altered, boundaries changed, and claims sold. There was every chance that the others believed this was Solomon ground.

Melissa had scarcely opened her bakery before Trevallion came in. She turned at his closing the door.

"Trev! Where have you been! It's been days! Weeks!"

He accepted the coffee and doughnuts she put out for him. "Hang on for a minute and I'll have Cookie fry up some eggs. We just got some in."

She sat down opposite him. She had filled out a little and was even more attractive. "I never see you or Jim any more. Where is he?"

"His business has grown, too." He sipped his coffee. "Have you seen Will Crockett?"

"No. He's been in only a couple of times since he lost the Solomon. He's a changed man, Trev."

"If you see him, tell him I want to talk . . . business. Important business."

She asked no questions. "He needs something. He's been wandering around like a lost soul. Anybody else would have taken a gun and killed Hesketh."

"It was business. Tricky business, but business nonetheless. One should never trust anyone too much." He put down his cup. "I'm a quiet man, and I'm much alone, but despite that, I like people. At the same time I know we are all subject to temptation and we are all human and you can always find excuses for what you do."

"So?"

He smiled. "I try to keep them from being tempted."

The streets were crowded now, and there was almost no place on the side of Sun Mountain that was not busy.

From high on the side of the mountain, he studied the slope below with his glass, and especially that area near the Solomon. When he had worked it out in his mind, he went back to his cabin and got several stakes together, then he went down to the Virginia House, inquiring for Will Crockett. He was not around. Dane Clyde was.

"Guess who just moved in? Al Hesketh just took an apartment here."

"Living it up, isn't he?"

"He's taking ore out of the Solomon that you wouldn't believe. That's the story, anyway." Clyde glanced at him. "He's going to be a rich man, Trevallion."

"No doubt." Trevallion was thinking of something else. "If you see Will, tell him I must see him. It's important."

"Have you met Sutro? If you haven't, you should. He's got some idea of running a tunnel to drain all the mines but he's not getting much help."

"He will have to work fast. The Ophir is down around a hundred and fifty feet and going deeper."

Tonight, he would have to move tonight. If he could bring it off—

Hesketh had guards around his mine, and at night they were apt to shoot first and ask questions afterward. Trevallion was quite sure that Hesketh had been assuming the area in which he was interested was part of the Solomon holdings, just as everybody else was. Hesketh had, Trevallion knew, picked up several adjoining claims, apparently assuming it had been part of the Solomon from the beginning. It would not be the first time such assumptions had been made. It was a small piece of land, but Sandy Bowers and Eilley were getting rich from a piece not too much different in size.

He wanted no gun battle if he could avoid it. Whatever he did must be done quickly, silently, and before it was realized what he was doing.

They went into the saloon and sat down. It was quiet, only a few businessmen drinking at the bar. Suddenly, Clyde said, "What I'd have given to have been here among the first!"

Trevallion permitted himself a rare smile. "You'd probably have done no better than the others," he said. "Alvah Gould, one of the original owners of the Gould & Curry, sold his piece for four hundred and fifty dollars, and thought he'd gypped the Californians. Another one ended up cooking in a sheep camp, while millions were being taken from the mine he'd sold for almost nothing."

"You could be rich," Clyde suggested. "Everybody says you know more about mining than any of them."

"That isn't true." He gestured toward Sun Mountain. "We're all learning. This is a new kind of mining, and we're having to find new ways of doing it. That mountain has a lot of tricks that we've only begun to learn about. If we don't find a new way to timber those drifts and stopes, the whole mine will come down on us."

"They're bringing in a man from California named Philipp Deidesheimer."

"I know him. I worked for him over in El Dorado County. He's a good man."

"He's expected to solve the problems," Clyde said. "Do you think he can?"

"If anybody can. He's a good mining man and a very shrewd one. He's a German," he added, "from Darmstadt."

Trevallion was watching the door. The man he wanted now was Will Crockett. Where *was* he?

Suddenly, he saw somebody else walk past the window. He swore.

Dane Clyde glanced around. "What's the matter? Something wrong with your drink?"

"No, I just saw a man I used to know." He got up. "Sorry to run. I've got to get over to the bakery."

Melissa was watching a new batch of bread go into the oven. Jim Ledbetter was having coffee.

"Melissa?"

She turned sharply at his tone. "Watch yourself. I just saw Mousel."

Ledbetter looked up. "You saw him *here*?"

"We should have expected it. After all, he claims to be a miner as well as a trapper. And he knew where Melissa was going. I'm only surprised he didn't come sooner."

"I'll be careful," Melissa said. "He doesn't frighten me any more."

"He's dangerous," Trevallion warned, "and he's full of hatred. The very fact that you've done well will make him worse. If he gives you any trouble, just let me know."

"Or me," Ledbetter said.

"Be careful your own selves. He didn't like either of you very much." She filled a cup and walked to the table and sat down. "I'm not surprised. I'm just wondering if he followed Alfie."

They both put their cups down. "He's *here*?" Ledbetter exclaimed.

She laughed at them. "Of course! He showed up yesterday, very elegant-looking and fashionable."

"No calluses on his hands, I'll bet," Ledbetter said grimly.

"He stopped by to see me. Said he was glad I was doing so well."

"I'll bet!" Ledbetter said.

She put her hand over his. "Jim, you're an old grouch! You never really knew Alfie. He's charming!"

"What's he doing for a living?" Ledbetter asked.

"He didn't say."

Trevallion said nothing, he was thinking of what he had before him and how it might best be accomplished. He looked around suddenly to find Ledbetter watching him. "What's on your mind, Trev?" he asked.

"Mining."

Ledbetter shrugged. "Be careful. Mousel's a rat, but a vengeful one."

Trevallion got up. "If you see Crockett, tell him to look me up."

He went to the door, paused a moment, and then went along to the corner of C Street. It was crowded with ore wagons, riders, and pedestrians. Miners, prospectors, stockbrokers, teamsters, and occasional drifting cowhands and businessmen, and mingled with them the usual corps of nondescript drifters who follow in the wake of any excitement.

At the MacNeale cabin he changed into digging clothes and went down the drift. He finished drilling the lifters at the bottom of the face, then came back on top and went into the cabin. It was a piecemeal way of working, and he did not like it much, but at least he was getting something done. He hefted the can of black powder; he would need more powder, and he was getting low on other supplies. He made a mental calculation of what money he had left and swore softly. He had been buying until his cash supply was almost gone. Yet he had some good ore and he should be getting some money from the ore left at the mill on his last visit.

Tomorrow, maybe.

Waggoner returned to Virginia City riding a sorebacked roan and in a foul mood. In his pocket there was an additional three hundred dollars and with it there had come a note: until Trevallion was killed, this was the last payment.

The town was crowded, and his arrival attracted no attention. Deliberately, he had developed no associations or friendships. Nobody cared whether he came or went, and that was the way he wanted it.

For the first time he was shying away from the job he had to do. He had killed other men, and would kill more, but not like this one. Trevallion bothered him, worried him, threw him off balance.

He should have had him that night at the gold cache. Four other times he had lain in wait for him, only to find he had taken another route or gone elsewhere. At first he had believed it was pure accident, but he no longer believed that. Trevallion knew somebody was gunning for him.

Waggoner had heard of the Sam Brown incident. That had demanded nerve of an uncommon kind. Also there had either been some organization or loyalty, because both Jim Ledbetter and Christian Tapley had been on hand.

Twice, when stalking Trevallion he had seen Tapley not far off. Watching him? Or just there by chance? If he raised a rifle, would Tapley have shot him? He swore bitterly. What's-his-name could do his own killing. Although, he reflected, it was his killing, too.

He kept out of sight and made his way to his old dug-out, only to find the lock broken and the dug-out occupied.

Leaving his horse ground-hitched, he opened the door and stepped in. Startled, a man looked up from a chessboard. Another man who had just slid down from a bunk was reaching for his overalls.

"Get out," Waggoner said, rifle in hand.

"Now see here! Just who—"

"I built this place. It's on my claim. You busted in where you've no right. You're claim-jumpers."

"You say this place is—" the chess player started to argue.

Waggoner kicked the chessboard out of his hands, and as the other man started to protest, he struck him across the face with the rifle barrel. "Get out," he repeated.

The miner whose face he had struck fumbled for his overalls, blood streaming from a broken nose. Shocked and hurt, he could think only of getting out, of getting away.

"We didn't mean nothin'," the other man protested, "the place was empty an' we—"

"You've got five minutes," Waggoner said. "If you aren't out of here and out of sight in five minutes, I'll kill the both of you."

Hastily, they caught up what they could, and with the one man only half-dressed, they stumbled down the trail.

Waggoner watched them go, rifle ready, then turned back to the cabin. For a moment he looked around, then he swore bitterly. The place was filthy.

With another glance out the door to be sure they were not returning, he opened the two windows to let in the air and then began to clean up. He swept the floor, dusted whatever needed dusting. He gathered up their bedding and carried it off the claim, dropping it in a heap. He found a six-shooter which had not been cleaned in months, and after emptying it, threw it out with the bedding.

The small stable, fit for two horses, had not been disturbed. He led his horse inside, stripped off the bridle and saddle, and forked down some hay. Back in the dug-out he placed a pistol on the table before him, and then stripped down his rifle and cleaned it with care. When it was cleaned to his satisfaction, he reloaded the rifle and started on the pistol.

Closing the windows and the door, he stripped down, and pouring water in the tin washtub, he bathed himself. He was a lean, hard-muscled man with massive shoulders and big hands. Naturally lazy, he disliked work of any kind and wanted very little. On Saturday night he wanted a woman, any woman, and he didn't care what she looked like. Occasionally he took a drink. Once every month or so he went on a tearing drunk that lasted four or five days, at which time he was sullen, silent, and vicious. Bartenders, recognizing the type, served his drinks and left him strictly alone.

At such times he was given to taking offense at the slightest remark, and on two such occasions had almost beaten men to death over some trivial remark. Sober he was cautious, careful, and avoided trouble. He stole whatever he wanted, killed if anyone got in the way, killing men as he would a hog or a sheep. The idea of carving a notch for each man killed would never have occurred to him.

His desire was simple. To kill Trevallion and return to the coast.

He had no plan. No doubt Trevallion was working somewhere around, probably on a claim of his own. He would find out about that first.

The three hundred dollars he had just been paid would last him for months. There was more coming when the job was done. He would have a year of no worries, no troubles.

The town was bigger, bustling and busy. There would be more people around, and he would have to take care not to be seen or suspected. Then a good, clean shot and a ride back to the coast.

Nevertheless, as he stretched out on his bunk he was uneasy. Getting a good clean shot was not easy with Trevallion. Just when you thought you had him, he did something different.

The worst of it was, Waggoner suspected Trevallion not only knew what he was trying to do, but knew exactly who he was.

If he started in again, suppose Trevallion decided to lay for *him*?

No question about it. No matter what happened he must do it, get it over with, and get out.

And there were other ways than the rifle.

TWENTY-TWO

All night long the wind blew. Stones rattled like hail against the walls and on the roofs of Virginia City, Gold Hill, and Silver City. The walls leaned away from the wind, and newcomers worried about their roofs and lay awake, frightened.

The longtime residents on Sun Mountain slept soundly, accustomed to the rattle of stones and the awesome sounds of the Washoe Zephyr. Their roofs might also go, but they knew there was no use losing sleep over it. Only the men in the mines were safe, and they had other things about which to worry.

Oozing layers of clay kept pushing into the empty tunnels, and unless trimmed back, would fill any space left available. The veins of ore widened, grew richer, and the problem of how to support walls and stopes became more serious. Up the street, beside a gas lamp, a German from Darmstadt labored over the problem. He thought he had it but was not sure. He got up, put on his hat, and went down the street to the bakery.

The bakers worked late, and the door was always open; the coffee was always ready. Philipp Deidesheimer wanted to talk. He needed another practical mining man, somebody like John Mackay, Fair, or Trevallion. He was sure he was right, but often a fresh viewpoint would bring up something he had failed to consider. Wearing his thick cap and heavy jacket, he went outside into the wind and a few spattering drops of rain. For a moment he stood thinking, and then walked slowly down the street. It was too late; he'd find none of the good ones out at this hour.

Neither Mackay nor Trevallion hung out at the saloons. Both dropped in, but were never late-stayers. Fair sometimes got to talking . . . it was almost midnight.

Only the bakery, where they were baking for the next day's business, would be apt to have anyone he could talk to.

He tried the door, and it opened under his hand. Melissa was not there. Hans, from Hofheim, was there. The German baker greeted him with a nod. "Help yourself." He nodded toward the big coffee-pot. "Always, it iss ready."

143

Trevallion was seated alone at the back table. He looked up and nodded. For a moment curiosity came. What was Trevallion doing around at this hour? Usually the hard-working ones were abed by this time.

Deidesheimer filled his cup and carried it to the table. He spooned in sugar, added some cream, and said, "I haff somet'ings to show you."

He took a square of paper from his pocket and put it on the table in front of them. "Vee haff a problem. To support walls and roof. The veins are wide and grow wider. I can t'ink of nothing. Nothing at all. Then it comes to me—the honeycomb!

"Vee built mit square-sets, one atop the other, and we fill in with waste rock for added support. I t'ink vee haff it."

"You'll need a lot of timber," Trevallion said, "more than now."

"Yah, much more! Before it iss only pillars here and there!" He pushed the square of paper toward Trevallion. "Look! You haff worked in Cornwall! You know somet'ings!"

Trevallion studied it thoughtfully. Formerly, working with timber pillars often of sixteen to thirty-odd feet, there was only poor support, and there was no way of working either above or below the pillars without risk of a cave-in.

No miner had worked a vein the width of those at the Comstock before this, and new methods were needed. "I see no reason why it will not work," he said. "I think you've got the answer."

"It is for the Ophir," Deidesheimer said.

"Everybody will be using it. Once they see how it works, it can't miss."

"You goot man," Deidesheimer said. "I t'ink it iss well to go into the timber now. Mit a flume to carry down logs. I t'ink you tell me once your papa did not want you to vork underground, yes? Cut timber and you get rich I t'ink."

Trevallion glanced at his watch. If he was to act, it must be soon. Deidesheimer finished his coffee. He got to his feet. "I am obliged. I wished for another opinion. I was afraid I had overlooked some obvious fault."

Trevallion shook his head. "Whether you know it or not, and I am sure you do, you have revolutionized mining. This will change everything."

"Perhaps." Deidesheimer gestured widely. "Much iss new here. The old vays are no longer so good. Vee must find new vays for new problems, no?"

Trevallion walked outside with him and watched him start off toward his home. He waited for a moment, studying the street, and then he went around the bakery and took a narrow footpath toward the east. When he had gone some thirty yards or so he stopped, and from beside a rock he took up several stakes and a double-jack. Following the footpath, he was out of the lights and away from any houses. The path passed near some dug-outs, but all was dark and quiet. Before him loomed the head-frame over the Solomon's shaft.

He waited, listening. He could hear the guard humming softly, then the sound of his boots as he walked. Timing his steps to sound with those of the guard, he walked up a small gully and past the Solomon's hoist-house. From the corner he paced off twenty steps, and kneeling, he built a small cairn of rocks. In the exact center and close to the ground, he buried a tin biscuit box with his claim notice inside.

Moving to a corner he thrust a stake into the ground, hitting it two short, sharp blows with the double-jack. The sound of the blows was muffled by a glove he placed over the end of the stake, so he moved on quickly to another. As he struck the second blow he heard a muffled exclamation, then the sound of running feet. Flattening out on the ground he waited, listening.

The guard came as far as the hoist-house, then stood listening. After a bit, muttering, he walked away. Trevallion placed the other two stakes without trouble. He was rising to leave when the guard loomed over him.

"Hah! *Got* you!" He swung with the butt of his rifle.

Trevallion, only starting to rise, threw himself to the ground on his shoulder and spun around as the blow with the gun stock missed. His instep caught the guard behind the knee. The knee buckled, and Trevallion kicked him hard alongside the kneecap with his other heel.

The guard grunted with pain and fell. Like a cat, Trevallion was on his feet and kicked the guard in the head as he fumbled to get his rifle in position. The kick knocked him sprawling, and Trevallion caught up the rifle.

"You're trespassing." He spoke very softly. "You're not on Solomon land any more. Now you crawl, you crawl to wherever you want to go, but don't come back here. Next time I might hurt you."

"You've busted my knee!"

"Not yet. It will be sore for awhile, that's all. Now get out of here."

"I got a job! I can't just—"

"You had a job. You won't have it after tonight. Now move!"

The guard tried to get up, cried out in pain, and fell. "Just crawl," Trevallion whispered. "You'll feel better that way."

"You just wait, damn you! I'll—"

"Tsk, tsk!" Trevallion said. "Don't you ever learn? If you talk that way, next time I'll have to be rough!"

He watched the man leave, then left himself, making his way back to the MacNeale claim. All was quiet. He waited, listening. No sound.

He went forward softly, pausing to listen at every other step. When he was inside, he lighted a lamp. Dane Clyde was asleep. Moving quietly, the lamp turned low, he got into bed himself. Then putting a hand half over the lamp-chimney, he blew out the light.

He lay still, wide awake, listening. He had heard nothing and he heard nothing now, but something disturbed him, something seemed wrong.

In the morning, he would find out in the morning.

He smiled suddenly, into the darkness. Tomorrow all hell would break loose.

The piece of land on which he had filed measured only a few feet, not much larger than the area covered by the Solomon hoisting-engine house, but unless he was mistaken it could prove to be the richest piece of the Solomon bonanza.

He closed his eyes, waiting for sleep. Outside in the darkness something stirred, but he heard nothing. A shadow appeared near the tunnel mouth and moved on cat feet past the cabin.

For a moment, when out on C Street, the shadow paused and looked back.

"Tomorrow," its voice said, "tomorrow it will all be over!"

And then San Francisco!

TWENTY-THREE

Albert Hesketh's breakfast was served in his room. He arose at eight, shaved, and carefully parted his hair, and by the time he was ready his breakfast was at the door. He studied his beard in the mirror. He kept it carefully trimmed in the Van Dyke fashion.

He regarded himself with some satisfaction. He had come a long way, but in another four years he would own the Comstock. He was perfectly aware that others had identical ideas, and that others had taken steps toward that end. He was interested but not concerned, for he was on the ground, while the others of whom he knew were operating from San Francisco.

He went into his sitting room where his breakfast was neatly laid out. The newspaper, only a few months in existence now, was placed beside his plate. This was the *Territorial Enterprise,* an amusing sheet but not to be taken seriously.

He took up the paper, glanced through it, and replaced it on the table. He glanced through the San Francisco papers as well. The stock of the Solomon was where he wanted it, down a few points. He wanted Will Crockett's stock or a part of it, and he wanted the stock price to be low so he could buy when the time came.

He knew more about Will Crockett's finances than did Will, and the man had little cash. Somehow he must contrive to live and to pay his bills.

Ten shares were outstanding, and those ten shares represented control until such a time as he could get all or some of Crockett's stock. He had already arranged for Crockett to be offered a loan, putting up stock as collateral. He would himself put up the money for the loan, strictly a secret thing, and he was sure that with Crockett's casual way with money the stock would soon fall into his own hands.

Nonetheless, that outstanding ten shares was a problem. They had worried him from the start, for they were the only shares on which he had no lead. There was no indication who owned them. They had been sold at the very beginning from a company Crockett had operated in California, a company which had purchased the Solomon. In those days Crockett had been able to sell stock to only a few acquaintances, and ·during their time together Hesketh had quietly tried by every means to find out who owned them.

He led Crockett into long, rambling tales of his youth, of his early days in the mining business, listening patiently, avid for names.

The trouble was that Crockett liked people and he had known about everybody and had been friendly with everyone, even outlaws and people from the theater. Nowhere was there the semblance of a clue. Nor was Crockett being secretive, he either did not remember or thought it of too little consequence, and Hesketh dared not ask him the direct question. He was afraid he might make Crockett suspicious.

Hesketh had reason to be pleased with himself. He now had control of a mine he believed would prove to be among the richest on the lode. He had stock in several others and owned some nearby claims. He had moved with care and until now had kept himself in the shadows. Now he was a mine owner and an important man. He had moved into the Virginia House where he could live like a gentleman, and when the International was complete, he would live there.

He had no intimates, rarely indulged in conversation, and secretly viewed all those about him with contempt. He used all whom he could, ignored the others. He trusted no one, permitted no one to get even an inkling of what he planned. He had no enemies, unless Will Crockett had become one, and but few worries. If all went as he planned, he would soon be untouchable.

Finishing his breakfast, he put aside the papers, donned his coat, and went down the carpeted stairs to the lobby. He paused only long enough for a glance and went into the street.

Since moving to the Virginia House he had begun a new lifestyle but one calculated to attract attention. Virtually without scruples, he was completely concerned with himself and his own plans. He believed all others were like himself, completely devoted to their self-interest—except, perhaps, such blunderers as he conceived Will Crockett to be.

That he had betrayed the trust of a man who had consistently helped him had never so much as come to mind. He had seen his opportunities and taken advantage of them.

Now, neatly dressed in a gray suit, he walked slowly along the street. From this moment on, he intended to move into a commanding position, and he wished everyone to see and know who was in command.

His walk on this morning ended at the Solomon.

He was scarcely in sight before the guard began waving at him. Irritated, he walked a little faster. What was all that frantic waving?

The guard was Joe Elsinger, a tough man. "Mr. Hesketh, when I got here, Alex was gone. Not a sign of him, anywhere."

"And look at that!" he pointed.

Hesketh had an angry reply on his lips until he saw the cairn. He started to speak, then stopped.

A cairn? A staked claim? Staked last night? By Alex? Not a chance. But by whom?

"Destroy it," he said, "knock it down."

"Mr. Hesketh? I can't do that, sir. They'd call it claim-jumping. I'd get hung—shot, maybe. No, sir. That's somebody's claim marker."

"That's part of my claim!" Hesketh said irritably. "Don't you suppose I know?"

"Sir? Begging your pardon, sir, but did you stake it? You, your-self? I knew of a case in Californy, sir, it was a case where the fifteen hundred feet seemed a mite long and some real sharpies, they measured it off and found it was eighteen hundred feet. So they staked the richest end of that claim, and they held it."

Hesketh's face was pale. *Crockett!* That damned fool! Couldn't he do anything right?

For a moment he felt sheer panic, then a blind rage that left him fairly trembling with fury. Desperately he fought for control.

"It will be all right, Elsinger. I'll handle this. There's been some mistake, I think." He paused. "When did you get here?"

"Seven, sir. That's when my shift begins. I came on at seven and there was no sign of Alex. I looked high and low, but I did find his rifle.

"And it looks like there was some scuffling. I mean the ground was tore up and there were a few drops of blood. Nothing serious."

"Thank you, Elsinger. Now you just stay on the job." He would have to see whose name was on the filing notice. He walked out, hesitated again, then lifted away several stones.

Crockett & Trevallion!

He replaced the notice and walked back to the hoist-house. For a moment he stood there, fighting the fury that gripped him. Crockett would never in the world have gall enough to pull something like this. It had to be Trevallion. That damned—

He stood very still. His eyes widened a little, and he touched his tongue to too dry lips.

Trevallion!

He must be careful, very, very careful. For this he would want an attorney. Trevallion was dangerous. He had heard that more than once, and Trevallion was no fool. He was no longer fighting just that blundering idiot of a Crockett but a shrewd, tough fighting man. He must be very, very careful! At the same time, he must have that corner. The richest ore might lie, should lie, right there under that cairn, or under the whole area they had staked.

He turned and walked back down the street to the Virginia House. Now he must think. Do nothing without thinking, nothing without careful planning.

Do nothing at all now. Within a matter of hours everybody in camp would know and most of them, a lot of sentimental fools, would sympathize with Crockett. So let them sympathize, let them have their day, and then, when some other sensation was holding their attention, he could move.

They had made a fool of him and they would pay, he would make them pay.

He returned to his room and ordered a pot of tea. He hated the stuff, but to him there was something cool and elegant about it. When the story was told, it would sound very good. 'What did Mr. Hesketh do? He simply returned to his rooms and ordered a pot of tea. You know how he is. Nothing disturbs Mr. Hesketh.' "

That was what they'd say, or something like it. He must be calm. He must wait. He must think.

Late last night was when it had been done. Probably after midnight.

Trevallion. So far as he knew he had never seen the man, although there were stories enough about him. He had faced Sam Brown. Maybe—

No. To do that he must approach Brown or somebody close to him, and that would not do. Besides, he wanted nothing to do with the man.

He must think, plan. Above all, he must keep cool. He must be in control.

When Trevallion awoke, Dane Clyde was already gone. Coffee was made, and there was some bacon at one side of the stove, keeping warm.

Today he would finish those holes he had started, load and shoot them. He had done too little work, and he was going to have to send some ore to the smelter.

Trevallion walked along the tunnel, pausing briefly at the niche where he kept his black powder. He remembered he had been running short when he fired his last round. He paused, hefting the can.

Light, very light. Well, he'd get a couple of holes drilled, anyhow.

He wanted to be around this day to see what steps Hesketh would take.

He walked up to the face. Several pieces of drill steel of successive lengths were propped against the wall, waiting for the changes he would make. One drill lay on the ground on an angle away from the face. He took up his single-jack, placed it near his foot, and reached for the drill.

He stopped, bent over, arms hanging; he looked at the drill steel again. Slowly, he straightened up. Now what the hell?

That was wrong, all wrong! Trevallion was a man of habit. When working alone, as he usually was, if he left a hole incomplete, he always left the proper length of steel in front of the hole as a reminder there was more to be done. It was one of those little habits men pick up, and it had been his way for years.

Always, he left the drill steel on a direct line with the hole, no matter where it was on the face of the drift, and this drill was lying diagonal to the face.

Could it have rolled? Unlikely. Then how— It was then he remembered the powder can. It had been light, too light.

He took up his candle and looked all around, very carefully. Nothing was disturbed, nothing out of place but that drill and the powder can that had been lighter than expected.

Taking up his tamping stick he thrust it into the hole, very gently. Not over eighteen inches, and if memory served him, he had that hole in nearly two and a half feet. He withdrew the stick, and squatting on his heels, he contemplated the situation.

Somebody had slipped in here during the night, or when both Clyde and he were gone, and had loaded that hole with a considerable amount of black powder. Without a doubt there was a cap there also, and the intent was obvious.

He had been expected to put a drill down that hole and hit it a crack with the single-jack, exploding the powder and killing him. The natural conclusion would have been that he had drilled into a missed hole, one that had failed to fire.

It was a not uncommon happening in hard-rock mining and would have called for no more than a shrug and a funeral.

The logical answer now would be to fish for the charge with a wooden or copper spoon to strike no sparks, or to drill another hole close by and let the second charge explode the first. He chose the second method.

In fact, the holes were already drilled. He loaded several, enough to break the ground properly, then spit the fuses.

Some time would be necessary to let the powder smoke clear out before he could go down again, but he had no wish to show himself around town and let them know their attempt had failed. At least, not yet.

He returned to the cabin, prepared a light lunch, and sat down to think it out.

Somebody had tried to kill him. It could not have been Hesketh striking back, because at that time he had made no move against Hesketh, and had Hesketh known what he was about, he could have brought men to stop him.

Who?

It had been months since that last shot had been fired at him, yet this might be the same man. Yet why wait so long? He had been out of town, somewhere.

Waggoner?

Trevallion resolved to drop all actual mining until he had blasted another way out. One attempt had been made in the mine, and he was vulnerable there, so another attempt would surely be made. He had planned another opening to insure a proper circulation of air, and he must let everything wait until that was done.

There was no way anyone could reach the mine now without going right past the MacNeale cabin, where he lived. Their only chance was at night.

Dane Clyde came in an hour later. He hung up his hat and coat and turned sharply around. "Well, it's happened! I've got a job!"

"You're lucky. What will you be doing?"

"Acting! What else? Their advance man is in town today, from San Francisco. Jeff's an old friend of mine from New Orleans. We've worked together before, and he knew I'd worked with Grita, so—"

"With whom?"

"Grita, Grita Redaway. It's her company. She's just arrived in San Francisco, and she will be playing there for two weeks, then she will come here."

He got out his carpetbag. "I haven't much of a wardrobe, but I'll get along. Somehow . . ."

"What will you need? You can always pay me back."

"A hundred dollars. I can make it work with that much until I get paid."

"All right." He let five gold eagles trickle from his fingers to the table-top. "I'll be shipping some ore by the weekend. Enough for a stake."

Clyde busied himself with packing and a continuous stream of chatter. Trevallion scarcely listened.

Grita, coming here! Of course, it might not be the same one. In fact, it was unlikely. Names were common enough. Everyone's name was duplicated somewhere.

Still, it was a long time ago. A long, long time, almost another world than this.

TWENTY-FOUR

It had been the end of an idyll. From their arrival in Gunwalloe to that other night in Missouri, it had been a bright saga of adventure. His father, usually quiet and untalkative, had spent hours talking of his work in the mines, of sailing ships, of the rocky coast of Cornwall. Trevallion had never guessed his father knew so many stories. Some were stories he told to Grita, later.

That had been the night he lost his father, not that day a long time later when he had died, gun in hand.

He had lost his father when he lost his mother, for when she died something had gone out of him, like a candle snuffed by the wind. He had been there, during those later months, but only the shell of him. Her love was gone, her spirit was gone, and it left only a hard and bitter man, eaten by loneliness, reaching out time and again to touch hearts with his son, and never quite reaching. Both of them wanted a closeness they could not find. And then, in the bloody fierceness of that terrible, unequal gun battle, he lost his father forever.

Well, two of the murderers were dead, and his father had taken two with him.

Five left . . . he must not think of that. Anyway, the day-to-day attrition of life in the mining camps might have eliminated some of them.

Yet one of them must be here. One or more. He had been stalked, shot at, and now somebody had tried to get him to drill into a loaded hole. Somebody who planned carefully.

"I'm going," Clyde said, "and I can't thank you enough."

Trevallion waved a hand. "Forget it."

"I'll pay you."

"If you can, when you can."

"Is there anything I can do for you? Any message for anyone in Frisco?"

He thought for a minute, then shook his head. He thought of Grita with a kind of wistful longing, then shook his head again. "No, there is nothing."

154

Who was he? Nobody. Because a small boy held a small, frightened girl in his arms once, a long time ago, that didn't mean
anything. No doubt she had forgotten. Better for her if she had.
Anyway, he had no claim on her, nor on her thoughts.

It was just that she was there, in the last moments of a life that was
gone.

Somebody said to him once, some woman back down the line
whom he met casually, somebody's wife who was a friend, she had
said, "Trev, I think you were born old."

Maybe, maybe that was it.

Dane Clyde went to the door. "When we play here, Mr. Trevallion,
I'd like you to come and see us. I am a pretty good actor, you know,
and, well, I haven't looked like much around here."

"None of us have," Trevallion said, "although it's our own fault."
He gestured toward the street. "It's all happening right down there,
Clyde, men are making fortunes, but what is more they are *doing*
something. They aren't sitting around griping about how things
should be better. They are making it better. From here on, that's
what I'm going to do."

Dane Clyde left, and walked down the hill to the Virginia House
where he would catch the stage they had running to Frisco now.

Trevallion got up and checked his gun. He was going to need it.
He walked down the hill to the bakery.

Melissa was there. A smooth, polished young man, handsomely
dressed, sat with her. Melissa's face changed. She looked like she'd
been caught with her hand in the cookie jar. "Trevallion? You
remember Alfie?"

Trevallion did not smile. "Well, I didn't see much of him. I guess
I do remember him."

Alfie smiled. "What's a man going to do when he's caught without
a gun?"

Trevallion glanced at him, remembering the derringer. "Not much,
I guess." He chose another table and sat down alone.

Almost immediately a man was standing over him. A man in a
tailored brown suit. "Mr. Trevallion? I understand you have filed on
a claim that belongs to the Solomon."

Trevallion merely glanced at him, then took up the coffeepot
Melissa had put on the table. He filled his cup.

"Mr. Trevallion! I don't believe you heard what I said!"

"I heard you talking." He did not look up. "What you said wasn't
worth answering."

"Mr. Trevallion," the man was growing angry. "My name is Peter
Metesky. I am a lawyer, and I represent the owners of the Solomon."

"All right. It is nice to know you are not unemployed."

"You are evidently unaware that the land on which you have filed belongs to the Solomon."

Trevallion sipped his coffee.

"Mr. Trevallion, I understand you are associated with William Crockett?"

Trevallion looked up into the hard blue eyes of the lawyer. Trevallion smiled. "I have filed on the claim you mention. Tomorrow morning I shall begin assessment work on the claim. My filing is legal. It has been recorded." He pointed across the room. "You have a table over there. I would suggest you go sit at it or get out. I did not invite you here."

"Young man, I am afraid you simply do not know the law—"

"If it is law you wish to talk about," Trevallion said, "I suggest you talk to Bill Stewart. He will represent me."

Metesky winced at the name. Stewart was not only one of the two or three best on the lode, but he was the toughest.

"I know Mr. Stewart," he said, "but it is you to whom I wish to talk!"

Trevallion stood up. He was an inch shorter than the lawyer and thirty pounds lighter. "Mr. Metesky, I don't believe there are any witnesses in this room." As he spoke, every man and woman in the room turned their backs. "So what happens between us is just between us. Now your table is over there. On the other hand, if you don't feel like sitting down, I will enjoy walking you to the edge of town and, if necessary, to California."

For a moment Metesky hesitated, then he turned on his heel and walked out. At the door he paused and looked back. "Go to hell!" he said savagely.

"Sorry," Trevallion said, "I can't go anywhere with you."

Trevallion sat down. "Your coffee's cold," Melissa said. "Let me get you some more."

It was late when he walked outside. For a moment he hesitated. Now the streets were lined with buildings, and there were lighted windows everywhere. From a dozen places he heard the sound of pianos or banjos. Further along, at the Virginia House, a man in evening clothes was helping a fashionably dressed woman into a carriage. Walking past him were two miners in wet digging clothes, lunch-buckets in their hands. A cowhand, spurs jingling, rode by on a paint cow pony, and the boardwalks were thronged with gamblers, drifters, speculators, and men and women of all sorts and kinds, all with an eye for the main chance.

He moved deeper into the shadow, a part of it all yet apart from it. Something moved in the shadows up the street, and he turned and started to go around the bakery. Abruptly, he halted; he had done that too many times. He walked up the street, pausing for a few minutes by the Bucket of Blood Saloon.

Trevallion felt curiously isolated from all about him. He was a part of this yet not a part. What had been a barren mountainside was now a thriving mining town with the unceasing pound of stamp-mills and compressors, morning, noon, and night.

Months had faded into months, and the town continued to grow, to build. Suddenly a man stood beside him, a man with a bandage across his face covering what was obviously a broken nose. "Are you Trevallion?"

Trevallion glanced at him, not liking what he saw. "And if I am?"

"Somebody told me you'd like to know. Waggoner's back."

"Thank you."

The man with the broken nose faded into the crowd. Somebody with a grudge, no doubt, but if Waggoner was back, that might account for the loaded drill-hole in his tunnel.

He would have to kill him or be killed.

The fact was there, and he could see no alternative, nor would the town recognize any other. Yet he shrank from it. He was tired of killing, tired of fighting. He wanted to work his claims, he wanted—

That would come. That would be for later.

He turned again and went back to his claim. From outside the cabin he looked down the slope toward the lights and excitement of the town.

He should be more like that town. At least it knew where it was going. Its mission was simple: get out the ore, turn a profit, build something with what was realized. Already Virginia City was changing the destiny of San Francisco. The town was becoming, realizing, changing. No matter that it might not last forever, for nothing did. It was what was accomplished along the way that mattered. Fortunes were coming into being down there, the world's mining methods were being revolutionized, men were building, creating, driving forward . . . who knew to what eventual destiny?

And what of him? He stood in the middle, torn between the urge to be down there doing, using his knowledge and using himself, torn between that and an old hatred, the rankling memory of evil unpunished, of evil that would continue to do evil until destroyed.

He got out his map of the town and studied it again. He had several claims now, some of them strategically located. Aside from his claims he had small investments with the bakery and with Jim Ledbetter.

The next step was assessment work on the claim near the Solomon. Once he had done some serious work there, his claim was established. If the claim turned out to be rich, as he believed it would, he would have struck a blow for Will Crockett, and for fair play.

At daybreak he was out in his digging clothes. He stepped out the door and Christian Tapley was sitting there, his rifle across his lap.

"Howdy! Reckoned y' all might use a hand! Sort of stand aroun' while you do the hard work."

"Welcome," Trevallion said. "How about your work?"

Tapley smiled. "I told my boss what I aimed to do, and he turned out to be a friend of Will's. He said I should bring his best wishes, and if you need any help, he'll send a crew up from the mine to do the work."

"We won't need 'em."

"Something else," Tapley said. "I was walkin' by when the stage was loading. I seen Hesketh getting aboard. Going to San Francisco."

Hesketh to San Francisco? Trevallion was puzzled. Unless something was to happen to Trevallion and he wanted to be out of town. But that made no sense. Not a half dozen people in town realized there was any antagonism, if you could call it that.

Actually, he knew nothing about him except that he had taken advantage of his position to cut the ground from under his employer, who was a decent man.

Nevertheless, he was worried. Hesketh did nothing without reason, and he was, apparently, a man who knew just what he was about, all the time. So why to San Francisco just when an important addition to his property had been lost?

It made no sense. Only, it did make sense to Albert Hesketh. If he was leaving town at such a time, he had a reason, a very adequate reason.

The guard at the Solomon merely glanced at them, then turned his back and ignored them. Trevallion had no idea of exploring at any depth or of opening any ore body. Unless he was quite mistaken, such an effort would entail many man-hours of hard labor and much equipment. He wished to do only enough to establish ownership of the claim. The rich ore, if any, would lie several hundred feet down unless all his knowledge went for nothing. The ore on the Solomon, as with several other mines, had gotten consistently richer as it went deeper, one of the few western mining areas where he knew this to be true.

As he worked he turned over every possible reason for Hesketh's sudden trip to San Francisco, and came up with nothing.

He talked it over with Tapley, while leaning on his shovel. "You can bet he's got somethin' in mind. He's canny, that Hesketh is."

"Will Crockett worries me," Trevallion said. "I wish he'd show up. I can't believe he just up and quit."

"He wouldn't. Not owning the stock he has." Tapley looked up suddenly. "D' you suppose that's it? That he's gone lookin' for more stock? There's some outstanding, they say."

"Nobody seems to know who's got it," Trevallion said, "although Will should know if anybody does."

"Some of it was sold back east, or to people who lived there. No telling what became of it."

A rider was coming up the slope, coming fast. He pulled up sharply as he came abreast of them. "War!" he shouted. "Fort Sumter's been fired on!"

Trevallion put down his shovel. "Where's Fort Sumter?" he asked.

"Somewheres over by Charleston, I reckon." Tapley spat. "Well, when they elected Lincoln, I figured somethin' like this was in the wind."

Tapley glanced at the hole. "You've got your work started. That'll stand in any Virginia City court. Let's go down an' get the news. The Pony must've come in."

He looked around. "You know, Trev? Back home I was all het up about all that there, but it seems mighty far off when a body gets out here. Seems like another world."

"Not to Terry," Trevallion said. "He'll be breathing smoke and fire."

"Be careful. He's a dead shot and meaner than Langford Peel, some say. He's killed a man or two, so be careful."

"Why? I'm not in this. I scarcely know what it's about."

"We're all in it," Tapley replied. "You, too."

PART THREE

TWENTY-FIVE

In the cool elegance of Winn's Branch at the corner of Washington and Montgomery, Grita Redaway was quite the coolest and most elegant. She was also very beautiful, and at the moment, very alert and very curious.

The man across the table was a stranger, introduced by Tom Maguire, and Tom Maguire was the power in San Francisco theater.

"Look, Miss Redaway," Maguire had said, "this man wants to meet *you*. Not any actress, but *you*. He is a friend of a man who is an occasional investor. Frankly, I don't like the man, and don't trust him, but of his friend, this Hesketh who wants to meet you, I know nothing at all.

"All I ask is that you meet him, have tea with him, something. Then get rid of him. Anything you like. It would be a favor to me. He's a mining man—"

"A mining man?"

"From Virginia City, actually. That's a coming place, you know. We're opening a theater there ourselves."

"And he asked to meet me?"

"You, only you. We knew how you felt about such things and suggested some other actresses. At least one of them might have been more, more agreeable, shall we say? The reply was a positive no. It was you he wished to speak to, you, and nobody else."

"Very well, I shall see him. For tea only, at Winn's Branch."

"Thank you. I appreciate it." He shrugged. "You've gotten me off the hook very nicely. There's one thing, though. This investor, I mentioned. He occasionally puts a little money in a show, but I've done other business with him. Canvas, rope, backstage gear of all kinds; he can let me have them much cheaper than anywhere else in town. Such things are often the margin of profit, so I do business with him."

He paused. "Between us, and just between us, I sometimes wonder how he can afford to sell so cheap."

"Thank you, Mr. Maguire."

It was a warning, or perhaps just a suggestion, but she appreciated it and intended to be a little wary. Anyway, she would see the man but once.

She was curious, but more than that she was, for the moment, willing to allow herself to drift with the current. From earliest childhood it had been in her mind to come to San Francisco and now she was here. There was a feeling she had that coming here was somehow important to her.

She had been thinking lately of a conversation with Rachel, in Paris. "You are very good, you know," Rachel had said. "You are in some ways the best of us, but you don't really want to be an actress. You handle each role so naturally, with such ease, almost without thinking."

"'That's not true."

"Perhaps not, but it appears so. But the thing you must decide, my dear, is what do *you* wish to do? If you are not to be an actress, then what? A mistress? That's a play where one never knows how long the run will be, so save your jewels. Put your diamonds away for a rainy day, or a lonely night."

Rachel glanced at herself in the mirror, frowned, touching her lips with a fingernail. "But you don't want that, either.

"A rich husband? Why not? There are many of them, married and unmarried, although the best ones are always married.

"America! I think you should go to America! Run off with one of those dashing cowboys one reads about! Or a handsome man who has his own gold mine!"

"I am going to America."

"Of course. We spoke of it, and I, too, shall go. To New York, at least. That woman, that Swedish singer. She has done very well over there."

"Jenny Lind? Yes, she did, but she's a type, Rachel. She's *different*. And then that man who took her over there, that P.T. Barnum, they say he is someone special."

"Barnum? But he is not even in the *theater*! Not really. He deals in fat ladies, dwarfs, and giants. Even elephants. Is that theater?"

"He has a skill, Rachel. He knows how to get the people to pay to see what he has. It is a skill."

She brushed it aside. "So? But what of you, Grita? I do not mean Grita the actress, but Grita the person! The woman! What will you do?"

"Long ago, when I was a very little girl, we started for California. We never got there. Now I shall go."

"But why? *Why?*"

"I really don't know. It's just, well, it's something unfinished. It was a dream we had then. Maybe I just want to see if the dream conforms to the reality."

"And then?"

She shrugged a shoulder. "I will come back. Take up my career—oh, I don't know!"

"There's a man in it somewhere. I just know there is."

"How could there be? I was a *child!*"

"I still say there is a man in it," Rachel insisted. "There just has to be."

So, after so long a time, she was here. She was in California, in San Francisco, and this was Winn's Branch.

The man walking toward her table was lean. He wore a gray suit, his light brown hair was parted at the side and had just a slight wave. His beard was neatly trimmed in the Van Dyke fashion. His eyes were gray-blue.

He bowed slightly. "Miss Redaway? I am Albert Hesketh."

"How do you do? Will you sit down?"

He sat down. "I want to thank you for agreeing to meet me. When I heard you were in the city I just had to meet you."

"Mr. Maguire said you were a friend?"

"Well, sort of. I am a mining man, actually, but I come here often on business." He glanced at her. There was something disconcerting about his eyes. "Have you been to America before?"

"It is an amazing country. I really knew nothing about it before I came over, and of course, everyone was talking about California."

"Of course, and its mines."

He gave the line a bad reading. Why the emphasis on "mines"? Or was it her imagination?

"Mines?" Her eyes were wide. "I thought, well, I understood there were no mines, that they just washed the gold out of streams with pans or something."

"There is that, too. The richest gold is, I believe, underground. They dig for it."

"I wouldn't like that. It must be very hard work."

He puzzled her. Accustomed to the attentions of men, she had become quite skilled in reading them, but there was something about this one she did not understand. A skilled actress, she had learned much about the use of the body in revealing or concealing what one was thinking.

"You should play Virginia City," he said. "We are all hungry for theater there, and as yet we have had very little. You could see some of our mines at first hand."

"I know nothing of mining." A memory returned. "I did hear some stories about tommy-knockers once."

He smiled. "All rubbish. There's no such thing. Some of the more superstitious miners believe in them."

He tasted his wine. She did not believe he liked it. "I am afraid my own approach is more prosaic. When I think of mines I think of investments, of mining stock. Of course," he added, "much of that old stock isn't worth the paper it is printed on. It is 'different now when we have some solidly established companies."

Deliberately she guided the conversation away from mines and mining to the theater, San Francisco, Paris, and life in Virginia City. Several times he seemed to want to get back to mining, but she avoided the topic.

The inner thoughts of people were often revealed by the usage of words or by slips of the tongue. Why the sudden reference to "old" stock? Nothing had been said about it, so there must be something in his own mind.

She glanced at her watch. "Oh! I didn't realize it was so late! Mr. Hesketh? Would you like to escort me back to the International?"

"Yes, yes, of course."

They started out, encountering James Stark and his wife. They paused, talking of his planned production of *Richelieu*, a play in which he had enjoyed considerable success. Hesketh stood aside, listening but understanding very little.

At the International she held out her hand to him. "It has been very pleasant, Mr. Hesketh. Thank you."

"May I see you again?"

She had started to turn away. Hesitating, she said, "We begin rehearsals soon. Perhaps. We will see."

"But how am I—"

"Just come by the hotel and ask for me. Or come by the theater, if you will. You see, Mr. Hesketh, my time is not my own. I am committed to play this part, and people are expecting me to do so."

Albert Hesketh turned away, irritated. He walked a half block and stopped, suddenly swept by an almost blinding fury. He hated frustration of any kind, hated resistance or anything that did not bend to his wishes.

From his room in the Virginia Hotel in Virginia City, it had seemed a simple thing to travel to San Francisco, meet Grita Redaway, and buy her stock from her. If she did, in fact, have the stock.

All he had accomplished was to meet her. They had talked, and he had learned nothing. He did not even know if she had the stock. All he knew was from a few notes he had found scratched in a ledger to the effect that Will Crockett had sold a certain number of shares to a person who proved to have been related to Grita Redaway, and that Grita had inherited the estate.

Did Grita Redaway still have the shares? Had she sold them? Thrown them away? And if she had them, did she have them with her? Actually in her possession?

He swore bitterly. Now what? He should be back in Virginia City and yet he dared not leave here. Someone else might come to her with a flat-out offer.

He could do that, himself. He would then know whether she had them or not, and if she would sell. At the same time he would be tipping his hand, and she would assume the shares had value and might even make inquiries. Remembering Grita, he thought she was very likely the type.

The more he thought about her, the more worried he became. His big chance was now. He had control of the Solomon. He could become an extremely wealthy, powerful man, and he had planned it that way, planned every step. Yet those ten outstanding shares could destroy him. He would have the income, but not the control, not the power.

What an exasperating woman!

He had to control himself. He had to see her again. Somehow he had to get those shares, but if she refused to sell, what then?

What, indeed?

The trail to Virginia City was improved, but still rough. Stagecoaches went over it now, and stagecoaches were occasionally held up.

If she had the shares, she might have them with her. If he could not buy them, he might at least keep them from the hands of anyone else.

Suppose someone went through her room at the hotel? A quick search, if carefully handled, might extract the shares and leave all else undisturbed. It might be weeks before the shares were missed.

He could not do it himself. There was too much risk involved. He needed a thief, a skilled thief.

Marcus Zetsev. He would know a thief. He dealt with them.

Hesketh shrank from taking anyone into his confidence, from permitting anyone to know what he was doing or planning. He trusted no one, yet there was no one else to whom he might go who would have the same kind of knowledge. Moreover, he and Zetsev were already allies.

But suppose Zetsev got the shares for himself?

Hesketh stopped at the corner and bought a newspaper. All the papers contained was talk of war. Now would be the time to make a pot of money, if a man had the capital to invest.

Leather, wool, metals, foodstuffs—all would be in demand.

He would see Marcus. He would know of someone. He had no need to tell him anything. Marcus could get one of those from whom he bought goods; he need only point him out to Hesketh. That would be the way.

In the meantime he would make an effort to see Grita again. She was, after all, an extremely attractive woman.

Marcus Zetsev was in his office when Albert Hesketh entered the ship chandlery. He could see him through the open door, and he sat watching him for several minutes. Marcus Zetsev had known and dealt with all kinds. He knew how to handle the tough ones, the tricky ones, the ones who might suddenly become deadly. And he was not at all sure about Albert Hesketh.

Zetsev trusted no man or woman, and least of all those who dealt with him. Usually, within a few minutes, he had each one catalogued. It was not so with Hesketh.

That the man was a thief he knew at once. That he was a plotter and a conniver he also knew. There were some other things he did not know. Hesketh might be harmless, but Zetsev suspected he was not.

Getting up he walked to the door. "Al? Come on in!"

Hesketh stiffened at the familiarity. Who was this upstart, this—

Hesketh relaxed slowly. *Don't be a fool!* he warned himself. *You need this man.*

When the door was closed, Hesketh sat down on the edge of his chair. "Marcus," he said, "I need a thief."

Marcus Zetsev was not surprised.

TWENTY-SIX

On the fourth day Grita moved from her room in the International to a small flat higher up on the hill with a lovely view of the harbor and the lower city. On that side of the house she had a small balcony, shielded from view, where she often sat in the morning. It was there she studied her lines.

Her view from the balcony allowed her to look across the roof of the house next door, which was lower down the rather steep hill, and on the right side it looked down upon the street, and on that side the wall of the balcony was shoulder height with a few thread-like interstices that provided a limited view of the street.

Thus she had the fresh sea air, occasionally the sunlight, yet privacy.

Sophie Edwin, a longtime favorite of the San Francisco theater, came to see the flat. "You will be robbed. Perhaps killed. It is not for a woman to live alone in San Francisco."

"Nonsense! I am not afraid." She gestured toward the bedroom. "I have my little friend."

"What? You? We had always heard that you had no man. I will admit that with a woman as beautiful as you are, I doubted that, but—"

"It is not a man." She stepped into the bedroom and returned with a derringer in her hand. It had twin barrels, one over the other. "See? It is a .44, and I should not hesitate to use it."

"Put it away! Please! I'm afraid of the things. There were several shootings in Sacramento when I was there. That man Trevallion—"

"Who?"

"Trevallion. He was a miner, I think, or a prospector. He was said to have killed a man named Rory over a card game. Caught him cheating, or something. You'd never have thought it to see him, either. He looked the perfect gentleman, and handsome! Had I been a few years younger—"

"You're young enough."

"Maybe." She paused, sipping her tea. "There was a story, though. Everybody was talking about it. There was some sort of conversation between them before the shooting, talk that had nothing to do with cards or the game. Something about some trouble back in Missouri. I never got the hang of it."

"Trevallion, you say?"

"It's an uncommon name. He was pointed out to me once, in the theater. He was always there, for every production. And always alone."

"You seem to remember him well."

"Who would not? He was a striking figure of a man, and then there was that night when Johnny Ferguson went up in his lines."

"We've all done that."

"Of course, and it was in an easy place. All he had to do was step off the stage, but the fool stood there gasping for words like a fish out of water."

"What was the play?"

"*Francesca da Rimini,* Boker's play. It was right at the end of the first act, and Johnny was playing Lanciotto. He got to the lines 'A neighing steed, a fiery onset, and a stubborn fight rouse my dull blood,' and he came up empty. He repeated it 'rouse my dull blood . . . rouse my dull blood . . .' and he stopped cold.

"Then it happened. Trevallion leaned over the railing and said, '. . . tire my body down
To quiet slumbers when the day is o'er,
And night above me spreads her spangled tent,
Lit by the dying cresset of the moon.
Ay, that's it; I am homesick for the camp.'

"I must say he read them damned well, too, and Johnny, thanks be to God, had the grace to turn, doff his plumed helmet, and give him as fine a bow as I've seen, and the crowd loved it. Johnny left the stage to the best round of applause he had all season."

"Is he living there? In Sacramento?"

"Who knows? He's the type not to stay anywhere long. We all heard about him, of course, as we heard all those stories about shootings and knifings.

"The Rory story stayed alive a lot longer because a friend of his was killed not long after. They were very bad characters and when the two were killed so close together the papers made a lot of it. This man Skinner and Rory had been friends in Missouri."

As though it were no more than an hour ago Grita heard his voice, his small boy's voice, but it was suddenly stern, and she had been frightened. She heard him say it. *I will kill them. I will kill every one of them. I will kill them or die trying.* "Did Trevallion kill Skinner, too?"

"Skinner? Oh, no! At least, I don't think he did. Nobody ever connected him with it that I know of."

"Is he—I mean, have you heard of him since?"

"No, it's like I said. He's a drifter. The chances are he's gone to the Comstock. That's where they will all be until there's a new boom somewhere."

Sophie glanced at her curiously. "Since when did you become interested in gunfighters?"

"I'm not, only—and please don't mention this, I think I knew him."

"Rory?"

"Trevallion. As you said, it's an unusual name. I think I knew him once when I was a very little girl. He sounds like a boy I knew. And that was his name. Only we called him Val."

That evening she received a gift of roses from Hesketh. They were very beautiful and only a simple note: *In admiration,* and signed with his full name.

Sunlight was dancing on the bay when she came out on her little balcony and settled down to go over her lines. After a few minutes she put the pages down and just sat, enjoying the mild warmth and the view over the bay, where several sailing craft were moving about.

Occasionally someone passed along the street below, and she was aware of them without really noticing. One man turned the corner and started up the street on the opposite side. Twice he paused and he seemed to be looking up at the balcony where she was. There was no way he could see her, however, as she was hidden by the high side. On the corner he paused, a lean, blond-haired man, sunken in the chest and sallow of complexion.

He lit a cigarette, continuing to watch. For the first time she really noticed him. There was no question about it, the man was watching her balcony, or at least her corner of the house. After a bit he went on up the street. Disturbed, she went inside and looked around quickly, for the first time realizing how vulnerable she was.

True, there was the derringer. She had found it among some things of her father's in an old chest. She knew how to load it and how to use it. If someone broke in while she was there, she would not hesitate to fire.

What if someone came when she was gone? She had very little jewelry that was of value and nothing worth stealing but that and what little money she had.

There were, of course, some old letters and papers that had belonged to her father and mother, and someone might assume they were of value because they were in an old wallet of her father's.

She had played too many melodramas not to know all the obvious hiding places under pillows, mattresses, or carpets, behind loose stones in a hearth or fireplace. The small dining area was separated from the rest of the room by colonnades made from yellow pine. The pedestal was four feet high, with leaded glass doors and a column about seven inches in diameter supporting a beam with a seven-inch drop. That beam was of panels, and when dusting on her first day, she discovered that the bottom panel in one of the beams would slide in its grooves.

Taking her packet of papers and a few odds and ends of jewelry, she slid back the panel and placed them inside the beam, sliding the panel back into place. It was not the best hiding place but might defeat a hasty search.

On her way to the theater she glanced back and saw the man standing on the street. He was not looking at her.

Probably, she thought, somebody who works in the area. Nonetheless she was disturbed.

The rehearsal went as they usually did; some of it went well, much did not. Nevertheless, the play was taking shape.

She was preparing to leave the theater when the stage manager put his head in the door. "A gentleman to see you, Miss Redaway. A Mr. Hesketh."

Later, in the foyer of the theater, he showed her some tickets. "For Tucker's Academy of Music," he said. "Lotta Crabtree is performing there tonight, and I thought you'd like to see her. I have three tickets," he added, "if you'd like to bring a friend."

Everyone was talking about Lotta, the little girl who had been entertaining in the mining camps and was rapidly becoming California's most popular actress.

Sophie had come to meet her. "You should see her," she said. "Lotta is very special."

"All right, tonight then?"

"And for supper, afterwards?" he suggested.

After he had gone, Sophie warned her. "You've never been to a melodeon, and most of them won't accept women customers, but when Miss Lottie is playing, they relax the rules.

"Mary Ann, that's Lottie's mother, won't stand for any nonsense, either. It's in their contract that one obscene word and they leave, and she means it. But the miners all love Lottie, so they like it that way."

"Is she really good?"

"She's the greatest natural clown I ever saw. Sings, dances, mimics— she's good, Grita. Very good."

"How old is she?"

"I don't know; fourteen I'd guess. She might be a year older. They never talk about age. But remember what I said about melodeons. They are very rough.

"But don't worry," she added. "I know some of the boys will be there tonight. The Knickerbrocker Hook and Ladder Company as well as the Lafayette outfit. I don't know who said it, but somebody did, that the fire companies were to San Francisco what the Cossacks were to Russia. And they like Lottie and nothing's going to happen while she's in the theater. You can bet on it."

The melodeon was jammed to the doors with a sweating, cheerful crowd, drinking, smoking, and shouting back and forth across the room.

One of the Knickerbrockers suddenly stood up and shouted. When he had the attention of all, he said, "When the little lady comes on the stage, we'll have no sound but applause, d' you ken what I mean? If there's anybody makes trouble, he'll be thrown out, an' if there's more trouble, the Knickerbrockers will clear the room."

"And the Lafayettes will help!"

The performance that followed was like none Grita had ever seen. Lotta might not be an actress; she was certainly a superb and talented clown. She sang, she danced, and worked with energy and skill.

"Now you see," Sophie said as they left the theater, "the kind of competition we have."

"She's very good," Grita said. "Very, very good, and she's still very young."

At Winn's Branch, over supper, the talk changed to mining and to Virginia City. "You should be thinking about the future," Hesketh suggested. "There are good investments in mining stock if you choose with care. I'd be glad to offer any suggestions I can. And certainly, as far as the Comstock is concerned, I know which mines are worth investments and which are not."

"I know nothing about mines," Grita said, "although it must be exciting to dig gold and silver right from the ground."

"You've never invested in stocks?" he asked.

Albert Hesketh, she thought, had a strange shading to his voice whenever he asked a pointed question. It was something she had detected at once, although she doubted that many did. He was not skillful in disguising his interests, and she was shrewd enough to know that while he might be interested in her as a woman, it was a secondary interest.

"Of course not," she spoke casually. "When one is in the theater, there's little chance to think of anything else. I've had my own company for only a year or so, and we have been reinvesting whatever we have made in costumes and equipment."

The talk changed to other topics and Hesketh was quiet, thinking. Could he be mistaken? Was he going to all this trouble for nothing?

Where was Will Crockett? Was he in San Francisco? Or worse, was the information from the records of the Solomon long out of date or false? Suppose even now Crockett was making arrangements to meet the owner of that stock and to buy it? Suppose Crockett was about to do as he had done, and pitch him right out of office? At the thought his face went almost white with a sudden burst of fury, and he looked up to see Grita Redaway looking at him.

"Mr. Hesketh? Aren't you feeling well?"

"Quite well." He stood up. "I must keep you no longer. Our carriage should be waiting."

Later, as she went up the steps to her door and put the key in the lock, she wondered again. He was odd, very odd.

She opened the door and stopped very still. Someone had been here.

Her flat had been entered while she was gone.

Suppose that someone was still here? She dropped her keys into her purse and took hold of the .44 derringer.

She took a slow, deep breath. *Careful now! Don't turn your back. Be ready.*

She put a foot against the door and pushed it shut.

TWENTY-SEVEN

Nothing happened.

She waited, listening. Her eyes swept the room. She had left a script open on the table with a pencil beside it for making notations. The script was still open but not at the place where she had stopped work.

Gun in hand she pushed open the door into the small kitchen—empty.

She looked across at the bedroom door, which she always left open when she was in the apartment alone. It was closed.

She started to glance up at the beam where her things were hidden, then averted her eyes. If someone was watching or listening they would expect her to check to see if her things were still hidden, and in that way they would find them. The lace curtains were drawn but the heavier curtains were not. If she went to that beam, somebody standing across the street on the sidewalk would see what she did.

Crossing to the bedroom door, she took the knob in her left hand and opened the door, pushing it wide.

Empty!

Carefully, she looked around, then ventured inside. The mattress was a bit askew, as if someone had looked under it and then hurriedly replaced it.

A complete search of the flat revealed that someone had entered, searched it very carefully, trying to leave behind no evidence of his entry. It had been very well done, and with someone less ordered the visit might have gone unnoticed.

She had been going through the script making notations and had left it open where she stopped work, with the pencil laid carefully alongside. Now the pencil was moved and the script open at a different page. Somebody must have brushed against the table and the script had flopped shut. He had hastily opened the script, having no idea of the page or that it would be noticed.

The next question was how he got in and if he would return. He certainly had found nothing, unless he had gotten inside the beam,

175

and she doubted that. Unless an extremely tall man, he would have to stand on a chair to reach it, and no chairs seemed to have been moved.

If he was just a thief, he would not come back. But what if he were looking for some one thing? Having not found it, he would certainly try again.

But what could it be? She was involved in no intrigue. She had no blackmailing letters or secret formulas such as used in melodramas.

She had nothing but a few old letters, kept for sentiment's sake, and that old stock. There was a letter or two from Val, also.

She drew the shades, turned the lights low, and began to prepare for bed. She kept the derringer close to her hand.

She propped a chair under the doorknob, pushing it up until it was snug and tight.

The balcony? She had not looked to see if a man could scale the front of the building, but all these houses had a lot of gingerbread decoration, so it might be possible. Also, someone might somehow come up the back and come over the roof.

All the while she was preparing for bed she thought of it, but it made no sense, unless that old stock had suddenly become valuable, and that was unlikely.

Yet Al Hesketh had mentioned stock several times, suggesting she invest, and asking if she had ever invested . . . but that was just talk. Albert Hesketh was a mining man, a businessman, and not a thief. Besides, he had been with her.

Turning out the lights she went to the beam, slid back the panel and felt for the stocks. They were still there. Tomorrow, in the daylight, she would examine them, then she would at least know what she had. She had kept them for sentiment's sake. Some had belonged to her father, some to her aunt. To be honest, she had always hoped they might be worth something, despite repeated assurances they were not.

There was that long ago letter from Val, when he told her of the money he had invested for her from that old debt owed to her father, or something of the kind.

She started to get into bed, then crossed the room and looked down into the street. All was dark and still. The street was ghostly at this hour. She started to turn away; did something move in the shadows over there?

She looked for a moment longer, saw nothing, and decided it was her imagination. She got into bed, keeping the derringer at hand.

When growing up in Paris, she had read the stories, basically true but highly colored, of the master detective and former criminal, Vidocq. Later, when active in the theater, she had often talked of him with d'Arlange, a French actor who had become her friend through her Uncle André.

"Look about you," d'Arlange suggested, "it is not necessary to have a gun or a knife to kill. Everywhere are weapons! Clubs with which to strike, cords with which to strangle! Any object that can be picked up can be a weapon!

"And for defense as well. Look about your room! Here there is a chair, there a table, a lamp! Study your room and the house where you live! Learn to know every room. Tip a chair in front of your pursuer, then hit him with anything when he falls! You can throw wine into the eyes! Or hot tea!

"Study your own room, your own house, your own neighborhood as if it were a battleground. Learn how to use it for defense, for escape, for counterattack!

"Have a plan! Know what you will do if your attacker comes through a door. Know what to do if he comes in through a window. Nobody need be helpless.

"I once knew a sea captain's wife who was much alone, and she was about to open a shop and had carpenters and painters in. She lived in a room above the shop, and one night she heard someone down below. She went down the steps and was just in time to see a man climbing through the window.

"She had no weapon, so she took the brush from the red paint pot and as he reached for her she slashed him across the eyes with her red paint brush! He opened his mouth to howl, and she thrust the brush down his throat, then she dumped the paint over his head and began flailing him with the empty bucket.

"He fled, and the police caught him only down the block, and he was in a sorry state, paint all over and cuts on his scalp, half blind and choking as well. And she? A few flecks of red paint on her flannel nightgown!"

She dropped off to sleep at last, and awakened with the sunlight streaming through the window.

After a while she sat up, propped pillows behind her, and returned to the examination of the script. It was a play she had not seen before, and interesting. In San Francisco there were a number of playwrights, far from professional, in most cases, yet quite capable. This play was by one of those, and there was talk of producing it.

Yet she could not concentrate. After a few minutes she put the play down and sat thinking. Suppose Albert Hesketh did believe she had some valuable stock? Suppose he had deliberately taken her to the theater to get her out of the flat so the thief could work? Nothing in life had impressed her with the idea that all motives were pure. It was distinctly unflattering for a successful actress, said to be beautiful, to be courted simply because she might have valuable stock, yet she would not be the first to be sought after for profit.

Suppose she led him to believe she did have stock, she could be vague about what and where, as she indeed was. Suppose she dangled the bait?

She got up, bathed and dressed, thinking about Albert Hesketh. What was it about him that made her uneasy? Was it his eyes, which were cold as steel marbles? Was it his features, that had too little mobility? Or that he so rarely smiled, and when he did it was stiff and artificial? She admitted, at last, that she had never felt comfortable in his presence.

Yet he was always the gentleman, if a little too precise, a little too perfect. He did and said all the right things, but somehow she doubted if he felt any of them. He puzzled her, but now she was angry, too. If he had, indeed, been responsible for the forced entry into her flat, she would be furious.

It was not that far, she decided. Today she would walk to the theater. She put the .44 in her handbag, closed and locked the door behind her.

She smiled ruefully as she turned the key in the door. A lot of good that would do!

It was cool and dark in the theater. The stagedoor entrance was unlocked and she went in, pausing for a moment, listening for sound. There was none.

She was early, but not much. They should be here by now. It was unreasonable that not even one was here. She crossed the stage in the dim light, glancing out over the rows of empty seats. Thank God she'd never had them empty like that for a performance!

Backstage she hesitated and looked around. It was eerie. For the first time she realized that never before had she been in a theater alone.

From behind her she heard a faint creak, as of a footstep. She turned sharply.

Nothing, only the vague half-light that filtered in from far-off windows, somewhere on the second story behind the balcony.

Opening her purse, she took the derringer into her hand. Its weight was reassuring, yet the silence was there.

Something stirred.

She looked back. Her dressing room door was behind her. If she got in there, closed the door, but what if the *something* was there? Waiting for her?

She was being a fool. There were always sounds in an empty building. Changing temperatures could make boards creak and groan, even pop.

She took a step back, reaching for the doorknob, her purse hanging over her wrist. Her hand felt for the knob and there was a sudden movement from behind. Her wrist was grasped by a strong, bony-fingered hand and jerked sharply, the handbag was jerked from her arm and she was shoved violently. She staggered forward, heard running steps, and she toppled and fell to her knees.

She looked up. For one instant she saw the running man on the stage, almost at the other end.

She fired.

He staggered, cried out, and dropped her purse, clutching his hand. She lifted the derringer for another shot, but he was gone.

She got up, staggered, and stood erect. Her purse lay on the stage and she walked to it, holding the gun in her hand.

From outside she heard running feet and then they were crowding in, her friends, the cast—even Dane Clyde. How long since she had seen him?

"Grita!" Rosie shrilled. "What *happened*?"

"A man tried to snatch my purse. I shot at him."

"You hit him, too." Clyde pointed at a drop of blood on the stage. Then he saw the derringer. "You mean you hit him with *that*? At that distance?"

Stunned, she put the gun into her purse. She must remember to reload it. That was her only thought. The gun, her only protection, was half-empty.

They were all around her, chattering, asking questions, saying how awful it must have been.

"He was waiting in my dressing room," she said. "He was waiting there, and there was no one around."

"We stopped to have a drink," Sophie said. "I'm sorry, but when someone is buying—"

"It's all right. I wasn't hurt. Just frightened, that's all."

"If you can shoot like that when you're frightened," Dane Clyde commented, "I'd not like you to shoot at me when you're calm!"

"It was luck, an accident. Just an accident."

The stage manager, Richard Manfred, crossed over to them. "All right, it's all over. Let's get down to business."

Later, when they stopped for tea, Dane Clyde walked over to her. "If you'd like, I'll reload your derringer. I've just come over from Virginia City and have my own gun in my carpetbag with some extra powder and shot."

"Oh, would you?"

He went for his bag, returned, and she watched him load the gun. "You're very good," she said.

"When you travel that road, you'd better know what you're doing.

Besides, there's been some trouble over there. It hasn't actually come to shooting yet, but—"

"Shooting? In the theater?"

He chuckled. "No, it hasn't gotten that bad, but I've some friends in the mining business, and sometimes things get a bit sticky."

Sophie and Rosie came over. "Are you all right, Grita?" Sophie asked. "You must have had a scare."

"If we just hadn't stopped!" Rosie complained. "But that nice Mr. Hesketh—"

"Who?" Dane turned sharply around. "Did you say 'Hesketh'?"

"Of course. He's a friend of Grita's and when he offered to buy—"

Hesketh, Grita thought. . . . Last night and now.

TWENTY-EIGHT

Grita turned to Dane. "Do you know him?"

"I know who he is. Albert Hesketh is a mining man from Virginia City, and he recently got control of the Solomon, one of the best of the mines. Be careful of him."

"What do you know about him?"

"When it comes to that, I know next to nothing. He has been in Virginia City for some time, and they say he came there from California. He was keeping books at the Solomon, and then all of a sudden he simply took over.

"Will Crockett trusted him and all the while Hesketh had been plotting to take the mine away from him. He did just that, and Will Crockett disappeared."

"Murdered?"

"I doubt it. We think he's looking for some missing shares of Solomon stock which, if he could get them, would return control to him."

"Unless Hesketh got them first?"

"Exactly."

After rehearsal Manfred joined her at the door. "Wait, and we'll walk home with you. You seem to be a target for this sort of thing." He gave her a searching glance. "Where did you learn to shoot like that?"

"I don't know how to shoot. I just fired."

"Sometimes instinctive shots are the most accurate. After all, it's just like pointing your finger and you have been doing that all your life.

"You hit him in the hand or arm, I think. That's just a guess, but he dropped your purse, which I am sure was not his intention.

"Back in East Texas, where I come from, we have a man named Cullen Baker who always shoots like that. He's very good."

Dane Clyde joined them and they started up the street. "Are you still planning to come to Virginia City?"

"Oh, yes! Mr. Maguire has scheduled us to play there for at least two weeks. We will do four different plays, two the first week and

181

two the second, and then probably a repeat, depending on how they do."

"The War doesn't seem to have affected business."

"Are many leaving from Virginia City? I mean, to go into the Army?"

"Quite a few, although President Lincoln is not pushing it. After all, the government needs the silver we produce. There's a lot of hard feeling, though, on both sides."

"We hear a lot of talk about it in Paris, but nobody I know really knows anything about it."

"There's too much loose talk over here, too. Actually, it is more a matter of States' rights than slavery. The importation of slaves has been against the law since 1820. Of course, there's some smuggling going on, principally through the bayous near New Orleans."

Clyde turned to Grita. "Sophie told me somebody tried to break into your flat?"

"He did not try. He did break in. He sprung the lock somehow and went through everything."

" 'Went through'? You mean he searched everything? What was he looking for?"

She shrugged. "I have no idea. He may have thought I have a lot of jewelry. From the audience some of the junk I wear looks very real."

"Last night and again today?" Manfred was skeptical. "That can't be coincidence. Somebody thinks you have something."

At the door, they paused. "Maybe," Manfred suggested, "we should come in with you."

"Please, would you?"

The lock on the door had been simply sprung by using a lever of some kind, a jimmy or a screwdriver or a pinch-bar. The flat was one of many, hastily built to handle the rush of people in the 1850s.

They made a quick search of the flat. It was empty.

Manfred paused at the door. "You're not afraid? I know Sophie would come to stay if you wished, and she's not afraid of anything. I saw her throw a drunk out of a theater once—bodily. I mean she just threw him into the street."

"I'll be all right."

Clyde did not wish to leave. He lingered. "Grita?" he spoke softly so that none but Manfred could hear. "Do you own any mining stock? In the Solomon, for instance?"

"Why do you ask?"

"Look at it. Hesketh has control, but Crockett has a lot of stock, too. If Hesketh can pick up those missing shares he will have control, he will keep control. If Crockett should buy them first, then

Crockett could oust Hesketh and take over again. It's no small thing, Grita. There's millions involved."

"If anyone believes I have stock in the Solomon," she said flatly, "they are mistaken. I *know* I have no such stock, and let's face it. I have never been out here before nor have any of my family."

She closed the door and locked it, then checked the windows, one by one. The one window which was impossible to reach, she left open slightly. The others she left locked. She went from room to room, carefully looking at everything. There was no evidence that anyone had been in the flat since she left.

Suddenly, she was angry. Someone had actually invaded and searched her flat, someone then had awaited her in the theater, had shoved her down and tried to get away with her purse.

She had no reason at all to suspect Albert Hesketh, except that he had somehow been involved, or seemed to have been, but she did not suspect him and she would not. He had simply taken her to the theater, and later had bought drinks for the company. It was merely coincidence that the thief had been around on both occasions.

Once more she put the back of the chair under the doorknob.

Whoever the thief had been, the same man would not come tonight, not with only one hand to use.

Marcus Zetsev looked across his desk at the thin, sallow-faced man. His right hand was bound in a bloody cloth.

"It was your idea, Mr. Zetsev. I didn't know the man. The way he told it sounded very simple, and of course, getting into that flat, it was nothing.

"I went through it, believe me, I did! I hunted every place where people would be apt to hide anything—they all use the same places—and came up with nothing.

"At the theater I had her purse and was getting away. Who'd think a woman like that would have a gun? Or could shoot like that?"

"What were you looking for?"

The slim man glanced at him slyly out of bloodshot eyes. "He made me promise—"

"Don't be a fool! You will never see him again. I am the one you will be seeing, and I want to know."

"I was hunting for a packet, a long envelope, something like that with some stock shares. If I found anything else, I could keep it. Hell, there wasn't anything else! I break in, then I lay for her and knock her down and get winged, all for nothing!"

Marcus took a twenty-dollar gold piece from his pocket. "There, I wouldn't want you to lose on the deal. If he ever gets in touch again, let me know."

"Are you crazy? I was fifty feet away and runnin' when she winged me! I want nothin' to do with her!"

When the thief had gone, Marcus tipped back in his chair. Hesketh had recently taken control of the Solomon, and the Solomon was worth millions. Hesketh wanted that stock and he wanted it bad; there had to be a reason.

Within the hour a friend from the exchange told him the reason. Those shares of stock meant control, and Hesketh had to have control. Just holding the stock would mean a lot of money, but handled just right—

Marcus Zetsev clutched the edge of his desk. Buying stolen goods was a petty business, after all, but to own a silver mine! And he could do it. His somewhat protruding eyes watered as he thought of that. Hesketh had failed so far. *He* would not fail.

Teem, the thief he had sent to Hesketh, was a veteran. Hence, if he had not found the shares in the flat, they were simply not there.

There had been no chance for Teem to examine the purse, but that was where they must be. Either in her purse or on her person.

Now she would be aware, she would be on her guard, and she could shoot. Marcus thought about it, playing solitaire meanwhile. He would have to get hold of that purse and, if need be, of her. And the place to do that was some night after the theater or, in a last resort, take her from the stage as she went to Virginia City. It was common knowledge that her next play dates would be there.

For two weeks the play had a successful run, but for two weeks there was absolutely no chance to get close to her. One or more of the actors was always about, and they were armed. His people were shrewd enough to perceive that.

Marcus had no desire to get anyone shot who might be taken by the police and forced to talk.

The show closed suddenly, and the newspapers reported that Miss Redaway's Company would be going to Virginia City, to Washoe.

Hesketh came by to order materials, and Marcus, his eyes guileless, asked if he needed another thief. "I do not," Hesketh said sharply. "It will not be necessary."

Grita Redaway met Albert Hesketh for dinner. It was an excellent dinner, and she enjoyed it, yet during the course of the evening she became sure of one thing, if no more. Hesketh, in one way or another, was not quite right mentally. The feeling came to her suddenly, and for the first time she was frightened.

"You must let me show you the Washoe, Miss Redaway," he said. "You must see them actually take silver and gold from the earth. In fact, I shall give you some on the day you come to the Solomon. I shall find a fine bit of high-grade for you."

"High-grade?"

"Very rich ore. In high-grade you can usually see the gold. The real, actual *gold*, right there in your hand.

"Although," he added, "I have seen high-grade that showed no gold at all, and one could tell only by the weight. Gold is heavy, you know."

"We will be going soon. I'd be honored, Mr. Hesketh." Suddenly she felt a vicious prompting, and she could not resist. "Isn't the mine actually owned by a Mr. Crockett?"

His eyes were momentarily ugly, then bland. He smiled with his too thin lips. "Mr. Crockett? Oh, he owns some stock, quite a bit of it, in fact, but he no longer has anything to do with the Solomon."

He glanced at her warily. "How did you happen to hear of him?"

"Oh? How did I know? It was that man, the one from the market. The exchange or whatever they call it. Mr. Maguire was asking him about the Solomon stock, and he mentioned him. He said that the *real* owner was Will Crockett."

"That's ridiculous!" Hesketh replied stiffly. "He no longer has anything to do with the mine. He's out of it, completely!"

"Will you be on the stage with us, Mr. Hesketh?"

"As a matter of fact, I probably shall. Yes, of course."

Later, as he was leaving the International, he heard a voice at his elbow. "Turn the next corner, Mr. Hesketh, and go into that saloon. There's a body wishes to speak with you."

He looked across the scarred redwood table at the sallow-faced young man. "For fifty dollars? What information can you possibly have that is worth fifty dollars to me?"

The sallow-faced man grinned, revealing a broken yellow tooth. "Maybe nothin'. But I got an idea that there Marcus—"

"What about him?"

"For fifty dollars?"

Hesketh hesitated, then irritably put the coins on the table.

"Marcus was curious, almighty curious, Mr. Hesketh. I seen him later, talkin' to a man from the exchange, and then to Pottawattomie Joe."

"Who is he?"

"Why, he's a sort of ridin' man, hangs out along the trail east of Sacramento. Stops stages, and the like. Seemed Marcus was almighty curious about that actress woman, asked a lot of questions.

"Then he had a long talk with Pottawattomie Joe. I sort of had an idea something was in the wind that maybe was worth fifty dollars to you."

Teem picked up the coins. "Another time, Mr. Hesketh. But you be careful, you hear me? You be careful. There's to be another man along with Joe, a man who sort of eliminates, if you get what I mean.

"Now what does Marcus need him for? You know he's not going to kill that actress-woman, now is he? But if they have Jacob along."

"Jacob?"

"Just Jacob. Whenever Jacob goes anywhere, somebody gets killed. Now, I wonder, Mr. Hesketh, who is to get killed this time?"

TWENTY-NINE

Albert Hesketh sat very still, his hands resting on the table. After a moment, he spoke. "Thank you. Yes, indeed, thank you very much."

The young man with the fifty dollars disappeared, and the waiter came over, a burly man with a bulging stomach and a mustache. "Here! Where'd he go? That one never paid his bit!"

Hesketh put a coin on the table. Beside it he put a twenty-dollar gold piece, but on this he kept one hand. "I need a man with a fast horse. I've twenty dollars that says you can find one."

"I know the man. Give me the twenty."

"When I have spoken to him. Have him here, now."

"To hell with you! I'll do no such a damn—" The waiter stopped. "All right, then."

He sipped his wine, ignoring the loud talk and bustle around him, trying to ignore the body odors and the coarse talk. His wine was half-finished when a slovenly, bearded man in a slouch hat dropped down at the table.

Hesketh looked at him with cool distaste. "I want a man who can beat the Pony's time to Virginia City."

"Can't be done."

"I have one hundred dollars that says it can."

"Cost me half that for horses. I can get Pony horses but I'll have to pay station-tenders."

"All right. I will pay fifty expense money now. You will get your hundred when the message is delivered."

The man in the slouch hat rubbed his nose, looked at Hesketh, obviously a prosperous man. "Who do I say the message is from?"

"You will say nothing. You will answer no questions and ask none. I like," he added, "a man who knows how to keep his mouth shut." He paused a moment. "I do not recall anyone who talked of my affairs on more than one occasion."

On a sheet of paper from a notebook he drew a rough diagram. "You will find the man at this cabin. His name is Waggoner. It is

187

possible he will not have your money in his cabin, but he knows where to get it."

When the man had gone, he finished his wine. Marcus Zetsev had put up part of the money for Hesketh to gain control of the Solomon. If something happened to Hesketh, Marcus would get that stock, and evidently Marcus had been doing some thinking. It was easy to deal with crooks, because you knew they would always try to steal from you, unless they were afraid of you.

Should he take the stage? Should he depend on Waggoner? Yet if he did not take it, Zetsev would have somebody to move against him, and this time he would not be warned.

He would take the stage, but he would take precautions, and he would be armed. Also, there would be women aboard, and road agents were notoriously shy about offending women. You could kill a man, but if one so much as made a too familiar remark to a woman, you could be hung.

Hesketh knew about Jacob. He was never around where thugs and outlaws might be found. When the Vigilantes started hunting for the bad ones, Jacob might well be one of the Vigilantes. Nobody seemed to know him or just what he looked like, but there were those who knew how to get in touch with him.

Albert Hesketh did not like killing when he had to do it himself, but there were times—

Marcus Zetsev kept a holster riveted to the side of his swivel chair. In that holster there was a .36-calibre Remington. The chair was always behind the desk, and very few of those who came and went in the office were aware of the holster and the pistol. A man had to stand close and look over the top of the roll-top desk to see it, and then only if the chair was turned just so.

The streets were dark and silent. Further north some of the rougher drinking establishments were filled with music and boisterous talk, and on the walks outside men gathered and talked.

Albert Hesketh, dressed in the rough clothes of a pioneer, walked down the street and turned toward the warehouse and office of the chandlery. The street was empty, as he had expected and hoped. There was the merest light from the office window, and he had to feel his way up the few steps. At the door he turned the knob. As expected, it was locked.

Now much would depend upon chance, and he did not like chance. He rapped very lightly. There was no response, so he rapped louder.

Inside something stirred, and he saw someone coming along the passage toward him, holding a lantern. He had not considered the lantern, and he did not want a fire, although—

"Who's there?" It was Zetsev's voice.

"Marcus? It's Hesketh. Something has come up!"

There was a long moment of hesitation, then a rattle of the bar being taken down and the knob turned. Marcus lifted the lantern and peered into his face. "What's happened?" he demanded, making no move to open the door. Obviously he was disturbed by Hesketh's arrival.

"I've found where the shares are, but I need your help. Look, don't hesitate. It means millions for us, but we've got to act quickly."

He might have brought the gun from the chair or he might have another.

The door opened wider and Zetsev stepped back to let him come in. It was not at all what Hesketh wanted, but he stayed close to the door, hoping Marcus would precede him. He made no such move, and reluctantly Hesketh stepped in.

Zetsev walked rapidly toward the office, his coat hanging loosely from his shoulders. Hesketh let the knife he carried up his sleeve fall into his hand. Inside the office he spoke, "Marcus!" He glanced from side to side; then in a hoarse whisper, he said, "We've got them, Marcus! We've got the shares! Look—"

With his left hand he reached into his inside coat pocket and drew out a sheaf of papers. Inadvertently, expectantly, Marcus Zetsev stepped forward, and Hesketh stabbed sharply upward with the knife.

The point went in below the rib cage and drove to the hilt. Zetsev's eyes bulged, and his mouth dropped open, but using the same hand that held the papers, Hesketh seized Zetsev's right sleeve and jerked him closer. Then he stabbed him again, driving the blade in a little higher and harder.

Their eyes were only inches apart. Zetsev's mouth worked as his lips tried to form a sound, but nothing came. Coolly, Hesketh shoved him against the desk and stabbed him twice in the throat, then dropped him to the floor.

The safe was open as he had expected, and he went to it, scarcely more than a large strongbox, and leafed through the contents. He found what he wanted, pocketed it, and glanced down once more at Marcus Zetsev. Bending down he wiped his knife clean on Marcus's shirt. Then he went to the door.

He lifted the bar and stepped outside and came face to face with four men.

They were, he was sure, members of the Sydney Ducks or the "Hounds," gangs of thugs who raided, robbed, and often set fires in the city to give themselves a chance to loot. Large sections of San Francisco had been burned in such fires on several occasions.

He paused, one hand still on the doorknob, half wishing he had taken the pistol from the chair inside. "If you're looking for loot," he said quietly, "help yourselves, the door is open."

"Who're you?"

He was already walking away. One of them started after him, calling, "Hey! You!" He continued to walk, turned a corner, and walked more swiftly. When he had gone a block he crossed the street and ran, then slowed up, seeing a rig. He hired it and returned to the hotel by a side entrance.

He examined his clothes but noted with satisfaction there were no spots of blood.

Once more he examined the papers. He had successfully brought away all record of his arrangements with Marcus, and Marcus himself was dead.

For a moment he thought with misgivings of the sallow-faced young man. Would he suspect? And what of the Hounds? The four men met at the door? No doubt they had ignored the body and stripped the place of everything of value. Their depredations were so known and this would be so typical, no other explanation would be sought.

Marcus, so far as he knew, had no relatives. Even if some should appear, it would not matter now.

Jacob would be looking for a businessman, hence he would go dressed in the rough clothes of a pioneer or miner, and he would be armed.

Albert Hesketh washed his hands and got ready for bed. If he thought of Marcus at all it was simply as a problem disposed of.

Suddenly he found himself thinking of Grita Redaway, and not as someone to steal from but as a woman, as a beautiful woman, not as sexually exciting, but as a part of the frame, of the setting he wanted for himself. He wished to be rich, powerful, and envied, and he wished to have the best of everything. And the best of everything was, he believed, no more than he deserved.

He had never thought to ask why he deserved anything. It was enough that he felt he did. His ego was walled, shielded, and guarded.

Once in his bed he slept soundly.

When morning came, a spatter of rain was falling and the harbor was obscured by mist. From her little balcony Grita looked for the last time over the view she had come to love. "I will miss it, Mr. Clyde," she said. He paused, holding her luggage in his hands. "We must play this town again."

"We will. Manfred's waiting below, Miss Redaway. We had better go."

"I'll be along." She lingered, and he went out, drawing the door shut behind him.

Quickly, she went to her hiding place and drew out her father's wallet. For an instant, she was worried.

Now it could no longer be hidden. She had it all with her. Whoever wanted those papers must realize that when she left San Francisco she would take the papers with her, and the shares. Still, Manfred was along, and Dane Clyde as well as several other members of the company. Others had already gone on before.

When their rig dropped them at the stage station the first person she saw was Albert Hesketh, yet he was so altered in appearance that she did not at first recognize him.

He smiled. "I am dressed as many of us do on the Comstock," he explained. "Actually, these rough clothes are easier for travel."

"Of course," she agreed, but was puzzled nonetheless. Hesketh had always seemed a dapper, overly neat man and one who seemed to think much of how he appeared to others. In these clothes he looked strangely out of place.

The spatter of rain turned into a steady drizzle that lasted through the day. The heavy coach creaked and groaned on its way, bumping over stones and rough places in the road.

Manfred was on one side of her and Mary sat across from her. There was a bulky, heavy man in a brown suit beside her, a man with mutton-chop whiskers and a mustache. Hesketh sat beside him and soon gave every appearance of being asleep. Dane Clyde was riding atop the stage and there were others inside and on top, how many she did not know.

Several times they stopped to change horses, and at one stage-stop, as they hitched the horses, she said to Manfred, "I am a little worried."

He glanced at her. He was a sharp, intelligent man who had traveled a great deal. "What is it?"

"Whatever they wanted from me in San Francisco they must know I am carrying now."

"I had thought of that."

"Nevertheless, if there is trouble, stay out of it. I want no one hurt because of me."

"We will see when the time comes."

A new passenger joined them there, a tall, clerical-looking man with sandy hair and thick sandy brows. He was neatly dressed in a hand-me-down suit still carrying the creases from the shelf. He was, she suspected, about thirty years old. He carried a small carpetbag and got quickly into the coach, ignoring them all.

From time to time others joined them. She had begun to wish she had taken the steamer to Sacramento.

"We will be here all night, ma'am," the driver said. "That there *ho*-tel is respectable and entertains lady guests."

"I thought the stages went right on through? Although I will admit the rest will do me good."

"All of us, ma'am. Yes, we do usually go through, but there's been some flooding and I won't chance those roads in the dark. I want to see what I'm gettin' into!"

She looked around. Hesketh had disappeared. So had the heavy man in the brown suit and the sandy-haired newcomer.

This was Sacramento. This was the town that letter had come from so long ago. Somebody here had owed her father money and it was invested, perhaps right here in town.

Manfred sat beside her at supper. "If there is trouble," he suggested, "it will be between here and Placerville, or after we leave there. Some of it is very rough country."

"You've been here before?"

He pointed toward the east. "My parents died over there," he said quietly, "not far from where we are going."

"Mine did not get that far," she said. "They were killed in Missouri, before they ever got started."

Manfred gave her an odd look. "Oh? I had no idea. I thought you were French."

"I went to school in Paris, but I am an American." She gestured around. "This is where we were coming. California was our dream."

"Mine, too. I wish my folks could have seen it."

Alone in her room, she wondered. Why that odd look? Simply because he had believed she came from France? Or was there some other reason?

THIRTY

At daylight, putting the last finishing touches to her hair, Grita looked around at Mary. "Have you a pistol?" she asked.

Mary Tucker looked up, surprised. "I do, Miss Redaway. I keep it by me."

"Can you use it?"

Mary smiled. "At home in Indiana there was little enough on the table and my pa worked in town. I had no brothers, so if we had meat the shooting was up to me. I kept meat on the table until I was fourteen, when the cholera took my family."

"Keep the gun where you can get it, then. I think we may have trouble."

"I will that. Is it after you they are?"

"It is. Or something I have."

"You seem very sure of yourself, ma'am." The Irish girl looked at her, smiling. "You'd think you'd been caring for yourself as I have."

Grita nodded. "I have, in a somewhat different world. When did you get into the theater, Mary?"

"When I lost them all I took a job for some people in Pittsburgh. The young man there, where I was maid, he was forever talking of the theater, and having folks to dinner from the theater. He didn't like girls much, he didn't, but he was nice and we talked a lot. One day I was speaking of one of the ladies who had been to dinner, and not knowing her name, I did an imitation of her that set him laughing.

"At supper a few nights later he told a man to look at me. 'She's the one you need,' he said. 'She will do the part better than anyone.'

"So they had me down to the theater to play a housemaid, a pert, snippy one, and they liked me. So here I am, four years older and an actress. 'Tis never rich and famous I'll be, but 'tis better than scrubbing floors."

"Do you never regret the farm?"

"I do. One day I'll put by enough to buy one, to own one of my own." She picked up her valise. "And you, miss? What will you do?"

"Who knows? Have you been in love, Mary?"

"Twice, I thought I was. Each time I came to my sense in time, thanks be to God. And you, miss?"

"No, not yet. There were some gentlemen I knew, very elegant gentlemen, too, but they were not for me. The trouble is, Mary, I'm like a lot of others. I don't know what I want."

"Who does, until you see him? And then you're like to be wrong."

Grita spoke suddenly, and without thinking. "I shall buy a ranch, Mary, and raise horses. I like the theater, and it's a challenge. There's no end to how good one can get, but none of us are good enough."

"It's good to hear them laugh."

"Yes, it is, but the crowd's a fickle beast. At least, that's what an old actor I knew often said, and I agree. Some actresses think the people love them, and that's nonsense. They love the roles you play or the way you play them, but not *you*. Tomorrow it can be another."

It was cold and damp when they reached the coach, and nobody was talking. The heavy man in the brown suit bobbed his head at them, but the sandy-haired one looked at nobody, he just waited.

They were seated before Manfred appeared. He got into the stage without a word and sat back against the cushions. He and the two girls were seated in the very back of the stage, facing forward and looking at the backs of three passengers who rode the center seat. Beyond them were three who faced toward the rear. One of these was Hesketh.

The driver's whip cracked like a pistol shot, and the stage started with a lunge.

"There's been some flooding," someone said. "The river's up across the road in places. We may have to take some other route."

" 'Other' route?" The voice was grim. "What other route?"

"There are trails." That was the man in the brown suit. "I've heard it said."

Waggoner heard the horse coming up the road and had a hunch. He rolled off his bunk and glanced out the window. Something passed between his cabin and the lights of the mine some distance away. A rider, no doubt. He hitched up his pants and slipped his suspenders over his shoulders. Then he belted on his gun, which had been lying on a chair close to the bed. He got out a cigar and lighted it. He smoked them rarely, but kept a few on hand.

The horse's hoofbeats slowed and stopped. The only other sound was the rhythmic pound of the stamp-mills and compressors. Occasionally, when a door opened somewhere down on the street, he caught a bit of tin-panny music from a saloon or dance hall.

After a moment there was a tap on the door, and he lifted the bar. "Come on in," he said, and stood back to look at the man as he entered. A stranger, a sallow-faced man with shifty eyes.

"I brung a message. You're to pay me."

Waggoner stared at him. He had an idea about the kind of payment needed.

He took the message. It was obvious to him the message had been opened and resealed. He looked at it, then looked up at the messenger and met a sickly grin.

> *Miss GR has shares. Offer usual terms before stage reaches VC. Rumor Pot Joe. Also specialist Jacob. Deal the high card to Jacob. Usual 3, delivery later.*

"Usual terms" meant he was to steal those shares. Pottawattomie Joe was a known outlaw, specializing in stage and wagon holdups, what was known at the time as a road agent.

Specialist Jacob, deal the high card— What sort of specialist? A killer?

Waggoner scowled. He knew of no one named Jacob. Still—

He looked up at the messenger. "I'm to pay you? I can do that, or you can lend a hand and make yourself a nice piece."

"How?"

"You read this?"

Teem hesitated, then shrugged. "Why not? A man better know what he's carryin' these days. There's a war on."

"You know what this means?" Waggoner held up the letter.

"Seems to say what it means."

"Seems to, but doesn't. 'Miss GR has some shares' don't mean nothin' like that. Chances are there's somebody on that stage with them initials, but that there's a code that tells me there's to be ten thousand in gold on that stage." He was lying, but he could use this man—for awhile. "I'll need a man to help." He jerked his head toward the town. "There's those down there would jump at the chance but you're here. Saves time."

"How much?"

"If we take the ten, you get twenty-five hundred. I got to give that much to my spotter, too."

"Half?"

"Not a chance. This here's my deal and I make the cut. You're in or you're out."

"I'm in."

"You got a travelin' horse?"

"I have. He's come a far piece." He had used Pony horses all the way over, horses rented from the spares the Pony Express kept. That enterprise was about over now and the hostlers were out to make every dollar.

"No matter. There'll be other horses." He was lying about that, too, but this joker would never know the difference. When the word was to pay him, Waggoner needed no interpreter.

Albert Hesketh did not like to kill, but only because killing left one open to be killed. He had never thought of himself as either a brave or an unbrave man. He simply did what had to be done if anybody got in his way.

He knew very well that he was riding into danger. Jacob undoubtedly had instructions from Zetsev to kill him, and was probably among those already on the stage. If not he would join it further along.

Had Jacob been paid? Or was he expecting to be paid later? Maybe if this Jacob knew that—

"There was a killing in San Francisco," he said suddenly, "a man I'd been doing business with. Named Marcus Zetsev. He sold equipment to mine owners, freighters, theaters, and such. The Hounds killed him, they think. They looted his place."

"I knew of him," Manfred said. "Tom Maguire bought gear from him, backstage stuff, canvas for scenes, ropes, pulleys, that sort of thing."

"That's the man. He always sold at a good price, so we'll miss him."

Now, if Jacob was aboard, he knew his employer was dead, and if he had not paid, he would not and could not.

There was talk about the Sydney Ducks and the Hounds and what ought to be done, then the conversation drifted into silence.

Hesketh was considering the road ahead. He had been over it many times, and his guess was that any holdup would come after Placerville, and probably after Strawberry. He was thinking carefully, coolly, of what he could do.

If Jacob was with Pottawattomie Joe, that would be one thing. If he was on the stage, he would have to bring about a shooting so he could kill Hesketh under cover of the firing. Yet that left open too great a chance that Jacob himself might be killed.

His hunch was that Pottawattomie Joe would wait until the last minute. There were trails up Fay Canyon and there was one cut-off from Carson Canyon. Joe could be back in his usual hangouts before anybody knew he was gone.

Waggoner could beat them to it, he must. It was good to know about men like Waggoner. They could save a man a lot of trouble.

The stage bounced and jolted, rocked and swayed, swung around precipitous cliffs and down into hollows, plunging through shallow streams. Several times they pulled out around tongues of flood water that had pushed back up some hollow or ravine. Dust sifted over their clothing.

Grita Redaway felt again for her derringer. It was there.

There were occasional mud-holes, but the higher parts of the road had dried out fast, and the usual dust was there, as if the rains had never been. At the top of a rise, the driver suddenly pulled up. Leaning over, he called to the passengers.

"If y'all want to stretch yer legs, now's the time! Got to rest my team!"

It was a small clearing on a knoll in the forest with pines all about and some great boulders and many fallen trees, their trunks lying parallel as though deliberately placed.

"Blown down," somebody said. "Wind comes down these canyons sometimes, flattens trees like they was grass!"

The stage driver, whip in hand, came over to them. He touched his hat to them. "Hope the ride isn't too rough, Miss Redaway. They are improvin' this road all the time, but the traffic's fierce! You should have seen it at first! Ma'am, you could no more get this stage over it than I can fly! A man had to go afoot or on horseback. Later they'd get wagons over it, but they'd often have to stop and almost build the road theirselves. It was sure enough rough!"

"Have you been here long?"

"Well, not so's you'd speak of it. I come out from West Virginny with my folks. That was in fifty-one. Lost my pa to cholera and ma, she set up a boardin' house over at Rough 'n Ready.

"We moved camp to camp there for awhile, along with ever'body else. I made the run to the Fraser an' like to got drowned up there, then got m'self trapped in a snowslide. Trevallion found me when I'd about give up—"

"Trevallion?" Manfred said. "I've heard stories about him."

"You'll hear aplenty of them. He's the kind of man who makes stories wherever he goes, and without tryin', too. I mean, he minds his own affairs."

"Does he have another name?" Grita asked.

"Never heard any other." The stage driver spat. "He don't need any other, ma'am. Folks just say Trevallion an' ever'body knows who they mean. They ain't another like him in the goldfields."

Grita turned to Hesketh, who stood near. "Have you met him, Mr. Hesketh?"

"No. I have had no occasion to meet him. He is a miner, I hear, and they say he is a good one. I hire miners occasionally, my foreman does. I rarely meet them."

Hesketh turned his back and walked back to the stage. The driver chuckled. "I reckon he don't like Trevallion none," he spoke softly, "kind of stole a march on him, Trevallion did.

"There's a mine," he explained, "called the Solomon, rich as all get out. Hesketh there, he was bookkeeper for Will Crockett, who owned it, or thought he did. All of a sudden his bookkeeper turned up with a controlling interest, and he kicked his boss right out.

"Kicked him out of his own mine, and he taken over. Seems all the time he was keepin' books for Will, this Hesketh was workin' to take over.

"Then all of a sudden one morning Hesketh goes to his mine and finds that Trevallion had moved in the night before and staked a piece of rich ground, maybe the richest, that Hesketh thought belonged to the mine. Trevallion staked it in his name and Crockett's, although I don't think Will knows a thing about it. So you can see why Al Hesketh doesn't care much for Trevallion!"

He looked around. "All right! Board up, ever'body! We got a long run ahead!"

"Driver?" Grita asked suddenly. "This man Trevallion? Did they ever call him Val?"

"No, ma'am, they never. Not that I heard of. He's just Trevallion. Called so by one and all."

THIRTY-ONE

The passengers were boarding the stage. The driver turned away but she put a hand on his arm. Surprised, he turned. Speaking in a low tone she said, "Be careful. I am afraid there will be trouble."

He had started to step up on the wheel, now he put his boot down. "What d'you mean, ma,am?"

"There are people who want something I have. I am sure they will try to get it before we reach Virginia City."

He took his time, knocking some mud from his boot against the wheel. "You got any indication of that? I mean, that there will be trouble?"

"There have been several attempts to rob me. In San Francisco they broke into my flat, and I was attacked in the theater there."

"You got any idea who's after you?"

"I do not. Richard Manfred, who is an actor in our company as well as stage manager, knows of it. So does Mr. Hesketh."

"What's Hesketh got to do with it?"

"Nothing that I know of. Except, well, he has been paying me a lot of attention."

The driver smiled, his blue eyes amused. "Now, ma'am, that can't come as any surprise. Most any man would pay his respects to you, given the chance."

"Thank you, but I suspect he has other interests." She turned toward the stage where the last passenger was stepping in. "I wished you to know as I want no one to be hurt."

"If they get what they're after, they'll—"

She turned. "Please understand me. I do not intend to be robbed, now or ever."

She got into the stage and the driver stared after her, swore softly, then climbed to his seat and took up the reins.

There was forest about them now, gathering clouds above. Under the trees, patches of snow; on the shaded side of the road there was a bank of snow. The air was crisp. A few lingering aspen leaves brushed their pale brown palms together in wistful memory of past beauty. The air smelled of pines.

"More than five thousand wagons working this road now, six to eight horses to the team, sometimes more."

They climbed steadily, the stage horses at a walk.

Hesketh had his eyes closed and seemed to be sleeping; Grita was sure he was not. A cold, methodical man, precise in his ways and movements, he gave her the impression of a man who walked a ragged edge, of a man somehow brittle.

What she knew of acting she had learned by observation. First there had been her natural instincts, followed by suggestions from her aunt and friends of her aunt, then a word here or there from an old-timer, and then studying other performers. Yet most of what she knew she had learned by observing people, picking up their mannerisms, gestures, and expressions. By watching people who were self-conscious, assertive, dogmatic, or conniving.

From the first she had the impression that the face Hesketh turned toward the world was in no way the true man. Always he seemed in control, in command. His decisions were quick, sharp, definite. His workers, she suspected, were afraid of him, and she detected, or believed she detected, a streak of cruelty under it all. Yet even that cruelty took second place to his contempt for all about him.

Now he seemed asleep, but there was no repose in his hands and their subtle, unconscious movements. His right hand he kept near the opening in his coat. Without doubt he had a gun.

The stage rumbled and rattled over the hard road, slowing occasionally for a patch of sand or a slight grade.

"Getting deeper into the wilderness," Manfred commented, and Grita knew she was being warned. She needed no warning. Several times her fingers had touched the derringer.

"Better let me handle it," Manfred said, quietly.

"It would not be fair. The trouble is mine."

"You are a woman."

"If women can be killed, women can fight. My own mother was murdered. She had no chance to fight."

"You never told me."

"There was no reason to tell anyone. It was a long time ago, in Missouri."

Albert Hesketh opened his eyes. Suddenly she was sharply aware of his attention. "In Missouri?" he said.

"We were starting west. My father had bought a covered wagon, and we were ready to go."

His eyes were unblinking, but his lips smiled a little. "You are sure it was murder? After all, you must have been very young."

She looked right into his eyes. "It was murder. I was there."

They were all looking at her now. The heavy man in the brown suit shifted a little. "Ugly," he said, "an ugly experience for a young girl. It is fortunate you were not killed, too."

"I would have been if it had not been for a boy who was with me. He hid me." *And held me,* she thought.

For the first time she really looked at that memory with all her attention. He had held her. Held her tight, shielding her eyes, whispering to her. For the first and perhaps the only time in her life she had felt completely safe, completely secure, protected. Her parents had been killed but he had been there, holding her, calming her, and he had lost a mother, too.

It was absurd to have such a memory after all these years, but of all her memories it was the most vivid. She remembered the scuffling in the wagons, the muffled cries, the thud of blows, and all the while those strong young arms holding her.

"You were lucky not to be killed. There were several of them?"

"Yes. They were renegades, scum that lived along the river, stealing whatever they could."

"You were lucky," the man in the brown suit repeated, "they would not have wanted a witness to be left for a crime as vicious as that. A rope is too good for men like that."

Hesketh turned his head to look out the window, and suddenly she remembered where she was and what was about to happen. She felt in her purse for the derringer. It was there, cool and strong to the touch.

"How far is it to Strawberry?" she asked him.

He glanced at her. "A long way yet," he said.

They overtook a long line of wagons, rolling up clouds of dust. The driver cracked his whip over the horses, and they raced on by to reach a small roadside station before the teamsters. The stage pulled up, dust sifted over them and past them. There were several horses at the hitching-rail and an Indian sitting down against the wall of the station.

Hesketh avoided her at the station, walking off by himself, but among the trees and away from the road. The driver came over to her. He jerked his head to indicate Hesketh. "There's an odd one. Keeps to himself."

He spat. "Canny, though. If I was some of them around Virginia, I'd look to my hole card. Will Crockett isn't the only one he'll have up a tree."

"Why do you say that?"

"He's hungry, that one. Hungry like a wolf who will eat until he busts, almost. Just takin' the Solomon from Will won't be enough. He'll want it all, and if I'm any judge, he's fixing to get it all."

"From what I hear he won't get far with men like Mackay and Fair. Or Sharon, for that matter."

"He won't try, yet. He'll just eat up the small fry. He hates Sutro. He wanted to get in on that tunnel idea of Adolph's, but no matter how much Sutro needed money to get on with it, he would have no piece of it from Hesketh. He never actually turned him down, just avoided him."

"If there is a holdup," Grita asked, "where do you think it will happen?"

He shrugged. "Somewhere between Strawberry and Hope Valley. If it's Pottawattomie Joe, who knows this country, he'll figure us to not use the Hope Valley route. Sometimes we go that way when the snow's deep, but I'm fixin' to turn north and go by way of the Kingsbury Grade.

"Plenty of trails where a rider can cut across country so they can pick their spot. There's a lot of places where a team can't travel no faster'n a walk, due to the grade."

With fresh horses they moved on at a good speed. Hesketh had returned to the stage and was the first man aboard. The man in the brown suit had buttoned his coat despite the fact that it was warm inside the stage. He now sat with his back to Grita and half-facing Hesketh. Manfred observed the change but offered no comment to her.

Now the trail became steeper, winding steadily upward. The snow under the trees was deeper. The air was chilly outside, but inside the stage it was close and warm. After a bit she dozed from time to time, absently wondering about Richard Manfred.

She knew nothing of him, nor did anybody on the show. He made vague references to companies in which he had worked in the South, was an intelligent and versatile actor and a better than average stage manager. Seemingly he thoroughly understood his business.

He was a man of medium height who looked taller, with dark hair and a dark, hawklike face, even white teeth and was attractive without being in any way handsome. His wardrobe was modest. He was quiet, unobtrusive, but not communicative about himself or his affairs.

He was especially good in the olios that followed the last act, in which each of the performers did some kind of specialty act, dancing, singing, or comedy. He seemed to do everything with equal ease, yet where he came from, his age, education, or background remained a mystery. Where some of the actors suffered from self-doubt and insecurity when off stage, Manfred was completely assured.

The sun's red setting colored the mountainside before them, and the stagecoach mounted a last steep grade and poised at the top of a

winding descent. The driver drew up, slowing his team without
actually stopping them, looking over the trail before him. He slapped
the lines on the horses' backs and started them moving at a faster
clip when a voice called from the trees.

"Hold 'em right there, Dave!"

He drew up, taking his time. Hesketh shrank back into the shadows inside the coach. Grita slipped her derringer into her hand.

"I'm not carrying anything," the driver said mildly, "the box is
empty, as you can see."

"Well, there's always the passengers," the bandit said cheerfully.
Two more men had come from the bushes on his right and left.

"I've got some women aboard, boys," Dave spoke mildly still.
"They're play-actresses. You know how the boys in Virginia set store
by their shows and such. I just want to warn you boys that you touch
one of those womenfolks and you're askin' for a hangin'."

The man doing the talking, whom Grita guessed might be
Pottawattomie Joe, gestured toward the stage with his gun. "You all
jus' step out here, nice an' easy like, an' nobody's goin' to get hurt."

Before a move could be made, Grita spoke. "You have three guns
out there, my friend, and we've got six in here. Do you still want us
to get out?"

"The lady's right. You boys just stopped the wrong stage. I suggest
you just back off and go to your horses."

Manfred's gun was in his hand as he spoke. "We don't intend to be
robbed. You might get one of us, but we'd get all of you. Now what's
it to be?"

Mary Tucker was holding her gun and so was the man in the
brown suit. Grita leaned back, looking at the men inside the stage.
"Be very careful, gentlemen," she said, "when you fire, that you
direct your aim to the outside. We wouldn't want any accidents now,
would we?"

Albert Hesketh held his gun low, but Grita's derringer was not
pointed toward the outside. She was looking right at him.

Pottawattomie Joe was in a quandary. Never in his long outlaw
career had he faced a stagecoach that held as many ready guns.
Usually they stepped down and handed over their valuables without
question, yet he had no desire to try his luck with a stage filled with
guns.

"You got me euchered, lady," he said cheerfully, "you surely
have. Why don't you just go along easy and we'll call it quits?"

Dave lifted his whip and the team started. He waved at the
outlaws and they waved back.

Albert Hesketh sat slowly back, very watchful. Pottawattomie Joe had struck unexpectedly soon, and he had failed. But who could have expected resistance? And such a show of guns?

Suddenly he was shaking with fury. That damned woman! That dirty— He fought himself back to normal, still trembling.

Nobody was looking at him, they were all chattering about the holdup. Only that Redaway girl, she was not talking.

Where was Waggoner?

THIRTY-TWO

The burst of fury passed and left Hesketh cold and empty, chilled through and through as if he had been exposed to an icy wind. For a few minutes his thoughts were confused, and he felt like leaping from the coach and running off into the woods.

His hands gripping his legs above the knees, he fought himself to calmness. The holdup had taken place and Jacob, if he was present, had not acted, which might mean that he still waited upon opportunity.

Waggoner would be next, but would Waggoner know Jacob? Yet Waggoner would get the shares from the Redaway girl, or would he?

She had acted with unexpected resolution and quickness of mind. Who would have believed that a mere play-actress could so suddenly bring all those guns into action? If she did the same thing to Waggoner, what could he do?

Hesketh, calm once more, tried to think it through. He *must* have those shares. He was positive the actress had them. During the months he had worked for Crockett he had examined everything in the company safe, every ledger, every paper, every letter. Tucked away in one of the drawers was a list of people to whom Crockett had sold stock when the company was still in California. Each shareholder Hesketh had tracked down over the months.

The idea of the holdup had seemed simple enough. He could not recall a case where the people being held up had not been relieved of their valuables without incident, unless there was a shotgun messenger aboard. The stage would be held up, among the things taken would be the shares, and they would be delivered to him.

Who would have expected a damned fool woman to take charge like that? He could not blame Pottawattomie Joe for backing down. It was the intelligent thing to do. The three guns outside could have riddled the stage, but the guns inside would have blown him out of the saddle and his men as well.

Waggoner, *where was Waggoner?*

With Marcus Zetsev out of the picture, Hesketh had been sure he could make a deal for the shares if they fell into hands other than his. Now it was up to Waggoner.

Inside the moving coach the passengers were settling down. Talk was dying out. Soon they would be relaxed, off guard, not expecting trouble.

If Jacob was aboard the coach, which one was he? Hesketh's eyes went from the slim, silent man to the man in the brown suit.

A bulky, heavy man, was it fat or muscle? Some of the most powerful men he had ever seen looked fat. The man smelled of stale cigar smoke, and he had blunt, strong fingers with the nails cut sharply off. His thick neck bulged against the stiff collar. A heavy gold watch-chain hung from pocket to pocket of his vest, and there was a diamond stickpin in the red tie he wore. When Grita had called Pottawattomie Joe's hand, the man in the brown suit had been very quick to produce a pistol, a .36 Remington.

Albert Hesketh was suddenly worried. Who *was* the man? He had produced that gun almost as if he had expected to need it, without hesitation and with a readiness for battle that surprised Hesketh.

The sandy-haired man, on the other hand, had sat very quietly, hands relaxed in his lap, not so much as a muscle stirring. Was he frightened? Ready? Or merely watchful to see which way the cat was going to jump?

He glanced over at Grita. She was relaxed against the back cushion, her eyes closed. Mary Tucker also seemed asleep.

The stage rumbled on, plunging down steep hillsides, climbing slowly, weaving a precarious way among trees and rocks.

They pulled up to Strawberry and the doors opened, letting light stream out over the hoofs of the horses and the wheels of the stagecoach. Sleepily, the passengers roused themselves and stepped down from the coach, Manfred lifting a hand to help Mary and Grita.

"Won't be much time, folks," Dave advised. "Grab yourselves some coffee and a bite, then we go on. We're runnin' behind because of that high water."

Dane Clyde stood beside him as the passengers went by.

Dave nodded toward Grita Redaway. "There's a cool one! Never seen the like! She stood ol' Pot Joe right on his ear!" He turned and glanced at Clyde. "Ain't you with her?"

"I'm in her company," Clyde said. "Miss Redaway goes her own way."

"I should reckon." He spat. "Take a man with hair on his chest to handle that one. They must've all had their guns in sight, because I never knowed Pot to back off so fast."

"I had mine out, too," Clyde said quietly. "It was time. And I never shot a gun in anger in my life."

"Well, you was close enough. Hard to miss at that range, although I seen it done, here an' there."

Grita went quickly to a table, and Manfred spoke to a waiter.

"Miss Redaway is to perform in Virginia City, and she is very tired. If you have time—"

"An actress? You bet! Say, I heard of her! She's mighty good, ain't she?"

"The best," Manfred replied. "If you will hurry now?"

He walked back to the table, pausing en route to glance around the crowded room. Hesketh had disappeared. The man in the brown suit had seated himself at a crowded bench by the simple method of crowding. The man next to him started to object, then seeing the bulk and manner of the newcomer he simply crowded over.

The floor was a mixture of sawdust and mud, and the room was full with booted men, two-thirds of them visibly armed.

A hawk-faced man in a battered slouch hat and a torn coat stopped near Manfred. "You come in on that there stage? Any room aboard her?"

"It's crowded," Manfred said. He pointed to the driver. "Talk to him. You might be able to ride the top."

Manfred moved over beside Grita and accepted a cup of coffee without sitting down. His eyes were restless, alive and aware, studying the men in the huge room.

The slouch hat came back and Manfred asked, "Going with us?"

"Can't say I am. Too rich for my blood. He wants five dollars to ride on to Washoe and I ain't got but three."

He started to turn away and Grita spoke. "Please? Do you have a minute?"

The man stopped, looking around at her. Quickly he removed his hat. "Sorry, ma'am, I didn't see there was a lady present."

"Do you want to go to Washoe?"

"Yes'm. I got to git there somehow."

She gestured toward his gun. "You look like a man who could use one of those. Can you? Will you?"

"I can, and I will," he spoke softly, "but I never shot no man without cause."

"There will be trouble before I get to the hotel in Virginia City. Mr. Manfred here can probably handle it, but I'd like him not to be alone."

"My name's Teale, ma'am. I've come on hard times. Fact is, I've never knowed much but hard times, all my born days. What is it you want?"

"I want to get to Virginia City safely, and without being robbed. I am Margrita Redaway and I believe there are plans to rob me."

"A man who'd rob a lady like you," Teale said, "must be pure-dee varmint."

"I'll give you—"

"Ma'am, you don't need to give me nothin'. My ol' mammy would turn in her grave did she think I was takin' money for protectin' a lady. You git me on that coach an' nobody ain't goin' to bother you. I'll get my possibles."

"Wait, have you eaten?"

"Yes, ma'am. I et the day before yestiddy."

"You'd better eat now. Get your things and come back."

"He won't wait, ma'am. I know he won't."

"He'll wait."

Teale glanced at her curiously, then walked away. A few minutes later he was back, carrying a rifle and a small, neatly wrapped pack of what appeared to be clothing. Food was on the table and he seated himself and began to eat.

"Richard? Will you see Dave? Tell him what's happened and that we will not be long."

Manfred hesitated. "You'll be all right?"

"Mr. Teale is here."

When Manfred had gone, Teale looked up from his food. "You're trustin' of strangers, ma'am."

"No, Mr. Teale, I am not. However, I do trust my judgment of character. I knew at once you were a man to be trusted, that your word was good."

"Well, now. I reckon I didn't know it showed."

"What are you going to do in Washoe? Work in the mines?"

"No, ma'am. I'd not be much account underground. There's mills and such and I might try prospectin' a mite. I've a brother there. He'll know what's available."

"All right, Mr. Teale. I shall be in Virginia City at least a month. I'll pay you forty dollars to work that month for me."

"Ma'am, I ain't dressed proper to be seen with a lady."

"You will have an advance from me. You can buy some clothes in Virginia City." She paused. "Mr. Teale, there is someone who believes I have several shares of mining stock that have become quite important. They will do anything to get those shares." Briefly, she outlined the attempts in San Francisco.

He finished his meal and gathered up his belongings. Dave was waiting, whip in hand. He glanced at Grita Redaway. "What a man will do for a beautiful woman!" he said wryly.

"Thank you, driver. I appreciate the consideration. Shall we go now?"

With a fresh team, the stage rolled out. There were scattered clouds across a sky spangled with stars. They were higher now, and the air was cold. Atop the stage Dane Clyde glanced at his new companion. "My name is Dane Clyde," he said, introducing himself, "I'm with Miss Redaway's Company."

"Company?"

"I'm an actor. Miss Redaway is an actress and a very good one. The company is hers."

"Well, now. I never knowed no actors or actresses before. You carryin' a piece?"

"If you mean do I have a gun, I do. I'm not very good with it. In fact, I never shot a gun. Trevallion told me I should learn."

"A growed-up man an' never shot a gun? Where'd you get your meat?"

"We bought it from a butcher shop. Or ordered it in restaurants."

"Now, what d' you know? Never heard tell of such a thing."

Huddled between the mail sacks to keep warm, Clyde told the story of the attempted holdup and its failure.

Teale chuckled. "So she stood up ol' Pot Joe? Wait until I see him!"

Startled, Clyde turned sharply. "The bandit? You know him?"

"I should smile, I do! Knowed him since he was a boy. Hunted buffalo a time or two with him. He knows me, too."

They talked no more. The stagecoach plunged through the night, racing across meadows, rounding tight curves above vast depths, splashing through streams, slowing for long climbs and racing to make up time where the dim trail was straight. The air was cold and still, the few scattered clouds were gone and the sky was amazingly clear, and always there was the smell of pines or of cedar.

Here and there they paused to give the team a chance to catch its breath after a long climb. Once they all had to get out and walk behind to enable the horses to make it.

At Yank's Station they changed teams. Hesketh got down and looked sharply around. *Where was Waggoner?* Only a little time was left.

For the first time he saw Teale. He glanced at him, then looked again. "Do I know you?" he demanded.

"No, Mr. Hesketh, you don't. You never saw me before."

"But you know me?"

"You're gettin' to be a famous man, Mr. Hesketh. Folks talk about you."

Something in the man's attitude and tone disturbed him. "You're sure we haven't met before?"

"Don't seem like it. I been around a good bit but I never knowed anybody named Hesketh, and that's a fact."

He paused a moment. "It was a great loss, Mr. Hesketh, a great loss. All of us will be the less for his passing."

"Passing? Who?"

"Why, Marcus, Mr. Hesketh. Marcus is gone, and we will sorely miss him. His place is gone, too. Burned by the Hounds, they say. But then everything that happens in San Francisco is laid to either the Hounds or the Ducks. It is a pity, Mr. Hesketh, but it is the way of things, in the midst of life there is death. Death is always with us, Mr. Hesketh."

Hesketh glanced at him sharply. "What are you talking about?" He was suddenly wary. There was something about this man—

"What are you talking about?" he repeated.

"Death, Mr. Hesketh. We were talking about death."

Everything in him seemed to go still. He waited a slow minute. "What did you say your name was?"

"Teale, Mr. Hesketh. Jacob Teale."

Jacob . . . ?

THIRTY-THREE

For a moment everything within him stopped. Hesketh had long avoided any situation he could not command. He wanted to turn his head, to look around, to see if any help was close by. There would be none. He was alone.

"Marcus is dead," Hesketh said, "but life, goes on."

"For some."

"I wonder if he left any debts unpaid? Or any contract work undone?"

"We all live in the midst of things, Mr. Hesketh. No man is ready for death. I suppose if a man contracted a job before he died there'd be no reason to call it off."

"There would no longer be a reason for it. Whatever reason there might have been would no longer exist."

Jacob Teale did not reply. From under the brim of the battered slouch hat his eyes looked like the empty sockets in a skull. His lean, cadaverous face accented the strangeness.

"I could use a man," Hesketh suggested.

"Got me a job. I'm workin' for that actress-lady."

"For Miss Redaway? But how could that happen? How could she know about you? And what in the world would she need of a man like you?"

"She seen me. I reckon she knew what she seen. She told me she was expectin' to be robbed and she didn't want it should happen. She told me I should see it didn't."

Hesketh was irritated by this man and by Grita Redaway. Everything had been planned so well, and there was no reason why it should not have gone off as planned. What in the world did a young woman like her see in this walking cadaver? Could she have guessed the kind of man he was?

"I would prefer there be no shooting while I am on the stage," Hesketh said carefully. "There is too much chance of innocent people being shot. It would be worth something to me if there was no shooting. Most road agents prefer not to shoot, I understand."

Teale spoke quietly. "Mr. Hesketh, that little lady seen me, she hired me, she trusts me to do the job. I figure to do it," he turned his eyes toward Hesketh, "no matter who gets shot.

"Mr. Hesketh, I don't know what's going on here. I ain't been in this country long enough, but let me tell you something in case you ain't noticed. That's an uncommon woman there. Nobody's goin' to fool her or take advantage of her. If she's got something you want you better buy it from her at any price she asks because you ain't goin' to get it any other way."

"She has nothing I want," Hesketh lied. "I scarcely know the woman. I just don't want trouble."

"Mr. Hesketh, I don't know you, either, but I know you left a trail somewhere an' I'm aguessin' there's blood on it. So we better understand each other. Mr. Hesketh, that little lady seen the kind of man I was, but she also seen I was in need. She come right out with it, no ifs, ands or buts, an' I like that. I really do. Now you understand this. I want nothing to happen to her. No shots in the night, no accidents, nothing like that. If I was you, Mr. Hesketh, I'd hope that little lady has a charmed life, because if she so much as stubs a toe an' hurts herself, I'm going to think it was your fault."

He turned abruptly and walked away. Hesketh stared after him, then he swore viciously, turned and walked to the stage, and getting in, settled himself in his seat.

The sandy-haired young man suddenly spoke into the darkness. "Lake up ahead. It's big and it's cold, and it's deep. Bigler's Lake some call it. Others call it Tahoe. Indians used to say there was a huge bird of some kind lived on the bottom. They called it the Ong and said it lived on human flesh. Finally it snatched some brave's sweetheart and he killed it after an awful fight."

Nobody said anything, and he lapsed into silence. And then for a long time there were only the creaking of the leather braces, the rattle of chains, and the sound of the running horses.

Jacob Teale, riding atop the stage, saw the movement. They had slowed for a last steep climb up a slight rise among the cedars. Van Sickles was not far ahead and they would soon leave the forest behind, and the trees. He had roused himself, expecting if a move was made it must be now.

He leaned forward and touched Dave on the shoulder. "No matter what, do not stop! Keep going!"

He was carrying a Merrill breech-loading Navy, a percussion rifle firing a .54-calibre cartridge. A new weapon at the time, Teale had bought it from a thief who had stolen it from a ship in the harbor. Settling down among the mail sacks and duffle bags atop the stage, he held his rifle ready. Suddenly a rider lunged from the brush and pulled up in the middle of the road. He shouted something and lifted a hand and Teale fired.

The horse leaped, the rider toppled from the saddle, and Teale drew his pistol, firing three quick shots into the brush where the rider had waited. And then they were by and racing down the trail. Hastily, Teale reloaded the rifle and then began loading the emptied chambers in the pistol.

Behind him Waggoner swore bitterly as Teem climbed from the dust, staggering and almost falling again. "Damn you!" Waggoner reined his horse around. "I told you to stop him, not to jump into the road!"

"They were ready for us," Teem said. "He blew the pommel right off my saddle! That damn' horse jumped an' I'd nothin' to hold to!"

He brushed himself off. "Hold on a minute. I'll catch my horse."

"You won't need him."

Teem pulled up short, half turning. "What? What did you say?"

He saw the starlight on the gun barrel, and Teem grabbed for his own gun. Too late he remembered it lay in the dust, where it had fallen when he was thrown. He dove into the dust, grabbing wildly for it. Waggoner turned his horse broadside to the fallen man and fired two shots into his back as he started to rise.

Turning his horse, Waggoner took a dim, little used trail that would take him across a shoulder of Monument Peak. With luck and some short cuts he might even beat the stage back to Virginia City.

The holdup had failed, but he had "paid" Teem as he was supposed to do. If his unknown employer didn't like that, he could get himself another man. Anyway, how did it happen there was a rifleman atop that stage? Had it been a trap?

No reason for a trap. He was no danger to his employer. He did not know who the man was and cared less. He did care for the money, which made his life easier than any he had ever known.

Blew the pommel off? That was shootin'! The man atop the stage was trying for a gut shot, and from the top of a bounding stage at a moving horseman, that was good shooting.

Waggoner had stabled his horse and was in a saloon having a drink when the stage came in after its stops at Van Sickle, Genoa, and Carson City. Once he had established his presence, he left the saloon and walked to his shack.

He stepped in, closed the door behind him, and stood very still; something was wrong.

Listening, he could detect no sound. After a moment he struck a match, lighting the coal-oil lamp. Nothing seemed to have been changed. He glanced into every corner, nothing.

Yet he knew what it was. The airless little cabin became very close and the air stuffy when long closed, and the air was fresh. Someone had been in the cabin, and that someone was not long gone. There was no other indication, yet he knew.

Who?

He must be careful. There might be a trap, something dangerous to him.

Waggoner put water on the stove for coffee and then looked around again, finding nothing out of place or disturbed.

He made his coffee and sat down at the oilcloth-covered table to think. He lit a cigar and gazed out the small window that afforded a glimpse of the town.

He had failed to rob the coach and get those shares, but how could he have succeeded? And who tipped them off? The first shot had been fired from the coach before Teem even lifted his voice. In other words, they were ready and waiting.

His unknown employer? It made no sense. There was no way he could be a threat to him, and he was needed.

Teem? Teem knew nothing until he told him and not much then, nor had Teem been out of his sight before the holdup.

He put down his cup suddenly and sharply. The stage was coming in. He would go down and listen to what was said. Moreover, he wanted to find out who had shot at him.

Closing the door behind him, he went down the slope, his boots crunching on the gravel. The stage was drawn up at the edge of the walk, and people were getting down.

The first person he saw was the most beautiful woman he had ever seen. He looked, then looked again. Another girl stood beside her, and two men.

Baggage was being unloaded. He strolled across the street and stood with the others who were watching, staring at the newcomers. His eyes went from one to the other, looking for a man with a rifle; he saw none.

Jacob Teale had drawn back through the crowd and was leaning against the wall, a seemingly uninterested bystander, lacking any association with the stage. Yet he saw Waggoner, caught a glimpse of him walking down the street with every indication of direction and purpose, now standing idly by, searching the crowd with his eyes, watching everybody who got off the stage.

Teale studied Waggoner with care. Now maybe, just maybe. The man had come down the street in a hurry as if he was to meet somebody, but now he was standing back and just watching. For what?

Manfred looked around. The streets were crowded, buildings were going up, there was the pound of stamp-mills and compressors. Everything spoke of money to be made.

"Isn't it exciting?" Grita exclaimed. "A real mining town!"

"There's money here," Manfred replied, "the place reeks of it. Give them entertainment and we can run forever."

She turned and for a moment her eyes touched those of Waggoner. She saw him clearly, a rough-looking, broad-shouldered man with strong jaw and cheekbones, a rock-hard face with big strong teeth.

She shuddered. "Richard, take me inside."

There was something in her voice that turned him sharply toward her. She was ashen, obviously frightened. "What's wrong? Are you ill?"

"No, just— It was that man," she said, and turned to indicate him. Waggoner was gone.

Jacob Teale was suddenly beside them. "Ma'am, if you need me, I'll be close by."

"Mr. Teale? Did you see that man? The large man who—"

"I seen him. You know him?"

"I . . . I've seen him. I'm sure of it!"

Hesketh had gone inside immediately. His apartment was here, and he went to it to change clothes. He was angry and a little frightened. He needed time to think, to plan, to do.

Everything, all he had planned for these past dozen years, was on the line. If Will Crockett learned Grita Redaway was in town and realized she had the shares, he would be relegated to second place, something he could not abide. Crockett would have him out, outside where he could do nothing.

Find Crockett somehow, and kill him. In any tight situation it was his immediate reaction, to kill whatever stood in the way, to strike out.

Nor could he take chances on Grita Redaway. She was lucky; something in him fought down the idea that she might be shrewd or clever. He would concede that to no woman. But she was lucky, and men liked to do things for her, all but him.

He would have to move fast. His chance was here. He was an important man on the Comstock. He knew nobody liked him, but that was of no importance because they feared him, and before he was through with the Comstock they would fear him even more.

If—a big if—if he could somehow get those shares. He needed control. Then he would take care of Trevallion.

Trevallion had enemies. If Waggoner couldn't bring it off, he'd find someone who could.

He dressed with meticulous care. He would dine in the main dining room tonight, alone. He would be served in princely grandeur, and she would see who he was.

He had a feeling she despised him. Well, he would show her!

He thought ahead to his next move. He had supposedly worthless claims that bordered on two of the best claims in the district. The owners were small fry. Soon, by one means or another, he would have those claims. He would avoid Hearst and the other big ones, for the time being.

For a moment he considered Crockett. The man was too trusting, but he was no fool. He was shrewd, intelligent, and not without guile.

Hesketh crossed to his desk and, getting out his key, inserted it in the lock. He turned the key, then turned it back. The desk had been unlocked!

He always locked it, and he distinctly recalled locking it before he left, yet it was now unlocked.

Somebody had been here, in this room. Somebody had opened his desk.

THIRTY-FOUR

Albert Hesketh had been born with another name in a tall two-and-a-half-story white house that stood in an empty field on the edge of town. His father was a slender, slightly bald man who clerked in a grocery store. The town itself was small, less than two thousand people.

Years later, when another name became necessary, Albert took that of one of the town's prominent families. In the town of his birth the Hesketh name had immediate identification. The Heskeths not only owned the most imposing house in town but were somehow connected with the bank as well as other enterprises. The Heskeths had no children.

Albert was a humorless child who did reasonably well in school, who made no friends and wanted none. Once, when he was seven, he was suddenly pushed over another boy's back. The boy had, unknown to Albert, dropped to hands and knees behind him and the other boy pushed him over his back. It was all in fun, but Albert's fall was shocking—to him. He leaped from the ground, and grabbing up a piece of broken board, he took a swing at the offending boy. The edge of the board caught the boy above the ear, knocked him down and out and cut his scalp. The cut necessitated several stitches, but when asked, the boy said he had fallen, and stuck to his story. Nobody ever pushed Albert again. Neither was he asked to play, to go hunting, or any of the things boys did.

His father rarely talked at the table, but when he did it was of business transactions of which he had heard and of which he always spoke enviously but seemingly without any desire to emulate them.

"Why don't you do that?" he asked his father.

"I haven't the capital," his father had replied. "It takes money to make money."

Yet later he heard men talking downtown, and one was telling how old Colonel Hesketh had made his money. "Trapped muskrats along the river," the man said, "sold his fur and bought a wagon-load of apples. He drove a rig into the country and traded those apples. Then he bought pigs and drove them to market.

"On one of his trips he saw this place, so he bought land here, built a store, and loaned money. Then he opened a bank."

Albert despised his father. His mother was a pale, sickly woman who was always "ailing." He was an only child.

At fourteen he began helping in the store. At fifteen he saw an old lady drop some money as she turned away from the counter. He picked it up and kept it. Here and there he managed to put his hands on little bits of money which he hoarded.

He hated the house he lived in and the town, and had but one desire, to be rich. Just what he would do when he was rich he had not considered. When he was sixteen, he left a back window at the store unlatched, entered in the dark, and took the money from the coffee sack in which it was hidden. He left some cans on the floor and carried away a few other things which he hid, not wanting them but to give the appearance of robbery.

When he left he broke the window near the latch to leave the appearance of forced entry.

A few days later he began inquiring for another job, and even went to a neighboring town to apply. All this was to give the appearance of a desire to move on, to better himself, so when he left no one would be surprised.

When he left he said no good-byes. He simply packed and caught a ride on a wagon as far as Pittsburgh, and then on a river boat. His first job was in Lexington, and he stayed, working as a bookkeeper and counterman in a supply store, for two years. By careful handling of purchases and accounts, he enriched himself by several hundred dollars before taking a steamboat to St. Louis.

He carried his money in a leather wallet inside his shirt. Emerging from the dining room, he started to his cabin when a roistering, loud-talking group descended upon him. "Come on! Have a l'il drink wi' us!" A man grabbed him in a rough but seemingly friendly fashion. "Come on! Join us!"

"No, thanks. I—"

It was with difficulty that he succeeded in pulling himself free of them. He got into his cabin and shut the door, then removed his coat. Suddenly his hands went to his waistband, feeling wildly about. The wallet was gone! All the money he had stolen and that which he had worked for was gone.

Rushing back to the deck, he looked wildly around. The wallet was there . . . empty!

He started for the saloon where he could hear shouts and boisterous laughter, then he stopped. Whom could he accuse? There had been seven or eight of them, perhaps more, and he had seen none of their faces because of the darkness.

In his pants pocket he had three dollars, in his cabin a carpetbag with a few items of clothing, and that was all. He dropped to his bunk and sat there, stunned.

Robbed! All his plans gone for nothing! All his carefully hoarded money *gone*!

He was swept by a blind fury. He started to his feet ready to rush out.

He stopped. Caution was what he needed. It was dark, the boat was quiet. Soon some of the men would be leaving their drinking, and if he could find one alone. . . .

It was cool and dark when he stepped outside. The deck was empty. He went to the window and peered in at the crowd around the bar. That bulky man in the broadcloth coat had been one of them, he was sure.

He would wait.

It was almost an hour before the man in the broadcloth coat staggered from the saloon and started toward his sleeping quarters. From a neat pile of wood for the saloon stove, Albert chose a stick, then quickly he went down the passage after him. Hearing footsteps, the man had started to turn when Albert struck him.

The man fell to his knees and Albert struck him again. A quick glance again to right and left, and he went through the man's pockets.

A five-dollar gold piece, no more.

Dragging the man to the side of the boat, Albert dumped him over. As the man hit the cold water there was a faint cry. If he was not conscious enough and a good swimmer, the stern wheel would take care of him.

There was no further chance. The others emerged in groups and went down the deck, lurching from side to side, arguing and protesting over something.

At last he went to bed, sleepless because of the sullen rage that gnawed at him.

He waited on the deck with the others, baggage in hand, while the steamboat pulled in to the dock at St. Louis. The talk around him was all of California, of the fortunes to be made in mining.

A man standing near him looked around suddenly. "Say! I don't see Sam. Suppose he overslept?"

Another man turned and started back toward the cabins. "I'll look. His wife will be waiting for him on the dock, with the kids."

Moments later, he came running back. "He's not there and his bunk's not been slept in!"

"What?" A ship's officer was nearby and the man went to him. Listening, Albert heard only a few words. "He wasn't drunk. Drinking, yes, but not drunk. Made this trip all the time. Moving to St. Louis now."

A low mumble from the officer, then the man replied. "Quite a lot, actually. Carried it in a moneybelt around his waist. Must've been a couple of thousand dollars."

Albert swore, softly, bitterly. *All that money? And he had missed it. Gone now, gone for good.*

All landing was stopped. One by one the passengers were questioned. Albert answered simply and directly. One of the bystanders said, "He left early, turned in. I saw him leave, so he wasn't even around when it happened."

"I was tired," Albert said.

One of the men turned his head and glanced at him, his brow puckered a little, but he said nothing.

"Fell overboard," the officer finally decided. "Happens all the time. A man's been having a few and he's walking down the deck, boat gives a little lurch and he falls. Too bad."

In St. Louis he found a job clerking in a store, and within a week he understood how things worked and was stealing, very little at first, then as his confidence increased, he stepped up what he was taking. Suddenly and without warning he was discharged. The owner simply said, "Take your money and get out. Don't come back, even as a customer. Just keep going."

He asked no questions, made no protests. He was getting off easy and knew it, yet it worried him in that he had no idea of how he had erred.

He found another job the following day and was careful to do everything correctly. He worked hard, became a skilled buyer of furs and hides, and learned all aspects of the business. Not knowing how much communication there was among various businessmen, he was careful to arouse no suspicion. He was a meticulous worker, keeping neat, exact books, and he made several suggestions that increased the business and cut the costs.

The great days of the fur trade were long past, but the trade in hides was just coming into its own. On Albert's advice the firm branched out into the sale of harness, saddles, and farm equipment of various kinds. He received a modest raise in salary, and he accepted it with thanks, mentally sneering at the amount. Meanwhile he read all he could find about mining and about California.

He became aware that the owner rarely made more than a cursory check of the inventory which fluctuated rapidly, so he began setting aside bundles of prime furs, buying at lower and lower prices from trappers who were in debt to the firm, and entering their purchase at the usual cost. By manipulating shipments he soon built a secret cache of bales of valuable furs, which did not exist on the books but which remained in the cellar warehouse. Nothing was missing from the premises, but he had secreted a large amount of valuable merchandise to be shipped at his discretion. If found, he would merely claim he knew nothing about them, and it had been some kind of oversight.

Men were growing rich in the mines, and Albert wanted to be among them, but he would need capital to invest. To work in the mines, to actually work with shovel and pan was no part of his plan of action.

As another winter drew to a close, he made his decision. He would go west in the spring. He would have his own wagon, his own supplies. Not only what he would need, but enough to sell when he arrived. The problem now was to get those bales of furs out of the cellar and to dispose of them.

Months before he had chosen his buyer, a greedy man not disposed to ask questions. Delivery of the furs was promised and arranged for, and Albert gave his notice.

He had talked of going to California, and many were going, so his decision occasioned no surprise.

Even at the low state of the market, the furs he had secretly stored would come to eight or nine thousand dollars.

Over a drink in a cheap saloon he asked the buyer, "Franz? Can you take delivery of those furs tonight?"

"Tonight?" Franz looked into his glass. "Why not?"

"I'll get a dray to haul them around," Albert suggested.

Franz waved a dismissing gesture. "I've my own man. I'll send him around whenever you like."

"You will have the money? I shall want cash."

"Of course."

Albert Hesketh was pleased. He would go to California in style. There would be no charges against him, all would be smooth, neat, and well handled.

At eight o'clock the streets near the warehouse were dark and silent. At ten the dray pulled up, and helped by the drayman, the bales of furs were loaded on the dray. As the dray pulled off, Albert started on his way to the saloon.

He went in, ordered a drink, and sat down to wait, and wait.

After fifteen minutes he began to fidget, after thirty he was up, peering out the window.

He waited for another hour, then two hours. Franz never appeared. Furious, Albert Hesketh went around to the hotel where Franz lived. He was sitting in the bar, holding a stein of beer.

"Sit down! Sit down!" Franz waved a hand toward a chair. "Where are your furs? We waited, and waited, but they never showed up."

"Don't tell me that!" Albert was ugly. "Your man took them. He had them all on his dray."

"On *my* dray? *My* driver? Well, I'll be damned! Maybe that's why he never showed up!" Franz sipped his beer complacently. "Just like I was saying to your boss the other day. You just don't know who to trust.

"I was asking him," he added, "if he had any prime fur for sale. He said he hadn't any right now, and he was sorry because he could use the sale."

Franz sipped his beer, wiped his mustache with the back of his hand, and then said, "I think you've been tryin' to trick me. You never had no fur. I've got your boss's word for it." His blue eyes were bland and smiling. "Well, better luck next time."

"Damn you! I'll—"

Franz waved a hand toward four men standing at the bar watching them. "If I were you I would just take a walk, a good long walk. If those boys got the idea you were thinking of getting rough . . . not that I couldn't handle you."

For a moment he sat there, trembling with suppressed fury. He wanted to get up, he wanted to tear the man to bits, he wanted to smash and smash and smash.

But Franz was larger, stronger, and the four men at the bar left him no choice.

He stood up, taking a long slow look at Franz. "All right," he said quietly. "All right."

He walked out and Franz looked after him, suddenly worried. One of the men came over. "Everything all right?"

"All right. Only I'd rather he had threatened me. Struck at me, something."

THIRTY-FIVE

O ver his wine in the hotel dining room in Virginia City, Albert Hesketh's eyes were hard with satisfaction, remembering that night. By dawn he had been miles on his way to Westport, behind him the sky was ablaze with fire.

That was the night Franz Halbert's warehouse burned with over a hundred thousand in furs and hides. Surprisingly, a steamboat and barge belonging to Halbert also caught fire, although they were moored a half-mile from the warehouse.

A St. Louis paper, read in Westport, informed him that Franz Halbert was wiped out by his losses. That the fire had spread and destroyed other warehouses was, to Albert Hesketh, inconsequential.

Yet he had been uncertain of what to do or how to move with the little money he had with him—until he saw the man with the gold.

Ancient gold coins, one at least a Spanish coin; where that was, there must be more. The man had undoubtedly come upon treasure.

That had proved a disappointment, for the man had no treasure, only a small handful of gold coins and objects along with a couple of small gems. Yet it had proved enough to outfit Hesketh for California and to establish him once there. Moreover, there had been something left which, hoarded, had given him his start toward controlling the Comstock.

Now he must think. He must plan. The Solomon was now controlled by him and he must keep that control, no matter what it cost. Only the shares of stock he believed to be in the hands of Grita Redaway were needed. True, he had not seen them. He merely surmised their presence in her hands, for it was she who should have inherited them.

Trevallion's filing on the adjoining claim was infuriating but no more than that. Trevallion was merely greedy for himself or had some childish notion of saving something for Crockett; in either case he could be handled or gotten rid of.

Suddenly uneasy, he shifted in his chair and refilled his wine glass. The trouble was not what Trevallion had done, but that *he* had done it. Was there some unrealized purpose behind it?

No matter. He would destroy them. Judge Terry might be the means. Terry was a shrewd, intelligent man somewhat blinded by his passions and his purposes. Terry wanted the gold and silver of the Comstock for the Confederacy. Even now he was plotting to seize it all.

If he tried there would be trouble, and knowing the men of the Comstock for what they were, probably shooting trouble. In the shooting Trevallion could be killed and his property seized and eventually new claims staked. So the thing to do was to help Terry. Quietly, secretly, with men and with guns.

A good meal and two glasses of wine and he felt better. True, he had failed to get the shares of stock, but they were probably here, and for the time being, Will Crockett was not. And that meant he had time, not much time, but some.

He was rising to leave when Grita Redaway came in, flanked by Dane Clyde and Richard Manfred. All heads turned as she was escorted to her table by the waiter. Her eyes caught his and he bowed slightly, then left the room. Grita Redaway had arrived on the Comstock and there was no question about it, she was radiantly beautiful.

Hesketh paused at the entrance, wondering why his heart was beating so rapidly.

PART FOUR

THIRTY-SIX

Sun Mountain had caught the first light of dawn when Trevallion came down the slope to the bakery. Ledbetter and Tapley were already seated with their coffee, awaiting breakfast. Melissa was nowhere around at this hour.

"Hear that Alf something-or-other is sparkin' her," Tapley commented. "She's doing well and honey draws flies."

"Ask Ledbetter about him," Trevallion suggested, "she's too good for him."

"Hesketh is back," Ledbetter said. "Came in on the stage last night with those show folks. The way he was dressed you'd of thought he was a miner. That Dane Clyde come back with them, too."

"I heard that Redaway woman is a looker," Tapley said. "I talked to a man saw them gettin' down from the stage."

"Odd," Trevallion said, "Hesketh dressed that way. He was never a miner, and never dressed like one."

"They had trouble," Tapley said. "Old Pot Joe tried to stand them up an' that Redaway girl backed him down."

"She what?"

"Seems she was armed, and so were several of those inside and when they presented their side of the argument Joe got the point and stepped back. There was another shooting after, somebody else seemed to have the same idea Joe did, but Jacob Teale was riding the top and he cut loose. That took care of that."

"Jacob Teale?"

Tapley shrugged. "Seems that show woman hired him on the trail. She just taken one look and put him on the payroll."

"Teale?" Ledbetter shook his head. "Well, I'll be damned."

"What's she want with a man like him?" Trevallion asked.

"There's but one reason for hiring Jacob Teale. You've got trouble and lots of it. But how did she know about him?"

Tapley spat. "She didn't. No way she could have. She just seen him and hired him, it's simple as that."

Ledbetter glanced over at Trevallion. "You know him, Trev?"

"I know him."

The coffee tasted good. He tasted it again and returned the cup to the saucer. Grita Redaway—unusual name, and could be the same girl. Waggoner had been out of town but would be back, by the looks of his cabin. Would he know who she was? Unlikely. But would she recognize Waggoner? That was unlikely, too, but he had been around the wagons a few times, and she could have seen him.

Anyway, she wouldn't need any help. A girl with the sense to hire Teale would do all right. He frowned. Why had she done it? Right quick like that? How could an actress, a city woman, have the sense to hire *him*? Had it been an accident, that she chose Teale? And why did she think he was needed?

Jacob Teale was odd. He was a peculiar man by anybody's standards, a solitary hunter, a killer as cold and remorseless as any he had ever known, but a religious, church-going man with a code right out of the Old Testament. He rarely took a drink, chewed tobacco occasionally and was never known to curse, at least not aloud.

Once up in the Modoc country they had been in an Indian fight together. Seven of them, all prospectors, had been trapped by a war party of young bucks out for some excitement. Two of the seven had been killed at the first volley and then it settled down to a daylong battle at long range.

During the night the others, believing Teale and Trevallion dead, had slipped away. The fight continued through another long, hot day, and then the Modocs, tiring of the game, pulled out and left them. Teale had been down to his last two cartridges, and Trevallion's rifle had but one ball left. He did have a pair of six-shooters with extra cylinders, however.

Their horses gone, they had to make their way out afoot, and twice on that trek back Trevallion had killed game with his six-shooter, the first time a big-horn at better than fifty yards. The shot had gone in behind the ear, dropping the animal in its tracks.

Teale had looked at it, glancing up. "Could have been an accident."

"It wasn't," Trevallion replied.

A few days later, short of meat again, he killed a mule deer with an identical shot. Teale looked at it, smiled slightly, and said, "I can believe in one accident, not two."

After a pause he said, "Wouldn't you say that was chancy? Wouldn't you say behind the left foreleg or a neck shot would be better?"

"Under normal conditions, yes. But I've seen a deer run a quarter of a mile after being shot right through the heart. Neither you nor me are up to a long chase right now, so I figured to drop them right where they stood."

Teale nodded. "Makes sense."

A few days later Teale killed a deer with a shot in the same place. He gestured at it. "An accident, maybe?"

"Could be," Trevallion said seriously. "If it happens again it will be no accident."

He had seen Teale only once or twice since. Each time they had but nodded or waved. He had begun hearing stories about Jacob Teale before that, and a time or two he had seen him in church.

Odd that Grita Redaway should choose him that way, obviously seeing something there that she trusted, or preferred to have on her side.

Restlessly he moved in his chair, glancing up the street. The town was booming, and he had a feeling he should be out and doing, but there were things to be resolved. Should he go to Grita Redaway? He was sure she was the same person as the little girl he had known, and she still must be very young, but when people had to shift for themselves they matured early. Look at Melissa, operating a growing, expanding business, and several successful mine operators whom he knew were not yet twenty. It was a time when you made it quick or you might not make it at all.

He glanced at Ledbetter. The freighter had changed. He was better groomed these days, wearing better clothes, was seen with Hearst, Mackay, Fair, and the others who were moving ahead on the Comstock.

Trevallion got up, and with a brief wave of the hand, walked out on the street. For a moment he hesitated, glancing up and down. Then he went back to his own mine and went to work.

Long ago when in the mountains he had staked some timber claims, and considering the way the Comstock was using timber, they could be worth a mint. He finished drilling the round, then loaded the holes, lit the fuses, and came on top. When he heard the boom of his shots he counted them.

Good, no missed holes. Yet it would take awhile to allow the powder smoke to dissipate. He had had too many headaches from breathing powder smoke in a confined space to want another.

For a week he rarely left the mine or his cabin. The vein was growing wider, the ore richer. With Tapley's help he made a small shipment, then another. Milling was no longer a problem as there were dozens, newly built, and hard at work. It was Tapley brought him word that Grita Redaway's play was to open.

"You need to get out of this hole," Tapley said. "Ledbetter's got himself a box at the theater and he wants you to join him."

"Maybe." He paused. "Is Teale still around?"

"He's here." Tapley bit off a chew and rolled it in his jaws. "Gets around, he does. And mighty quiet about it. What kind of a man is he, anyway?"

"You've known his kind, Tap, but he's an odd one. He lives by the Book, up to a point. Or maybe it's just that he reads it his own way. I've traveled with him, worked and fought beside him. He's good at any of it, but if he thinks a man needs killing, he'll kill him. He will take money for a killing, but only if he thinks it needs doing."

"No sign of Will Crockett. There's talk around that he may have killed himself, or been killed."

"I don't believe he'd kill himself."

"Nor me. Hesketh eats supper every night at the hotel. He's moving ahead. Bought a mill that was having trouble and he's milling his own ore."

Tapley got up. "What will I tell Ledbetter?"

"I'll be there. Meet him at the bakery."

When Tap was gone he went and got out his black broadcloth suit. It was wrinkled from being packed, so he heated up a tea kettle and when it was steaming, held the spout close to the suit and slowly worked the wrinkles out, with much reheating of the water, moving the spout up and down over the fabric.

Then he got out a white shirt and a collar, collar buttons, and cuff links. He hadn't been dressed up in over a year, the last time for a funeral.

He never missed a theatrical performance when he was in the area, and having a quick, accurate memory, he had learned parts of the plays from often hearing them. His reading consisted of whatever books or magazines were floating around the mining camps, which was generally good literature. Coming west in a wagon where every ounce of weight must be carefully judged, those who brought books brought the best, those which would stand continual rereading.

Leaving his cabin, he took a path that led between buildings and across lots to the bakery and was just emerging on the street when two men rode past.

Abruptly, he stopped. They were dusty from the trail, and their horses showed signs of hard travel. They passed him only a few feet away and one of the men had a missing little finger and a bad scar on his hand.

It was a hand one would not forget.

THIRTY-SEVEN

The hall was crowded, with every seat filled. About one of every twenty was a woman. Trevallion followed Ledbetter, who was following the usher to a box at one side of the theater, if such it could be called. In a space suitable for four chairs, there were seven.

John Mackay was seated in a box across the theater. He nodded briefly. Jim Fair was with him.

Langford Peel strode down the aisle and took a seat in the third row, and one by one they filed in and took their places, the rich and the ones becoming rich, the bold, the dangerous, the acquisitive, the boisterous, and the shy.

Trevallion glanced around, looking for Jacob Teale, but there was no sign of him. No doubt he was backstage. Trevallion found a seat at the back of the box and against the wall. Ledbetter looked around as he sat down. "I hear this Margrita Redaway is a handsome woman," he said.

"I don't think I've ever seen her," Trevallion's tone was mild. "Dane Clyde spoke of her."

"He's in the company," Ledbetter gestured toward the stage.

Trevallion glanced around at the crowd. He was uneasy, but that was probably because he did not like crowds, and never had. There were familiar faces, and a few strange ones.

Bill Stewart, the attorney, came in. A big, broad-shouldered man with a shock of red hair. He glanced about, glimpsed Trevallion, and walked across the back of the theater and came over to the box. Dozens of people were coming and going or merely standing and talking. Stewart stopped by the box, glanced around, and then said, "How's things, Jim?"

Ledbetter nodded. "Good enough. Snow on the pass already."

"There's going to be trouble, Jim. Terry's got something on his mind."

"The war. That's all he talks about."

"It has to do with that." Stewart glanced at Trevallion. "Where do you stand, Trevallion?"

231

"I've never become involved in politics," he replied mildly. "I'm a Cornishman."

"You're a citizen, though?"

"I am. And pleased to be one. What's the problem?"

"Lincoln's going to need help. Are you Union or Confederate?"

"I'm for the Union, Bill. It took awhile to put this country together. It would be a shame to tear it apart, no matter what the reason."

Stewart rolled his cigar in his jaws. "They tell me you can use a gun and that you'll stand your ground. I'll need some good men."

"You can count on me," Ledbetter replied.

"I'd have to know more about it," Trevallion said. "When a man uses a gun he'd better have a good reason, even if he does have a good lawyer."

"What I have to do will be done with the sanction of President Lincoln, and at this juncture it is very important to his program and our victory. All I want is to keep trouble off my back for a few hours, maybe less.

"Ordinarily I fight my own battles, but this time I will be busy and I don't want to be interrupted."

"When you can, tell me about it. All about it. If it is legitimate, you can count on me."

After Stewart had gone, Ledbetter said, "He's a good man, Trev. One of the best."

"I agree, but I let no man make my decisions for me. Not when it comes to what's right or wrong. When there's law, I obey the law. When there is no law I follow my conscience."

He glanced around. "They've a full house, certainly. What is the play?"

"It's been suddenly changed, I hear. They will play *Francesca da Rimini*. Why the change, I do not know."

He knew the play and liked it. If Margrita was playing Francesca, as he assumed, she would not appear until the second act. Dane Clyde he recognized at once, although appearing as an older man and made up accordingly.

At the end of the first act, a waiter came around to take orders for drinks. He was ordering a beer when he happened to look past the waiter's shoulder and saw Waggoner.

The big, rawboned man had come in, sitting down across the aisle and two rows ahead of where Trevallion sat. The seat had been empty throughout the first act.

The curtain went up on a scene between the Cardinal and Guido, Francesca's father, and a moment later, Francesca entered.

Trevallion was startled. She was a beautiful woman, but beyond a doubt it was the same Grita he remembered.

As an actress her style was different, lacking the bombast and extravagant gestures of the other players. He scarcely heard the play through watching her. Although he knew it well, he had never heard it played as it was by this company. Moreover, the costumes were new, colorful, and a complete change from the worn and tattered costumes so many traveling companies possessed.

He had papers that belonged to her, yet he found himself curiously hesitant to meet her. What could he say? He had known a frightened little girl, and this was a woman, beautiful, accomplished, and accustomed to a life far from mining camps and the cold streams where men washed for gold.

If she remembered him at all, it would be a memory associated with horror.

Should he go backstage? There was small chance he would be admitted to see her. How then? At her hotel?

A man naturally reticent, he found himself even more so now. In his own world he was prepared for any situation that might arise. He had hunted, trapped, prospected for gold, defended himself; he had planned long journeys, coped with the wilderness. He had mined and was knowledgeable about ores, timber construction, shafts, winzes, raises, and the new square-sets, but he had no formal education, and his awareness of her world was from his limited reading only.

Yet what had he to do? Deliver some papers that indicated her possession of certain properties, that was all. Nothing more was needed than what any messenger might perform.

In his own world he was known, respected for his courage and his abilities; in her world all that counted for nothing.

He was scarcely aware of the play, well as it was done. She was good, far better than he had expected, perhaps better than anyone he had seen. She had presence, making the whole play seem suddenly exciting and alive.

The man who played Lanciotto seemed strangely familiar. Sitting up, he leaned forward; what was it about him? Dane Clyde was there, playing Malatesta, the father of Lanciotto, in rather heavy makeup, but Lanciotto? Why should he seem familiar?

The play ended and they filed out onto the street. He stopped, looking around. Should he go backstage?

Ledbetter glanced at him sharply. Then he said, "She's good, isn't she?"

"Very good. Very, very good."

"She'll do well on the Comstock. Been a long time since we've seen a woman that beautiful." Then he added, "I was surprised not to see Hesketh. He rarely misses a play, and he knows her. Rode over from Frisco on the same stage."

"I wouldn't know him if I saw him. I don't believe we ever met."

"Hesketh? God knows he's at supper every night at the hotel. Makes a thing of it, he does."

"I rarely go there." There was no use trying to see her, anyway. Her papers were back at the cabin, hidden with some belongings of his own.

"Want some coffee?" Ledbetter asked.

"Not tonight. I'm going to get to bed. Thanks, though."

He turned and walked away up the street. Tapley came up and joined Ledbetter. "I seen the play. Good, wasn't it?"

"It was." He jerked his head toward Trevallion. "I wonder if anything is wrong? He seemed preoccupied."

"He better not be," Tapley replied. "Waggoner's back in town and so is Hesketh."

Grita Redaway was dressed and adjusting her hair when Dane Clyde knocked and entered. "You made quite a hit out there tonight."

"We all did, Mr. Clyde. They seemed to like us."

"They're hungry for entertainment, and especially any show with beautiful women. They see too few of them and they're far from home. That's why Lotta has been so successful, ever since she was a child. She played mining camps where those men hadn't seen a child in months, maybe years. And many of them had youngsters at home. They used to give her nuggets, dust—everything."

"Let's hope they haven't changed," she said. "Have you seen Mr. Manfred?"

"He'll be along. We thought we'd both better walk you and Mary back to the hotel. This can be a rough town."

He paused. "Oh, by the way. That friend of mine was out front tonight. Trevallion? He was sitting toward the back of the lower box on the right."

"Oh? I saw him then. I was looking at the audience before the curtain went up, a dark man in a black suit?"

"That's the one. He was a good friend when I needed one."

She made no reply. Together they went to the stage door. Manfred was waiting there. He gestured to indicate the town. "Look at that! The streets are crowded and it's nearly midnight. It's easy to see why Tom Maguire wants a theater here! The town's booming!"

"It should be," Clyde said. "They are taking millions from the ground! The Ophir, the Potosi, the Hale & Norcross—there's a dozen more, all taking out tons of ore, and listen to the stamps. They never stop, day or night, crushing ore to be sent through the mills."

"Why here?" Grita asked.

Clyde shrugged. "It just happens that way. If what I hear is correct, there was a huge fissure formed ages ago, from an earthquake, volcanic explosion, or something of the kind. I'm no geologist. Hot springs shot steam, mineral water, and gas up through the fissure and they brought along with them, in solution, a lot of silver. The fissure was about four miles long and from fifteen hundred down to less than three hundred feet wide. There were a lot of cracks that broke off from the sides of the main fissure and they filled up, too. Chunks of rock from the mountain fell into the fissure, dividing into sections here and there. They're saying here it is one of the greatest mineral discoveries in history."

"Did you ever do any mining, Mr. Manfred?"

"No," he said, after a minute, "although I planned to."

"Can we go into a mine?" she asked.

Clyde shook his head. "I doubt it. Most miners think women are bad luck in a mine, but some have gone down. You wouldn't like it. It's steaming hot, muddy, and in some of these mines there's clay that keeps oozing up through the cracks. It breaks timbers, forces its way in, and if it isn't constantly removed it would fill a tunnel in time."

"I wish . . . I'd like to walk down the street. Is it safe?"

A voice came from the shadows near the theater's entrance. "It will be safe, ma'am."

"Oh! Mr. Teale!"

"Yes, ma'am. You go where you're of a mind to. I'll be somewheres near."

"Thank you." She turned to the others. "Mr. Clyde? Mr. Manfred? Shall we?"

At every step there seemed to be a saloon or a dance hall humming like bells with loud talk, laughter, and tin-panny music. Batwing doors swung wide and a man, obviously drunk, staggered onto the walk. He saw Grita Redaway and blinked, then he stepped back and with elaborate courtesy doffed his hat and made a deep bow. "Madam, your carriage awaits!"

"Thank you, sir!" she said, laughing.

They walked on down the boardwalk and men moved back as they approached. One man also removed his hat and bowed slightly. "A fine performance, Miss Redaway. We are honored."

"Thank you," she replied, smiling.

A step or two further, Dane Clyde said, "You *have* been honored. That was Langford Peel."

"Who is he? I don't know the name?"

"He's the 'Chief' as they call him. Supposedly the best man with a gun on the Comstock. He's killed several men. He was a soldier, I think, before that."

"The best man with a gun? Is he what they call a gunfighter?"

"Very much so."

Teale spoke quietly. "He ain't the best, an' he doesn't claim it. He's just handled what trouble came his way, and never hunted it to the best of my knowledge. Anyway, he ain't the best man with a gun on the Comstock."

"No?" Manfred asked. "Who is?"

"Trevallion is. I've seen him in action."

Grita paused and turned toward him. "You have seen him kill a man?"

"Yes, ma'am, although he don't know it himself, and I never mentioned it to no one. It was a man needed killing."

"Was that over a card game? I've heard stories of that," Clyde said.

"No, but I heard about that. Caught a man cheatin'."

"There was more to it," Manfred put in. "Some words passed between them, something relating to Missouri."

Grita Redaway thought for a moment her heart had stopped beating. She swallowed. "Missouri?"

"Some old grudge. Some say Trevallion knew he would cheat and wanted an excuse to kill him. Well, he done it."

THIRTY-EIGHT

S he waited a moment, wanting to know yet almost afraid to ask. "You said you saw him kill a man?"

"Yes, ma'am," Teale said. "It was out on the trail. I'd headed for the settlements and was plumb beat, so I just turned off the trail into the brush, staked my horse out of sight, and bedded down.

"A horse comin' along the trail woke me. Then there was another horse from the other direction. Well, ma'am, I got enemies here and there, so made out to ready myself for trouble.

"I could see them plain. One of them was Obie Skinner. He was a runnin' mate of that man who was killed over the card game, I don't recall his name. That Skinner was a bad one, real bad. He wasn't afeered of anything, and he was almighty good with a gun.

"The other one was Trevallion. It was that Missouri thing again. Trevallion brung it up and Skinner went for a gun. I'd of bet my shirt on him but he didn't have no more show than a jack-rabbit at a coyote picnic. Trevallion blew him out of his saddle."

"Please," she turned to Manfred and Clyde. "I'd like to go back to the hotel now."

In the lobby she turned suddenly to Teale. "Mr. Teale? Will you sit down with me, please? I want to ask you a few questions."

She turned to Manfred and Clyde. "Thank you, gentlemen. Tomorrow, then? At the theater?"

"If you'd like us to wait?" Clyde suggested.

"No, I will be all right. I just thought of something I've been wanting to know about mines. Mr. Teale can tell me, I'm sure."

When they were gone, she turned to Teale. "Will you sit down, please?" When they were seated she said, "You are an interesting man, Mr. Teale, and a curious man, are you not?"

"Whatever a body knows can't hurt him an' may be a help. When I'm hunting buffalo, I try to learn a buffalo's habits. It's the same with beaver."

"And men?"

"Yes, ma'am. Men have their ways, too, an' each one a mite different. I try to know the ones who might be trouble for me."

"Like Trevallion?"

"Yes, ma'am. But he will never be a trouble to me. He's a good man."

"He's killed men?"

"So have I, ma'am. Sometimes it's necessary. Sometimes they invite it, comin' at folks the way they do. I don't look for men to shoot unless they are comin' at folks. Then I take steps."

"Trevallion?"

"I listen well, ma'am, and sometimes I prompt. I sort of nudge folks who might know something. Trevallion killed those men for something happened a long time back. Well, there was a man kept a trading post down off the mountain. Been there a long time. He's gone now. Sold out. But he knew Trevallion when he was a boy. Knew his pa.

"Seems Trevallion's pa was killed by some men who come ridin' in, Trevallion's pa got two of them but they killed him. They'd have killed Trevallion, he was just a lad, if they had time, but folks was acomin'. They taken out."

"Do you know what was behind it?"

"Yes, ma'am. Trevallion's pa told this man who ran the trading post some of it. He got more from some who came across the plains with him. Seems Trevallion's ma and another woman had been set on an' killed back in Missouri. That other woman's husband was killed, too."

"How well do you know Trevallion?"

"Sort of. We come down the trail together a time or two. He ain't one to talk. Minds his own affairs. Does his share an' a mite more." Teale looked up at her suddenly. "Ma'am, I'd not say this to many, but I size a man up. I say if that thing had not happened back there in Missouri, Trevallion would be one of the biggest men on the Comstock. He knows mines and he's sharp. He's got it in him."

"Does he have so much hate in him then?"

"Maybe, maybe that's it, but maybe it is something else. Maybe it is just that he doesn't want evil to go unpunished and be free to commit other evils."

"So he takes the law into his own hands?"

"Where there's law, I say let the law handle it, but out in wild country like that, ma'am, out in wild country where there's no law, a man has to be the law. He has to administer justice.

"This here's a fine, big, beautiful country, and men like Bill Stewart are bringing law into it, but they've got a ways to go, and they cannot punish crimes that taken place far away and long ago."

"I see." She stood up. "Thank you, Mr. Teale. I wanted to know. Please do not mention the subject of our conversation."

"No, ma'am."

She turned away, then paused. "Mr. Teale? What will Trevallion do now?"

He shrugged. "Kill the rest of 'em, although I think he's kind of out of the notion."

"Out of the notion? Why do you say that?"

"Because there's at least one of them in town. He knows it an' he ain't killed him." He hesitated, looking around for a spittoon. He found it, spat, and then added, "Fact is, two more of them just rode in, and he doesn't know *that*."

"Why? Why do they come here? Now?"

"That I don't know, ma'am. I only know they come in, bold as brass, and by now they will have found Waggoner."

"Waggoner?"

"He was one of them, ma'am. One of that crowd back in Missouri. He was there in the crowd tonight. I seen him."

"At the theater? Watching my show?"

"Yes, ma'am. He was there. Trevallion seen him, too." He paused. "Ma'am? I don't figure to scare you, you bein' the kind of woman you are, but Waggoner didn't take his seat until just before the second act. He sat down just before you come on stage."

She was silent, thinking. After a moment she got up. "Thank you, Mr. Teale. You have been most helpful. I am not frightened, and I wish always to know when there may be trouble. Otherwise, how can I prepare for it? I had believed myself a bystander, now I realize this is not the case. He must be aware of me. He must know something about me, or want something I have."

"Ma'am, don't you worry. I'll be around. Them others, those actors? Will they stand?"

"I believe they will, Mr. Teale."

"That one? The tallest one? I seem to have seen him someplace before."

"It isn't likely, unless you've been to the theater in other places than the frontier." She paused. "Thank you, Mr. Teale. And good night."

Alone in her room, Margrita—she had dropped the Marguerita long since, shortening it and making it simpler—undressed and prepared for bed. Looking at herself in the mirror, she thought of what had taken place.

She was, she supposed, a beautiful woman. She had been told so often enough in the past few years but was unimpressed by it. The world in which she had grown up had been one where talent and intelligence counted for much more than beauty, and the idea of being beautiful was one that had never impressed her.

Now she was asking herself why she had come here. Had she not been doing well enough abroad? Well, to tell the truth, no. Not as well as she wished, nor as well as she must. As much as she loved the theater, it was a means to an end rather than a way of life. She wanted to find a place for herself, a place where she belonged, that was hers.

From all she had heard, the quickest way to some sort of financial security was in western America. Now she was no longer sure. Jenny Lind had found great success in America, but hers was a special case. The same was true of Lotta, who had done well and, thanks to her watchful mother, had kept most of what she had gotten.

Of course, part of it might be the wish to complete something she had begun, or her parents had begun. They had started west, to find a new home in California. It had been a dream, a dream they had all shared, and a dream suddenly aborted on that awful night.

Yet she was here. If not in California, she was as close as one could be, and she had already made up her mind it was to California she would return.

Tonight had been good. They had played to a packed house, and they were sold out for the week. True, the La Plata Hall was not large, and the makeshift boxes she had installed were not much of a help. She must vary her bills and she would need another woman, an older woman. The new costumes had been a good idea, even if it had cost her a good bit; the people liked the glitter and color.

Waggoner, who *was* he? Why was he interested in her? The old nagging memory was there, of a face once seen, of someone who had stared at her mother back on the streets of Missouri, of being frightened.

She shook her head to dispel the memory. Absurd. It was some fancied resemblance. Yet, why was he interested in *her*? Was he somehow tied in with those attempted robberies? But those had been in San Francisco.

She turned out the gas and started for bed, then she stopped and walked to the window, looking down into the dimly lit street.

The saloons were still open, casting some light across the boardwalks; there was still a sound of music, and between numbers she could hear the rattle of poker chips.

The pound of the compressors was like the pound of her heart. Even up here, even at this hour, she could feel the excitement, the restlessness, the eagerness.

She wanted to be down there in the street, she wanted to be part of it. She wanted to own a mine, to see the silver ore coming to the surface, to see it being milled. Impatiently, she turned to her bed and got under the covers, realizing for the first time how cold it was up here at night.

She lay still, then turned on her side and closed her eyes. They opened suddenly.

That boy, he was a man now. He was Trevallion. Didn't he have a first name? Nobody called him anything but Trevallion.

He had been in the theater, why had he not come around to see her? It was not as if they were strangers. Well, not completely strangers. And what of that money of hers he was taking care of? He might at least give her an accounting.

It probably wasn't much. All gone now, no doubt. Anyway, he would not remember her after all these years. Why should he? They had been children. It was silly of her to even—

He might be married!

She punched her pillow into a different shape. Well, what if he was?

Trevallion, the name had a sound to it. But what was a name? It meant nothing until you made it mean something, just like you yourself were only what you made yourself become.

But Trevallion did have a sound, and that was because it stood for something to the men who spoke it.

Those mining shares she had were for some company in California. Did someone tell her that company was now operating here? Maybe she was already in the mining business!

Trevallion took a roundabout route back to the cabin, and before entering, he checked the thread he had tied across the tunnel mouth. It was still there.

He unlocked his door and stepped inside. A small fire still showed red ashes in the stove. He added a few sticks, stirred it up, and sat down on the edge of the bunk to pull off his boots.

A beautiful woman . . . a beautiful, beautiful woman!

And a fine actress. Not really the best he had seen, but close to it. And she had a way about her, the way she moved, the way she talked.

He checked his gun as he did every night and placed it on the chair beside his bed. He put his boots close, too. He always kept some clothing ready to hand, and had ever since that earthquake in '57, when he was down in the Tehachapi country.

Waggoner, should he call him?

He had been one of them and he had tried to kill him; now he was watching her. But he could not guess that she had been there. Waggoner would not even know there was a little girl.

Suddenly there was a sharp rap on the door. He lifted up on one elbow, his hand reaching out for his gun. "All right, what is it?"

It was Tapley. "Didn't want to bother you, but there's going to be trouble in court in the morning. Bill Stewart's got one of Sam Brown's friends on trial, and Sam says he's going to run the jury clear out of the country. You know Bill won't stand for that."

"I'll be there."

Sam Brown—well, it was time. Trevallion turned over and closed his eyes. If he knew Bill Stewart, Bill wouldn't need any help.

Not even with Sam Brown.

THIRTY-NINE

Trevallion was saddling the black mule when Tapley came into the stable. "Jim's joinin' us as we ride through town," Tapley explained. "A couple of the other boys rode down last night."

"They're trying the case in Genoa?"

"That's right. Sam Brown's been loud talking about what he'll do to that court, and he's taking a bunch with him."

Ledbetter was waiting outside the bakery. He stepped into the saddle, and they rode rapidly out of Virginia City and down the mountain. The morning was cold, the sky clear, and the stars very bright. Nobody talked.

"What d' you want us to do, Trev?" Tapley asked.

"Stewart will have to deal with Brown. If anybody starts to interfere we'll stop them. Keep your eyes on the crowd."

"Stewart's got nerve. He'd charge hell with a bucket of water." Ledbetter spat. "He's about six-two and he weighs maybe one-ninety. He's a Yale man who took his postgraduate courses in the toughest mining camps in California. When this Territory gets to be a state, he's the man we want for senator, or governor."

The courtroom was crowded when they entered. Standing along the wall on either side of the door, they could observe all those who were seated before them. Sam Brown had deliberately taken a seat in the first row where he could glower at the jurors.

One of the Brown faction looked around as they came in and nudged the man beside him. Both turned to look. Trevallion hooked his thumb behind his belt a few inches from his pistol butt. He did not look at the Brown men when he did so, but he knew they were watching.

Judge Cradlebaugh was presiding. He did not like Sam Brown, nor was he afraid of him. Some of the jury obviously were quite afraid, having heard Brown's threats to come down and clean out the place. When preparing for a fight, Brown always braided his long whiskers and tied them across his throat as some protection from a knife. He had done so now.

Suddenly, he stood up. What his intentions were he never had a chance to disclose, for Bill Stewart, acting as prosecuting attorney, turned sharply around. In each hand he held a .44 derringer. "All right, Brown," he said, "get your hands up!"

Startled, Brown lifted his arms. "You," Stewart indicated the bailiff, "disarm him."

Whatever else Brown was, he was no fool. He knew that if he made a move Bill Stewart would kill him. He stood perfectly still until Stewart gestured with a gun. "Take the stand."

When Sam Brown was seated, Stewart approached the stand. "Sam, you have made your boast that you would come down here and swear your friend free. That you would scare the living daylights out of judge and jury, and you'd walk right out of here with your friend."

Stewart held up a Bible. "Sam, do you know what this is?"

"It's a Bible," Sam muttered.

"A Bible. You are correct, Sam. But what is a Bible?" Stewart leaned toward Brown. "Sam, this Bible is *the Word of God!*" He thundered the last words, then turned sharply. "Bailiff, swear him in! To tell the truth, the whole truth, and nothing but the truth!"

Stewart stood back until the swearing ceremony was complete. "Now, Sam," he said, "you have sworn to tell the truth, and the whole truth. You have sworn that on the Word of God.

"The Good Lord watches over us, Sam Brown, and he is watching over us now. *He* knows the truth, as do you. You have sworn to tell the truth and you must, no matter what."

Stewart paused, then more gently, he asked, "Sam, did you ever kill a man?"

Brown laughed, looking around the room. "I reckon," he said.

"How many men, Sam? And remember, you are under oath."

"Well, sixteen, maybe. I forget."

"Sixteen men. That's quite a few, isn't it, Sam? I don't suppose many men ever killed that many, do you?"

"Naw! That there Peel, him they call the Chief, he never killed half that many!"

"I suppose not. I guess you've killed more men than any of them, Sam. Now take the one you killed down in the saloon a while back? The one you cut up with a bowie knife? And then you laid down on the billiard table and went to sleep, was that it?"

Sam looked around proudly. "Why not? Killin' a man doesn't mean nothin' to me!"

"I guess not. I imagine you're about as tough as they come, Sam. I've seen you around town, and I've told myself, 'Now there's a really hard man!' "

He paused again. "That man you cut up, Sam? What kind of a knife did he have?"

"Him? He didn't have no—" Sam stopped abruptly, looking around uneasily. "I don't know what kind of knife he had."

"Sam, you're under oath now. About a week ago I saw you come out of your house, and then you backed right into it and came out the back door. Why, Sam?"

"Why? If you seen it, you don't need me to tell you! It was a big black cat ran across in front of me!"

"Of course, Sam. I did see it. A man would be a damned fool to invite bad luck that way. You did the smart thing, Sam. A man as bright as you are could see the danger right off.

"Of course, you also know that having a black cat cross your path isn't one-tenth, not one-hundredth the bad luck that it is if you break your oath. You know that, don't you, Sam?"

"I know it!"

"Sam, that man you killed? He wasn't carrying a knife, was he?"
"No."

"What kind of a gun did he have, Sam?"

"He didn't have no gun, he—"

Sam stopped again.

"Unarmed, then you killed an unarmed man, Sam. You killed a man who didn't have a chance to fight back, didn't you, Sam?"

"I—"

"And he was drunk, too, wasn't he, Sam? He was falling down drunk, isn't that so?"

Stewart paused. "Now, Sam, you aren't afraid of me, are you?"

"I ain't afraid of nobody!"

"Of course not. And if someone claimed that you were testifying up here because you were scared, that wouldn't be true, would it?"

"No! Why the hell should I be scared of you?"

"Exactly! Some might say I am intimidating a witness, Sam, but you aren't intimidated by me, are you?"

"Hell, no! I ain't ascared of nobody!"

"Of course not. So you're not afraid to admit that man you killed was unarmed. No weapon was found on him, was there, Sam?"

"None I know of." Sam was uneasy. His brow was beaded with sweat. He mopped at it. "I don't know. He might have had somethin'. I don't know."

"He was unarmed. That makes you a murderer, Sam. Not a chief. Not a gunfighter who gives a man an even break, but a murderer."

Brown started to rise. "Now, you see here!"

Stewart lifted his derringers. "Sit down, Sam. And remember, you're still under oath. If you lie while you are under oath, Sam, you'll have no more good luck. Not ever. Not one bit.

"The truth of the matter is, Sam, that most of the men you killed were either blind drunk or unarmed.

"In fact, Sam, at the Battle of Pyramid Lake you threw Baldwin, a wounded man, off his horse so you could escape. You thought that was pretty smart, Sam, but the fact is that you showed yourself for what you are.

"You're a coward, Sam, a dirty, low-down, stinking coward, not fit for human society! Now get out of here! And if I ever find you in a courtroom again, unless you're on trial, I am liable to lose what little patience I have left. Get off the stand! Get out! And take that rabble with you!"

Soaked with sweat, Sam blundered toward the door and into the street. For a moment he paused, staring wildly about. He made a half move to turn about, then went down the road toward the store. After a moment the others followed, very subdued, looking neither to right nor left.

Trevallion walked to the door and watched them go. Ledbetter lit a cigar. "That'll finish Brown. He's got to either face Stewart and kill him or leave the country."

"He'll try to kill him, or somebody. Nobody will be afraid of him now."

Once in the saddle they turned toward Gold Canyon. Ledbetter rode in silence for some distance and then he said, "Trev, by the looks of the ore I've seen from that hole in the ground of yours, you've got a good mine. Why don't you bring in some more men and really sink her down? If it is capital you need—"

"I've been thinking about it," Trevallion admitted. "So far it's been paying its own way, allowing for the work I do. To strike the main ore body, I think I'd have to go down at least two hundred feet, and that's expensive."

"You give it some thought. I'd go in with you."

Trevallion hesitated. "Nobody I'd rather go partners with, but you know how I am, Jim. Least thing and I am liable to take off."

"I know nothing of the kind," Ledbetter replied testily. "There's no harder working man on the Comstock! And that wandering off, that's kid stuff. It's time both of us settled down, and you know it."

Ledbetter paused. "Moreover, we need you here. With the war on, the President is going to need silver. You're worth a sight more here than anywhere else.

"You say you're a Cornishman, but this is where you make your living, and this is where you've chosen to live, and you're a citizen. The most important thing right now is keeping the country together."

They rode on in silence and then Tapley said, "Trev? You know that Eldorado Johnny? They tell me he's ridin' into Virginia City huntin' Farmer Peel."

"The worst of it is," Ledbetter added, "he'll find him. Langford Peel never backed off from anybody."

"He's been talking about it for months," Trevallion said. "Peel's heard about it, and if Johnny comes to Washoe, Peel will know what he's come for."

He rode on a short distance. "All right, Jim. We'll try to make that hole of mine pay for itself. I'll hire some men in the morning, and I'll work two shifts as long as the money lasts."

"Anybody heard anything of Will Crockett?" Tapley wanted to know. "Melissa's worried. She thinks somebody had him killed."

"Who would want to?"

"You know as well as I, Trev. Al Hesketh can never sit easy as long as Will is around. He's an easygoing man, but he doesn't like to have his nose rubbed in the dirt by a man like Hesketh. He will be back."

"If he's alive," Tapley added.

"Speaking of Hesketh," Trevallion asked. "He was bookkeeper for Crockett, but what was he before that? Where did he come from?"

"He was around the camps in California, the same as all of us. Who cares who a man was? Or where he came from?"

Trevallion turned in his saddle and glanced back along the trail. Somehow, talk of Hesketh always made him feel like that—why?

Melissa was in the bakery when they entered. She gave them a quick, almost frightened glance and then turned to get cups. She set them out, then poured coffee, turning away quickly before he could say anything. She went to the stove, busying herself. "Would you like some eggs?" She half turned toward them. "I have some and was about to scramble some for myself."

"I'd like that," Ledbetter said. He watched her as she moved about the room, and Trevallion was surprised to see an unexpected wistfulness in Jim's expression. He caught Trevallion watching him and said quickly, "Any news of the war?"

"I've been with you," Trevallion replied dryly.

"Well, I was wondering. We're getting news faster now with the telegraph in. Old Abe is having his troubles. It's a wonder he was ever elected, homely as he is. Folks can't seem to realize that it isn't a smooth talker we need in there but a steady man, a man with judgment. Any medicine-show man can spout words, if they are written for him. It takes no genius to sound well. To act right and at the right time is something else again."

As he talked his eyes were following Melissa. "Something's bothering her," Trevallion commented. "She's got something on her mind, something more than coffee and scrambled eggs."

She returned to the table. "Baynes will serve us in a minute." She sat down opposite them, glancing from one to the other. "I want to thank you boys," she said, "for helping me get started here. I've done well."

"In another five years," Tapley commented, "you'll be really rich. This boom has just started."

"Well," she hesitated, "everybody doesn't feel that way." She looked from one to the other. "I am selling my share to Baynes, selling out while it is still worth something."

"Getting married?" Trevallion asked, mildly.

She flushed. "Yes, if you must know. I am."

Trevallion kept his eyes from Ledbetter. "Who is the lucky man? Is it Alfie?"

She flushed. "Yes," her chin lifted, "it is. I know," she added defensively, "that you don't think much of him, but he's changed. He's doing very well, and he wants to take me back to San Francisco to live.

"Some of the mines," she added, "are playing out. Alfred thinks this will be dead and forgotten in three years." She looked from one to the other again. "I'm sorry, but I want more of a life than I have here. Alfred thinks I've been working too hard, and that I need to play a little."

Jim Ledbetter got up suddenly. "Just remembered," he said, "I've got a mule train going out this morning." He touched his hat, and went quickly out of the door.

"You've hurt him," Trevallion said.

"Hurt Jim? How?"

Trevallion put down his cup. "Haven't you realized? Jim's in love with you. He's been in love with you all this while."

FORTY

The dining room of the hotel was sparsely occupied at that hour, which was the way she preferred it. Grita had risen early and had already spoken for a horse, as she wished to ride through the town and see a little of the surrounding country.

She had told no one, wishing to be alone on this ride, as there were problems she had to resolve, and riding alone would give her time to think.

The coffee was hot and strong, stronger than any she had drunk, but she found she liked it.

Suddenly she heard boots on the hard floor, and the jangle of spurs. She looked up.

He was a young man, very boyish-looking, with unruly hair which had reluctantly submitted to a comb. He was clean-shaven and unbelievably neat, considering the time and the place.

"Ma'am? Miss Redaway? I'm Eldorado Johnny."

From the way he spoke, he obviously expected her to recognize the name. He was shy, embarrassed but determined.

"Yes, Mr. Johnny?"

He flushed an even deeper red. "Ma'am, it ain't, I mean it isn't Mr. Johnny. It's Eldorado Johnny." Then with more confidence he said, "I'm a pistol-fighter. Maybe the best there is."

She was puzzled, but he seemed a nice young man. "I am afraid I don't understand."

"Ma'am, it's like this. I been thinking about it for months, longer. I decided now was the time to be Chief of Virginia City. Chief of Washoe."

" 'Chief'?"

"Yes, ma'am! *The* Chief. I am going to challenge Langford Peel. You see, he's the Chief right now. I am going over there tonight and I am going to call him out."

"Won't he shoot you?"

Eldorado Johnny smiled tolerantly. "No, ma'am, because I'm better than him. I'm better than anybody with a gun. So I come into town last night and this morning I went to the barber shop, first

249

thing. I told that barber to give me the works—shave, haircut, shampoo, everything. Even his best colon*ee*. I wanted to smell nice, too.

"You know what I told them, ma'am? I told them I wanted the works, because before the day was over I'd either be Chief of Washoe or the best-lookin' corpse in the graveyard!"

"You really mean that, do you not? But is it worth it? What is it to be Chief, after all?"

He was appalled. "Ma'am? What is it worth to be Chief? Ma'am, you just don't understand!"

"I am afraid I do not. After all, Washoe is just one small spot on the map, and to be Chief in Washoe does not mean that you are Chief anywhere else."

"But I'll be Chief in Washoe, ma'am, and that's what counts." He ran his fingers through his curls. "Ma'am, I was wonderin', I wanted to know, I was sort of hopin'. . . . Well, you're the most beautiful woman around, maybe the most beautiful woman there is, and I was just wonderin' if after I am Chief, I was wonderin' whether you'd have dinner with me?"

He was blushing furiously, and his brow was beaded with sweat. "I mean, please? Would you?"

"Johnny," she said quietly, "I do not have dinner or supper with men I have just met, and if I did, it would not matter whether you were Chief or not."

She paused. "However, you seem a nice man, Johnny, and if you will just forget being Chief and trying to kill Langford Peel, I will have supper with you. Here, tonight, after the theater."

He backed off a step. "No, *ma'am*! It wouldn't be fitten. To have supper with you a man's got to *be* somebody! I ain't just one of these no-accounts, ma'am. I got ambition! Why, I've been to the barber an' everything!"

He backed off. "No, *ma'am*. I got to be Chief in Washoe tonight."

He turned swiftly and went out the door, the sunlight glinting on his highly polished boots.

Johnny went down to Pat Lynch's saloon, and Johnny went up to the bar. He ordered a drink and he took the drink and he turned half around and said, "Is there a Chief in the place?"

And Langford Peel, in his black frock coat, took the cigar from his lips. "They have sometimes said that I was Chief. Is the question you ask for me?"

"I told them down at the barber shop I'd be Chief of the town tonight." Johnny spoke lightly and a smile showed around his lips. "I'd be Chief in the town tonight or the best-lookin' corpse in the graveyard."

"We'll step into the street then, Johnny. Do you mind?"

Johnny went down to the street then, but the Farmer stopped in the door. Johnny turned as he reached the street and drew on his Colt .44.

Langford shot him dead in his tracks with his gun half-drawn from his holster. Langford shot him down where he stood, then holstered his gun and said, "He was a handsome lad, and a neat one, too, so you can fix him up with the best, a hardwood casket with velvet lining that will give him a place to rest.

"Have the boys and the girls out to see him on his way, and whatever the bill is, bring it to me. He was a good game lad, and it might have been me."

Margrita came down the steps to where Dane Clyde waited at the foot. "Did you hear the shots?" he asked.

"I did, but with all this noise—" she paused. "Was it Eldorado Johnny?"

"It was Johnny, all right, but he won't be Chief in the town tonight, nor any night."

"He seemed nice," she said.

Clyde shrugged. "It is a strange sense of honor and pride they have, but they live hard and they die game, and according to their lights that is the way it should be."

Her horse was a dappled gray, and she rode sidesaddle with her skirt spread wide over the horse's flank. Men turned to look as she passed and some nodded, unsmiling and grave, but admiring her beauty. She rode up the canyon, looking about her to see the workmen at the mills and mines. The air was clear and cold off Sun Mountain, and she saw a road turning off to her right and took it, but after a short distance it became a road without people, empty and still.

She drew up, listening. Although still so close, the pound of the mills seemed far away. She walked on, the only other sound the creak of her saddle and the click of her horse's hoofs on the rocks. Twice she drew up, looking at the bare rock walls where the sunlight lay warm. It was a strange, empty land, but she loved it.

Riding on, she suddenly paused. Here was a place where someone had worked. There was a hole dug near what must have been, in wet weather, a stream. Nearby there was a clump of cedar.

She heard the horse before she saw it and was suddenly aware that she was alone and far from anyone. She opened her saddlebag and started to put her hand in for her gun.

"You won't need that."

She turned her head sharply. It was Waggoner, sitting a big, rawboned horse and staring at her. His face was expressionless. His big hands rested on the pommel. "Ever since I seen you I knew it had to be."

"I beg your pardon?"

"Don't come that high an' mighty on me. I don't care nothin' for that. Besides, I ain't ready yet."

She turned her horse, but he blocked the way. She was sorry now she had not drawn the gun. It was there, near her hand, but could she reach it in time?

He just stared at her from his sombre eyes in that gaunt, hard-stretched face.

"When I'm ready," he said, "I'll take you." He snapped his fingers, "Jus' like that. You ain't nothin' special, you know. There's fifty women on the Line that's better."

"Will you move out of the way, please?"

"When I'm damn' good an' ready. Like I said, you're nothin', but I want to drag you in the dirt, I want to show you how damn little you matter.

"I been waitin' for you," he added.

Everything went cold inside her. Her breath caught, and then she said, very quietly, "Now what does that mean?"

His grin was insolent. "I knew you'd come back. I just knew it. Somethin' inside me said it. You was only a little tyke, but looked at me like I was dirt, you did."

"I do not know what you are talking about, but if I looked at you that way, obviously my judgment was correct. Now I am going to ride out of here. Move your horse out of the way."

"When I get good an' ready. You jus' sit tight, lady, or I might decide not to wait. You figure you're somebody, you figure you're mighty proud an' strong. Well, you ain't nothin'. When I get through with you, you'll be crawlin' to me in the dirt, beggin' me."

Inside she was cold and still. The man was not just talking. He meant what he said. She was frightened, but not into inaction. She must get her hand on her gun. It was only the derringer, which meant she must be close to him before she fired. He knew she had a gun, and would be careful, yet if there was a sudden movement of their horses she would be able to get the gun.

She was thinking that when they heard a horse walking.

Her hand, poised and ready, her heel ready to touch the spur to her horse's flank on the side away from him, her mind made up to act. To try to get by in front of him would be impossible. His horse was much the heavier, and he was undoubtedly a fine horseman. A quick turn and slash at his horse's rump, then by him and down the trail. She was inwardly poised and ready when they heard the horse's hoofs.

She saw the sudden surge of anger and impatience in his eyes, and he started to speak when the rider appeared. He was riding a black mule.

Trevallion took in the situation at a glance, but instantly he told himself, *not now!* No gunfight here, not if it could be avoided. She could be hurt.

"Good morning!" he spoke pleasantly, walking the mule toward them. "Miss Redaway? I was just looking for you. If this gentleman will excuse us?"

Waggoner fought down the ugly fury that started to rise inside him. Cold common sense warned him. He did not doubt his ability to kill Trevallion, but Trevallion was no tenderfoot, and he would be sure to get off a shot or two, and at this range he would score.

"I reckon I'll have to," Waggoner said, "although I'm sure lookin' forward to seein' more of her. Business comes first, doesn't it, ma'am?" He smiled insolently. He turned the big horse and for a moment he looked right at Trevallion, who said, "We have some business together, Mr. Waggoner, and I believe you owe me about five hundred dollars. Would you mind getting it ready for me?"

Waggoner rode on by, then for a moment an almost blinding rage swept over him. *Why not now?* Why not—

He pulled up his horse and started to turn, but Trevallion had a rifle in his hands now, almost casually pointed in his direction. Waggoner rode on.

Not against a rifle, not now. There would be other chances. Right in the street if necessary. But it had to be done soon, not only for himself, but his unseen employer had sent him two impatient notes.

Grita and Trevallion sat quietly, listening to the diminishing sound of his horse's hoofs.

Then their eyes turned back and they looked at each other. For a long moment, neither spoke, then she said, "I am glad you came when you did. He is not a pleasant man."

"I've seen him around."

She was beautiful, but more than that there was something about her that he liked, instantly. Suddenly he remembered what he had said, so long ago, that he wanted to marry her. He flushed at the memory.

"You came for me?" she asked.

"Dane Clyde said you had ridden this way and would I suggest that you come back. It has something to do with the theater. I was riding this way."

He was embarrassed, not knowing what to say. Did she remember him? He turned his mule and she rode up beside him. Together they started back down the canyon.

He felt unreasonably awkward and tongue-tied, and they rode in silence until they had almost come to the hotel. Then he said, "I have some business, your investments. We must talk about that."

"Is that all?" she asked.

"I don't know," he said, "maybe—"

Dane Clyde came up to them.

FORTY-ONE

Albert Hesketh had made up his mind. Too much depended upon what happened in the next few weeks. He must move swiftly, resolve all his problems within that time, and be prepared to go forward in the way he had planned.

He had tried and failed to locate Will Crockett. Many believed Crockett dead, but Hesketh did not. Yet, if he could be found and killed, no one would even wonder. It was a case of out of sight out of mind. Crockett was rarely even mentioned any more. Business was moving forward, new mines were opened, the older ones developed, new discoveries were being made.

The War, Sutro's projected tunnel to drain the water from the lower levels—these were the subjects of conversation.

Crockett's estate—who would inherit? Had he not some relative in California? Hesketh had been through everything in the files at the mine and could recall nothing. So, if he died, Hesketh might himself lay claim to whatever Crockett held. Still, he should have something, he should have a note, a will, a letter, something giving substance to a claim. Uncontested it would fall into his lap like a ripe plum.

Like most men with a criminal turn of mind, Albert Hesketh planned for success, not failure. He did not even consider the idea that anyone might see through him or be aware of what he was doing.

What was to be done must be done, at once. He had control of the Solomon and must move to be certain he continued in control. Within the next few days they would move into bonanza. The ore was there, and he had samples of it, and once the Solomon began shipping that ore, the stock would skyrocket. His holdings would overnight triple or quadruple in value.

Margrita Redaway worried him. If she did hold the stock as he believed, why had she not come forward? What was in her mind? To Albert Hesketh nothing happened by accident or whim, all was planned, and the planning was directed at him. He saw plots on all sides. When people conversed in low tones in his presence, they were talking about *him*.

Inconsistently, he believed all of those of whom he expected to take advantage to be fools, and for them he felt nothing but contempt. At the same time he avoided any contact with George Hearst, John Mackay, Fair, Sharon, or the bigger men on the Comstock. He wanted to be considered one of them but felt uneasy under the cool, direct attention of John Mackay.

Give him time, he told himself. They would come later, and for the present, he had his plans.

He had bought several small mines, considered worthless. These he would salt with ore from the Solomon or elsewhere, and when the shipments started, their stock booming, he would sell. After a while he would let the shipments fall off in quality, the value of the stock would drop, and he would buy it back again and do the same thing. There were always dupes in a hurry to get rich quick.

Yet Margrita Redaway disturbed him. He had never been interested in any particular woman and cared for nothing but money and the power it represented. He found it difficult to think clearly in her presence. His mind, usually clear and incisive, became blurred and confused when she was around. At the same time he was irritated by the feeling that nothing about him really reached her. Ordinarily he would not have cared, but somehow he did care, and that irritated him, too.

If she had the stock, she could offer it for sale. It would be worth a great deal of money, and it was his experience that everybody wanted money. What was she thinking of? What was she planning? He refused to admit that any woman had intelligence, but at the same time he was confused, trying to decide what was in her mind.

Then he had seen her with Trevallion. He had seen them ride into town together and was alarmed. How had they gotten together? She had ridden out alone, he had seen that, but she had returned with him.

Trevallion was his enemy. He felt this instinctively, yet Trevallion had never spoken against him nor acted against him, except in the one matter of filing on the claim adjoining the Solomon. Trevallion might *know*.

The thought came to him, and then he hastily averted his mind. He must not think of that. He would not think of it. Too many years had passed, and even if Trevallion knew, he could prove nothing. But would Trevallion want proof?

The fact remained that Trevallion could destroy him. Now, at last, Albert Hesketh—for he now thought of himself by that name—had become someone. He was a mining man, a mine owner. He was a wealthy man, well, almost, who could become wealthier. People looked at him with envy. He walked into the dining room at night and took his seat like royalty. He dined in solitary dignity, aloof from the crowd, envied and admired. It was thus he saw himself.

He did not guess that nobody really cared. That they accepted him as one more odd character in a camp filled with even odder or more flamboyant ones. He was a very dim page alongside the likes of Sandy Bowers, Pancake Comstock, Ol' Virginny, Langford Peel, Tom Paisley, Bill Stewart, and Judge Terry, to name a half-dozen from a camp where oddity was a rule rather than an exception.

To himself Albert Hesketh was a man of dignity and poise, a commanding figure in the business of mining, a man who someday might decide to run for the Senate. He was special, and therefore Margrita Redaway should have noticed him. She should be paying attention. She had actually met him, been taken to dinner by him.

He shook her from his mind. It did not matter. She did not matter. He had the Solomon and one way or another he would make sure of his hold and of his control.

Trevallion must go. He must locate Will Crockett and eliminate, once and for all, that threat to his future.

Also, he would build a home. He would build the best home, the grandest home of them all.

Ralston, the banker, had the best home now. He had heard of it, wanted to see it. Belmont, it was called, and it was somewhere near San Francisco. The grand balls and parties given there were already legend. He must see it. Then he would know what he had to do.

Trevallion stood in his way. So, and he returned to the idea reluctantly, did Margrita Redaway.

If the shares he wanted had not been found, it must be that she carried them on her person. Therefore she must be killed, and searched.

He shrank from the suggestion. The idea of touching the body of a woman made his flesh crawl. He did not know why he felt as he did, but it was something deeply ingrained in his being. He had touched but one, and it remained a moment of shuddering horror to him. Whenever the memory or the thought returned to him, he turned quickly away from it. He shrank from the memory.

He had never gone in for self-examination. He had never wondered why he was a being virtually without appetites.

Hesketh thought of Trevallion. The man should have been dead. Why was he not? Every day he lived the danger became greater. At first, even when resolved to have him killed, he had not pushed. If it was to be done right, it must be done with care. Yet nothing happened. Not even any rumors of attempts upon him.

Suddenly, his thoughts shifted. Why had that Redaway woman hired Teale? What would an actress need with a killer?

A bodyguard? Well, maybe. There had been attempts to rob her.

Manfred. Hesketh had only seen Manfred once or twice, but something about the actor disturbed him. He did not seem to be an actor, yet he obviously was.

For a moment he thought about trying to hire Teale, then pulled back from the idea. There was something about Teale that disturbed him. The man was a killer, and he had killed for hire, but he himself decided when and if he would kill and by some weird reasoning of his own.

Albert Hesketh returned to his rooms. They were as he had found them, rich with hotel opulence, but without character. The only thing he had changed in the room were the locks. On the door he had two locks placed, each opened by a key that he alone possessed. He let the maid in, and he let her out, remaining there while she did her work. He had an abhorrence of anyone handling his clothing or of investigating his few belongings. He watched while she worked, and when she was finished, he locked the door again.

Once the door was locked and he was alone, he sat down in an armchair to think. Slowly and with care he began to study his situation, thinking out every aspect of it. He knew what must be done and the question was how to do it.

Melissa was gone from the bakery, and Alfie with her. Jim Ledbetter no longer came by, and Trevallion, when he went anywhere but home, went to the International. They no longer had to wait for the Pony. The telegraph was in and they heard the news much sooner than before, although the gossip of the mining camps was still to be heard around the saloons.

They were the clubs of the common man, they were the clearing-houses, the places where information was passed out and deals formulated. There were few secrets on the Comstock. There was always a miner fresh out of the hole to relay news of the latest strike. As soon as he had a few, the story came out.

It was the same with the mill-workers. A man with his ear to the ground heard all he needed to buy stock or sell it. The people in San Francisco, going wild dreaming of fortunes to be made, had no such source of information.

Pack trains were few now, for most of the freight came in huge wagons with jerk-line teams. The old trail had been widened, and gravel had been packed into the clay, until it was as solid as pavement during most of the year.

Trevallion had returned to his cabin and slammed the door. He stood, hands on his hips, looking around his sparsely furnished bachelor quarters. Suddenly he swore, he swore slowly and with exasperation. Then he went to the cubbyhole he had hidden in the rock at the back wall and got out his notes.

He looked over the figures. He did not have much. For months now he had been living from hand to mouth, working a little ore, selling it, placering a little. He had small investments in the bakery and in Ledbetter's freight operation. He was not a poor man, but he was far from wealthy.

He thought of Ledbetter, who had offered to throw in with him, but he did not want to risk Ledbetter's money, and he did want to go it alone.

He would have to work. He would have to work as he never had. He took off his coat, hung it on a nail, and then took off his gun belt.

That Waggoner, what was going on there, anyway? Had he not come up when he did—

Waggoner needed killing, and he had it to do. After all, Waggoner had been one of them.

Shocked, he dropped to his bunk. Waggoner—did he know who Margrita was? But how could he? He had not seen her, and anyway, she'd been only a child, a very small child. That was absurd.

He had started out to kill them all. What had happened to him? Waggoner was here, Waggoner had even tried to kill him, yet he had done nothing.

He undressed and fell into bed, but he did not sleep. His thoughts returned to Margrita. Suddenly, from where the idea came he did not know, but probably it had been lying in his mind for some time, he knew she was the only woman for him. And he had nothing for her.

He had known it when he saw her on the stage. He had known it when they rode back to town together. He had known it in that brief moment when he interfered out there in Six Mile Canyon.

She was already a success, and he was nothing. He was a miner, a man who worked with his hands. So they had known each other before, but then they had been mere children, babies. Briefly their lives had been joined by a night of horror and the following sorrow. She had stayed in his mind, and once he had written to her.

He thought then of her papers. He must go over them, and he must get in touch with Will.

Will? Where the hell *was* he?

He stared around the small room. This was one night when he wished he could go down to the bakery and sit there, smelling the bakery and coffee smells, with Melissa nearby and Jim sitting across the table. Not to talk, just to have a presence. Not to be alone.

What the hell was the matter with him? He had been alone half his life!

In the morning he awakened and went down into the hole. With cool detachment he studied the layout, studied the ore samples, and knew he had to face it. The ore looked good, but unless there was a sudden breakthrough into something better, this was not going to make him rich. And suddenly he wanted to be rich. He wanted very much to be rich, at least a little bit rich.

His gut feeling told him he was in good ground. It told him there was rich ore somewhere down below, but he did not have it now, when he needed it.

He would need money, a lot of money. That was why the first discoverers had sold out, because these were claims that demanded development. A prospector likes to *find*, but he is rarely the man to develop a mine, and he rarely has the money needed.

So what then? Keep the boys working as long as he could, hoping for a break. And to go to work himself, somewhere where he could *earn* some money.

He did not want to go underground again, but he would have to.

Waggoner? What about Waggoner while he was underground? Hadn't somebody said two men had just joined him?

Maybe there were three of them in town now.

And that gun he had found so long ago, a gun that might have been lost by one of the killers, the one he still had, with the name *A.X. Elder*.

Who was A.X. Elder?

FORTY-TWO

A t daybreak Trevallion was climbing over the rock shot down by the previous round, and checking the face of the drift. The round had, as usual, extended the tunnel by another three feet, but the vein looked no better.

Using planks laid end-to-end as a runway for his wheelbarrow, he mucked out the rock, clearing the approach to the face. It was time to lay some track and do away with the wheelbarrow, but track cost money.

As he worked he considered his situation. He always thought better while working, walking, or riding. Somehow physical activity was conducive to thinking, at least if the activity called for no particular attention.

Today was Sunday, and he was alone. Some of the mines and mills worked Sundays, too, but he never had, although occasionally he puttered around as he was now doing. A quiet day would give him time to plan. For weeks he had been making resolutions, telling himself what he must do and should do, but other things had interfered. It was those interferences, no matter what they were, that he must push aside. They were time-wasters.

Thus far he had been pushing his tunnel back into the mountain, but with few exceptions the best ore on the Comstock had been found at the deeper levels. To sink a shaft would cost money.

So far the little he had made placering along with the few ship-ments of ore had been sufficient for his needs. He was a man of simple tastes and required little, but unless he intended to let his years waste away, he had better get on with it.

He could borrow money. He was a hard worker, a steady man with a good reputation in the mines, and he knew the money would be available, but it was not the way he wanted it. He would be beholden to no man. Keep clear of debt, his father had warned him when he was very small. Once you are in debt, his father advised, you are carrying another man's weight, and it will be him who sits in the saddle and his hands on the reins.

He sorted the rock he had shot down and put the best-looking stuff to one side. When he had enough, he'd mill the lot. It would not come to much, but it would be walking-around money, anyway.

He swore suddenly, bitterly. If he only had that five hundred dollars Waggoner had stolen! Of course, he could prove nothing, and if he hunted him down and killed him, he would be no better off.

As he worked, he considered his situation and what might be done. There were jobs enough, but at four dollars a day; even the six he might get as shift-boss would not amount to very much. He could do better by himself.

He could return to one of his claims but that meant leaving Virginia City, and he was reluctant to be away from town just now.

He had gone into the mine without breakfast, but now he came up, stirred up the fire, and sliced bacon into the pan. He had coffee on when there was a rap on the door. He took his gun from its holster, which hung over a chair back, and slid the six-shooter behind his belt.

Standing to one side of the door he asked, "Who is it?"

"It's me, Tap."

He opened the door and Tap stepped in. "Brisk out yonder," he commented. Then he glanced at him. "Heard the news?"

Without waiting for a reply, Tapley said, "Sam Brown's dead. He got all charged up, figured he had to show his hand since Stewart made light of him, so he threatened Van Slyke."

"Van Slyke killed him?"

"Got him a shotgun and rode down the road and waited for him. Blew him right out of the saddle."

"I'll be damned! Van Slyke? The least likely man in camp, I'd say. Well, you never can tell."

"Bill Stewart kind of showed him up," Tap said. "Once that happens a man had better run, because everybody will be after him. The trouble with a reputation is that you have to back it up, and once you slip, you've had it."

"Had breakfast?"

"No, and that bacon smells almighty good." Tap glanced at him. "You're in your diggin' clothes."

"I've been down in the hole. Worked a little. I'm going to sink a shaft. Going down three or four hundred feet."

"Never work on Sunday myself," Tapley said, "least it's an emergency." He paused. "Reason I came by is that I saw Waggoner down on the street with two strangers. Hard cases if I ever saw them."

"So?"

"Trev, those men were Bald Knobbers. At least one of them was. Another's an Arkansawyer. Spotted him right off because he's from my neck of the woods. I figured you ought to know."

"Thanks."

Trevallion served the bacon, some toast, and put the molasses jug on the table. "How are things at the mill?"

Tapley shrugged. "I like workin' for you better. If you're going to sink a shaft, maybe you'd need a good man."

"I can use you, but I don't know how long the money will last. Maybe you'd be better off sticking to a steady job."

"Maybe, but I like workin' for you." He paused. "You an' Miss Redaway gettin' acquainted? Seen you ride into town together."

"We knew each other long ago," Trevallion replied, and then at Tapley's surprised look he explained, telling the story from the beginning.

Christian Tapley swore softly. "It do beat all! I heard there'd been some trouble back down the line." He glanced at him quickly. "Then, did you kill Skinner?"

"I did."

"I'll be damned. And you figure Waggoner is one of them?" He was silent for several minutes, chewing slowly, thoughtfully. "You know, Trev, I seen it happen before. There's some crimes that are never forgotten. For some reason they scar ever'body they touch. This is one of them.

"All those years, and then Rory dead, and Skinner. You say your pa killed two of them?"

"He did."

"And you figure there's five left?"

"Four or five."

"You better figure on five, Trev. If you only count to four an' quit that could be fatal. That fifth man—"

"I'm figuring on five, with or without the one who started it all."

"You think you know who it was?"

"I think it was that man with the pale eyes, the one who was curious about pa's gold. He looked like the man who shot Grita's father. I'd have sworn it was him. Yet I did not see his face."

"Then it could be anybody, anybody at all." Tapley started to fill his cup, then stopped, coffeepot in hand. "Waggoner's been around awhile. He isn't workin', but he has money. Where's he get it? What's he livin' on?"

He finished pouring the coffee. "Trev, he tried to kill you up in Six Mile or wherever you were. At least, you figured it was him. Well, why'd he try to kill you? Because he knew who you were! He spotted you. He remembered you."

"He couldn't have. I was only a boy."

"Why else would he take a shot at you? And you said somebody rigged a missed-hole for you. If it ain't him, it's somebody else. You got any other enemies around?"

"None that I know of."

"You staked out that claim up there next to the Solomon. Ol' Hesketh couldn't have been too happy about that."

"That was after. And I don't know Hesketh. I've never even seen the man, not to know who he is."

Tapley finished his coffee and got up. "I'll be around come morning to start work. You take care, you hear? That Waggoner's a mean, tough man."

Christian Tapley walked down the slope frowning. Suddenly, on the spur of the moment, he turned toward the International. He was walking across the lobby when he saw Teale watching him from the door of the billiard room. Turning he crossed to him. "Want to set a minute? We've got talkin' to do."

When they were seated, Tap said, "Supposin' you just listen an' let me talk a bit? There's something you should know."

Teale did not reply, he simply waited. Tapley gestured to indicate the upper floors. "You're watchin' over Miss Redaway. You let her ride off by herself."

"She wanted to ride alone. She said she wanted to think."

Tapley told about her riding up the canyon. "Trevallion rode up after her, and when he came up to her she was cornered by this here Waggoner. He came up just in time to know there'd been hard words betwixt 'em without him hearin' anything. Waggoner seemed almighty put out when Trevallion showed up, but after a few words, he rode off. Trev rode back to town with her."

Tapley explained his feelings about Waggoner, and repeated the story Trevallion had told him. Teale held up a hand. "I know the story," he said.

He was thinking back, remembering other things. He got up. "There's no show tonight. Tapley, could you stay here, take over for me until about tomorrow afternoon?"

"I've promised Trev to lend a hand over there."

"One more day won't matter. I got things to do. You take care of her, you hear?"

"I hear."

Jacob Teale went to the stable and saddled his horse. He was going to do something he had meant to do before this, and should have done. He had been remiss. Only, Margrita Redaway had needed him.

He was leading his horse from the stable when he saw Langford Peel across the street, watching him. Peel was smoking a cigar, and when he saw Jacob had seen him, Peel strolled across the street. "Ridin' out?"

"A ways."

"Stage trail?"

"Could be."

"Hear there was some shootin' out yonder the other night."

"A mite."

"That explains the body, then."

Teale was quiet for a moment and then he said, "I fired, but I had nothing certain to shoot at and I didn't kill anybody."

"Didn't say you did. Just figured you might want to know about the body they found alongside the trail out there. He was lying on his face in the dust, and he'd been shot twice, in the back."

"Anybody we know?"

"Frisco man, runner for a dive down there, sneak-thief, whatever. He was riding one of the express ponies. Horse showed up at his stable, and the hostler made inquiries. Whoever the dead man was, he made a fast ride from Frisco to Virginia City, switching horses often." Peel dusted ash from his cigar. "He didn't know he was riding to his own death."

"Thanks, Peel."

Peel touched his hat with a finger. "Professional courtesy, Mr. Teale, simply professional courtesy!"

Jacob Teale camped in the woods that night and was on the ground shortly after daybreak. The sign was several days old, but except for the trail it was an area where few people came. He found where two riders had waited, one of whom had smoked many cigarettes, obviously nervous.

They were the men he had shot at from the stage-top, for the position was the same, as he expected. But then one man had murdered the other. Why? In a fit of rage, when the holdup failed? But why? It had not been the one man's fault, unless—

That horse had leaped into the road. That might be it. But they had waited calmly. It had been the nervous man who was shot, not the other. And from the tracks, the other man had ridden swiftly away.

Teale picked up the trail and followed it across a couple of short-cuts. The man knew the country. A big man, riding a big horse. He would remember the tracks.

Jacob Teale was quite sure he knew who the strange rider had been. What he did not know was why he had been there to attempt a holdup, or why the other man had been killed.

But he had a pretty good idea.

He rode back to town and relieved Tapley, thanking him. Tap asked no questions, and Teale sat down to think and to wait for Miss Redaway to come down the stairs.

The night the stage had come in, Teale had dropped off the stage and stood back among the crowd. He had seen Waggoner, the man who hurried until he reached the stage and then no longer hurried. To see who had shot at him?

Waggoner was not a road-agent, so why was he acting as one on that night? Was he there to hold up the stage or to kill someone?

Margrita Redaway came down the stairs, and Jacob Teale stood up and moved toward her.

"How do you do, Mr. Teale? A lovely evening, is it not?"

"It is, ma'am. Shall we go?"

FORTY-THREE

With Tapley working with him Trevallion's drilling went much faster. With one man holding the drill while the other struck with the eight-pound double jack, the drilling was easier, even allowing for time to clean out the holes. When they paused to "take five," Tapley commented, "You're a good hand with that sledge. Ever get into one of the contests?"

"A time or two. I used to box some in the celebrations, too. Or do some Cornish-style wrestling. I don't know who started it, but every Fourth of July there was always a contest going. But I preferred the boxing."

"You win?"

"Uh-huh, here and there." He hefted the sledge. "Swinging this is good for the punch, and I was on the end of one of these from the time I could lift one. The same thing with a muck-stick—shovel, to you."

"Yeah, I'm no miner. Worked at it here and there, but I like it up on top. I've timbered, though, and laid a lot of track."

Tapley paused. "Want some coffee? I'm fixing to go on top and make some."

"All right, but be careful up there. They might think you're me."

Tapley indicated the hat Trevallion wore. "I got to get me one of them hard hats."

"You don't get them, Tap, you make them. You just get a common felt hat and stiffen it with linseed oil. Takes a lot of work. Some favor resin. In fact, I do myself. Rub it into the hat again and again, and after a while it builds up. Better do it if you're going to work underground. It will save a lot of raps on the skull."

Tapley took his candle and started for the ladder. At the foot of the ladder he stopped, took his gun-belt from a peg driven into the wall, and slung it around his hips.

Trevallion spooned out the holes they had completed and stepped back, studying the layout. Then he loaded the holes, spit the fuses, and went back along the drift. He slung his gun-belt over a shoulder, not waiting to buckle it on, and scrambled up the ladder. The first shot boomed before he reached the end of the tunnel, snuffing out his light. As he could see the light at the end of the tunnel he did not bother to light it again.

Suddenly he paused. He was still well back inside the tunnel and he was, as he made a half-turn, facing toward the new ground he had bought from the Dutchman. There was nothing to attract him at the point, but he made a decision. He would hold off on his freshly begun shaft and start drifting into the Dutchman's claim.

"Makes no sense," Tapley said, "but it's your claim."

Trevallion shrugged. "In my time I've done a lot of things that made no sense. Call it a hunch."

"Your money's in the pot, son," Tapley said. "Whatever you want. But if you'll notice, that ground falls away over there, and you keep on going very far and you'll be right out under the stars again."

Trevallion smiled. "Maybe that's the idea."

He bathed himself as best he could, shaved, and putting on his dark suit, he went downtown. In his inside coat pocket he took the papers he must discuss with Margrita.

He glanced toward the bakery. He had scarcely been near the place since Melissa left. There had been no word from her except a card to Eilley Bowers. It was from San Francisco.

He took out his watch and glanced at it. The play was more than half over, so he directed his steps toward the theater. The street was crowded as usual.

A big ore wagon rumbled past, drawn by six head of mules. He had started across the street and suddenly he glimpsed the boots and legs of somebody on the other side of the wagon, waiting for it to pass. Turning sharply, he walked toward the head of the slow-moving wagon, then running, he ducked around ahead of the team and stopped.

A man stood in the center of the street with a drawn gun, staring wildly about.

"Looking for me?"

People had stopped, watching as the man turned, lifting his gun. "Yes, damn you!"

Trevallion's side was toward him. He stood tall and alone, waiting.

Only seconds passed, yet it seemed like hours. With a kind of curious detachment, he saw the man's gun coming up, he heard somebody yell, and there was a surge of people on the street, some rushing to see, some crowding to get out of the way. They were the smart ones.

The man's back was to the light, his face in darkness. The gun was lifting. Trevallion drew and fired.

The man's gun went off, the bullet striking the earth with an angry *splutt* only inches from his boot. Gun in hand he walked slowly toward the fallen man, watching but unworried. He knew where his bullet had gone.

People crowded around. Among them was Peel. He glanced at the body, then, with an odd smile, at Trevallion. "Bucking for my job?" he asked lightly.

"No, Farmer, but I think he was."

Somebody turned the man over, and it was Kip Hauser. "I'll be damned," Peel said. "He always struck me as a sure thing man."

"I believe he thought it was," Trevallion said mildly. Then he walked on across the street and to the stage door.

They stopped him there. "I want to see Miss Redaway," he said.

"So do a couple of hundred others," the doorman said, grinning. "Sorry, but—"

"Let him in." It was Jacob Teale. "Let him in any time he wants to come."

The doorman shrugged and stepped back.

"Heard some shootin'," Teale said. "What was it? Some drunk?"

"I don't think he was drunk," Trevallion said, "I think he was paid."

"Want to wait here?" Teale asked. "She'll be finishing up in just a few minutes." He pointed. "Stand in the wings if you like."

Albert Hesketh received the news over a late supper in the International. He was seated alone at his table when he heard the shots. He paused a moment in his chewing, then continued.

John Santley came into the dining room, and seeing him, crossed to his table. "I have the information you wanted, Mr. Hesketh," he said. "The Sandusky is—"

"Please!" Hesketh's voice was sharp. "Not here. I never talk business over food." Then he added, "Just leave what you have and I'll go over it." He looked up. "You are late, Mr. Santley."

"Yes, sir. There was a crowd in the street, sir. There's been another killing, sir."

"Yes?"

There was a hint of question in the tone and John Santley said, "It was a Kip Hauser, sir. He was one of Sam Brown's crowd."

"He killed someone?"

"No. Oh, no, sir! He was killed. *Two* shots, sir, fired so rapidly they sounded as one. They were all talking about it. Two bullets, one through the heart, one in the throat."

"I see. The other man was arrested?"

"Oh, no, sir! It was self-defense, sir. A dozen men said Hauser had his gun drawn before the other man made a move."

"I see."

His face was utterly still, not a flicker of emotion. Inside he was seething. What a pack of fools! Couldn't anybody do anything right?

"The other man was very calm, sir. He walked down the street and went into the theater."

The theater? God *damn* him!

The curtain came down and the applause was deafening. Virginia City enjoyed its theater and liked the performers, but above all it liked a good time. Especially it appreciated the freshness of the Redaway Company costumes and the ease and naturalness of the players.

Margrita came offstage, flushed and lovely. She saw Trevallion at once and stopped abruptly. Then she walked toward him, both hands outstretched. "Val! How nice of you to come!"

"You'd better go back," he said. "They are still applauding."

"You'll wait? I'll only be a minute!"

She returned to the stage and the curtain went up. Four more curtain calls and then she came offstage.

"Val? Will you have supper with me? Mr. Manfred has some business to discuss, so he and Mr. Clyde will be with us for a few minutes, then we can talk. Is it all right?"

"Of course. I am afraid mine is business, too. At least," he added, "part of it is business."

"Can't we skip that part? I want to know what you've been doing all these years."

She went on into her dressing-room, and Val turned to see Teale approaching. "Are you going to be with her for supper?" Teale asked.

"I believe so. At least, I've been invited."

"Good! I need some time and she will be safe with you." He hesitated. "Who was it got killed out there tonight?"

"Kip Hauser."

"Had it coming for a long time, but that's a bothersome thing. Somehow he didn't seem likely to end that way. I mean, he was careful, real careful. He was mean, but he wasn't quarrelsome."

"I think he was paid. I started across the street and all of a sudden I see somebody on the other side. It looked too quick to suit me, so I ran around the head of the team. You know there's a grade right along there, and those heavy ore wagons move pretty slow.

"Hauser had a gun in his hand and seemed startled when I wasn't there. He'd planned to have me at point blank range and surprised. The way it happened, I spoke to him and he turned, and *he* was surprised."

"I reckon. Him an' that crowd run roughshod over everybody while Sam Brown was alive. Now they've come on hard times." He paused. "She know it yet?"

"No. It will be a shock. She's not been raised the way we were, Jacob."

"No, sir. Surely not. They still shoot each other now and again, but they do it all formal-like, with challenges, callin' cards, and seconds and all."

Teale turned away. "Hope she ain't too upset by it. Women do take on, sometimes, although she seems a common-sense sort of person."

He looked back at Trevallion. "She does beat all. The way she hired me, just seen me and hired me. I can't figure it out."

"I can, Jacob. She's learned to read people and she saw that you were a good man, a trustworthy man, and one who would stand." He paused again. "Jacob, I have a bad feeling about this. They tried to rob her in Frisco, I hear, and they tried to rob her on the way over. Whatever she's got, somebody wants it mighty bad."

"That's my thinkin'."

"You were on the stage, Jacob. Do you remember who was with you?"

"Ever' one. Hesketh was there, and two strangers. I ain't seen either of them since, which doesn't mean they ain't around.

"Mr. Trevallion, I wouldn't tell this to anybody but you, but there was a man on that stage somebody wanted killed. The word come to me and the price. Now I was right down to bedrock and showin' no color, but I don't do that kind of work. If a man needs killin' I ain't one to balk at it, but I knowed—knew—nothin' about Mr. Hesketh, and I knew a lot about the man who wanted him dead. That man was in San Francisco.

"Now I was ridin' the top and somethin' didn't smell right about the whole affair, so I laid ready, and when that man showed up along the road, I cut loose. I wasn't shootin' at anything, just tryin' to show whoever was there that they should pull in their necks. They done so.

"Later, a dead man was found up there but he was none of my killin'. He was a San Francisco man, sort of a runner for some of the Barb'ry Coast outfits. He'd been shot in the back."

"You found him?"

"Well, I scouted around. There'd been two of them. One was a big man on a big horse. That man came back to Washoe."

"Do you know who he was?"

"Mebbe I do an' mebbe I don't, but I asked a few folks, and it seems that San Francisco gent rode in here in an awful big hurry. To get where they were they had to ride out almost immediate. Whatever they were to do had to be done right away, whether it was rob Miss Redaway or kill somebody."

"But one shot the other?"

"Uh-huh. The San Francisco man got shot. Now why was he killed? Did he jump the gun by gettin' out into the road like he done? Was the other man mad because of that? Mebbe.

"But there's another thought, too. Supposin' that other man was killed because he knew who sent him to Washoe?

"Mr. Trevallion, I think Miss Redaway is in more trouble than she guesses, and I think whoever is after her or what she's got isn't one to stop at anything.

"The man who tried to hire me is dead, his place burned and him with it. Accident, they say. Mebbe.

"The man who carried word over here is dead. Shot apurpose.

"Somebody hires Kip Hauser to kill you, an' anybody but you or me or somebody like us would've been killed.

"Seems to me there's something mighty big at stake here, somethin' bigger than we'd guess, and whoever's on the other end will stop at nothing. Not nothing atall."

Jacob Teale buttoned his coat. "Mr. Trevallion, I'm scared. I'm scared for the both of you."

FORTY-FOUR

The dining room of the International was almost empty when they reached their table. Only a few late diners were scattered about the room, and none were seated close by.

Trevallion drew back Grita Redaway's chair and seated her, then went around the table and sat down opposite her.

For the first time there was a moment when she could really look at him. He was, she realized, a very handsome man. Dark, perfectly poised, and very self-contained. Their conversation was at first in trivialities, as all such preliminary conversations are apt to be.

"You know," he said suddenly, "you are a very lucky person, and you do not realize how lucky. Your father, or whoever it was who loaned that money those many years ago, used remarkable judgment."

"I don't know what you mean."

"He loaned money to a man who was in financial trouble, a very shrewd man and an honest one. You will remember that you wanted him to reinvest the money for you, and he agreed if I would be partly responsible."

"Well? What happened?"

"What happened is that you are very well-off. I won't say wealthy, simply well-off."

The waiter came, and they ordered, then he continued. "You helped to provide capital to a man who knew how to use it.

"Being possessed of capital and knowing what to do with it are not necessarily twins. This man was a shrewd, intelligent investor and he proceeded to go into the business of supplying tools, clothing, and food to miners. From that he bought land, began farming on a rather large scale, shipping wheat to Alaska and to China.

"He bought land for you, also, but a part of your capital he kept working with his. He had reverses from time to time, all of which he outlined to me and which I understand, knowing the country and the times, but what matters is that you now own a comfortable home in Monterey, a ranch in southern California, and a small piece of his produce and supply business."

"I had no idea! You mean all the time I was growing up —"

"That little bit of money was growing, too. I might add, nobody knows this except the gentleman himself, you, and I."

"I don't know what to say. I'm overwhelmed. I knew there was a little money there, but—"

"That little money has been in the hands of a very shrewd man for about fifteen years. The Sacramento River flooded out crops on two occasions, and a shipload of grain was lost at sea."

Trevallion reached into his pocket. "This list," he put a finger on it, "is your holdings. It looks quite impressive, but what you will understand is that the dollar value is not so great as it might appear. All of this," he indicated the list, "is growing and should be improved or simply let alone. Ten years from now, if you hold all this, you will, indeed, be a wealthy woman."

"I had no idea." She looked directly at him. "And you? What of you?"

He shrugged a shoulder. "I have little. A mine that has good indications, several claims that have only possibilities, and a few minor investments."

He was embarrassed. "I have not done as well as I should have or could have. I, I've been preoccupied."

Trevallion paused, then he asked, "Miss Redaway, do you hold shares in the Solomon? I was told you had some mining shares, and from what has been happening I believed you might."

"No, I do not. I do have some shares in mines, most of them worthless, I believe. I also have some old debts owed my father and my aunt. I am afraid they are useless also."

"Several attempts have been made to rob you?"

"Yes, at least two attempts in San Francisco, and an attempted stage holdup."

"Why?"

"I've no idea, unless they assume I have something I do not."

"You must be careful. They may want something more than just a possession."

"You mean they may wish to kill me?"

He was surprised at her calmness. "That might be it."

"I have suspected as much, although I have no idea why."

"You don't seem frightened."

"I am, I suppose, and I should be. I've learned that fear can be one's first line of defense. One has to be aware of danger to defend oneself against it."

He smiled. "You know," he said, "I like you."

"I like you, too," she replied seriously. Then she added, "I don't know what it is in me. Perhaps it is something left from that terrible fear I felt as a child, but I accept the fact that life is a jungle."

"Is that why you hired Jacob Teale?"

"Yes. I saw him and I liked what I saw, a very dangerous man but a *man*, and I had a feeling if he gave his word it would prove good."

"You gave him something that meant more than anything else could. You trusted him and you respected him. His kind of man wants little else."

"And you?"

He shrugged. "I don't know. All these years, I—"

"You started out to kill those men."

"Yes. For years I thought of little else except that they had destroyed so much that was beautiful and good, and that they were going free. It became an obsession."

"And now?"

He shrugged and did not reply. He wanted to kill no one. He wanted an end to all that. He wanted only to work, to build, to do. He looked across the table at Margrita. "It must be ended," he said abruptly. "It has gone on too long."

She nodded. "It is strange how this one crime's effects have lingered. How many crimes have those men committed? How many have been killed? But this one has gripped all of us. You, me, and yes, them, too. They are obsessed by it. They cannot forget it. Why else would they try to kill me?"

Trevallion tasted his coffee. "I think someone has much to lose. That can be the only explanation. Rory was nothing. A card-cheat and a thief. Skinner was no better. Yet both of them were obsessed by what they had done. They are dead.

"Who is trying to kill me? I know it is the man who cornered you in the canyon. If he is not stopped he will kill us both."

"Who is behind it?" Grita asked.

"I've no idea."

Grita paused a moment. "Albert Hesketh was in San Francisco when the attempts were made to rob me. He had invited all the cast for a drink when the second attack was made."

"Coincidence. He may be angry with me for staking that claim; but to have me killed? It makes no sense."

For a few minutes they ate in silence and then she said, "You're a strange man, Val. I've never forgotten that night when you held me. I was so frightened and you were so strong. Terrible as that night was, I have never felt as safe as I did then."

"It was your need that made me strong," he said simply. "I was afraid, too, but I had to be brave so you would feel safe."

He gestured around them. "This was what we were looking for. We all wanted it. The pot of gold at the foot of the rainbow and most of us passed it by and went on to California. All the time it was here, waiting for us. I sometimes think this place was our destiny, yours and mine.

"You, you were gone so long from it, yet you are here at last, and I am here. So," he added, "are those others, whoever they are."

"Maybe it is only that man, that Waggoner."

He shook his head. "It was not him tonight."

"Tonight?" She was startled.

"Tonight, on the way here, a man tried to kill me. A man who would have had to be paid, and paid well. A man who had to believe he could do it in safety."

"What happened?"

"He failed. I have lived too long with trouble."

"Was it those shots I heard?"

"There are always shots. Yet, I suppose so."

He put down his cup suddenly. "It is late. You have another show tomorrow, and I have work. And there is something else. I must end this."

"End it? How?"

"Discover who is behind it. Find out what they want and put it forever beyond their grasp. I don't know, only that I can sit no longer. There are things to be done."

She arose. "Val? Be careful."

"I shall." He looked at her, his face cold and serious. "I have things to do, things I must complete, and something I must become."

They said no more but parted at the foot of the stairs. He looked at her for a moment, touching her fingers lightly with his, and then he walked toward the door.

Teale was there. "All clear," he said, quietly. Then he added, "You were mighty good tonight. Two shots and either one would have been enough. He thought he had you, cold turkey."

Trevallion went into the street, yet he did not turn toward home but walked up the street and began to make a round of the gambling houses. All were crowded. The bars were lined two and three deep, the games were busy. He walked among them, unnoticed for the most part, but looking carefully. He wanted a man who knew Kip Hauser, one of the old Sam Brown crowd. None of them were visible.

He gave up at last and then suddenly, without planning, he stopped in at the bakery. A stranger served him.

He was drinking his coffee and thinking when a baker came from the other room, wiping his hands. "Hey! Ain't seen you in a while! The ol' place ain't the same with M'lissa gone."

"What d' you hear from her?"

"Nary a word. Like she dropped off the end of the world. And that's bad."

"Bad?"

"If'n she was happy she'd be writin' to tell us. That's the way folks are. An' she was never one for complainin'."

"She's a good woman."

The man looked at him, then sat down. "Heard you killed a man tonight."

"A man tried to kill me. I defended myself."

"Had it comin'. Hauser was always a thief. Knowed him for years an' all that no-account lot he drifted with."

"Have you seen any of them? I want to talk to one of them, any one."

"They're scared. The whole lot of them took to cover after you killed Hauser, scared to death. The word's around it was a put-up job, an' Hauser had gold on him. *Gold*, an' he ain't pulled nothing for days. That's the word."

"Who paid him?"

"Who knows? None of his friends do. Look," the baker leaned toward him, "I know some o' that bunch. They talk to me. Nary a one o' them has any idea who paid him, if'n that's what you're after. They just don't know."

The baker drew a cup of coffee and came back. "Anyway, that ain't the big news. The big news is the Solomon."

"What about it?"

"They blew into a stope of almost solid silver! Kind of a natural hollow in the ore body, but sheeted with silver! They say it's the richest ever! That there Hesketh, he's goin' to be the richest man on the lode!"

FORTY-FIVE

Trevallion put his cup down. The news could not have been worse. Unless his judgment was completely wrong, that new discovery would have been made on the side where he had filed his claim.

If such was the case, development of the new area could not proceed very far without crossing the line. The old argument about one lode or many would rear its head once more, and he might well lose that claim. It was not as if he had depended upon it, for he had filed largely to benefit Will Crockett, but he hated to be defeated and especially by a man like Hesketh.

Worse, it would provide Hesketh with almost unlimited financing, and he was a man who would know how to use it.

Trevallion sat very still, thinking it through. Bill Stewart immediately came to mind. He had used that law in defeating Terry and would understand all its ramifications.

At the moment it appeared that Hesketh might seize that claim for his own as a continuation of his own lead. Trevallion had never bothered to learn the legalities of mining. He had been basically a discoverer, finding a claim, then selling it and leaving the development to others. Discussion of the fine points of mining camp law were always taking place but he had rarely listened. Now he regretted he had not paid more attention.

Albert Hesketh would move fast. Trevallion had been slow to realize the man's potential, for he had kept a low profile, seemingly content to slowly enlarge his possessions.

John Mackay had commented once, "I'd have no dealings with him. A man who would do what he did to Will Crockett is without basic decency or principle."

The discovery of bonanza ore would provide unlimited credit, giving him freedom to move in any direction he liked. So how would he move?

Trevallion thought again of that claim he had staked alongside the Solomon holdings. Now, more than ever, Hesketh would need that claim.

Trevallion got up and started for the door. He opened it with his

278

right hand then lifted the hand to push the door wider. As he did so the baker called out. "Hey? Ain't you goin' to finish your coffee? I was just about to scramble you some—"

Trevallion had turned back, his hand still on the opening door.

Three bullets smashed through the door and the opening. One ripped a gash in the door-jamb, another went through the door within an inch of Trevallion's hand, and the third tugged at the back of his collar, smashing crockery on the back shelf.

Trevallion hit the floor, scrambling, pistol in hand, toward the side entrance. He pushed it open, waited an instant, then lunged outside and ran to the corner of the street.

Several men had stopped in the middle of the street, staring wildly. Newcomers, obviously, or they would have been out of sight or under something by now. A door closed down the street, then an ore wagon rumbled up, drawn by several teams of oxen.

Nothing . . .

He went back inside, holstering his pistol. "I'll have those eggs," he said, "an' better give me a fresh cup of coffee, something to quiet my nerves."

The baker refilled his cup which rattled in the saucer. "You ain't got no nerves." He was shocked and pale. "Ain't had no bullets come that close since Chief Winnemucca's braves opened up on us." He stared at Trevallion. "They surely wasn't shootin' at me. My bread ain't *that* bad."

"And your coffee's good, so it must have been me."

"From what I hear any man who starts shootin' at you don't have his head screwed on just right."

Trevallion did not reply. He was thinking it over. Two men had been shooting. His mind told him that, for there had been a faint difference in the sound of the shots. If the baker had not spoken, he would be dead and the fault his own. He had allowed himself to be distracted, to be thinking of something else as he started out the door. In other words he had been a plain damned fool.

He finished the eggs and coffee and looked around at the baker, who was working alone tonight. "Anybody back in Melissa's room?"

"You want to spend the night? Ain't nobody there." The baker paused, sheepishly. "We're holdin' it for her, hopin' she'll come back."

"I don't want to stay. I want to use her window. The doors don't seem very safe."

"I'd say!" The baker jerked his head. "Go ahead. It's on the house."

Trevallion got up and, avoiding the windows, went into the back hall and then opened the door to Melissa's room. It smelled faintly of perfume. He closed the door and crossed to the window, standing to the left and then the right to look out. Reflected light made the slope faintly visible and he saw nothing. Lifting the window he stepped out, closing it quietly behind him. For a moment he stood against the stone wall of the house.

Waggoner? Some friend of Kip Hauser? He slid away from the wall and into the night.

Back at the cabin with the door closed, he checked his gun from old habit.

Working with Tapley, while two others continued sinking the shaft, he began to drift toward the outside. They needed a better circulation of air, and there was a good showing of ore in the direction in which he was drifting. After three days he had a wagon up and loaded twenty tons of ore in several trips to the smelter. It ran sixty dollars to the ton.

"Can't figure it," Tapley said suddenly, pausing to rest at the face of the drift. "That Waggoner, now. He's around town, never does a tap of work, always has money. Eats in restaurants, mostly, an' eats well, drinks when he's of a mind to, sees a girl now an' again. Where's he get it? The money, I mean?"

"Somebody's paying him."

Waggoner showed up at the stage the night Margrita Redaway came in, Trevallion thought. Why?

"Waggoner's obviously not scared of you huntin' him down. You've been in town for weeks, months, even. And you've done nothing. He can't be scared of you tellin' what he done, because it's too long ago and far away. So if he's not worried, who is?

"We've been over this time and again and it always comes up to the same thing. Somebody wants you dead and that somebody has something he doesn't want to lose. Also, my guess is that somebody is *here*."

"In Virginia City?"

"You bet. You just bet your life."

"Looks like I have," Trevallion commented wryly.

They returned to work. Oddly enough, his hunch was paying off, for the ore they were taking out of the new drift was somewhat better than from the shaft, and he could use it.

As he worked he turned the matter over in his mind. He was a man to whom decisions came easily, and he had been decisive all his life, yet now he was irritated by uncertainty. Waggoner was a problem with which he could cope, but Waggoner was his only lead to the man behind the violence.

Who wanted him killed? Why? Who instigated the attempted robberies in San Francisco? And why?

Trevallion forced the thoughts from his mind and settled down to drilling. Later, when they had paused briefly to catch their breath, he said, "Don't mention this work."

Tapley indicated the two men working in the shaft. "Shall I speak to them? They'll keep their mouths shut?"

"Do that." He leaned on the end of the sledge handle. "The ore we're finding was sheer luck. I've just had an uneasy feeling about having only one way out of this mine. It will increase the circulation of air, too, but what I'm looking for is another way out, and nobody will know we have it."

It was dark before they emerged from the mine. He stripped to the waist and bathed in slightly heated water while a cold wind came off Sun Mountain. His digging clothes were stiff with dust and sweat.

He got out the bread and cut several slices, then sliced beef from a large roast and put on the coffee. A couple of years ago he could have taken his six-shooter and gone hunting for Waggoner. Now Washoe was shying away from gunfights and trying to settle itself down to an orderly existence.

Orderly in a disorderly way, for the town was a haven for rough-necks. The trouble was that a bum today was tomorrow's millionaire. A man tossed out for not paying a board-bill might return a few days later and buy the place to fire the manager.

The mines were opening up bonanza ore on every side. The Ophir, the Yellow-Jacket, the Gould & Curry, and the Savage were rich beyond belief. The enormous success of these mines had aroused an optimism that knew no limits. Trevallion was a mining man, which most of them were not, and pleased as he was with the success of the Comstock, he knew how quickly some lodes were worked out, or failed to continue. Again and again he heard bar-side miners comment that there was no end to it. They'd found the greatest lode of all time.

There were miners who worked and miners who talked, and hundreds of deadbeats, petty thieves, and the usual drifters that follow booms. Despite that, there was a core of solid, hardworking men who were developing the mines. And there were some, like John Mackay, who were not only developing the mines but themselves as well.

They met rarely. He had worked beside Mackay in California and was amazed at the man's progress. In that short time his grasp of basic mining techniques had increased, and of mining geology as well. He talked little, went about his business, but knew what he was doing and where he was going.

All the talk was of new developments. At parties given at the International, champagne flowed like water. The superintendent of one of the mines drove a handsome coach drawn by four matched black horses with a harness studded with silver. The carriage lamps were bright with silver and gold. Another had his horse shod with silver.

The days of the shacks and dug-outs were gone, although here and there a few remained. Now the mining magnates lived in Victorian mansions with doorknobs of solid silver, Persian carpets, and Brussels lace curtains at the windows. The Gould & Curry was employing more than 2,000 men; several other mines had almost as many. In that year $20 million in bullion traveled over the old trail, now graded and surfaced, to the markets of San Francisco.

Albert Hesketh enjoyed his new suite at the International. He had never cared to smoke, now he ordered Havana cigars. He had never drunk, now he had champagne. He was an important man, he told himself. He had more money than the original Heskeths had ever had, but he had no such position as they, and it rankled.

Yet, he could be governor, or even a senator. He had money now, he had position. There were no limits. Only . . . there was the fear.

A fear he lived with every waking hour, a fear that caused him to awaken in a cold sweat and lie wide-eyed and staring in the middle of the night.

He could be exposed. Even if after all these years they could prove nothing, he could be exposed. The story could come out and all he had become could be shattered like thin glass. He could be destroyed.

He suffered no remorse for what he had done, he suffered only fear of discovery, of exposure. One man and one woman lived who could, perhaps, expose him.

Murder and rape.

Murder might be forgiven, rape never. He must destroy them, they must both be killed, no matter how.

Yet, why kill her? She was a beautiful woman. She was the right setting for him. She could add grace and beauty to a home, and she could not but admire him. After all, he was a success. He was making millions. Well, not quite millions, but they would come. And she knew nothing, she could know nothing. She had been too young, and she had not seen him. No one had.

Trevallion?

He hated the man, and the man worried him. The very thought of him was an irritation. Trevallion had killed Rory and he had killed Skinner—so much the better.

Yet, how had he known who they were? Of course, he had been older than the girl, and he had seen them again when they tried to kill his father. Nevertheless, two men were dead and who was next?

What the hell was the matter with Waggoner? What was wrong? Why had he not killed Trevallion? And that fool Kip Hauser, to let himself be caught flatfooted.

Now Margrita Redaway was here, and she had been seen with Trevallion. What did that mean?

But Trevallion knew nothing of *him*, could know nothing. Of course, he might remember him from that encounter in the street. Why had he been such a fool as to ask to see that coin?

The moment he had seen it he had known it for what it was and was sure the senior Trevallion had found Spanish treasure. He was sure there was much of it in the wagon.

There had been so little in comparison to what he had expected and hoped for, but still there had been enough to outfit him for California and to give him a start, and still enough left to enable him to buy shares in the Solomon. Albert Hesketh stared across the room, thinking.

Two men, Will Crockett and Trevallion.

They must be killed, and if necessary he would do it himself.

FORTY-SIX

Trevallion awoke in the middle of the night. He lay perfectly still, listening. His life had been such that he slept with awareness, quick to awaken at any slight sound or strange movement.

The door was barred from within. The window was large enough for entry but was closed but for a crack at the bottom.

He put his hand over to the chair where his holster hung from its gun-belt and slid the six-shooter into his hand. He waited a long moment but heard no further sound, if it was a sound that had awakened him.

Easing from under the covers, he put the gun down on the bed and slipped into his trousers, then slung on the gun-belt and returned the six-shooter to its scabbard.

All the time he was careful to keep himself in complete darkness, and not to lift his head high enough to be seen through the window. Knowing the position of what little furniture he had, he avoided it and got back into a corner from which he could see out of the window.

Nothing, then a moving shadow, a glimpse only.

He waited, listening, poised and alert. A shadow moved, but he was not such a fool as to shoot. It could be a friend not wishing to disturb him; only a fool shot at what he could not identify.

Was there one man out there? Or were there more?

There was a slight pressure on the door, but the bar permitted no give and the door was firm. One attempt, then no more.

A friend or acquaintance would knock or call out. A shadow moved outside the window. Trevallion's left hand dropped to the poker. Outside the window he saw the faint shine of a gun barrel, then a face pressed against the window, peering in. He swung the poker with his left hand.

Glass shattered but the poker struck something hard beyond the glass. There was a faint cry, then a moan of pain and staggering steps.

Somebody else swore, swore bitterly. There were muttered words and Trevallion waited, feeling the cold draft from the broken window.

284

He heard boots on gravel, muttered protests, and more anguished moans. Trevallion hung an old coat over the broken window, and opening the stove door, he added a couple of sticks to the coals within. At once the fire blazed up and he glanced at his watch . . . two A.M. He took off his pants and got back into bed, listening to the pound of the stamp-mills. His pistol lay beside the bed on a chair and within easy grasp.

At daybreak he was outside, repairing his window. There was shattered glass on the ground outside and some flecks of blood. There was also a six-shooter with well-polished bone grips on the butt. He took up the gun and carried it inside, then locking the door, he went to work in the mine.

Tapley arrived a few minutes later and joined him. They had been working several minutes before Tapley straightened up and said, "M'lissa's back."

"Back?"

"She came in last night. She's back at the bakery."

"Does Jim know?"

"He does. He brought her back. Seems she got word to him somehow. She fell sick and that man of hers taken out. He left her."

"Ought to be shot."

"Jim'll do it, if he sees him. He's that mad. She got word to him somehow and he went for her. Found her in a cheap hotel with no money."

"Seem like old times, havin' her back."

"If she gets well."

"Now if we could only find Will Crockett."

"I think he's dead," Tapley said. "Why would he leave like that? Where could he be, and no word from him at all?"

"He might have gone back to California. He might be mining there. You know he had a mine there, sold stock in it, and—"

Trevallion broke off. "Tap, what was the name of that mine Crockett had in California?"

"Damned if I know. I never knew him, you know. I saw him around town a few times and down at the bakery or over at Eilley's, but I never knew him well."

"I've got to know."

"Ask Hesketh. He would know if anybody would. He knew all about Crockett's business."

"No, not him."

Trevallion put down his double-jack. "Tap, I'm knocking off for the day. I've got some questions to ask, and not of Hesketh."

"You want me to keep workin'?"

"Yes, but watch yourself. I had trouble again last night."

Tapley looked at him. "I saw your window was busted." He put his hat on again. "I'm goin' with you."

At the house, Trevallion gestured toward the gun. "Know who owns that?"

Tapley shrugged. "Might be a dozen of 'em around, but I seen one of those newcomers who run with Waggoner wear a gun like that."

Trevallion changed clothes and belted on his gun again. "You mind the store, Tap. I don't know what's going on, but I think all hell's about to break loose. I've just had a hunch."

He went down the street to the International.

"Miss Redaway?" the clerk said. "She went for a ride, I believe."

Trevallion turned sharply from the desk, then looked back. "Was Teale with her?"

"I believe not, sir. I believe she went alone."

Where was Teale?

"Sir?" Impatiently, he turned on the clerk. "Are you Mr. Trevallion?"

"I am."

"She left this for you, sir."

He took the letter from the clerk and ripped it open.

Val:

I have had a note from a man named Will Crockett. He has asked to see me. He said he was ill and could not come to me. He is in a shack at the north end of Bailey Canyon, near the spring. Mr. Teale had business in Gold Hill and has ridden over there.

I realize this is foolhardy of me but Mr. Crockett's condition is such that there is little time.

Grita

A trick? He turned swiftly and went up the steps on the run. As he turned into the hall on her floor, her door was just being closed from within. He reached it an instant before the lock clicked shut and shoved it open.

The man closing the door staggered back, a slender man with glasses and a pointed beard, well-dressed and apparently not at all alarmed.

"Sir! You very nearly knocked me down!"

"I am sorry, but as Miss Redaway is absent, I could not imagine who was in her suite."

"Absent? Oh, I am sorry! I was hoping to talk with her this morning, business talk. The door was ajar and I thought I heard her call out to come in. I must have been mistaken, but there is so much noise outside, you know how it is."

The cold blue eyes measured him. "You are a friend?"

"I am, and shall be seeing her soon. If there is any message . . . ?"

"No, no, it is business. I will arrange to see her later. Now, if you please?" He stepped around Trevallion and went down the hall.

Trevallion stood, thinking. Now who the devil— He turned quickly to get the man's name but the hall was empty.

He must go, but he did not like to leave the rooms empty. With her out of the way, and that might have been the idea, they could be searched at leisure. Still, the man he surprised certainly looked like anything but a sneak thief. A businessman, as he professed to be, or, what was it about the man that disturbed him?

Mary!

Of course! He would get Mary, and she lived on the same floor. He went down the hall. Which room was it? He rapped.

She opened the door a crack, her hair done in curlers, a flowered wrapper clutched about her. "Oh! Mr. Trevallion!"

"Mary, there isn't any time. Miss Redaway has ridden off and I've got to find her. She may be in trouble. Will you stay in her suite while she is gone?"

"I will that." She turned hastily and began gathering up things. A pistol lay on the bureau top.

"Is that yours?"

"It is."

"If you can use it, take it along. This could be serious."

"Guns are always serious, Mr. Trevallion. I will take it, indeed, and if trouble comes, I shall use it. I'm a poor country girl, Mr. Trevallion, and I grew up shooting varmints."

At the stable he saddled the black mule. He was riding out when Ledbetter rounded the corner. "Trev? You're not leaving, are you? Bill Stewart wants to talk to you."

"Later." Quickly, he explained.

"Bailey Canyon? I haven't been up there in a year or more, but last I heard that cabin was empty."

Trevallion did not go by the longer, roundabout route that turned off above Seven Mile Canyon but cut across, riding west toward the head of Bailey.

Smoke was coming from the cabin chimney. There were two horses in the corral and one, the one Margrita had ridden, tied to a hitching-rail outside the cabin.

He pulled up, swung down, and tied the black mule. Slipping the thong from his six-shooter and carrying his rifle in his left hand, he went up to the door.

The door stood open, although there was a chill in the air. Margrita sat on an empty box near the bed on which lay a man. Another man stood near the stove.

Margrita got up quickly when she saw him. "Val! Thank God, you've come!"

He stepped to the bedside. It was Will Crockett all right, but a man wasted and frail, his cheeks sunken, his eyes hollow.

The feverish eyes caught the movement as Trevallion entered. "Good! Good!" he whispered hoarsely. "Tie to him, miss. He's a good man. I should have listened to him, and to Melissa. They told me. They warned me."

He caught at Trevallion's hand. "She has it! I gave it all to her! Her folks bought stock in my first venture! Bought when I was desperate for money! She has the controlling shares! Now I give her the rest of it on condition she throw him out, Hesketh. Throw him out and keep him out!"

Crockett dropped Trevallion's hand and reached for hers. "Careful! You've got to be careful! He's left a trail of blood! It was his man shot me!"

"Which man?"

"The big, lazy-moving man, blondish. Figured I was dead. I wasn't. Been nigh onto a week since. Had to live! Had to beat him!"

"Dragged hisself a couple of miles," the man by the stove said. "Must've been headed toward Virginia from over nigh Steamboat Springs. I done trailed him to where he fell from his horse. Killer chased after his horse, shot the horse, ripped open his saddlebags an' dumped them out. I gathered up what lay about. It wasn't much."

"Be careful!" Crockett's voice had grown hoarser. "Kill you, don't care. Kill anybody."

His eyes flared open and his hand flew out toward the paper on the rough table. "Sign it! Sign it! You're a witness! I give an' bequeath, all to her! Every bit!

"I looked for your aunt, ma'am. I surely did. Then for you. I needed that, those shares.

"Take charge. Put him out like he put me. Lock, stock, an' barrel! Frisco! There was a man in Frisco died in a fire. Whoever set that fire thought it was all destroyed but it wasn't! Find heirs! Buy rights! They'll take anything, anything!"

"Take it easy, Will," Trevallion said quietly. "We will handle it. You get some rest now. We'll get a wagon over here and get you down to town." Trevallion looked up to the man by the stove. "Ride in and get hold of Jim Ledbetter. Tell him about this. But tell nobody else."

"Sure will. Jim? I know Jim. Used to work for him."

Margrita rinsed out a cloth and lay it on Crockett's forehead. "I remembered him, Val. He used to come to our house when I was very small. He was much younger then, but a good man, and a good friend.

"My father loaned him money, so did my aunt. She bought shares in his first venture in California, and he gave stock in the Solomon for those original shares."

They listened to the clatter of hoofs as the man rode off.

"You examine him?"

"No, not really. Enough to know he's been shot twice, and I suspect he's lost a lot of blood. I think he has pneumonia now, too.

"Mr. Faber, that's the man who was here, he found him and brought him here. Sent a friend after me. They were afraid to noise it about for fear they'd come back and finish the job."

"And so they would." Trevallion glanced out the door. "We've got to be careful, Grita."

Trevallion walked outside and looked around. He saw nothing but that did not mean nothing was there. If it was so much as suspected that Crockett was alive and had the additional shares to reclaim possession of the Solomon, there would surely be an attempt to kill him. As for himself, he had been shot at several times and knew his number was up.

"Stay inside," he warned. "I'm staying under cover myself."

Suddenly he thought of something. "Where is Jacob Teale?"

"He asked if he could take time off to ride to Genoa."

Of course, the man needed some time to himself. And he had a small ranch near that town.

Impatiently Trevallion paced back and forth, irritably looking at the mountains, up the canyon, and down the trail toward town. "It will take at least an hour and a half," he said. "Probably more. By the time Faber gets into town and they get a wagon out here, closer to two hours."

She changed the cool cloths on Crockett's brow, then came to stand beside him. "This isn't a play," she said, "this is real."

"It is," he agreed, "but you're playing it as though you had rehearsed it all your life."

She took hold of his left arm, very gently. "I have," she said.

FORTY-SEVEN

Albert Hesketh ate his breakfast at the International and then walked the few blocks to the offices of the Solomon.

Santley had the reports from the mine on his desk, all neatly laid out. He must, Hesketh was thinking, buy another mill. There was money to be saved, and he suspected the mill operators were not as honest as they should be.

He had been a fool to enter Margrita's rooms at the hotel, but time was running short and he needed those shares. Every bit of evidence he had accumulated indicated they were in her possession. Knowing she was coming here, she surely would not have come without them. Yet a moment later and he would have been caught going through her desk.

Trevallion, now he had seen the man. He was different than he had suspected, much sharper, cool, and there was something about the man's eyes that disturbed him. It was Hesketh's nature that he despised all men and held them in contempt, yet this man, this Trevallion, was dangerous.

The coolness displayed at the killing of Kip Hauser was not what he would have suspected. From first to last, by all reports, Trevallion had been in command of the situation, quick to perceive danger, and acting with deliberation and no sign of panic. Such a man, who lived with awareness, would be difficult to kill as Waggoner had already discovered.

There was a knock on the door, and at his call, Santley entered. "We've opened Number Three, sir, and the men have begun stoping it out. The vein at that point is thirty-five feet wide and very rich, the best yet."

"Thank you, Santley. That's good news."

Santley lingered, and Hesketh looked up. "Was there something else, Santley?"

"Yes, sir. There's a rumor in town, sir, that Will Crockett has turned up. He's been badly hurt, but he's said to be alive."

For a moment his heart seemed to stop but his face showed nothing. "That's very fortunate," he said, "now we can get down to business."

"Yes, sir."

Santley turned to go. Obviously, Hesketh thought, Santley had expected more reaction.

"Where is he staying, Santley? Do you know?"

"No, sir. I believe it's your own hotel, sir. It was Miss Redaway and Trevallion who brought him in, in one of Jim Ledbetter's wagons."

"Thank you, Santley. If you hear any more of this you might let me know."

When the office door closed he got to his feet and walked to the window, looking out over the mountainside. He fought down the panic that surged up inside him. There was more than sixty thousand dollars in this safe and his private safe at the International. Why not take it and run?

It was a fleeting thought, quickly pushed aside. What he wanted was here, power and position. So far he had won, and now at this setback he must not weaken.

If Margrita Redaway did have the missing shares, and if she was with Will Crockett, then they had the power to unseat him, to take over. He still would have income from the mine and he had other claims, although nothing like the Solomon.

He had been so sure that Crockett was dead, although he had never stopped worrying. Waggoner had his instructions, and Waggoner would know that Crockett was back in town.

Badly hurt, Santley said. Wounded probably, maybe dying. That would be of no use if he made some arrangement with Margrita Redaway.

The situation was desperate, and it was a time for desperate measures.

Everything he had worked for, connived for, all of it was at stake. Whatever was done must be done now.

All three of them must die, and when they were killed he himself must be much in public view, totally unconnected with whatever happened. It had to be quick, it had to be decisive, and it had to be immediate.

How?

The first thought was Waggoner, of course. He was close, he was convenient, he could be had. He had failed in the past, but in other cases he had succeeded. He had to reach Waggoner, and some means must be set up to dispose of all three.

Somehow he had to get them out of the International, at least two of them. If Crockett was in such shape that he could not be moved, he would have to be disposed of right where he was.

It was then he thought of Mousel.

Hesketh did not remember when he had first heard of the trouble in Placerville. It was one of countless items he heard and filed away in his memory for future reference. Mousel had been about to kill somebody and Trevallion had stopped it. Mousel, it was said, carried a grudge against Melissa Turney, the man she had recently married, and Trevallion.

Mousel, for the past several weeks, had been a mucker in the Solomon, a sullen, disagreeable man and a lazy one. Several times the shift boss had wanted to fire him, but Hesketh suggested keeping him on. Now he knew why.

Dismissing all else from his mind, he worked on plans for the Solomon, the new developments, shipping of ore, and assembling some of the figures pertinent to construction of a mill. All the while at the back of his mind was the problem of Crockett, Trevallion, and Margrita Redaway.

When Santley came in, Hesketh asked, "How much ore do we have that is ready for milling?"

"A hundred and fifty tons or so, and we will take out almost that much today."

Hesketh sat back in his chair. There was cash on hand, unbanked. He would move that to his safe at the hotel, just in case. He would reduce all the ore to cash as quickly as possible. He had no intention of losing the Solomon, but if he did—

He thought of Mousel. He knew the type, a man who nursed grudges, who lived by his hatreds and through his hatreds. Such a man could be useful.

For a time he sat quietly, thinking of what might be done, fighting down the panic that kept creeping up on him.

All he wanted was here. For a brief time he had held the Solomon, even if by the thinnest of threads, and now they would try to take it from him.

How long did he have? A day? A week? A month?

Put on another shift, he told himself, work around the clock, mill the ore at once, and ship the metal. If he lost the Solomon he could take the money and disappear.

To leave the Solomon? Bitterness was an ugly taste in his mouth. He lunged to his feet, half in panic, half in fury. He would kill them all!

To leave meant that he would lose not only the Solomon but also Margrita Redaway.

But he did not have Margrita, and he had a feeling she despised him. Yet, how could she? *He owned the Solomon!* Women loved power and they loved money, so how could she not admire *him*?

As long as he held the Solomon.

Why did Crockett have to return *now*? He had been so sure he would not come back. Couldn't they do anything right?

Santley had been gone for an hour when Hesketh locked the office door and walked down the hill, down along the street to the International. To leave would be unthinkable. Somehow, he must find a way.

Crockett was in the International, they said. He must find out where. If necessary he would kill him. No knife, a pillow. They would believe he had simply died.

But he must be careful, very careful, indeed.

He must have some more men. He must find a man who could recruit for him, who could gather a tough, hardbitten bunch who would be ready to act when he needed them.

Santley? No. Santley knew little, let him know no more. Never let the left hand know what the right is doing. Let things seem to happen, and be surprised when they do.

When he entered the hotel it was being decorated for a party. He paused, irritated. "What is it? What's happening?" he asked.

"A party, sir." The clerk was respectful. "Sandy and Eilley Bowers are back from Europe."

Hesketh lifted an eyebrow, a faint expression of distaste on his face. He glanced quickly around the lobby. Jacob Teale was nowhere in sight, and he considered that. Had she disposed of his services? Was he off upon some other task? A chilling thought came: perhaps he was guarding Will Crockett?

He went to his floor on the elevator. One of two elevators west of Chicago, of which the hotel was inordinately proud.

He had brought some money from the Solomon, and he opened his own safe, and stored it carefully away. From the safe he took a derringer and a sleeve-holster. From now on he would wear it wherever he went, and he had always carried a boot-knife ready for instant use.

Again he thought of Margrita. She must be killed, too. Reason argued with his desire to possess her as a showpiece, to parade her as his wife. Physical desire had nothing to do with it. He had never felt such things nor cared. He wanted power and power only, not secret power but obvious power. He wanted people to fear him, to obey him, to step aside for him. He wanted not only power but the trappings of power. A palatial home, a beautiful wife, but above all the power to crush, to destroy.

And now he was on the verge of losing it all. If the Solomon was taken from him, he must build it all over again, if he could.

Yet he had no patience for building from the ground up. The basic work, the hard work on the Solomon had been done before he seized it.

Sandy and Eilley Bowers were giving a party. The thought returned to him suddenly. He liked neither of them. They were strong, hearty people of little taste, warmhearted and generous, but they were boors—in his estimation, they were boors.

Yet they had friends, and they were generally well-liked, even loved. Hesketh understood that without accepting the reasons why. Their party would be attended by everyone, or almost everyone. The hotel would be crowded, champagne would be flowing like water, and there would be much drunkenness. It would be a night when anything might happen, when anything *could* happen.

Perfect.

Waggoner might come but he would not stay, for Waggoner was unsocial. He preferred his own company to that of anyone else. He would enjoy the free food and drinks and then go back to his cabin; so for a time he would be gone.

Hesketh knew what he would do. The details of the plan fell neatly into place. The panic was gone now, and the blinding rage. He was still, he was cold, he was sure.

He would pick up a newspaper and he would speak to the headwaiter.

For a moment he hesitated, thinking it all over carefully. Yes, it was the way. It all depended on timing and a certain amount of chance. But he could gamble. He had gambled before this.

Albert Hesketh bought a newspaper at the cigar stand and turned toward the dining room. The hotel was already beginning to fill with the Bowerses' guests.

"I shall be down," he glanced at his watch, "in thirty minutes. I shall want my usual table."

"But, Mr. Hesketh, Sandy Bowers has taken over the dining room. He is paying for everything. He will arrange—"

"My usual table," Hesketh replied coolly, "nothing but that. What goes on here tonight is no concern of mine. I shall dine as usual, and I shall return to my rooms. I shall want my usual dinner for Friday nights. No more, no less. And I shall pay for my own dinner."

"Yes, sir. Of course, sir."

When he returned, he left his door open just a crack to listen to the movements in the hall outside. There was almost no sound as most of the patrons of the hotel were already down on the lower levels sharing the Bowerses' hospitality. He waited an instant then stepped out, shut his door carefully, and walked down the hall to the stairway. He glanced back. The hall was empty. Swiftly he went down the stairs. He'd had no trouble discovering what room Crockett had been given.

The lower hall was empty, too, so he walked along briskly and tapped lightly at the door. He waited a moment and tapped again, no answer.

He tried the knob and it turned easily in his hand. He opened the door and stepped inside. If anyone found him here, he had just come to see if there was anything he could do for his former employer. After all, he'd say, we had our troubles but I really liked the cantankerous old—

The shades were drawn. A dim light burned at the far side of the room, but other than the man lying on the bed, propped up by pillows, the room was empty.

There was an empty chair near the light and a newspaper folded beside it, as well as a half-empty cup. The nurse, or whoever had been here, must have just stepped out. He had very little time.

A spare pillow lay on the floor near the bed. He picked it up and stood for a moment, looking down at Will Crockett.

The trouble was, he wanted Will to know. He wanted Will Crockett to see him in that last, flickering moment. To see the man he would order around no longer.

Smiling, he touched Will on the chest, shook him gently.

"Will? It's Al Hesketh, Will."

FORTY-EIGHT

The dining room was crowded with men and women clad in all their tawdry best, most of them standing. At an improvised bar champagne was being poured, and men were three deep, awaiting their turn.

Easing through the crowd, speaking to no one, Hesketh went to his usual table and sat down, opening his *Territorial Enterprise* to the inside. As a harried waiter passed he spoke quickly, "Waiter? How much longer must I wait?"

"Oh? Sorry, sir. We've been busy with the party. Right away, sir. I'll see to it."

"You might bring me some more coffee. A fresh cup, if you don't mind." He handed the waiter a cup, left standing on the table by some passerby at the party.

He straightened around in his chair and took up the newspaper, yet his eyes did not focus.

Will Crockett was dead. One of the three was gone. One more, at least, must go. He doubted whether anyone in the constantly shifting group in the room had noticed when he had arrived. In any event, they would not be noticing the time.

Will Crockett was dead. Actually, it had been remarkably easy, perhaps the easiest thing he had ever done. At his voice, Crockett's eyes had flared open and he seemed about to speak or cry out, but the pillow had descended, smothering any outcry, smothering life itself. He could still feel Crockett's clutching hands grabbing his arms. But he was strong in the hands and had always been.

He had been in the room less than a minute, and then back to his own room, down to the main floor and the dining room.

It was done, finished.

He had hated Will Crockett as he hated anything that stood between him and what he wanted.

Sandy and Eilley Bowers came into the room, glancing his way but neither came over. The fools! Running through their money like a couple of drunken sailors! Didn't they realize it wouldn't last forever?

The waiter began to serve his dinner, and he folded his paper and

296

placed it further over on the table. Uneasily, he felt his forearms. Those fingers, he could still feel them.

"Cold, Mr. Hesketh?" the waiter asked.

"No. No, certainly not. Why should I be cold?"

Upstairs, in Will Crockett's bedroom, the nurse had returned to her station. All was quiet. Mr. Crockett seemed to be sleeping, and it was just as well. She had slipped out for a quick glass of champagne; she had never tasted the stuff before and was faintly disappointed, expecting something more. She opened her book and began to read. More than a half hour passed before she became disturbed. Pausing as she started to turn a page, she listened.

Odd, he was sleeping so quietly she couldn't even hear him breathe. He . . . she got up quickly and went to the bed.

Deliberately, Albert Hesketh took his time over his meal, ignoring the bustle and stir around him. He wanted everybody to be aware of him, and that he had been there a long time. Nobody, he was sure, would remember just when he came in, only that he seemed to have been there forever.

Finally, he took up his paper again, ordered another cup of coffee and a brandy, and sat back slowly, relaxing.

Over an hour; by now they should know, by now they would have discovered that Will Crockett was dead.

Hesketh finished his coffee and was about to rise when he saw Waggoner.

The big man was across the room, standing alone, a glass of champagne in his hand. Waggoner's eyes swept over the room, passed him, never even halting. Of course, Waggoner did not know him, and would not know him unless there had been some fleeting memory.

The thought made him remember his brief meeting with Trevallion in Margrita Redaway's rooms. There had been a flicker of something in Trevallion's eyes, of doubt, the stirring of a memory, of suspicion.

Trevallion had seemed on the verge of recalling something, of remembering.

It did not matter. Trevallion must go. If Waggoner could not handle it, others could. He might even do it himself.

But at once, for now, there was no more time.

Trevallion wore his black suit and his gun. He met Margrita in the lobby where she was talking with Clyde and Manfred.

"I am sorry," he said. "I am afraid I am late."

"Will Crockett is dead." She turned to him as she spoke. "Mr. Manfred believes it is murder."

"How did he die?"

"He was smothered." Manfred's eyes were like ice. "I have seen the look before. No matter what the nurse says, she must have left the room."

"She denies it?"

"She does. I believe she came down to get a drink. In fact, one of the waiters remembers seeing her."

"Where was Hesketh?"

"In the dining room, in very plain sight, being served his dinner as always, in the same seat as always."

"He wouldn't do it himself, anyway," Clyde said.

Manfred glanced at him. "Of course he would. Have you ever really *looked* at him? I have. He would kill you without turning a hair."

He turned slightly, looking from Margrita to Trevallion. "You two are next, believe me, I know. Look at it seriously. He now has possession of the Solomon. It represents a lot of money and if one wishes to use it, that money means power. Will Crockett's return threatened Hesketh's control. Crockett is conveniently dead. So who threatens him now?"

"I suspect that I do," Margrita said, "or so somebody seems to believe."

"And you do," Manfred said to Trevallion. "For some reason you worry him."

"I've been worrying somebody," Trevallion replied mildly, "ever since I came to Virginia City."

"Ever since you came *back*," Manfred said.

Trevallion gave him a sharp glance. "What's that mean?"

"Hadn't you been here before?" Manfred pointed down the canyon. "Isn't your father buried down there?"

He had their attention now, but suddenly his manner changed. "We're none of us here by accident. Oh, maybe Clyde is, but we are not. This place," he gestured widely, "it has a fatal attraction for us. Trevallion and me because we remembered the place, and Miss Redaway because her family was coming west for gold and something drove her to complete what had been begun.

"Don't ask me why, except, well, my family are buried down there, too."

"I had no idea," Margrita exclaimed. "Somehow I never suspected."

He shrugged. "Nobody does. Because I lived abroad for a while they all believe I'm a bloody foreigner. I'm not."

He stared at Trevallion. "I remember you, although you don't remember me. I don't think you even saw me, although I was around."

"Saw you? Where?"

"On the wagon train, coming west. My name wasn't Manfred then. I owe Lord Byron for that. I borrowed the name from his poem because that Manfred sold his soul to the devil and got away with it. When the devil came to take possession, he had become too strong for him, and refused him. I did that, too, in a way. Only I wasn't strong enough so I ran away. I got away."

"You were on the wagon train with us?"

"Yes. My name was Thompson then."

"Thompson! But Thompson was the family that drove off into the basin after a mirage."

"Exactly. My father was a bull-headed, foolish man, Mr. Trevallion. That does not say he was not kind or a good provider. Also, he was not a trusting man, and that, at least, I inherited from him."

He paused, looking around, then he added, "One thing you must grasp. Albert Hesketh is a completely self-centered man in its most extreme sense. He has nothing of what we call conscience, and fear in its usual sense is utterly foreign to him.

"My father took us off the trail into the desert after a mirage. By the time he realized the lake we thought we saw kept receding before us, it was too late. He tried to turn the team around and got bogged down. He had valuable tools in the wagon and would not leave them.

"We tried to get him to take the oxen and walk out but he refused. Working in the blazing sun, fighting to get the wagon turned, his heart failed him and he died right there.

"The heat was frightful and we had no water after the first few hours. We buried my father and just doing that took a lot out of us. Two of the oxen died there and we unhitched the others. I got my mother on one of the oxen and my sisters on the other. We'd come miles, and going back was mostly up hill.

"My mother had been ill a lot, and she lasted longer than I expected, but she went, too, and then my sisters.

"I buried them, after a fashion. And then this man came along. He was alone but he had six pack burros. He gave me a little water, when I had almost passed out, then he gave me more.

" 'Where you from, boy? Where's your wagon?' I pointed and he told me to get up and we'd go back. He asked what was in it and I told him and he started back. I didn't want to go. 'You want to get out of here don't you, boy? You help me and I'll take you out.'

"We went back to our wagon, and he had me help him load everything of value on those burros. Then he asked me where the money was. I asked 'What money?' and he said, 'Don't give me trouble, boy, or you can stay right here an' die. Everybody has a little money. Where is it?'

"I wanted to get out. I wanted to live, and I was scared of him. Ma had given me what money she'd had from pa when he was dying, so I gave him that.

"We started out and I suddenly realized he intended to kill me or leave me to die, but he needed my help right then.

"Before we got to the trail—he wasn't using the main emigrant trail—we found another wagon. There was nobody around, so he went through the wagon, taking everything of value and loading it.

"I was exhausted and wanted to quit, but I knew if I did he'd leave me. After a while, it was almost dusk, we started on. He seemed to pay no attention to me and didn't stop even when I fell. Finally when it was almost dark he called to me. He'd stopped back of a big old sand dune with some rocks around, and some brush. I was scared of him and when he called again, I ran.

"I was behind the mules which were following him, and he had to ride out from them to see me, and I dropped behind a rock and then began to crawl. He started for where I was, and I ran again. He shot at me, and I fell just like I'd been shot, then I rolled over and crawled. There was a big old rock there with a kind of shelf out from it. I crawled under that. He finally gave up hunting and rode off."

"Some of those people," Trevallion commented, "planned to return and pick up their wagons."

Manfred shrugged. "So? He didn't care. He looted them and sold whatever he got from their wagons, sold it later, in California."

"And that man was Albert Hesketh?" Margrita suggested.

"It was."

"Has he seen you now, here?"

"He may have. Of course, I am older now and I've changed a lot." He paused. "That was over three hundred dollars he took from me. God knows how much he got from others, or other wagons."

"There's Eilley Bowers," Margrita said. "I must speak to her. Will you excuse me?"

Clyde went with her and Manfred stood alone with Trevallion, who said, "Odd, how we were so close then and never met. But then, how many people on a wagon train ever know the others? A few, maybe, and that's all."

"What I told you wasn't all," Manfred said.

"No?"

"He caught me again. He made me go with him into the desert and loot wagons. Once I helped him bury a man who'd been shot in the back. When we picked him up his body was still warm, and it was at night. That man had been killed within the hour."

"By Hesketh?"

"Who else? Nobody was around, he took me right to that wagon. Knew right where it was."

"What about you?"

"He shot me one evening, just casually turned and shot me. The bullet knocked me out and cut my scalp very badly. I was all blood and he believed me dead, so he just rolled me over into a dry wash and caved the bank over me.

"It was night and he did not see that part of my face was uncovered. When I became conscious I crawled out and got away to California, picked up by a wagonload of actors, as a matter of fact."

Laughter and the clink of glasses came across the room. "He killed Crockett," Manfred added, "although I am sure it cannot be proved.

"One thing we must remember. Albert Hesketh is a very fastidious man. He likes every package neatly done up with all the loose ends cut away."

Manfred glanced from Margrita, standing across the room, to Trevallion. "And we three? We are loose ends."

FORTY-NINE

Trevallion sat over a cup of coffee in the bakery with Jim Ledbetter. "Like old times," Ledbetter said.

Trevallion gestured toward the town outside. "It's changed. It's a city now, where it used to be just a bunch of squatters on a barren mountainside, living in the brush like a bunch of jackrabbits."

Melissa came to the table. "Mind if I sit down?" She put her cup down, and then joined them. "I'm sorry about Will. He was a good man."

"He was that," Ledbetter agreed. "Too good."

The coffee was hot and it tasted good. Trevallion put his cup down and thought of Margrita, useless thoughts for him. Now, as soon as she took control of the Solomon, she would be a wealthy woman, and a wealthy and beautiful young woman wouldn't want a man from the mining camps.

It was time to drift, time to go off down the trail talking to himself. It was deep enough.

He spoke the words aloud, without thinking. When a miner said it was deep enough it meant he was pulling his stakes.

"You leaving?" Ledbetter said.

"A few loose ends," he said, and then recalled Manfred's comment.

The door shoved open, slamming back hard. A man stood in the doorway, swaying a little. His clothes were muddy as though he had fallen, and he was very drunk. It was Alfie.

Melissa stood up quickly. He stared at her, swaying. "Good ol' 'Lissy! 'Lissy, I'm broke. I need some money. I—"

"I am sorry. I have nothing for you."

The smile left his face. "What you mean you got nothin' for me? Now you listen here!"

"Alfie," Melissa spoke quietly, but with dignity, "I must ask you to leave."

He stared at her. "You don't tell me to leave. You don't—"

"Leave, Alfie, and don't come back. You took all the money I had and left me sick in bed. Go away."

He started forward but suddenly Ledbetter stood between them.

302

"The lady said you were to go. Now go or I'll give you a horse-whipping!"

Alfie stared at them, sullen with anger. "I'll go, damn you! But you ain't so much, you—"

Jim Ledbetter was a mild man, but his fists were not. Jim Ledbetter knocked him down, and then, taking Alfie by the collar, he dragged him to the door and put him outside, closing the door as he returned.

"Thank you, Jim," Melissa said.

"That's all right, ma'am."

At the Bucket of Blood Saloon Mousel thrust his hand into his coat pocket, hoping to find the price of a beer. His hand encountered a piece of paper, the corner of an envelope, actually. In it were tucked two gold eagles and on it was written, *"You are going to shoot him, anyway. Why not now?"*

He stared at it, blinking slowly. Then he stepped to the bar. The bartender, his mouth open to refuse, saw the gold piece and drew the beer.

Mousel gulped some of the beer. Somebody was using him. Well, he'd be damned if . . . but, why not? He *was* going to, he had come to town with that intent, so why not?

Forty dollars was not much but it was more than he had coming at the Solomon.

Why not? And why not now?

The pistol he had now was a Remington Navy. It was a good pistol, too. He drank more of the beer. He should shoot her, too. She was the one. Got real uppity, didn't she? Well, he'd show—

The door swung back and Alfie came in. Mousel had the beer in his left hand but as their eyes met, Mousel reached for the Remington in his waistband and drew it. He glimpsed the look of startled horror on Alfie's face, and Alfie's hand came up, thrusting toward him, palm out.

Mousel fired.

Men turned from the bar, startled. Mousel was gripping the Remington; Alfie was dead on the floor, his hands empty.

A man bent over him, then he straightened up slowly, rubbing his hands down the front of his pants. "He's dead, all right," the man spoke quietly but sternly, "and he's unarmed. He has no gun."

Mousel's chin began to tremble. All eyes were on him. "Now, look here!" he protested. "This man—"

He turned and stumbled toward the door, only as he opened it, a man was coming in. A man wearing a badge.

"It's murder," one man said, "shot an unarmed man."

Mousel's flabby cheeks trembled and his eyes watered. "It ain't like that!" he protested. "He . . . that man . . . well . . ." The words trailed off. "He stole my woman," he managed at last.

Trevallion stood in the door. "That's not true," he said, speaking to the officer. "I was there, Hank, and so was Jim Ledbetter. The lady to whom he refers hired a mule from Ledbetter and came in with one of his caravans. I was riding in the same bunch. The dead man was nowhere around when the lady left Placerville."

Searching Mousel for a weapon, Hank found the corner of the envelope, the other gold piece and the change. "Paid for it? Forty bucks? You bought yourself a noose for forty dollars?"

Hank turned to Trevallion. "Did you ever see Bill Stewart? He's been asking for you."

"I'll look him up." He was standing near Hank and he spoke softly. "Looks like an open and shut case. He shot an unarmed man. All this talk about a woman, that doesn't have to be mentioned, does it?"

Hank shrugged. "Not so far's I'm concerned."

"Have you seen Tapley?"

Hank shook his head. "Not this evenin'. You want him?"

"I do."

"I'll send him along if I see him, but you see Bill, it's important—to all of us."

"Hank? Can I see that note? The one you found in Mousel's pocket?"

Hank showed it to him. "Know the writin'?"

"No, no, I don't."

Hank turned to Mousel. "Who gave you this?"

Mousel's flabby cheeks were sagging, his eyes were wide and frightened. "It was in . . . in my pocket. I jus' found it there."

"You're a liar," Hank said contemptuously.

"He may not be," Trevallion said. "He may be telling the truth. I just think he killed the wrong man."

He went back to the hotel, walking with awareness. Will Crockett was dead, murdered. Alfie was dead, too, but who would care about Alfie? Nobody wanted Alfie dead. At the worst he was merely a nuisance. He had gambled a little, cheated a little, lived off women. Nobody cared enough to want him dead. Whoever had slipped that note into Mousel's pocket, or had it slipped there, had believed Mousel would kill somebody else.

Him. Mousel had it in for him, too, and whoever had slipped that note and the money to Mousel had thought he would kill Trevallion.

Stewart was not in his office, and Trevallion returned to his mine. Tapley was already at work, and there were three men with him. Two were working in the new drift, drilling holes for a round of shots. Trevallion was restless and worried, and in no mood for work.

Back in the cabin he hung his gun-belt over a chairback and heated some water for shaving.

He had it to do. Waggoner and the other two had tried to kill him, and he knew where Waggoner holed up. He should find him, now. He had no desire to spend the rest of his life expecting a bullet in the back or being on guard every second.

He lathered his face, thinking about it and the possible reaction if he hunted them down and shot it out.

Grita? How would she feel? What would her reaction be?

He stropped his razor, tested the edge, and began to shave. He wanted no killing. He hated no man, not even the killer of Will Crockett, although the man should be punished.

Suddenly he thought of the man he had found in Grita's rooms. Could that have been Hesketh? And if so, what was he doing there? Looking for the shares?

He stropped the razor for a fresh edge, lathered his chin again. That could have been Hesketh, he had looked like a businessman. Carefully dressed, freshly shaven—odd eyes, very piercing.

He paused, razor poised; those eyes, where had he seen them before? Or had he? He rinsed his razor, wiped it dry, his mind empty, receptive, waiting.

Footsteps sounded outside, then a brief rap on the door. Putting down the razor, Trevallion turned to face the door, the gun-butt within inches of his right hand. "Come in," he said.

Manfred stepped in. "Sorry," he apologized. "I don't mean to interrupt."

"Sit down. I was just finishing."

"I've been thinking about Hesketh. There's no way we can get at him. Legally, I mean. I know he looted those wagons and it wouldn't sound good. Like you pointed out, many of those people planned to go back for their belongings. We all knew that and they were left alone. The fact that he looted wagons that were seemingly abandoned, there's nothing we can do about that.

"As for killing—and I'm dead sure he killed at least two men who weren't dead and might have been saved . . . there's nothing anybody can prove. I know what I know, but a good lawyer would tear that evidence to shreds. We'd get nowhere.

"Nor is there any evidence he killed Crockett. He's been involved in some shady dealings and has taken advantage of people, but that's about all, and you can't arrest a man for that."

Trevallion placed the razor in its case and closed it, then tossed the pan of water out the door. It would help to keep down the dust at the approach to the tunnel.

"Have you talked to Grita?" he asked.

Manfred shook his head. "I'm worried," he admitted. "Albert Hesketh is dangerous. He's like a sidewinder, vicious, poisonous, and always poised to strike. By now he probably knows that Grita inherited everything from Will Crockett. That leaves her in possession when she wishes to take over. She can throw him off the premises, and she should. He'll steal her blind, otherwise."

"And if something should happen to her, he will be left in possession until her heirs can decide what to do."

"Nothing will happen to her," he spoke positively. Then he turned sharply. "Who is with her now?"

"Clyde. But Teale is in the lobby."

Trevallion was thinking as he put on his shirt. Word would have gotten around and by now Hesketh would know. Furthermore, he would be moving to change the situation. Which meant both Grita and himself were targets of the first opportunity; of course, that had been his position for some time.

"Manfred," he said slowly, "you're in this of your own choice, so go back to the hotel and stay close to Grita. He will surely try to kill her, not he himself, but somebody sent by him."

"I'll go." Manfred got up. "And you?"

"I'll be along," he said, "but be careful."

"I shall," Manfred said. "Remember, I know the man. He hasn't an iota of mercy in him. He is absolutely cold. He has no respect for human life or anything that stands in his way."

"What will he do if he's backed into a corner? As he is now?"

"He will fight, I think, in his own way. The man's uncommonly shrewd."

When Manfred had gone, Trevallion buckled on his gunbelt. Uncommonly shrewd? No. Possibly not shrewd at all. Perhaps only a man who moved into whatever opening appeared, taking every advantage. Often the man appears shrewd who is only ruthless and without scruples.

The day was pleasantly warm. Trevallion walked outside and looked down the street toward the main part of town and the International. He could see people along the streets, miners going to work, and huge wagons hauling ore from the mines to the mills. A gentle breeze rustled the leaves on some coarse brush close by. The sky was blue with only a few remote clouds.

Had all his days led but to this one? In the mine behind him men worked, digging out ore for him. Somewhere a tin-panny pianolike sound came from the town below. What awaited him down there, he did not know, but he had an uncomfortable feeling that he faced some sort of a culmination.

He remembered the look on Waggoner's face when he had interrupted him in his meeting with Margrita. There was some brutal, indomitable force in the man, a man who could envision no defeat, no failure.

Turning, Trevallion looked again at the mine, at the cabin. Then he started down the slope. He went first to the International.

Teale was in the lobby, and he arose from his chair and crossed the room to intercept him.

"Trevallion? You can't see her. Not now."

"Is she busy? It's quite important."

His features were without expression. "She's up there with him, with Hesketh. She asked not to be disturbed."

Hesketh? Alone with Albert Hesketh?

Trevallion started forward but Teale laid his rifle across in front of him. "Like I said, Trevallion. She asked not to be disturbed."

FIFTY

When she returned to the sitting room of her suite, Albert Hesketh was seated on the edge of a chair, his hat on his knees.

"You wished to see me?"

He stood up. "I do, of course. You are an uncommonly beautiful woman, Margrita."

It was the first time he had addressed her by her given name, and she did not like it. If he was aware of her reaction, he indicated no evidence of it. "Thank you," she acknowledged.

The man who called himself Albert Hesketh had never in his life had time for the social graces. He had rarely talked to women and, generally speaking, despised them. He thought about them rarely and had in his mind several opinions of what they were like. His own fight had been for money and position, and he was quite sure that was what any intelligent person wanted, and women most of all.

"Margrita, as you may know, I have become a very rich man, and I shall be even richer." There was something in the way he spoke that irritated her, but she made no reply. "Since our first meeting I have come to know you, and you are just the wife I have been—"

"What?" She stared at him in total disbelief. "Are you proposing?"

He smiled. "Why, as a matter of fact, I am." He was, as he had told her, a very wealthy man, and these actresses were— "Yes, of course. I plan to build a home here, the most beautiful home. Of course, I shall have one in San Francisco, too. We must entertain, you know. There will be financiers out from New York or London, and you are just the woman to preside in such a place."

He sounded so smug she almost laughed. She was young in years, but in her few years she had seen more than most and had looked upon the actions of people with the eyes of one gifted in the analysis of character. Each one might be a part she would one day be called upon to play, and she had always felt there was more to be learned from observing the characteristics and motivations of people than in any other way.

"Why?" she asked.

He was startled. "Why . . . what?"

308

"Why do you wish to marry me?"

He smiled. "You are beautiful."

She was amused. "Perhaps, Mr. Hesketh, but that is very little on which to build a marriage. There are many beautiful women." She turned her head to look at him. "And why should I wish to marry you?"

Why? The question irritated him. Why? Why not? Of course, she would wish to marry him! He was a wealthy man. He was somebody. He was attractive, and he was a coming man. Yet when he sought for words to explain himself he found none, and that irritated him even more. He had assumed—

"You would have a beautiful home," he persisted. "You would have position. You would be somebody."

"But I am somebody, Mr. Hesketh. I am *me*. I like being me, and I need nobody to make me somebody. I need no setting. As for a home, I can build my own. As for position, each of us finds his own."

He smiled a tight little smile that could not quite hide the anger in his eyes. "To build a home, Margrita, is very expensive. It is not—"

He tightened his lips. Didn't this little fool realize what marriage to him would mean? Couldn't she *see*? He fought to maintain that icy control on which he prided himself. "Don't you see? You wouldn't have to parade yourself on the stage any more. You wouldn't have to—"

"Mr. Hesketh? You don't understand. I like the theater. It is exciting and interesting to me. If I leave, it will only be for love, and because I am very sure that I have found the right man. Whether he is wealthy or not would never be a consideration, just that he's someone with whom I could be happy, someone I could respect."

Margrita Redaway had known many men, most of them only in passing, but she sensed there was something here that was totally beyond her experience.

For the first time she realized that Albert Hesketh was not very bright. She had thought of him as intelligent, perhaps shrewd in a business way, but now she realized, quite suddenly, that he was so completely self-centered as to be obtuse, blind to the feelings of others, and concerned only with people as they affected his plans. Yet there was something else, too, some quality that made her uneasy, unsure of herself. There was something in the man— something—something that was wrong, that was out of kilter.

He was staring at her. Couldn't this little fool understand? He was offering to *marry* her!

Underneath his impatience something else was stirring within him, something that held panic. He had to marry her. It was the only way out, unless—

"Perhaps I shall build a home of my own, Mr. Hesketh. Possibly in California. There are some beautiful places there."

"If you like," he said, "we could—"

"No, Mr. Hesketh. It is not 'we.' If what you have been doing is considered a proposal of marriage, my answer is no. Very positively *no*, Mr. Hesketh."

He stared at her, shocked. Until a few days ago he had not seriously considered marriage at all, although in the back of his mind he realized it was a part of the total picture he wished to present. But to propose marriage to this, this *actress*, and to be refused—

"You're being a fool!" he said sharply. "A complete fool! How long do you think you can continue this parading around? Far better to marry and have a home."

"Perhaps, Mr. Hesketh, perhaps you are right. I may do just that; if the right man should ask me I might quit tomorrow, as much as I enjoy my work.

"As for money," she added, "I have nothing to worry about." She flashed him a smile. "Haven't you heard, Mr. Hesketh? *I own the Solomon!*"

He stiffened sharply as if slapped across the mouth. His throat tightened so he felt as if he might strangle, clutched as he was by a blind fury. His face went white, and when he tried to speak the words would not come. Finally they did come, choking and stumbling.

"No! No, you do not own the Solomon! You will never own it! It is mine! *Mine!*"

She was very cool, very quiet. "When Mr. Crockett was found, wounded and sick, he willed his portion of the mine to me, Mr. Hesketh, as I am sure you are aware." She looked up at him. "And I had ten shares of my own, you know. That leaves me in control, Mr. Hesketh, and I believe it was you who first put up a sign to keep others away. I am afraid that is just what I must do, Mr. Hesketh. I must ask you not to trespass on the premises."

"You . . . you can't do that."

"If I am not mistaken, Mr. Hesketh, that sign is even now being put in place and my guards are replacing yours."

It was a struggle to retain his composure, yet so much was at stake. "Don't you see? If we were married we would own it all! Just you and I!"

"I am new to Nevada, Mr. Hesketh, and I may be mistaken, but in many states you, as my husband, would control it all. I have no doubt you have thought of that, but the answer is *no*."

She glanced in the mirror, touched her hair lightly, and, looking at him in the mirror, she said, "I have no doubt you will do very well on your share, Mr. Hesketh. We shall work the mine with great care."

She turned to face him. There was something, something about him . . . something not quite normal. Something about him had always left her uneasy.

The derringer was in her purse, across the room from where she stood.

She touched her hair one more time, then turned and took her wrap from the back of the chair. "I am afraid, Mr. Hesketh, that you must excuse me." She crossed the room to her purse, feeling his eyes upon her. "I have people waiting." She stooped and took up the purse and turned to face him, opening the purse as she did so and taking out a handkerchief. "Of course, if you wish to sell?"

"No!" His voice was hoarse with emotion. "I'll not sell! It is mine! It is all mine! You will see! I shall have it all!"

He hesitated a moment, staring at her. She replaced her handkerchief in her purse and took hold of the derringer.

"My friends are waiting, Mr. Hesketh, and I believe we have concluded our business."

He turned toward the door and when he reached it he turned to look back. "You have been very foolish," he said, "but no doubt you believe you know what you are doing. I am sorry for you."

He stepped out and pulled the door shut behind him. For a moment she stood very still, clutching the butt of the small gun. Then, slowly, she relaxed.

He had gone. It was over. What was it about him that bothered her?

He was insane. No, that was ridiculous. Yet the thought persisted. In any event he was strange. His smile never seemed natural; it seemed set, forced, as if he were telling himself to smile.

She shrugged. She would probably not see him again, nor was there reason for it. She snapped shut her purse and turned to the door.

Albert Hesketh walked directly to his suite and placed his hat on the table; then he sat down, knees together, feet side by side. His folded hands rested on his knees, and he started to think.

There was an answer. There had to be an answer. At this stage, with victory so close, he must not be defeated. He must think . . . think. . . .

She must be killed. Killed, of course. He had decided upon that some time ago, even before he had thought of her as a possible wife. He would, he told himself, have killed her anyway, eventually. The thing was what to do now, for just killing her would do him nothing but harm, unless—

Unless the mine were left in his hands while her estate was settled. Seated, his hands folded in his lap, he considered that possibility. It could be done if there was no suggestion that he was responsible for her death, and of course, he would take precautions to see that nothing of the kind occurred.

The chances were that she had told nobody of her action here today, unless it was Trevallion. She might have told him, although he doubted that. One thing he had noticed about Margrita Redaway was that she was closemouthed. She did not tell her business to every comer.

Killing her was something he wanted done, yet it would do no good unless he were left in control of the mine. Even if he eventually lost control, there might be a year or more in the meantime, and during such a time he could siphon off much of its wealth. The machinery for that was already in operation while Crockett was still around.

He would not go near the mine, and therefore there would be no one to say he could not go there. He did not wish to be publicly turned away, for that would arouse talk and would be generally known. If not generally known he could, if anything happened to Margrita Redaway, brush it off as mere nonsense.

The problem was how, when, and where. There was also the problem of obtaining what papers she had and discovering just who had witnessed Will Crockett's last testament. Yet, even that did not matter. Accept the fact that the mine was willed to Margrita, but that she had transferred it to him.

Trevallion would know better, but Trevallion would be dead.

He took out his watch and checked the time. It would soon be time for dinner, and he must be there, in his usual place.

A mine, perhaps the Solomon? Margrita Redaway had mentioned wanting to descend into a mine, and women were said to be bad luck in a mine. Suppose she was the one who had bad luck? Once in a mine there was so much that could be done.

Possibly she and Trevallion together? He smiled. That would be a fortunate coincidence. He could just hear the old miners commenting that he, of all people, should have known better.

That new Forty-Niner tunnel. They were having trouble with oozing mud there, anyway. It was a dangerous spot, but there was rich ore back where it ran close to the old workings. Crockett had always wanted to open up the old workings as he had seen samples that looked good. Albert Hesketh had deliberately talked him into delaying that project.

He smiled again, thinking of it. Albert Hesketh had done pretty well, up to now. Yet the fat was in the fire and he had to act.

Santley. He had never trusted Santley, although the man had worked faithfully. Santley was an apple-polisher, and once he realized, as he was sure to, that a new hand might be in control he would seek to curry favor. Santley had seen the samples from the new workings, and only last week Hesketh had found him examining old samples from the old workings.

None of them trusted him, so he would simply let it work for him. If this plan did not work, he had another. He sat down at his desk and wrote swiftly.

Mr. Santley:
If Miss Redaway suggests going into the mine, please advise her not to enter Forty-Nine. At all costs, keep her out of that area. Say nothing to arouse her curiosity.
                                    Albert Hesketh

He smiled as he looked at the note. If that would not do it, nothing would.

And there was no better place.

If anything was said, had he not tried to keep them out?

FIFTY-ONE

Waggoner stood up and stretched. "You boys take it easy. I got me a little job to do."

The man with the scarred hand looked up from the cards. "Never figured to see you working in a mine, Wag. What's come over you?"

Waggoner smiled. "Pays well. At least my kind of work does."

"What about Trevallion? We can take him any time we want, Wag. Sure, he's supposed to be good, but against three of us?"

"You jus' set back an' let me handle it. Maybe none of us will have to. There's more than one way to chop wood but the thing most needful is a sharp Ax."

"Ax?"

"Why not? Who's any better? Peel? Not on your life! Nobody's any better and nobody has more reason. He's in it as deep as any of us."

"I ain't seen him in years. How'd you know where to find him?"

"I got ways." Waggoner suddenly sat down. He pushed his hat back on his head and poured whiskey into a waterglass. "Or somebody does. Les, who knew about that? Back there in Missouri, I mean?"

"Hell! Nobody knew! How could anybody?"

"Somebody does know, Les, somebody knows ever' damn one of us."

Les placed his cards carefully on the table. "You mean Trevallion?"

"Him, maybe. That's why we're here. But somebody else, too."

"Who could, Wag? You ain't thinkin'. Who was there? Baldy an' Pete were killed by the feller at the blue wagon."

"That was Trevallion's pa."

"All right. That's Baldy an' Pete. Trevallion's killed Rory and Obie Skinner. That's four gone. There's us, that makes seven, and the Clean-Cutter, which is eight. That's all there was."

Waggoner tossed off his whiskey, made a face, and refilled his glass. "Where'd the booze come from, Les? We were broke, remember?"

314

The other man looked up from the gun he was cleaning. "We got the booze from that busted wagon, don't you recall? The one with the busted wheel. I was wantin' a drink real bad and somebody says there was a jug in that busted-down wagon. Sure enough, there was. That was how we all got liquored up."

"Who tol' you about that jug?" Waggoner asked.

"Hell! How should I remember? There was a lot of us around. Somebody said it was there, that's all I know. I wanted whiskey an' I wasn't about to ask no questions."

"Same with me," Les said. "What difference does it make, anyway?"

"Maybe none atall. Maybe a lot. What I'm askin' myself is how that whiskey happened to be there in an empty wagon? Does somebody leave a jug o' whiskey just asettin'?"

"How should we know? What the hell, whiskey is whiskey. I take it where I can get it."

"That's what he figured."

"Who?"

"Boys, we been euchered. We been set up an' taken. We done what we done but somebody else got the money. Did you get any money, Les?"

"Hell, no."

"Well, neither did I. Neither did anybody unless it was him who left the whiskey there. Who was it yelled that somebody was comin'? That a whole gang was comin'?"

Les suddenly swore viciously. "Damn it! Damn it all to hell!"

"See? Somebody suckered us into it, somebody got away with all that money."

Rig, who was cleaning his gun, began to reload. "That's past. What the hell? So we were suckered? That was years ago."

"I don't like it," Les complained. "I don't like being played for no sucker."

"Think back, both of you. We got to remember who told us about that liquor."

"What the hell difference does it make now? That's over an' done with."

"It makes a difference," Waggoner said, "because he's here. He's right here in Washoe."

They stared at him. He tossed off his drink. "I got a job to do." He thumbed a roll of bills from his pocket. "See that? It's from him. It's got to be from him."

"Then you know him!"

"No, I don't. I don't know him at all, but he knows me. He knows you all, too. He knows who we are an' what we done."

Les picked up the cards again and began to shuffle them for

another turn at solitaire. He started placing the cards, then looked up. "He had to be there. He had to be in Missouri at the time. He had to be right there in town." He glanced at the man cleaning the gun. "Got any ideas, Rig?"

"Uh-huh, but you've got to remember, there must have been two dozen wagon trains outfitting to head west, and there were others just like us who were hangin' around to see what we could latch onto." He put his gun into its holster. "What difference does it make? If he hasn't said anything up to now, he ain't liable to. Anyway, that was years ago. How they goin' to prove it?"

"Lynchers don't need much proof," Les replied.

"You give it thought," Waggoner said, "I'm busy. I got a job to do."

"You say he paid you that money? Then you must've seen him."

"One time, several years back. He met me out in the hills and he was all wrapped up so's I couldn't see his face or guess his size, except for height. He got word to me and I met him." Waggoner jerked his head to indicate the east. "Over yonder." He paused again. "He wanted Trevallion killed."

"That must've really hurt your feelin's."

"He told me Trevallion knew us all, that he'd killed Rory and Skinner, and it was get him or Trevallion would notch his stick for us. It made sense. Besides,' Waggoner smiled, revealing his big, strong teeth. "He give me three hundred dollars. Ever' time something like that come up, it was three hundred."

"No wonder you ain't killed him."

"I tried. Believe me, I tried. Kip Hauser tried it, too, and Kip's dead."

"Kip was no gunfighter. Never knew him to kill anybody he couldn't stick. He was a knife man."

"He tried it. You got to remember Skinner, too. Obie was mighty damn good with a gun. Trevallion is no easy job."

"The three of us," Rig said. "We could box him."

"Wait, let's see if this does him in. This could do it."

"Hold on, Wag. Wait just a minute. Who is this gent who comes up with three hundred dollars ever' now and again? Where's he get his money? What's his stake in this?"

Waggoner took up a tin pail and began packing a few odds and ends for his lunch. "Asked myself that. I figure he was in it, too. He's scared of Trevallion. Wants him dead."

"You think he was the one who got the money?"

"Well, I think he's well-off now." Waggoner paused, considering. "Maybe a gambler. They have money."

"More than likely it is somebody else, somebody with something to lose. If you're goin' into that mine to do what I think you're plannin', how is he so sure Trevallion will be down there? That ain't Trevallion's mine. I think he's after somebody else."

"I'd be curious," Les suggested. "I'd be wonderin' who this gent is who knows so much."

"Look," Waggoner said. "Every now and again he has something needs doing. Each time I get three hundred. First time, that time I seen him, he warned me against tryin' to find out who he was, said he'd have me done in.

"Hell, what do I care who he is? I been livin' it easy. You think I want to nose around an' mess that up? You got to be crazy."

"Whoever it is," Les insisted, "he's got something to lose. Maybe he's away up there, big mining man or businessman."

Waggoner opened the door and stepped outside. "You fellers want to earn your keep, you kill Trevallion. I can get you a hundred dollars apiece for that."

Waggoner started down the trail, and Rig stared after him. "What's he talkin' about? A hundred dollars?"

"That's a summer's work punchin' cows," Les said. "You an' me both have killed men for less, a lot less."

There was silence in the room and then Rig said, "I don't like it, Les. I don't like somebody knowing about that thing back yonder. I don't care who he is."

"What we goin' to do about it? We don't even know who he is, nor what he is."

"Trevallion knows. He knows some of us, anyhow."

"How could he? Nobody was around."

"That's what we thought. He was probably hidin' in the brush, scared to death." Rig stuffed his pipe and tamped it down. "If he killed Rory and Skinner like they say, what's he waitin' on? He must know Waggoner's in town. Maybe he even knows about us."

Rig was uneasy. He struck a match and lit his pipe. "We got to get him, Les. We got it to do, and before he can get us. He's planning something, you can bet on it."

"To hell with him!" Les held an ace in his fingers, looking at the cards before him. "I'm thinking about the other gent, the one who can afford to pay Wag three hundred dollars ever' now and again. Why should Wag get it all?"

"What's on your mind?"

"Well, if he's so doggone anxious to have Trevallion killed, it's because he's scared himself or he's afraid he'll be exposed. We got us a pigeon, Rig. This man is *some*body. He can't afford to have his past brought up; maybe he'd pay real money to have it all kept quiet.

Maybe he'd pay us five thousand dollars to keep quiet, and then after a little while, another five thousand?"

"What about Wag?"

"You seen him givin' us any of that three hundred? And he won't, neither. *Five thousand,* Rig, split right down the middle. That's a lot of money, Rig."

"I never seen that much. Never in my born days have I seen five thousand dollars all to oncet." He took his pipe from his lips and spat into the fire. "Don't do no good talkin'. We don't even know who he is."

Les was silent while he studied the cards. "No, we don't, but we're goin' to find out. We're goin' to study on it. We're goin' to do a little *ree*-search, as the fellow said."

"Hell! There must be ten thousand people on the Comstock! How do you pick one out of all that bunch?"

"It won't be easy, but let's study on it. There's a whole lot of deadbeats, cardsharks, and crooks. We know who they are, and it won't be one of them. It's got to be somebody who *is* somebody, or seems to be. That narrows it down.

"It's got to be somebody who was in Missouri in '49 or '50, long about that time. There's a whole lot who didn't come out until much later, and there are some who were in California before. And it's got to be somebody who was here in '59. You look at it that way, and the field's mighty thin."

"What do we do?" Rig asked.

"We go down to town. You go one way and I'll go the other, and we find some of the oldtimers and just get them talkin' about the good old days. Names will come up; if they don't, we bring 'em up. No time at all we will know who is still around, and from them we don't have much trouble sortin' out those who've done well, and so have somethin' to lose."

He brought the deck together with a swift gesture and placed the deck, squared and neat, at the side of the table. "You an' me, Rig, we're goin' to have us some money!"

Together they closed the shack and started down the rocky street toward town. Pausing at the corner of A Street and Union, Rig said, hesitantly, "Les? Just suppose he won't stand still for it? Suppose he decides to have *us* killed?"

"Hell," Les said, "he won't know who we are. Anyway, who are we? A couple of chickens? We don't kill easy, Rig. We can take care of ourselves. Anyway, who would he hire to kill us—Wag?"

They started down toward C Street when Rig stopped suddenly. "Les? What about Wag? Supposin' he did hire Wag? Are we worth three hundred dollars apiece to Wag? The way he figures it, that's nigh onto two years of lazy, easy livin'."

Les stared out over the town, thinking. "We got to think about that, Rig. We got to keep an eye on Wag. If this pigeon of ours doesn't come through, and quick—"

"Yeah?"

"Then we kill Wag. It'll be him or us."

FIFTY-TWO

Trevallion was waiting when she came to the lobby. She hesitated a moment, watching him in conversation with Teale. He was a remarkably handsome man in his own rugged way, and he possessed a certain air, a certain style that was his own.

That he would be wearing a pistol she knew. Here, in the quiet precincts of the International, those who wore weapons kept them from sight, and they were rarely seen unless worn by someone just in off the trail and seeking a drink or a room.

Trevallion looked around and saw her, and the men crossed the room to where she stood. "You saw Hesketh?"

"I did, and gave him his walking papers. I let him know that as of now he was no longer welcome at the Solomon and orders were to refuse him entry."

"How'd he like that?" Teale asked.

"He didn't. He was very angry, I think. I shall ask Mr. Teale if he will guard the mine for me, and—"

"No," Trevallion interrupted.

There was such finality in the word that she was startled. Teale had turned his eyes immediately to Trevallion.

"I want Teale with you," Trevallion said. "I'll get one of Ledbetter's boys to stand guard at the Solomon. You'll need at least two, one to spell the other so that he can rest. Teale must stay with you. I wouldn't feel safe with anybody else on the job. There isn't anybody in Nevada going to bother you with Teale around."

"It shouldn't matter now," she protested. "He knows that he has no business there now, and he certainly will have none with me. I have laid claim to the mine and shall see that it is announced in the *Enterprise.*"

"Do you believe that?"

She hesitated, then shook her head quickly. "No, I don't. I think he is a mean, revengeful man who would stop at nothing. I offered to buy him out," she added.

"And—?"

"He was furious. It is obvious he believes the mine is his, stockholders or no."

"Maybe I'd better go up there and look the place over for you," Trevallion suggested. "It has been some time since I've been there."

"We will go," she smiled at him. "*We* will go, Mr. Trevallion. After all, the mine is mine, or the largest piece of it."

Margrita turned to Teale. "You can have something to eat. We won't be gone long, and you can take me to the theater."

Teale nodded. "All right, ma'am. Some grub would taste right good." He started to say something else, but they were walking away.

From his window in the International, Hesketh watched them go, taking out his watch to note the time. "Something else," he muttered, "I need something else."

Had their guard arrived yet? He thought not. His own men would be gone. Santley would be there, but Santley always left early on Saturday afternoon to buy groceries for the coming week.

The theater? There was no play tonight, as there had been a minor fire and some damage done, yet it was likely she would return to the theater to see how repairs were progressing and to check damaged scenery. It had been very little, after all, and they should be ready to open Sunday night.

He permitted himself a little smile. They would be ready to open, but they never would. Not unless they had a new leading lady.

He tapped lightly on the table, thinking carefully, trying to run an assay on every aspect of the problem.

Teale, Teale had not gone with them, and Teale was a most careful man. Something must be done about Teale.

He shook his head irritably. Too much, too close together. And he must take his walk at the wrong time if the message were to go out. He disliked breaking a pattern. It might be noticed. Still, there was no way he could be connected with any of it. He would be dining at his usual hour, in his usual place, and if all went smoothly it would be a clean sweep, and all must go well.

One phase of his plan was already in progress, and the second phase must be the elimination of Jacob Teale. That elimination could be the something else he needed, the something that would distract attention and keep people from wondering what had become of Margrita and Trevallion.

Margrita's guards would be in place soon, but only after Trevallion and the girl had reached the mine, and probably would be unaware of their presence there.

The removal of Teale was of first importance as Teale would be suspicious, and he could not be distracted from what he conceived to be his duty.

As he straightened his tie in the mirror, he was pleased with the reflection. He had planned well, although he did not like spur-of-the-moment planning. He liked time to consider, to gloat, to enjoy all the subtle details. On this occasion too much depended on the actions of other people, something for which he had a basic distrust.

He was not worried about Waggoner. He had come to have absolute confidence in the big man. Waggoner took his time, he did what he was told, and he left no loose ends. Waggoner's part presented no worries. Of the other two he was not so sure. He knew them too little, but after meeting Teale there was a good chance he would not have to worry about them later. He would surely kill one and perhaps both. The important thing was that he be killed himself.

Now for the note. First he composed it in his mind, then he printed it in neat block letters.

FIND AND KILL JACOB TEALE. OUTSIDE INTER-NATIONAL. $250 EACH. $500 IN ALL. MUST BE DONE TONIGHT. $200 NOW. REMAINDER WHEN JOB DONE.

He read over the note. It was being done too swiftly, but there was no other choice. It was now or never, and he hoped his message would not be lost on Les and his partner.

Two hundred fifty dollars each, $500 in all . . . in other words, the survivor might find himself with the whole $500, and no need to share. Might that not be a temptation too great to resist when a lot of shooting was going on, anyway?

Waggoner would be at the Solomon or returning. The others would probably be at some saloon, yet even if they saw him, something he did not wish to happen, they would not long be around to enjoy their knowledge. He put on his hat, took up the cane he had begun carrying, and went down to the lobby.

As he left the International he saw Teale from the corner of his eye, seated on a bench near the hotel door, where he often was.

Virginia City was, even in late afternoon or evening, a noisy, busy town. Stamp-mills were going, compressors were pounding, teamsters cursing their mules, and the usual sounds of laughter, pianos, and bawdy song from the saloons.

He had worked out several methods of getting messages to Waggoner, but none of these would work with Les and his partner, for they had not been instructed beforehand. He must take the risk and deliver the note right to Waggoner's cabin.

What if Waggoner discovered it first? Well and good. Teale would be eliminated in any event, but then Teale might kill Waggoner and this Hesketh did not want. Waggoner he needed, for a little while longer.

He wore his neat gray suit, and he strolled casually, pausing from time to time to look at the face of the city. He knew he would be observed and expected it, but he had already set the stage with his previous walks. They would dismiss him at a glance.

There was no light in the window, although it was early for that, and there was no sign of activity. He paused, twice he picked up bits of rock and examined them before casting them aside. That, too, was the usual thing in Virginia City where everyone at the time had minerals on the mind.

Pausing to study the rocks, he studied the cabin. It looked safe. After all, he could just say he was looking for a miner, he wanted more help at the Solomon.

In his pocket was the note, and in his pocket was the gold. He hated to pay out money, but in this case there was at least a chance he would never have to complete the bargain. With luck they would take care of both Teale and each other.

He paused again, touching his brow with a linen handkerchief. Still no movement. The place was probably empty.

He knew where the note should go, as he had used the place before this. It was a mail slot made of an open-ended cigar box built into the wall. On the outside there was a little wooden door. He had never seen the inside.

He glanced around. Nobody was around. Nobody was watching. He stopped in front of the cabin, lifting his fist to knock, then dropping his hand to open the slot. Inside he placed the note and the gold.

He lowered the little door and turned away. He had not taken a step when he heard the door open behind him. He had taken a second step before he heard the voice.

Inwardly, he cringed. He felt the muscles in his back tighten and he fought down an impulse to run. Then he turned as the voice said, "Well, look what we got here, Rig! We got us a visitor!"

He knew their faces. They were older now, their features seamed with the tracks of years gone by, but they were the men he remembered.

"How do you do, gentlemen? Can I help you in some way?"

"You can tell us who you are."

"I believe that would serve no purpose for either of us." The message was there, the gold was there. To attempt to play the innocent would be absurd. A bold face was needed. "We have little time for nonsense. Who I am or who you are does not matter. There is a note in the box. There is also the sum of two hundred dollars in gold. I would suggest you read the message, put the gold in your pockets, and do what is suggested. If you want the other three hundred."

"He's talkin' money, Les. He really is. Maybe we should listen."

"This money for us or for Waggoner?"

"It is for you, but you must act quickly. The day after tomorrow, even tomorrow, and you'd be wasting time."

"How'd you know about us?"

"I make it my business to know useful people. I need an expert job done now, and I mean *now*. I'd prefer it be done within the next two hours."

"And you got three hundred more when it's done? That's two-fifty apiece. Who is this guy?"

"His name is Teale." Briefly, he described him. "A few minutes ago he was sitting on a bench down by the International. I would suggest you give him no warning."

They both looked at him. "What's that mean?"

"Only that he is armed, and I would presume such a man might be dangerous. So why get hurt? You can always say he was going for his gun. Or that he killed your maiden aunt back in Memphis."

"Five hundred dollars? Way I heard it you didn't pay so much."

"There are two of you. It must be done at once. You men are expert in your, your profession. For top work, I pay a top dollar."

He drew out his watch. "I must be going, gentlemen, but I'd prefer the job be done within the hour. Tomorrow morning your three hundred dollars will be in that box."

Rig leaned his shoulder against the door jamb. He had a sly, taunting look in his eyes. "Suppose we just keep the two hundred an' do nothin'?"

Hesketh smiled, and it was not a nice smile. "Then it would be my problem, would it not? Fortunately, I have had it happen but once."

Abruptly, he turned his back and walked away. When he was back on C Street he paused. Now, they would have to die, one way or another.

He went inside and seated himself at his usual table in the dining room. The *Territorial Enterprise* and a San Francisco paper were folded neatly beside his place.

He unfolded the paper and sat back in his chair a little. He was suddenly frightened.

That man, that Jacob Teale, the way he had looked at him as he came up the steps. Almost as if he *knew*.

But that was nonsense. How could he know? How could he even guess at what was to happen in the next few minutes?

Nonetheless . . .

Albert Hesketh folded his newspaper and placed it beside him. That fellow Twain was writing again, the one so many thought amusing. So far he had said nothing about the Solomon or about him, but if he did—

He glanced at the menu, but it had not changed from the day before. He ordered, indicated his wine glass should be filled, and composed himself.

Any time now . . . just any time.

His brow was beaded with perspiration. Keep cool, he told himself. Just keep cool.

The waiter filled his glass. He watched the wine flow into the glass. Red, like blood.

Blood? What was the matter with him, anyway? He had been through this before. It was nothing. They would come and—

Somebody dropped a plate and some silver and he jumped as if shot. Then slowly, he settled back.

God! It had to work! It must work!

The sharp barking roar of the guns was almost anticlimactic. Three rapid shots, so close together they could scarcely be distinguished, then a single, final shot . . . and silence.

FIFTY-THREE

When Trevallion and Margrita reached the Solomon, it lay warm in the afternoon sun. The cluster of buildings huddled together on a miniature plateau where the road ended. A long building on the left housed three offices, designated by doorplates: *Superintendent*, *Business Office*, and *Assay*.

At the backside of the small plateau was the hoisting-engine house and in front of it the head-frame and the collar of the shaft.

Facing the offices on the other edge of the flat surface were the blacksmith shop, toolshed, and the bins where the ore was dumped when hoisted. The Solomon was, as yet, a small operation and not to be compared with the Hale & Norcross, the Savage, Ophir, or many another along the lode. Will Crockett had listened too long to Albert Hesketh, and Hesketh had deliberately hindered development to gain control with less trouble.

"If the mine is to be worked properly," Trevallion suggested, "you will need capital. You need to go deeper, drift into my claim—"

"But it is your claim," she protested.

He shrugged. "We can face that problem when we come to it. I filed it in my name and Will Crockett's, and as his heir you would own part of it, anyway."

"But you did that for Will. I wouldn't hold you to that."

"I don't welsh my bets," he said. "I'll retain my half but we can work it together."

The door of the business office opened, and Santley stepped out. "How do you do?" he addressed Trevallion. "I know you by sight, but I don't believe we've met."

"I'm Trevallion. Mr. Santley, this is Miss Redaway."

"How do you do? I hope you are not thinking of going into the mine, Mr. Trevallion? The men are all off work now. If you could come back on Monday—"

"If I want to go below," Trevallion said, "I'll climb down the man-way."

"Well, but it is dangerous, you know, and we had a note from Mr.

Hesketh particularly warning Miss Redaway not to go into Forty-Nine. It is a closed area."

"Why?" Margrita asked. "Why is it closed?"

"Because it is dangerous, I presume. Mr. Hesketh does not communicate with me. I mean he makes his own plans and keeps them to himself."

"You've seen the assay reports?" Trevallion asked.

"No, sir. They go directly to Mr. Hesketh. Mr. Shinmaker, he's the assayer, he has orders to talk to no one, and he won't. Not a word."

Santley glanced around. "I shouldn't be saying this to you, ma'am, but Mr. Hesketh stopped work there very abruptly, in Forty-Nine, I mean. For no reason that I can think of. Just ordered the men out and closed it off with some timbers. A fencelike . . . but nothing one couldn't go past, if one wished."

He paused again. "They may have had some trouble with mud, you know."

"We'll just look around," Trevallion said. "Miss Redaway has never seen a mine."

"Of course." Santley glanced at his watch. "I was just about to close up. Will you be needing a key?"

"We will, thank you. No need for you to stay. We'll not be long."

Trevallion showed her the offices, explained a little about assaying, and when they emerged the sun was going down.

She turned on him suddenly. "Val? I want to go down!"

"In the mine? At this hour?"

"Well," she said, "it won't be any darker down there at night than in the day. Can't we take a pair of those lamps?" She indicated a row of them hanging on a small rail near the assay office. "We wouldn't be long."

"Wait, come back in the daytime when somebody is around. One should never go into a mine unless someone else knows you're there."

"Oh, come on, Val! We'd only be a few minutes. I want to see what's so strange about that Forty-Nine place."

He hesitated. It was foolish. Yet he was curious, too. What was the mystery about Forty-Nine?

"Well—"

"Come on, Val! We'll only be gone a few minutes! You've been down in this mine, haven't you?"

"It's been months. Will had me down to look it over just before he was dispossessed. No doubt there have been a lot of changes since then. It's deeper, I know, and they've run some drifts. Let's go back inside for a minute."

He had noticed the layout of the mine-workings on Santley's desk and he went back, bending over it. He had no trouble locating Forty-Nine.

He studied the situation with care, not liking it. Still, they would be down but a few minutes.

"You will get very dirty," he warned, "it's wet and muddy down there."

"I'll change at the hotel. I've been dirty before." She laughed. "Come on, Val! Show me!"

"You'll have to climb ladders," he warned again.

"I've climbed mountains in the Alps," she said, "and I've done a lot of rock climbing. You needn't worry about me."

"We won't bother with the lamps," Trevallion suggested. "They drip oil and can be dangerous. We'll take candles. Three of them will last ten hours, but we'll take twice that many, just for luck." He hung his coat on a hook and took a miner's jacket that hung nearby, dropping extra candles into the side pocket, and a spiked candleholder for fixing candles against a wall.

It was dark and still in the mine. Margrita was excited and interested but a little frightened, too. There was no sound but the drip of water, and an occasional rattle of falling rocks. They picked their way along the narrow track on which the ore-cars ran, and at a fork in the drift, Trevallion picked up a shovel.

He was thinking of the chart of the mine-workings he had seen in the office. They should be nearing Forty-Nine.

When he had taken a few more steps, he paused so suddenly that she bumped him from behind.

"What's wrong?" she asked.

He stooped and picked up something from the floor. "That's odd. Santley said they weren't working in Forty-Nine any more but this is a piece of Bickford fuse, used in blasting."

"They could be working close by," she suggested. "Let's hurry. It's awfully hot and I want to get back on top."

He chuckled. "Whose idea was this, anyway? It should be right ahead, though."

Forty-Nine, he recalled, was the beginning of a cross-cut between two tunnels, started to permit better circulation of air, something that must always be considered. Also, the cross-cut enabled them to sample rock from a wide triangle that lay between two tunnels.

He paused at the opening, looking up the drift that lay before him. He gestured. "That's a deadend. Or so the chart showed. They ran into some barren ground. It might be just a 'horse' but there's no telling."

"What's a 'horse'?"

"The Comstock Lode lies in a fissure or crack that developed millions of years ago. Roughly, it's some four miles long, and after the crack occurred, gases bubbled up from below. There are hot springs all over this area, and they deposited the gold and silver. Occasionally great chunks of country rock would fall off into the crack, so you'd have what the miners call a horse—a stretch of barren rock dividing several mineralized areas.

"When you come upon such a place underground you have a decision. You must decide whether to continue working, hoping for mineral on the other side, or to stop where you are, taking it for granted the barren ground will continue."

He led the way into Forty-Nine, pausing occasionally to look around. "We're wasting our time," he said, after a bit. "There's nothing here."

"Then why—"

"Just what he said. It was bad ground and no use working it. Hesketh wasn't telling an untruth. He was being honest for once."

He gestured toward the ground at his feet. All along the wall there was a thick black and smooth stretch of mud at the foot of the wall, projecting almost to the track. "It's creep. At least, that's what some of us call it.

"Sometimes there's layers of mud or earth between rock strata. Naturally, there's great pressure on it, and when you run a tunnel into it, the pressure squeezes it into the open space."

"Then what?"

He shrugged. "It just keeps squeezing. The mud keeps oozing, and in areas like that you usually have one or two men busy all the time cutting it out with shovels and carrying it away. Or else in time it would fill the tunnel."

"You mean it would fill all this space?"

"Uh-huh. There's some water in it, of course. It just keeps creeping unless cut out and carried away. I have seen it in only one place other than the Comstock, and that was an old mine in Oregon I was asked to check out. Mud had crept in, filling some of the old workings, even broke timbers and pushed them over."

"Can nothing stop it?"

"Nothing, until it fills all the available space."

She shuddered. Turning quickly, she said, "Let's get out of here!"

They had taken no more than two steps when there was a dull thud somewhere ahead of them and a sudden puff of pushed air that put out their candles.

Grita clutched his arm. "Val? Val? What is it?"

She could smell dust, and something else, a vague smell, totally unfamiliar.

"There has been an explosion, Grita," Trevallion said. "Stand perfectly still until I light up."

"That smell, what is it?"

"Powder smoke," he said. "I think we're in trouble, Grita."

She could feel her heart pounding. She was afraid, deathly afraid.

He fumbled for a match, struck it, and lighted his candle, then hers. "Let's see how bad it is," he said. He led the way back along the track to the opening of the cross-cut. Only there was no opening. Where the opening into the tunnel had been, there was a pile of muck, broken rock, and splintered timbers.

He lifted his candle. The charge had been so placed as to block both the cross-cut and the deadend tunnel. He studied it thoughtfully, trying to recall the formation he had glanced at as he entered the tunnel. How much had been shot down? How far were they from the other side?

Too far, probably too far.

"Grita," he said, "put out your candle. We'll need the air."

"Are we trapped, Val?" She fought back the fear in her voice.

"Yes, we are. And that was the whole idea, Grita. That must have been the reason for the note. It was deliberately written to arouse our curiosity, to get us in here."

"But they'll find us, Val! They'll find us when they come to work tomorrow!"

"Tomorrow is Sunday," Trevallion said. "Nobody will be working. And of course," he could see it all clearly now, "Hesketh will dismiss the miners, saying we'd want to hire our own crew."

"What about Mr. Santley?" She was grasping at any chance, any possibility.

"He lives near Genoa. He won't be back before Monday at the earliest. If Hesketh doesn't find some reason to keep him away even then."

He took her by the arms. "Grita, let's face it. Nobody is going to come looking for us. Nobody will even ask questions. Not for a while."

"Then, then, this is all there is? We will die here?"

His smile was grim. "Why no, Grita, it just means that we know where we stand. We just know nobody is going to come looking, so whatever is done we have to do ourselves."

He gestured. "Sit down over there and think some good thoughts for us. I'm going to work."

FIFTY-FOUR

Melissa was sitting at her back table when Jim Ledbetter came in. "Hello, Jim! Come and sit down."

"Thanks." He removed his hat and ran fingers through his hair, then walked back and sat down across the table from her. "Seen Trevallion?"

"He hasn't been in. Come to think of it, it's been days. I think he's in love, Jim."

"Might be it. I'm worried, though. I figured he'd be around as soon as he heard about the shootin'. How's Teale? Have you heard?"

"He's in bad shape. I don't see how he did it, but he killed both of them. They came in on him like the two sides of a triangle. One of them called out something and when he looked around, the other man shot him. Then they both opened fire. He killed one of them, fell on his side on the walk, then just raised up on his elbow and took careful aim and killed the other. Never seen anything like it."

"You saw it?"

"I did. I saw it comin' before Teale did, started to yell at him and was too late."

"Jim, I've got to warn Trevallion."

"Warn him? Of what?"

"Jim, did you ever hear of the Clean-Cutter?"

"The Ax? Sure. He killed a man up near the Oregon border when I was out there. What about him?"

"He's here. He's in Virginia City."

"They all come here sooner or later, Melissa. This is where it's happening."

"That's not the point, Jim. I think he's come after Trevallion. I saw him talking to Waggoner, the big man who was asking about Trevallion? The one Trevallion believes got his gold? They greeted each other like old friends.

"They were in here, and I am almost sure I heard Trevallion's name mentioned. They were talking about Rig and Les, whoever they are."

LOUIS L'AMOUR

Ledbetter looked up sharply. "They're the two that tried to kill Jacob Teale. They were batchin' up there with Waggoner."

"The Ax knows Trevallion, Jim. Remember when we were first coming over the trail? It was back there at Dirty Mike's or Strawberry, I've forgotten which, but there was a handsome blond man rode by and he gave Trevallion a good, long look. I've seen him since, in California. It was the Clean-Cutter, Jim. It was the Ax."

Jim Ledbetter drank his coffee. It was all surmise. Still, it could be. The Ax talking to Waggoner, and Waggoner batching with the two men who tried to kill Teale. It did all tie together.

"I'll take a look around, Melissa. If Trevallion comes in, tell him what you've told me. Then no matter what he will be ready."

When Jim closed the door behind him, Melissa went to the window and watched him walk away up the street. Trevallion had said that Jim was in love with her. It seemed preposterous, but it might be. He was a good man, a straight, honest, decent man. Why was it she was only attracted to the others?

Christian Tapley was just leaving the mine when Ledbetter arrived. "Trevallion? I ain't seen him, Jim. Fact is, I was waitin' to see him. Figured we might go see how Teale is doing."

"Nobody can see him. He's in bad shape and needs rest. The way the Doc sounds, I don't think he's holding the right cards."

Ledbetter filled his pipe. "Tap, I don't like it. What's become of Trev? He hasn't been down to the bakery and he ain't here."

Tapley chuckled. "Led, give it some thought. It's that play-actress woman. Don't you know he's sweet on her?"

"Maybe. Come to think of it, I ain't seen her, neither."

"See? What did I tell you?"

"Well," Ledbetter said, "I'm going to turn in. If you see him, tell him to be careful. The Ax is in town. Maybe because of him."

In the blackness of the cross-cut called Forty-Nine a candle flame flickered. The charge had been set off at the place where the cross-cut left the main tunnel, but the resulting rockfall had not closed off access to the tunnel. However, only a few yards further along the tunnel ended.

The end of the cross-cut was only a few feet behind the rock where Grita Redaway sat. The air was still good. The candle burned with a steady flame.

Trevallion was on his knees as high as he could get on the rockfall, tugging rock after rock from its place and letting them roll back behind him. The stuff was too large for a shovel to be of any use.

His coat, vest, and shirt hung on the shovel which was standing against the wall.

"Val? Can't I help? I'm strong."

"Later. It's going to be a long job."

Dust had fallen over his back and shoulders, sweat had run down his back and chest, leaving little trails in the dust. He chose another rock, worked it loose, and let it roll back behind him. It did not go far.

"It's ten o'clock, Val. Hadn't you better rest?"

"I'll rest when we get out."

He worked steadily, carefully, with no unnecessary moves. He did not think, for there was no thinking to do now. He had known immediately what must be done and he went about it. He must open up a hole to let air come in before they exhausted what remained.

They could expect no help. By now the guards Margrita had ordered would be on the job, and they would permit no one to approach the mine.

Ten o'clock. He did not recall just what time it had been when they entered the mine, except that it had been late afternoon, say, four o'clock.

Six hours, minus, say, the thirty minutes or so spent looking about before they became trapped. He came down off the muck pile and sat down on a rock.

He was tired, but not as tired as he would be before this was over. Once before he had been briefly trapped in a mine cave-in, and some passing Indians had dug him out. He remembered how close the air had become, how the candle flames had burned lower, the struggle for breath as the air grew thinner.

"You're quite a woman," he said, looking over at her. "No hysterics, no complaints, no crying. So I am going to lay it out for you.

"There may have been more than one charge. Several small charges may have been placed at intervals along the drift. Remember that piece of fuse I found? Somebody was in a hurry and was careless."

"You believe it was done purposely?"

"Of course. Nobody leaves unexploded charges in a mine if it can be prevented, and if there was a missed hole it could not go off spontaneously. Somebody was watching, somebody who came into the mine and spitted a short fuse behind us."

"If more than one charge was set off, there will be more piles like this?"

"Yes. Or one continuous pile. More likely the first. In such a narrow drift it does not take much of a charge to block passage, and if they had several charges, which could have been exploded almost simultaneously, there may be fifty or sixty yards of rock to get through."

"It seems a lot." She was watching him. It was amazing how cool he was. She could almost see his mind working, and she knew that when he talked to her he was posing the problem for himself, facing it, selecting eventualities. He had commented that she had not gone into hysterics. Well, he hadn't either. She had never seen anyone so calm.

"Too much. If they did that we'll not make it without help, and there will be no help. In a way," he added, "that makes it easier."

"*Easier!*"

He smiled. "Of course. Then we don't sit around waiting for something to happen. We know that if it is done, we will have to do it."

"Do you think Albert Hesketh did this?"

"Who else?"

"Why should he hate us so much?"

Trevallion shrugged. "I doubt if he does. If I measure the man correctly, we are a nuisance he is eliminating. He removes us just as he might remove a boulder from a road or a spot from his coat."

"He bothers me. Sometimes I almost think I've seen him before somewhere."

"I think you did. I think you saw him on the streets back in Missouri."

"In Missouri! That's preposterous!"

"Maybe. It's been worrying me, too. There was a man back there who saw my father had some gold—one of those thick, old-time gold pieces. A doubloon. He was very curious about it."

"So would I be."

"This was different. And somebody instigated those men to do what they did. They don't even recall who it was, themselves."

He got up and went back to work. Steadily, methodically, he pulled the rocks loose and rolled them down. Sometimes he had to crawl back and clear them still further back. He did not look at what he had done, he did not consider the enormity of what remained to be done. He simply worked.

At twelve o'clock he stopped again. "Get some sleep, Grita." He used her first name without thinking of it. "Use my vest for a pillow."

"I don't think I'll need it."

"Use it," he said. "I'll work for a couple of hours longer."

"What do you think?"

He shrugged. "It doesn't look good." He took up the candle and held it close, peering into the hole he had made. There were more rocks beyond. The candle flame did not flicker.

"We've got some distance to go yet," he said. "Get some rest. It will help later on."

She made a sort of bed near the face of the cross-cut, and strangely, she slept.

He worked steadily, hollowing out a place no larger than necessary, just a crawl space, actually. Several times he stopped.

When he rested he tried to visualize the layout of the mine as he had studied it in the office. There had been an old working, nothing very much, yet a place where some previous prospector had sunk a slanting shaft into the earth not very far from where they now were.

But where?

And the cross-cut? He mopped the sweat and went back to work.

Work on the Comstock had never been easy. Several times miners had encountered hot springs deep underground and had to run to escape a flood of boiling water. The cross-cut was being dug to connect two drifts or tunnels that spread from the main tunnel in a Y formation. The cross-cut would connect the two arms of the Y, so it was unlikely there would be any danger from hot springs in that direction unless from overhead. Still, a man never knew. Mining on the Comstock had ever been tricky, and all a man could expect was the unexpected.

He worked steadily. His muscles ached with weariness, sweat dripped into his eyes, and they stung from the salt. He found himself resting more and more often. Was he imagining it, or was the candle flame burning lower?

He backed out of the hole again. He was in over fifteen feet and the roof above him seemed fairly solid. He mopped his face and chest with his shirt. Margrita was sleeping, and thank God for that.

His watch lay on a flat rock where she had removed it from his vest before using it as a pillow. It was after two in the morning.

The work had been painfully slow. Each rock he removed had to be pushed behind him, and as he worked deeper, the rocks had to be taken from his improvised tunnel.

He sat down heavily, blinking the sweat from his eyes. He belonged nowhere and was accountable to no one, hence would not be missed for some time. Nor would Margrita be missed until play time tomorrow, for this was already Sunday. If the air was going bad now, as it seemed to be, how much longer could they last? Another twelve hours? It would not be enough, unless, but who would guess where they were?

Teale!

Of course, Teale would return to the hotel and when he found she was gone he would make inquiries. Or would he? Not for a while, at least. He would assume she was resting.

Twice in the next two hours he had to detour around rocks too large to move. Whoever had placed the charges had been shooting down rock, not trying to break it for running through a mill or for mining purposes.

It was nearly five o'clock when he was struggling with a rock when he heard one fall away ahead of him.

He put out a testing hand.

Emptiness!

He backed out hurriedly, got the candle and crawled back, holding it out before him. Hope vanished in a cloud of despair.

About fifteen feet of space, and then another wall of broken rock.

He crawled slowly back to where Grita lay, and sat down.

Another barricade of rock, and then perhaps still another.

He felt empty and exhausted. Resting his arms on his knees he lowered his head and closed his eyes.

He was tired . . . so very tired. . . .

FIFTY-FIVE

Albert Hesketh awakened on Sunday morning with a sense of well-being. He shaved and dressed, thinking with satisfaction how well events had moved forward.

True, Teale was still alive, although badly wounded, but he was out of action for some time. Rig and Les were gone, removing a complication that had annoyed him.

Margrita Redaway's guards were in place to prevent anyone from approaching the Solomon, and Margrita and Trevallion had been disposed of. Or he believed they had.

Twice he had gone to her door and rapped. Once a maid had told him, "She's not in, sir." Then with a knowing little smile, "She went out with a young man. Right handsome he was, too!"

"Ah, well," he had smiled, "the less said the better, then. Don't you agree?"

"Oh, of course, sir! I'd say nothing, nothing at all!"

"Of course." He put a small gold piece in her hand. "I know you'll be discreet."

He dressed with his usual neatness and rode the elevator down for breakfast. Perhaps a dozen others were at breakfast, none of whom he knew. Salesmen, or mining men, in town to look over the prospects.

Albert Hesketh folded his newspaper and placed it beside his plate. He was thinking, coolly and carefully, of what must now be done.

He had cleared the decks of obstructions. From here on, it should be smooth sailing. As the largest surviving stockholder, he would have little trouble regaining possession of the Solomon. The tactics had already been established for skimming off the richest ore from the mine, but he would go further. He would file a claim on the Trevallion-Crockett claim adjoining the Solomon and use that to take out the best ore both from the new mine and the Solomon.

He watched while his cup was refilled. He was safe. He had been nowhere near the Solomon.

He took out his watch. Perhaps sixteen hours they had been down there now. If not killed in the explosion, they should by now be approaching their end. How long could they last? How much air was there, actually?

What would happen next? No doubt by tomorrow somebody would begin inquiries for Margrita. He could suggest to somebody that they had eloped. Such stories had a way of traveling, and soon everyone would accept it as fact. When he resumed work in the Solomon, he would start with a different crew and he would open new workings. Their bodies might never be found.

Trevallion was a tough man. As the thought came, he put his cup down sharply. At a nearby table a man turned his head, glancing at him.

Tough, but not tough enough. Yet, how long could a tough man last? How much air was there? Trevallion would certainly try to escape, which meant he would exhaust the air that much faster.

Had they left any sign on top? Anything to indicate their presence down below? He shook his head. Not a chance. What could they leave? And after all, his letter to Santley was there, warning them against going into Forty-Nine. He smiled. That had been a nice touch.

Albert Hesketh was pleased with himself. Despite all obstacles, he was in command. Will Crockett was gone, and now these two. Even the "tools" who might offer some kind of a clue were gone. Only Waggoner remained, the massive, stolid, uninterested Waggoner, and he knew nothing, and cared less.

The drift should be closed. Even if someone discovered what had happened, and there was no way, it would take a week of hard work to open up that tunnel. Four separate charges, and the amount of damage done to the tunnel would be extreme. The drift had been run into brittle quartz and clay, dangerous stuff at any time, and the relatively small charges would bring about a collapse much more extensive than in other types of formation.

He accepted a refill of his coffee cup and opened his newspaper. He had never liked loose ends. He was a man who preferred neatness. He wanted all the packages neatly tied and the ends tucked in. And he had done just that. Within a few hours, perhaps even now . . .

Opening his paper, he glanced across the top of it, and somebody was looming over the table. Despite himself, he looked up.

"Hello, Mr. Hesketh. Mind if I sit down?"

"I am afraid," Hesketh's throat was tight, "I do not know you."

"I think you do. We were on the stage from San Francisco together, Mr. Hesketh. My name is Manfred. I am an actor in Miss Redaway's company."

"Oh, yes! Yes, of course. What can I do for you, Mr. Manfred?"

What was it about his eyes, the chin, the way—

"You can do quite a lot, Mr. Hesketh, but first you can tell me where Margrita Redaway and Mr. Trevallion are."

"Oh? They are around some place. I, I am not among their circle of friends, I'm afraid. You will have to ask elsewhere."

"I am asking you, Mr. Hesketh, and I want an answer. You see, I know all about you, Mr. Hesketh, all."

Albert Hesketh was icy cold. It could not be. This could not happen. Who was this Manfred?

"That's very nice. I had no idea I was so interesting, Mr. Manfred, but then it takes very little to interest some people."

"I've been interested for a long time, Mr. Hesketh. For more than fifteen years, Mr. Hesketh."

With a careful hand, not to spill a drop, Hesketh filled his cup. Then he looked up. "Coffee, sir? If we are to talk we might as well relax."

"No coffee," Manfred said.

"Fifteen years? It seems a long time. I don't seem to recall—"

"You used to talk of loose ends, Mr. Hesketh. You never liked loose ends. Well, I'm one of those loose ends, Mr. Hesketh. I am a loose end that never got tucked in as you like them done. I am one of your mistakes, Mr. Hesketh."

Hesketh smiled. "Mistakes can always be rectified," he replied.

"Where are they, Mr. Hesketh?"

"I have no idea." He folded his newspaper. "I am afraid, sir, we must terminate this conversation. I have other matters to attend to."

"Of course, Mr. Hesketh. You have to do something about me, do you not? You have to rectify that mistake."

"I am not amused." Inwardly he was trembling with anger. Who was this interloper?

"You're such a *little* man, Mr. Hesketh. Really, a very petty little man. You have fancied yourself an important mining man, Mr. Hesketh, but you are not. Look around you, Mr. Hesketh. Take a good look because this is as far as you're going."

Albert Hesketh stood up. Inside something seemed to burn with a white heat. He fought to retain his coolness. "I am sure, young man," he said, "you have some sort of delusion. Go take a hot bath and lie down for a few hours. It will pass off."

Manfred smiled. "I shall find them, Mr. Hesketh. You can bank on it. The rest of the company are out now. We are looking, checking. We will find them."

Hesketh shrugged. "I hope you do, if it will make you feel better. They have probably eloped, gone off to Genoa or somewhere. Maybe even to Placerville."

"I think not." Manfred arose. "Trevallion's mule is still in the stable. So is Miss Redaway's horse. We're going to find them, Mr. Hesketh."

Hesketh went to the elevator and then to his room. He was trembling with fury tinged with sheer panic.

Who *was* this man? Why did he look familiar?

Again he consulted his watch . . . *eighteen hours*.

How much longer?

He must, somehow, get word to Waggoner. How, without being seen and recognized?

Suddenly, standing by his window, he saw the answer to his problems.

The Ax—the Clean-Cutter!

He was down there on the street now, but could he be reached, and would he act as wished? The Ax had always been the least known, the least understood of them all. Moreover, he traveled alone and had never hung out with any of the old Missouri crowd.

Most of that Missouri crowd had actually been drifters from elsewhere, men who congregated at the points of departure of the wagon trains. The Ax was a different sort from the others, seemingly better educated, always better dressed, and very likely the most dangerous of the lot.

Manfred would know nothing about the Ax, hence would not suspect him.

On a Sunday morning at the bakery, all was quiet. Melissa arose late, attended church, and then returned to the bakery. Only one baker was on the job this morning, a thin, tall man with sandy hair and bushy eyebrows who was a New Hampshire man, who dreamed of making his pile and returning to the coast to spend the rest of his life fishing.

"Harry? When you get the bread in the oven come back and sit down." Melissa sipped her coffee and glanced out the door. Across the street a blond man in a black broadcloth suit was tying his horse to the hitching-rail. As was often the case in the west, she noticed the horse first and the man after. It was a splendid animal, far better than the average drifter might have. It was the sort of horse only a wealthy man or an outlaw would be apt to have. Outlaws needed horses that could run fast and far.

The man looked up and down the street, then started across to the bakery.

"Harry? We've a customer. Draw him a cup of coffee and after he's gone, tell me what you think of him."

The door opened and the stranger stepped in, removing his hat as he did so. He was a handsome, blond man with a wedge-shaped face. She had recognized him the moment he turned to face the bakery as the man who had waved to them on that long-ago day.

"Oh? I am sorry, ma'am, but you are open for business?"

"We are. Come and sit down. Harry? The coffee if you please."

He seated himself at a nearby table, glancing around. "Warm," he said, "and pleasant. I don't know when I've seen a pleasanter place." He looked at her. "Or a prettier woman."

"Drink your coffee," she said.

He flashed a quick smile. "I will." He waved a hand. "Quiet today?"

"It's not noon yet. Most of the noisy ones are still sleeping off last night."

"Was that when the shooting was?"

"Shooting? Oh, that one! No, it was earlier. Broad daylight."

Harry walked over, stirring sugar into his coffee. He spun a chair around and sat down astraddle of it, putting the coffee on the table before him. "Figured they had him boxed. Come in on him from both sides, an' him expecting nothing."

"They got him?"

"Nope. They surely didn't! That ol' Jacob Teale's a foxy one! They come in at him and went for their iron, and he nailed both of them. They got lead into him, and he may die, but he settled their hash. Done it quick an' smooth."

"What was it about?"

Harry shrugged. "Who knows? They were newcomers. Nobody knowed about them but their first names, Les an' Rig."

The stranger sipped his coffee. "Must've been a reason. Teale work for somebody?"

"Yep. Bodyguard. He was bodyguard for that actress. Redaway, her name is."

"Redaway? Well, what d'you know! I've heard of her. I know that name. Young, is she?"

"Twenty, twenty-one, along in there. And beautiful. Best-lookin' woman you ever did see."

Melissa was not talking, she was watching the stranger. He was not just making talk. He was looking for information.

At that moment the door opened and Jim Ledbetter came in. He took a sharp look around, noticing the stranger, who looked up, smiling. "How do you do, sir?"

He emptied his cup and got to his feet. "Well, I must be off. Enjoyed the coffee." He placed a coin on the table and took up his hat. He shot a quick, sharp glance at Ledbetter who had stopped just inside the door.

"Lookin' for somebody?" Ledbetter spoke around the cigar tucked in the corner of his mouth.

"Well, now. I might be. I just might be! Ledbetter, isn't it? The man who operates the mule trains?"

"Among other things," Jim said dryly.

"You tell Trevallion that the Ax is lookin' for him. A.X. Elder's the name."

Ledbetter rolled the cigar to the other side of his mouth. "He knows your name. He read it off a gun you dropped when runnin' away."

Elder's smile vanished. "I won't be running when I see him again," he said.

"Then you ain't as smart as you used to be," Ledbetter said.

"Maybe you'd like some?" Elder suggested.

Ledbetter held out his right hand toward the counter where Harry stood. "Hand it to me, Harry."

Harry handed him a shotgun with two barrels.

"All right, Mr. Elder. Any time you're ready."

FIFTY-SIX

Trevallion felt a hand on his shoulder. "Val? Val, are you all right?"

He sat up quickly. "Sorry. I fell asleep. I was dead for it."

"I can imagine." As he stood up their eyes met. "Val, tell me. I'm a big girl now. Is this all of it? Are we not going to get out?"

"Not that way." He nodded his head to indicate where he had been working. "I broke through last night. There's just a small gap and another pile of rock. If we get through that, there will be another."

He stooped and took a pick from the floor. "I found this, though. Some miner had left it standing at the wall, God bless him."

She stared at him, not comprehending.

"Grita, do you remember that cross-section of the cross-cut we looked at up in the office? Did you really *look* at it?"

"I think so."

"Look," he said, "this cross-cut is like a bar across the top of a Y, or almost the top. How wide was the top of the Y, do you remember?"

"I don't know. I just glanced at it. I think—maybe it was fifty feet. In fact, I am sure it was."

She turned away, then grabbed his arm. "Oh! Val! *Look!*"

From under the planks that sheathed the walls on the right, clay was oozing, a long roll of it like the body of a snake that thickened and visibly grew as they watched.

"Aye," it was an expression his father used, "given time it will fill the place where we stand. It seems to come from nowhere, but it's in many of the mines on the Comstock. It's been lying there thousands, maybe millions of years, imprisoned between layers of rock, then somebody opens a space and it finds some place to go. Maybe it's been building behind the planks, or maybe that last explosion gave it just the start it needed. There are mines where men are assigned to doing nothing else but cutting that stuff away with their shovels and mucking it into cars to be hauled out."

He took up the pick. In the low blue light of the candle, her eyes were dark hollows in the pallor of her face.

"You believe that chart we looked at showed this cross-cut was to

343

be fifty feet when finished. Well, I stepped it off, and I've sized it up a good many times since we've been in here. It's forty feet or more from the other end of the cross-cut to the face, here. I think it is more than forty feet. That means the other tunnel may be no more than seven to ten feet from the face."

"But it's rock, Val! It's solid rock!"

"There's many kinds of rock. This is like most of the Comstock, it's decomposed feldspar and clay. Sometimes whole sections of the roof will fall in. It's pretty flaky stuff.

"Sit back a ways, and pray. Some boys in one of the other mines near here drilled into a boiling hot spring and shot boiling water and steam for thirty feet. Believe me, they got out in a hurry."

"There are hot springs here?"

"Uh-huh. There's places where the rocks are so hot you can't touch them. Several miners have already died from the heat."

He chose his spot and took a tentative swing at the wall. Just an opening, just a hole of some kind, to let the air in. Trevallion did not know if Grita realized what that blue flame meant. The candle was burning lower, the flame bluer, which meant the air was worsening.

He swung the pick, tearing loose a chunk of rock. With a double-jack it was about fifty blows to the minute. He wouldn't do that well with a pick, in this air.

He worked steadily, not thinking. The dim light shone on the wall, picking up stars from bits of mica. When he stopped working there was dead silence except for their breathing. No sound could reach this place, and no air. If anybody realized they were missing, they could not know, and in this mine might be the last place they would think to look.

He struck the pick into the rock and pulled away a good-sized slab. "I've got to be careful," he spoke half aloud and to himself, "or I'll break this pick-handle."

His body dripped with sweat, water he could ill afford to lose. With a cold, desperate fury, he attacked the rock wall. Pieces broke off and fell at his feet, some of them gleaming with silver. His body shone with sweat, his pants were dark with it. The heavy thuds of the pick and the gasps of his breathing were loud in the small space.

For an hour or more he worked without a letup. Then suddenly he backed off and sat down, his breath coming in great, wrenching gasps.

"Val?" Her voice was a whisper. "Are you all right?"

"All right," he did not look around at her, "had to rest."

He tried not to look at the face. He had made some progress, but pitifully little. The trouble was he had to open a fair-sized hole to allow use of the pick.

Grita got up. "Let me try."

He shook his head in protest, but yielded the pick. She swung it awkwardly, then began to get the way of it. Yet after a few minutes she backed up and sat down. "Give me a minute. I'll have to rest."

He took up the pick.

The sullen hours retreated behind them, the opening seemed pitifully small. Slowly, heavily, he swung the pick. His lungs sucked at the air. He could swing but once or twice, then he would have to rest. Again and again Grita tried. Her hands became blistered, the blisters broke, blood stained the pick-handle. He did not remark upon it, and she scarcely noticed the hurt.

The candle flame was bluer now, and smaller. He swung the pick and pulled off a good-sized slab. Once he would have been excited by it, only hours ago. Now he scarcely noticed.

They no longer talked, they no longer wished for freedom from the darkness, they scarcely even thought of air, they just *were*.

He swung the pick because he knew no other way. All his life there had been a battle, and all his life he had worked. He would go down working, go down fighting, go out trying as he had always done. Had he known how, he would have quit, but life had taught him everything but that. Savagely yet sullenly, like a dumb brute, he attacked the mountain. Bits of it splattered into his face, and sometimes it was wet.

The muscles, into which the swinging of double- and single-jacks had built power, ached desperately now. His hands were like claws, shaped only for the handle of the pick. Sometimes after a blow he fell against the wall and rested there a moment, feeling the hard face of his enemy.

Manfred pushed through the door, bumping the man who stood with his back to it. Not until he was in the room did he see the shotgun in Ledbetter's hand.

"Another time, Mr. Ledbetter," Elder said, and went out the door behind Manfred.

"Thank God," Melissa gasped. "You stopped a shooting," she said to Manfred.

"Maybe," Ledbetter said. "I don't think he would buck a shotgun." Then he saw the expression on Manfred's face. "What's the matter?"

"They're gone," he said. "Grita and Trevallion are gone, and I think Hesketh knows where they are."

"You mean they're *dead*?" Melissa demanded.

"I don't know, but I know *him*. I know that cat-that-swallowed-the-canary expression on his face. If they are not dead they are in extreme danger."

Melissa sat down slowly. "Jim? Where could they be?"

"How long since anybody saw them?" Manfred asked.

"It's been hours."

"What about Tapley? Has anybody seen Tap?"

"I'm here." He came into the doorway. "I was looking for Trevallion."

"So are we all."

"He was goin' to the *ho*-tel. He was meetin' that actress-woman, Miss Redaway."

"They might have gone up to the Solomon," Jim suggested.

"No reason for her to go up there," Tapley said. "What's a woman goin' to do at a mine?"

"She might be curious," Melissa said, "after all, she owns a good piece of it."

"Even so," Tapley argued, "why would they stay? There's nothing up there to keep them. Santley ain't there. I seen him down to the store and he was headed for his place down in the valley."

"Teale would know. He was at the hotel with them," Melissa said. "He always knew where she was."

"But Teale got himself shot," Tapley said. "How would he know?"

"He mightn't have been shot until after," Ledbetter said. "Maybe that was the idea. With him dead nobody would know."

"It's the mine," Melissa said. "It's got to be the mine. You boys better go have a look before it gets dark."

Manfred turned. "Dane Clyde is supposed to meet me here. Ask him to wait, will you? We won't be long."

"Be careful," Melissa warned.

Ledbetter started to put the shotgun back on the counter. Harry shook his head. "You keep it. You need it more than we do."

They started up the street together. Farmer Peel stepped out of a gambling hall and shaded his eyes after them.

"Cash me in," he said over his shoulder, "I've business to attend to."

He turned back to the street. "Jim!" he called. "What's the trouble?"

"Trevallion's missing. So's Margrita Redaway. We think they're trapped in the Solomon!"

"Hold on! I'm coming!"

Two miners, carrying lunch-buckets and still dripping from the heat of the mine, turned and followed. Along the street word passed from man to man, place to place.

Two more broke off from a crowd and followed, then another one, then three, one of them a gambler in his shirtsleeves.

From this place and that they came, gamblers, bartenders, teamsters, miners, and superintendents of mines.

"He's always been game," one man said. "I was there when he
brought the gold back from the Modoc country," another added.
"He was always there when anybody else was in trouble," somebody
else said.

Waggoner saw the line. He stepped to the door of his cabin and
shaded his eyes. *What the hell was going on?*

Several dance-hall girls, the madame from a popular parlor house.
Soon there were fifty, then a hundred, and a hundred and fifty.

Somebody ran past. "Hey!" Waggoner called. "What's going on?"

"Trevallion's trapped in the Solomon! We're goin' to get him out!"

Waggoner started to speak, glanced at the long and growing line,
then he stepped back inside and closed the door.

For a long moment he stood inside the door without moving.
Somewhere a little warning bell was ringing. *Get out! Get out fast!*

He shook his head, irritably. Why? He had left nothing to indicate
his presence, nothing at all. Everything he had taken into the mine
had been left there, and none of it belonged to him. How could he
be connected with it? And what was all the fuss about, anyway? Who
was Trevallion? And who was she, that actress? That kid from back in
Missouri grown up?

He had left his horse down at the stable to be shod. If he went
after his horse now everybody would wonder why he was leaving
town at this hour.

Sweat broke out on his forehead. He was being foolish. The thing
needed now was calmness. If the falling rock had not buried them,
they would have suffocated by now. They were dead. Nobody would
ever know.

Yet, any mining man would know somebody had placed those
shots, and not for any mining purpose. Questions would be asked, of
everyone. He thought nobody had seen him go up there, but how
did he *know*? There was always somebody throwing slops from a
door, shaving close to a window—who knew?

He passed a hand over his brow and brought it away dripping.
What was the matter with him? What was he afraid of? Yet he knew
what it was. The last time he had seen a bunch of men together like
that it was a lynch mob, but before they reached his place he was
gone.

He was all right. Nobody knew anything, except the man who sent
him here.

Nobody but him.

But why was the Clean-Cutter in town? Waggoner had never liked
the Ax. Too cocky and too sure of himself. He never saw the day

he could stand up to Waggoner. At least, so Waggoner told himself.

But why was he *here*? There had to be money in it or he would not have come. Whose money? For what job? And who would have known how to reach the Ax?

Probably a number of people, but one man certainly. The same man who had reached Waggoner. But why the Ax? What could the Ax do that he, Waggoner, could not?

There was one thing. And Waggoner was not a trusting man.

FIFTY-SEVEN

The guard stepped into the path as Ledbetter, Tapley, Manfred, and Langford Peel reached him.

"Sorry, boys. Nobody visits the Solomon."

"How long have you been on guard?" Ledbetter asked.

"Yesterday afternoon sometime. I been relieved once, then I come back."

"Anybody go up there?"

"Nobody. Orders were to let nobody go by unless with an order from Miss Redaway."

"You haven't seen her? Or Trevallion?"

"Nope. Nobody." He paused. "Well, come to think of it I thought I saw somebody over on the back side, but when I walked around there was nobody there. On a job like this you get to seein' shadows."

"We've reason to believe Miss Redaway and Trevallion may be trapped up there. We're going up."

"Now, see here!" The guard was sweating. "You just can't—"

"You want to stop me, Tom?" Peel asked mildly. "Or," he turned and gestured, "all those?"

Tom shook his head. "No, and if Trevallion's down in that hole, I want to help."

"We don't know he's there," Tapley said, "although I don't know where else they'd be."

Ledbetter turned to Manfred. "You've worked with her. Would she go down in a mine?"

"She'd go any place she chose to go," Manfred replied. "That's a woman knows her mind."

Ledbetter tried the door of the office. "This is open. Somebody's been here."

"They wouldn't walk off and leave the office open. Not even with guards about."

Ledbetter pushed open the door and went in. Manfred followed as Tapley walked toward the hoisting-engine house.

349

Suddenly Peel called out. "Boys? He's here all right. Here's his coat!"

Ledbetter started for the door but Manfred's voice arrested him. "Jim? Look at this!"

Manfred had the cross-section of the cross-cut before him. "This drawer was open and this had been taken out. At least, it was on the table. And see here—" He pushed Hesketh's message to Santley toward him.

"Forty-Nine. He says don't go near Forty-Nine and here's the chart, the layout, as if somebody had been studying it."

"All right, it's something. Let's go."

Outside Ledbetter recognized the coat. "That's surely his."

They were all gathering now. Ledbetter looked around. "Anybody here who ever worked in the Solomon?"

"I did." A big red-haired miner in damp digging clothes pushed to the front.

"What's wrong with Forty-Nine?" Ledbetter asked.

Red shrugged. "Nothing more than anywhere else. There's a lot of dangerous ground on the Comstock. Everybody knows that, but it's no worse than a lot else."

"Let's have a look." Ledbetter paused. "Better only six of us go down so we don't clutter everything up." He looked around at the assembled faces. "Please stand by. We may need you.

"Peel? Will you stay up here and keep an eye on things? I don't want anybody in that office. You, too, Manfred.

"Red, I'll take you and Tap, and Red, you pick out three good miners to come with us."

"Build a fire," somebody suggested. "If they find them they'll be cold when they hit the night air. Comin' out of one of those hot mines is an invitation to pneumonia."

"I'll get some blankets," somebody said, and turning, ran off into the night.

With lighted candles the six disappeared into the opening. Sticks were broken, a fire started.

Red led the way into the mine. "Been a few months," he spoke over his shoulder. "I quit. Didn't like the way they operated."

"Did you know Hesketh?" Ledbetter asked.

"Never saw him but once or twice. He stayed in that office of his. But he sure knew the mine. Used to come down and prowl around after the last shift went home. Sometimes him or somebody did some work around, cleanin' up, usually. I never knew why, but we'd see the signs when we come on shift at the change."

He gestured with a hand. "Forty-Nine's up this way." For several minutes they walked in silence, then suddenly the tunnel was closed by a slanting wall 'of muck.

Red held his candle high. "Well, I'll be damned! Whole damn roof fell in!"

"It didn't fall, Red. It was blasted. Look here," he held up a slab of rock, putting his finger on a small half-moon of a hole, "drilled, an' see? That band of quartz ran right over the top." He turned it. "Some good values in it, too."

"Maybe," Red agreed reluctantly, "just maybe. But what would a man do that for?"

They looked at each other. Finally Red said, "They had trouble with this area. She was always flakin' off. I was pushin' a car in here one time, and a slab that must've weighed three hundred pounds fell. Hit the front end of the car. I was all bent over pushin'. If I'd of been one step further, it would have wiped me out."

"If they're back there," another miner said, "they've had it."

"How far from here to that cross-cut? To Forty-Nine?" Ledbetter asked.

"Hundred and fifty feet. Maybe more. Been awhile since I worked in here."

"This is fresh," Red said. "I can still smell powder smoke." He gestured with his candle. "Let's go back to the other branch. We got to try it."

"No need, Red." The miner speaking was a stocky, deep-chested man they called Blaine. "That cross-cut opened up this drift, and they hadn't broken through on the other end yet. This is the only way into Forty-Nine and nobody has gone this way."

"Unless this was done after they went in," Ledbetter said. "Somebody has tried several times to kill Trevallion. Took some shots at him."

"If they are back of that," Blaine gestured back toward the cave-in that stopped them, "they aren't going to get out in a hurry. I know that roof, and if any of it went, fifty or sixty feet went. When we start to muck it out, more is going to come down. It's bad ground, believe me."

At the main tunnel Ledbetter paused, turning to shine the light of his candle up the other side of the Y. "You don't think we should look up this way?"

"No use," Blaine said. "That cross-cut hadn't come through. We'd do a damned sight better to start getting muck out and gettin' some timber ready. That tunnel will have to be shored up."

Red hesitated, then said, "What the hell, Jim? Come on."

Two of the miners stopped. "You have a look. We'll go topside and start things rollin'. We're in for a lot of digging."

Red led the way, commenting, "Be hell if we dug all the way back there and he showed up all hale an' hearty."

"He won't," Ledbetter said, "I know him. He never left anything hanging out, and never left a door unlocked. He's a careful man."

Their boots splashed in the pools of water between the ties. This tunnel was wetter than the other, and water dripped from the roof. It was dark and wet and very hot. Jim Ledbetter thanked all his gods that he had never taken up mining. How they stood it he could not guess.

"Ain't far now," Red said. "They put a few rounds in from here just to mark the spot." He paused suddenly. "Say one round. There it is, only three feet or so from this side."

They stood side by side looking at the beginning of what was to be the cross-cut, like a narrow, arched doorway in the rock.

Jim mopped the sweat from his face. "Hell!" He was exasperated and disappointed. "I was hoping maybe there was an opening all the way through."

In silence they stood, listening to the slow drip of water. It was utterly black where no candlelight shone, and water dripped everywhere. In most of the mines they had pumps going all the time to keep water out of the tunnels. He wanted to get out, to get away. To get back under the stars.

"Red, I don't see how you do it. You must have more guts than a country mule."

"Mined all my born days," Red said. "I've been underground more than I've been on top. My wife's always after me to quit, but what could I do? I don't know anything else."

He turned his head and the light from the candle on his cap shone for an instant into the arch of the cross-cut. "I—"

"Red." Jim's voice was choked. "For God's sake, Red, *look at that!*"

They turned their candles.

A hand—a white, slim hand—was sticking out of what appeared to be a solid rock wall!

FIFTY-EIGHT

Albert Hesketh straightened his gray silk cravat, pulled his vest down, and regarded himself in the mirror with satisfaction. The part in his hair was absolutely straight, every hair in place, his appearance impeccable.

Deliberately, he opened the door and walked down the hall to the elevator. All things were moving to his satisfaction. He was not only pleased with himself, but with the future which opened before him.

He would control the Solomon. By the time he lost control, if he ever did, he would have the mine thoroughly gutted.

Moreover, he had other properties awaiting development. A lot of men were going to become rich on the Comstock, and he would be one of them. George Hearst, they were saying, had already made over a million. It was probably true. Hearst was a shrewd man, and he bought well and worked hard. He had known what he was doing every step of the way.

And so had he. Hesketh permitted himself a complacent smile. His way might be different, but his way had been successful, too.

The dining room was almost empty when he took his usual seat. This was surprising, for this was a night when it began to fill up rather early. It was the custom for those who could afford it to dine at the International on Sunday evening.

The waiter came to take his order, then ventured a comment. "I didn't expect you this evening, sir. I thought you would be up at the Solomon."

Hesketh glanced up. "The Solomon? Why?"

"Well, it is your mine, and everybody is up there, sir. The word is that Mr. Trevallion and Miss Redaway are trapped up there."

Something cold seemed to turn over in the pit of his stomach. So soon? They might even be still alive. No, not hardly. "Oh? I hadn't heard." He paused a moment, knowing what he said would be repeated. "There's been some litigation, you know. Temporarily, at least, I've been denied access.

"Trapped, you say? How could that be? I understood the mine was closed and there were guards."

353

"I don't know, sir. The whole town's up there. They're very popular people, you know, so everyone who is free has gone up there."

The waiter went off to fill his order and no doubt to spread the word that Albert Hesketh was at dinner, "as usual."

His paper lay unopened beside his plate. Slowly he took the napkin from its ring and placed it in his lap.

Too soon. Altogether, too soon. He had not expected them to be found until tomorrow. The incoming shift would find the roof collapsed on Monday morning, and then there should have been an investigation. What had gone wrong?

He frowned, suddenly furious. He felt the burst of rage and frustration within him. To be balked, to be thwarted in any way sent him into a fury, but outwardly, he appeared as always, cold, without expression, the master of his destiny. It was so he thought of himself.

He ordered a glass of wine, sipped it slowly. All depended now on what was discovered. Nothing could lead to him, of course. Had he not expressly warned that they not enter Forty-Nine? That had been a nice touch. Rethinking it, he was pleased with himself. Even if they were alive, a possibility he doubted, other steps could be and would be taken.

He must think, must plan. He thought of Waggoner, then dismissed him. No, save him for later. He wanted to save Waggoner for Margrita Redaway. It would serve her right. It was Waggoner, Hesketh believed, who had precipitated the rape and murder back there in Missouri. This was a job for the Ax.

Trevallion was reputed to be good with a gun, but the Ax was better, better than Langford Peel or any of them.

He was having his dessert when the door burst open and a man came in. "They found them! They're alive! They're all right, and they're coming down the hill right now! They're coming *here!*"

There was a flurry of excited questions, and from the talk Hesketh gleaned a word here and there.

". . . almost through. Trevallion was cutting his way out with a pick. He'd gotten a hole through so's he could get air, then he passed out.

"That's the way I heard it. Had one hell of a time, I guess. Been trapped in there for hours."

"Done apurpose," somebody was saying, "shot down after they went in."

"Who? Ain't hard to figure out. Who stood to gain? Who could get into the Solomon?"

His back was to the speaker and he knew there were people

between them. Obviously, the man did not know he was present, or if he did know, did not care.

Hesketh placed his napkin beside his plate and arose very carefully and without turning around went quickly from the room. He did not wait for the elevator but went up the stairs, his heart pounding.

Keep out of sight—out of sight, out of mind. There'd be a flurry of excitement over this, but some other sensation would take it from their minds. In a few days it would be an old story.

How had they discovered the roof had been blasted? He had intended it to look like a natural cave-in, which happened often enough to warrant no comment. Somehow, Waggoner had botched the job. Hesketh swore, and he was not a man given to swearing. He swore slowly and with emphasis. Waggoner was a fool.

The Ax, the Ax was the man he needed.

He'd been only a boy then, a lean, slender boy of sixteen but with a thin edge of viciousness showing, and grown men stepped carefully around him. There had been a man who spoke contemptuously of him back in Missouri, and the Ax had cut him open. Just turned and slashed him across the belly with an Arkansas toothpick.

He was quick as a cat, utterly without mercy, and on tiptoe to resent any injury or slight.

Over the years that had remained the same. The difference was that he had become a dandy. He dressed carefully now, made every effort to appear the gentleman, and he had become efficient with both pistol and rifle. He combed his curly hair carefully and kept his hands and nails as clean as a girl's.

Hesketh nodded slowly. He must have the Ax. But how to reach him? How to pay him? The Ax was here. He was not only in town, he was in this very hotel.

Trevallion lay on his back in bed, his eyes closed. Once out in the open air he had recovered rapidly. Now he was simply tired.

He relived again that moment when his pick broke through and he felt the rush of air against his face. He had managed a deep breath, then he had enlarged the hole, and lifting Grita with his last strength he held her at the small opening where she could inhale deeply. He had fallen to his knees then, only half-conscious. He remembered a murmur of voices from somewhere, but he could not rise. It might be delirium.

It had taken them only minutes to make an opening large enough to get him out. Once in the open air he did not want to move, he just wanted to breathe, to breathe long and deeply.

Grita had come through it even better than he. Of course, she had not worked as hard or as much. She was at the hotel now, with Mary.

He lay with his eyes closed, tired in every muscle, but relaxed, thinking.

This had been a definite attempt to kill them both. The time had been well-chosen, the holes drilled, the charges planted, knowing they would inspect the mine. And that note, warning them not to enter Forty-Nine. As had been guessed, that would be all that was needed to arouse their curiosity.

In that loose formation where slabs were flaking off constantly, only a small charge or two was needed. Finding the pick, left by some miner's carelessness, had saved them.

Who?

He sat up suddenly. There in the tunnel, toward the end, every swing of the pick was a major effort, when he swung, struck home, slowly recovered, and swung again. He was stupid with fatigue, lack of oxygen, and exhaustion of spirit, and still something within him drove him on to try, and try again. How long he had stayed there at the face he did not know. Again and again he struck with the pick, sometimes with seemingly no effect, sometimes to see whole flakes of rock come away.

During all that time something kept nagging at his awareness, something striving for acknowledgment, for recognition. His brain was a vast, empty void, it seemed, where only the one thought remained, to keep trying. Yet from somewhere that nagging something, a shadowy face, a thin, pale face with strange blue eyes and a voice saying "May I see that?"

See what? There had been a man in a carefully tailored suit, a man looking for Margrita Redaway, a man who—

The same man. They were one and the same. The man in the street who wanted to see the gold doubloon and the man he had discovered in Margrita's hotel room were the same man.

He shook his head to clear it. Now wait a minute. Think it through. If the faces were the same, what of that other face, half-seen in the dark by the glow of a burned-down camp-fire? The face of a man who stood over Margrita's father and shot him dead?

The same man.

Trevallion swung his feet to the floor and reached for his socks. Slowly, carefully, he dressed, and as he dressed he put it all together.

The several attempts to kill him, at least one by Waggoner. And Waggoner had been one of them. Waggoner had money. Where did he get it? He never worked, but he was always supplied with cash. The obvious answer was that somebody who had money was giving it to him to keep him around where he could be used.

Trevallion finished dressing and reached for his gun-belt.

It was not there.

Then he remembered. He had removed it when working in the mine. Unless somebody had brought it out, it was still there.

He rummaged around in his duffle bag and came up with another gun, the one that he had found in the leaves after the man fled who had killed his father. On the butt was carved a name: *A.X. Elder*.

He thrust the gun down in his waistband and went out, closing the door carefully behind him.

Waggoner and the other man, the instigator of it all, Albert Hesketh. It had to be. It fitted.

An hour earlier, across town, Jacob Teale heard the story of the rescue of Trevallion and Margrita from the Solomon.

They must have gone to the Solomon, of course! They had been going there when she suggested that he have something to eat, that they'd be right back. He could have been the only person who knew they were going to the mine. Right after that he had been attacked by two strangers, and without warning.

There were two other beds in the room, but both were empty. Jacob Teale sat up carefully and swung his feet to the floor. His clothes were hung very neatly over a chair and he dressed himself, praying neither the nurse nor the doctor would come in before he got out.

He belted on his gun, checked the loads, then took up his rifle.

By the time he reached the International, his knees were buckling. He got through the door and crossed the room to the nearest table, where he sat down quickly.

A waiter came over to him. "Sir? Your rifle, sir? We don't permit them in this room."

Teale's eyes held the faintest flicker of a smile. "I won't keep it here long. Can you get me a drink?"

"Whiskey, sir?"

"Rum, I think. Some of that Haitian rum. Always wanted to try it and never have. When I was a boy I used to hear a lot about rum."

"Yes, sir. Just a minute, sir."

Teale leaned back and closed his eyes. Weak, he was weaker than a cat. Thank God, they had that elevator. It had never seemed of much account before. He had disdained it. In fact, he had never ridden an elevator in his life.

He heard the waiter coming and looked around. "I'm going to change my order."

"Yes, sir?"

"You know how to make a Kill Devil?"

"A what, sir?"

A black man who was setting the next table turned around. "I know how to make one. Let me make it for the gentleman."

Jacob Teale looked up. "Two parts light rum, one part brandy, a bit of honey, and just a pinch of ginger. Is that the way you make it?"

"Yes, sir. Sometimes there's a discussion about how much ginger, sir."

"Just a pinch, no more."

As the black man left, the waiter said, "Your favorite drink, sir?"

"No." He spoke carefully, hitching himself a little higher in his chair and feeling a sharp stab of pain. "I never had one in my life. An old man, I worked for him long ago in Louisiana, he drank Kill Devils when I was a boy. Always was wishful to try one."

He sat very still, holding himself tight against the pain. When the black man came with the Kill Devil he looked at Teale, then looked again, more sharply. "Are you all right, sir? Would you like me to call a doctor?"

Teale smiled. "I've had one," he said.

The Kill Devil tasted good. He tried another sip. He watched the black man setting another table and he sipped his drink carefully.

"Have you seen Mr. Hesketh this morning?"

"He was in for breakfast, sir. I have not seen him since then." He looked at him again. "Aren't you the gentleman who got shot outside a few days ago?"

"I am afraid I am."

He closed his eyes, resting them. His head ached with a dull, heavy ache, and his mouth tasted bad. Or had until he drank the Kill Devil.

He finished his drink and seeing the elevator come down he crossed, got aboard, and went up to the floor where Albert Hesketh had his room. He walked down the hall, rapping on the door. There was no response.

With his bowie knife he forced the bolt back, entered the room, and closed the door again. Then he crossed the room and sat down in a dark corner.

He was tired. He was very, very tired.

He leaned back in the chair and closed his eyes, his rifle across his knees.

When Mary opened the door, Trevallion was there. "How is she?"

"She's been asking the same question about you. Come in."

She closed the door behind him, and he heard Grita call out, "Who is it, Mary?"

She came out and, seeing him, crossed the room, her hands outstretched. "Val! You look wonderful!"

"I don't believe that. Not the way I feel. My mother used to say, when somebody looked very bad, that he 'looked like he'd been dragged through a knothole' and that's the way I feel."

"That awful place. I'll never go in a mine again."

"Grita? It was intended to kill us, you know."

"I know."

"And it was Hesketh. Grita, I know him now. It all began to come to me down there in the Forty-Nine. He was the man who killed your father back there in Missouri."

"Are you sure, Val? I've always had a feeling I'd seen him before."

"Be careful, Grita. Don't go out anywhere without Mary and Manfred. Four eyes are better than two, and six even better. This isn't over."

He glanced at her. "Do you remember Waggoner? The man who made trouble for you up in Six Mile? He was one of them, too."

"I know he was. He told me. There was some way he said we looked at him, my mother and I, that made him hate us. I'm sure it's all imaginary, because we never *looked* at anybody except in passing. He's a brute."

"And he's still around. There's another man, too. A good-looking blond man. I don't know him but he knows me, I think."

"I wish it was all over."

"Be careful."

She was so very lovely. He stood, wanting suddenly to reach out and take hold of her, but he did nothing of the kind. "We will never have peace until they are gone," he said, "and all these years I've known this day would come."

"Be careful yourself, Val, and come back when you can. In fact," she added, "I'll be at the theater tonight. Why don't you come by for me when the show's over?"

"Depend on it. I'll be there."

He went down into the street, glancing into the dining room as he went out. He saw no one. He paused a moment surveying the street with a quick glance. Nobody. He went down the street to the bakery.

Melissa got up when he came in. "Trevallion! Are you all right?"

He shrugged. "Why not? It was just like doing two weeks' work in two days, that's all. Jim been around?"

"He's around, somewhere. He's worried about you."

Trevallion ordered coffee and sat watching the street. It was a warm, busy day. Ore wagons went by, men on foot and horseback. Two beautifully dressed women passed on the opposite side of the street accompanied by a man in a dove-gray suit.

The town was changing. He could feel it. He looked over at Melissa. "The wild old days are gone," he said. "It will not be the same again."

"I know." Her tone was almost regretful. "Some of the boys are heading for Pioche and some for the Reese River diggings."

"They can have them. No more wild frontier towns for me. I'm settling down."

"With her?"

He glanced at her. "You women, always romantic. What makes you think she'd have me?"

"She will. She's no fool."

He waited, thinking. Yes, that was the way it should be, and deep inside him he had known it ever since that long ago time when he had held a trembling, frightened little girl in his arms, trying not to be frightened himself because he had to help her be brave. So much had happened, and so much had still to happen.

"Somebody tried to kill us, you know," he said. "That somebody is still here. But it isn't only him. There are three of them."

"I've heard the talk. I heard it when they went up to the Solomon the other night. There are fifty men in this town you've helped out of scrapes, men like Jim Ledbetter whom you found in the snow, like Dane Clyde whom you staked to a new start. They'd hang anybody who attacked you."

He glanced at her. "That isn't the way it is, Melissa. Every man blazes his own trail, saddles his own broncs. They can pick up the pieces, but what has to be done, I'll do, and they know it."

"Is—is that big man one of them? The man with the scar on his face?"

"He's one. There's a blond man, too."

"I know him. He was in here the other day. They call him the Ax, the Clean-Cutter."

He touched his waistband. "I know. I've got his gun right here. I'm going to give it back to him."

Waggoner locked his cabin door, crossed the street, and went down an alley between buildings. In the space behind one, he went into a stable where he rented a stall. He dumped some grain into a bin and wiped down his horse's back with a couple of quick strokes to smooth down the hair. Then he swung his saddle into place and tightened the cinch.

"Eat up, horse," he said, low-voiced, "you got a ways to go before daylight."

He stepped out of the stall; taking out his six-shooter, he spun the cylinder. Then he reholstered the gun and went to the door. From where he stood, although it was some distance off, he could see the back door of the hotel. For a few minutes he watched it, then shook his head.

He took out a big silver watch and looked at it, then slid it back into his pocket. Closing the door after him, he went down the alley and crossed the street. He waited for a minute, watching the theater. Nobody was around, but a janitor who was sweeping up. The door stood open.

At this time every day the janitor crossed the street for a beer. Waggoner waited patiently, watching. When the man went into the saloon he crossed and entered the darkened theater and went backstage to the dressing rooms. He found the room used by Margrita Redaway and entered. There was a clothes closet in the back. He entered, pulled a small box back into the room, and sat down.

He had been planning this for some time. She always came early and was usually dressed before the others even arrived. He had watched her, watched the theater, learned the habits of all the others. Now he would wait, and when she came—

First the mother, now her.

He settled back in the darkness. He had over an hour to wait.

He could afford to wait. He had waited years for this moment.

FIFTY-NINE

Trevallion stepped out on the street, removed his hat, and ran his fingers through his hair. He stood for a moment, thinking, the wind stirring his hair. Bill Stewart had been asking for him. He must see him.

His eyes scanned the street, missing nothing. He put his hat on and hitched his belt a little, easing the position of the gun. He had reloaded it, just to be sure.

It was all going to end here, today. He knew that, smiling a little wryly when he considered that he, too, might end right here. They had killed his mother and his father, destroying their dream of a new home in a new land. Would they make it a clean sweep and get him, too?

Albert Hesketh worried him most of all. Hesketh would never draw a gun and so give him a chance to shoot him. Nor was there anything he could prove. Supposition, yes. He knew that Virginia City would know him guilty, but there was nothing he could prove.

He had no doubts about Waggoner or the Ax. They were men who used guns, strong men, confident men, each dangerous, each very sure of himself, and with reason.

He no longer wished to kill anyone, yet he had no choice. They had tried and would continue trying to kill him. Moreover, they had tried to kill Grita. He was a fool to stand so long in one place and started up the street.

Virginia City was going about its business, mining ore, mining money from the pockets of stockholders, freighting ore to the mills. The stamp-mills were pounding, people were coming and going, all oblivious of what was about to happen. Generally speaking, it was none of their business, but after it happened it would be, for a few days, a topic of conversation. Then some other interest would develop and it would become history, referred to occasionally as "do you remember—?"

Trevallion knew it all. He had been there before. Suddenly a rider pulled up beside him. It was Ramos Kitt.

"Heard you were in trouble. I come arunnin' but you were already out."

"Thanks, anyway."

"Trev? Why are you my friend? You are, you know. It was on your advice that I started guarding gold. When I tried for a job, I found you'd recommended me. You knew I'd been an outlaw. Why?"

Trevallion was embarrassed. He shrugged. "I just knew you were too good a man to go to waste. A man does a lot of things when he's a kid he wouldn't do a few years later. So I put in a word here and there. It wasn't anything."

"You're in trouble, Trev. I'm good with a gun."

"You're damned good, but you just stay with what you're doing. A man's success he can share with others, his troubles are his own. I've got it to do, Ramos. You know that better than anyone."

Ramos Kitt turned his horse, then stopped. "It's the Ax, you know. The Clean-Cutter. He's fast, Trev, he's very fast. Don't try to match him, because nobody can. Take one if you must, but kill him. You may only get one, so put it where it matters."

He paused again. "His big fault—I've seen it—he *wants* to be fast. Prides himself on it. He will, most of all, want to beat *you*. He's so anxious to be fast that sometimes he misses that first shot. It's something to remember.

"And watch yourself on the street, like this here. If he can, he'll do it where it can be seen. He's awfully good, maybe the best ever, but he's a show-off, too."

"Thanks, Ramos. I'll remember."

Kitt rode on, and Trevallion turned the thought on the spit of his mind. He did not consider himself a gunfighter. He had never wanted the name or prided himself on the things he had done. A man doesn't sleep well on the bodies of the dead.

He wanted no part of the Ax. The man who concerned him now was Waggoner. Waggoner was a sullen brute, and he had made a vicious promise to Grita. Crossing the street, he took a passage between two buildings that let him out on a vacant lot. He skirted some old lumber and a pile of rusted tin cans and walked up toward Waggoner's cabin. There was no movement, no sign of life. His rapping on the door brought no response. He peered in the window, and the room was empty.

He peered again. Something about the room worried him. Some bachelors were notoriously untidy, others were as neat as any old maid, but this room was too neat. It looked like the room of a man who was leaving for some time, everything put away, even the coffeepot.

He faced away from the cabin, then started down the hill. A

woman, carefully nurturing a few flowers in her dooryard, straightened up. "You looking for him? I think he's left, gone."

Trevallion removed his hat. "Thank you, ma'am. What makes you think so?"

"He took his rifle and a blanket-roll and went down to where he keeps his horse."

"And where would that be?"

She pointed. "He rents stall space from the same stable my husband uses. He's riding a big roan now. Grains it a lot."

"Thank you, ma'am."

The stable door was closed but he went up to it, unlatched the door, and swung it open.

There were three horses in the stable who rolled their eyes at him, showing the whites. One was a big roan, weighing twelve hundred pounds if an ounce. The horse was saddled, blanket-roll tied in place, rifle in the boot. So Mr. Waggoner was packed, saddled, and ready to go someplace—but something must be left undone.

Grita . . . Waggoner was not so eager to kill as to demean, to crush her pride, to see her crawl. He had followed her up Six Mile Canyon, had cornered her there. Only Trevallion's arrival had saved her then, or so she believed.

Trevallion closed the stable door, putting the hasp in place. He headed for the International. There were a few people sitting in the dining room but he knew none of them. He went up to Grita's room. There was no reply when he knocked.

He swore softly. Now was when he missed Teale. Had Teale been with her he would not have worried. Now he was worried.

Where was Waggoner?

Trevallion returned to the street searching up one side and down the other. He stopped in all the saloons, and Waggoner was in none of them. He returned to the stable; the saddle horse was still there, waiting for its rider.

When he came to the bakery Trevallion went inside. From there he could watch the street, the doors of some shops. Ledbetter was there, talking to Melissa. "Did you ever see Bill Stewart?" he asked. "I don't know what he's got in mind but he's been talking to a few of the men whom he respects. He has something for which he needs our support."

"Not today," Trevallion said, "any day but today."

Ledbetter glanced around at him. "Trouble?"

Trevallion was watching the street. Trouble, of course, but his trouble. At the lift of a hand or a single word he could have help, but how would he feel if Ledbetter got killed? And there would be killing today. He could feel it.

Virginia City was going about its business, mining, buying, selling, drinking, eating, smelting ore, planning law suits. The problem was his own, not Ledbetter's, not Melissa's, or even Virginia City's.

"I'll handle it," he said.

He had scarcely touched the coffee when he lunged to his feet and went out the door fast. The *theater*, of course! What was the matter with him? Waggoner would be at the theater.

It was still some time before the theater opened, but Trevallion remembered Margrita's habit of arriving before everyone else. After all, it was her company and she wished to see everything was made ready. Unfortunately, if Waggoner had been watching her he would know that was his perfect opportunity to strike.

Trevallion hurried toward the theater. Ledbetter stood up, staring after him. "Now what the hell?" he wondered.

"Jim?" Melissa said. "Don't go. Please don't go."

He turned to look at her, wondering at the tone of her voice. "He said he could handle it. He knows I'm ready." He backed up a step and sat down, looking again at Melissa. "You sounded worried there for a minute," he commented mildly.

"I was, Jim. I don't want you to get hurt."

He shrugged. "Wouldn't matter much. There's nobody who'd notice. A man like me, he doesn't leave much space when he dies."

"I'd miss you, Jim."

Startled, he looked up. "You? Miss me?"

"Very much, Jim. I'd miss you more than anything."

He looked at her again. "Well, I'll be damned. You mean that, don't you?"

"With all my heart." She paused. "I've been an awful fool, Jim. It took Trevallion to make me realize."

There was a long silence, then Jim Ledbetter said, "And he's goin' out there alone, against God knows what."

"He's always been alone. Maybe he will always be alone."

"No," Ledbetter said after a minute, "I don't think so. He's found his woman."

"I don't know her, Jim. Is she all right for him?"

"She is, I think. Maybe she's the only woman alive who would be."

"Why, Jim? Why her?"

"She's been there," Ledbetter said, "since they were tykes. It's her, all right. It's her because she's the only person who ever really needed him. That's the secret of it, Lissy, to be needed."

"But she has everything."

"No, Lissy. She's an empty woman, and he's that kind of man. Since they were youngsters, I think, there's been a memory of something lost. Now they've found it."

The evening sun was leaving blood in the sky, the shadows were reaching out to reclaim what they had lost at daybreak, and the red faded to rose and pink. It was an hour and a half to show time when Grita unlocked the side door of the theater. The janitor was long since gone, but he had done well. She glanced around, making a quick inspection, walking down the aisles and checking under some of the seats. He was a good man, that janitor, despite the fact that he liked his little nip now and again.

The house was already a sell-out. The people of Virginia City loved their theater, which amused her, for the life they were actually living was so much more exciting and dramatic than any play.

She thought of Trevallion with sudden longing, remembering him as he had been when they were entombed, his calm acceptance of the situation and then the efforts to do something about it. No time wasted in recrimination. His strength had fed her strength.

She walked down the aisle and crossed to the left, mounting three steps to pass through the curtain to the backstage area. She turned to rearrange the curtains a bit, and she caught a glimpse of something on the floor. She pushed the curtain back for more light. It was a tiny bit of horse manure and hay.

That janitor! Just wait— She had let the curtain fall and had taken three steps toward her dressing room when she felt a stab of fear.

She opened the door and stepped in, putting her coat over the back of a chair. Suppose somebody had come in afterward? But who?

Somebody who had been in a stable. But none of her people had been riding today, that she knew. So if someone had been here, it was some outsider.

Within the great barnlike theater all was deathly still. The only sounds discernible here were the pound of the stamps. No sounds of passing teams, no voices. It had to be that way, or outside sounds would drown what was being said onstage.

She had to get out. She had to get out now. Somebody had been here, and might still be here.

Leave the coat. Leave her purse. But her gun was in that purse!

Nevertheless, leave it. If she showed any indication of leaving he would come at once.

Come? From where? The closet. If he was here, he had to be in the closet. If she started to run in this dress and her high-heeled shoes he would overtake her in a half-dozen steps.

There was a chair. It was flimsy, but if she could get it propped under the knob—. But to do that she had to move deeper into the room, up close to the door itself.

She could, of course, just walk out of the room. But it was a long way to an outside door and she had locked it on entering. She could never do it. The chair under the knob, lock him in the dressing room and then go for help. But suppose there was nobody there? What of it? People might say she was seeing shadows, but what if they did?

Pulling off a long glove, she stepped into the room, crossed to the closet door and taking the chair by the back, lifted it over and started to thrust it under the knob. And then the door burst outward and he was there—Waggoner.

"Cute," he said. "Pretty damn cute." He was even larger than she had remembered. He smelled of stale sweat and unwashed clothing. "How'd you know I was here?"

Fear was the last thing she must show. "Because you're filthy," she said quietly. "You left some horse manure back there. Nobody would be coming here right from the stables."

He chuckled. "Sly," he said, "pretty durned sly!"

The dressing room was small. No matter which way she turned he was within arm's reach of her. She had put her hat on the table. If only she could reach one of the hatpins! But he was going to give her no chance, none at all.

"Heard you lock the door," he said, "mighty nice of you. Gives me more time. Not that we haven't got aplenty." His smile showed big yellow teeth. "I been watchin' this place. Them other actors never come much more than thirty minutes afore curtain time. Thirty to forty. So I got you all to myself for nigh onto an hour."

"If I were you," she replied coolly, "I would leave now, while you still can. The men in this town will hang you for what you've already done."

"They won't hang me. I done pretty much what I wanted all my life." He put his big hands on his hips, staring insolently. "I'm goin' to do what I want with you, right here, right now."

Her derringer was in her purse, behind her on the table. If she turned her back on him . . . She dared not do that, nor to reach back. She must wait; maybe if he came toward her a step back would seem natural. If she could just get her hand on that purse.

Suddenly, completely without warning, he slapped her. It was like being hit with a club, and it knocked her sprawling. Before she could move, he kicked her. She just barely managed to turn her hip to catch the force of the kick and protect her stomach. It was not playful, but brutally hard.

Then he reached down and grabbed her by the shoulder. Long ago she had been taught a little about defending herself, and she knew better than to pull back. Instead, she caught his sleeve and jerked him toward her.

The action was totally unexpected, and he fell, sprawling. Like a cat she was on her feet. She was angry now. She knew she could not outrun him, so she pushed the chair into him, and as he was struggling to get up from it, she grabbed for her purse.

His flailing hand knocked it to the floor, and she kicked him in the face. He grabbed at her leg, but it slipped from his grasp. She grabbed wildly, for something, anything, with which to hit him. Her hand caught up a bowl of face cream and she smashed it on his head. He came up with a lunge and knocked her sprawling, her head ringing from the blow. He leaped to get at her, and she rolled over quickly and scrambled up.

Maddened, he glared at her. "I'm goin' to take pleasure," he said, "in chokin' the life out of you!"

"You're a cheap coward," she replied coolly. "I doubt if out in the open you could whip a full grown woman."

He swung a huge fist, and in dodging she fell over the fallen chair. He started for her, and just then there was a pounding on the outside door.

He stopped, and for a moment his eyes were wild, then they cooled down. "You call out," he said, "and you'll just get him killed, whoever it is."

Carefully, her eyes on him, she got to her feet. Her dress was torn, her hair in disarray, but she found she was surprisingly cool. *Think!* she told herself. *There has got to be a way.*

"I am going out of here," she told him, "don't try to stop me."

"You make a move toward that door," he replied, "and I'll break both your legs before I do anything else. And then I'll break your fingers."

He would do it, of course. She had no doubt of it. The banging at the door had ceased. Had he gone away, whoever it was? But who could it be, at this hour? Her purse lay on the floor. If she could only get that gun!

An hour ago she would have been horrified at the thought of killing anyone, now she realized she wanted to kill him. She even hoped she could. This man was one of those who had attacked her mother.

Suddenly she moved toward the door, but he was quicker. For such a big man he moved like a panther. He slapped her again, his hand open. His palms were large and thick, and he slapped her with utter contempt on his face.

"Think you're somethin' special, do you? Well, I'll show you—"

"I wouldn't." The voice was low, from outside the dressing room.

Waggoner turned like a cat, palming his gun as he turned, and Trevallion shot him twice.

He fell back, catching himself on the edge of the dressing-table with his left hand, his right still holding the pistol. Both bullets had hit him just three inches below his belt buckle.

Trevallion held his pistol casually, almost carelessly, it seemed. "Grita," he said, "you'd better step outside."

She moved behind him, took up her purse, and backed out of the door.

At the door she stopped, turning to face them. Waggoner was staring at Trevallion. "You seen it," he said hoarsely. "You saw all that, back there in Missouri?"

"We were back at the edge of the brush, Grita and me. I was holding her so she wouldn't cry out."

Waggoner's breathing was a rasping, ugly sound. His eyes never left Trevallion's. "If I'd of seen you I'd of stomped the life out of the both of you."

"No doubt. You were never anything but a brute. I'd not disgrace an animal by calling you that." Changing the subject he said, "Was it Hesketh who was paying you?"

"Hesketh?" Waggoner was obviously surprised. "Hesketh from the Solomon? Well, I'll be damned. Then it was him. He left the whiskey in that ol' wagon apurpose. Got 'em all drunk. Except me, nobody needed to get me drunk. I'd of been down there whether the rest come or no. That woman and the girl yonder, they passed me by like I was dirt. I figured to show 'em."

His gun swung up, but Trevallion had been waiting for it. The swinging barrel of his own pistol caught Waggoner's wrist halfway, and the gun went spinning into a corner. Stepping over, always facing Waggoner, Trevallion scooped up the pistol with his left hand. He stepped back into the doorway.

"You haven't got much time, Waggoner. I'd spend it trying to make peace with the Lord. If by some chance you should live, you'll hang."

He stepped out and pulled the door shut.

At the edge of the stage he paused to reload his pistol and thrust it behind his belt. Waggoner's gun he put behind his belt at the small of his back. He slid out of his coat. "Your dress is torn. You'd better wear this into the hotel." He put his hand on her arm. "Are you all right? Not feeling faint?"

"Shaky," she admitted, "but I'll be all right." She turned to face him. "If I'd had anything to fight with, I might have whipped him. I had no idea I could do that well!"

He laughed. "Let's go," he said gently, "you need some rest. You did all right."

The reaction was setting in, and she was trembling. He put his arm around her. "It's only a little way," he said.

She clung to his arm. "Val, I was so frightened! He's so, so evil!"

"Not any more."

"You—he will die?"

"Yes."

Ledbetter was coming up the walk. "You all right? I heard shooting."

"It was Waggoner. He's back yonder in the theater. He's in bad shape, and by now the shock is wearing off, and he's beginning to feel it."

"We had some shooting, too. In the hotel, I mean. Albert Hesketh is dead."

"*Dead?*"

"Jacob Teale was in his room, waitin' for him. When Hesketh came in, he killed him."

"Just like that?"

"Well, not exactly. Teale was in bad shape. How he even got over to the hotel from the hospital is hard to figure, but he done it.

"Hesketh must have been full of his own thoughts because he came in, hung his coat over a chair-back, and went to the sideboard for a drink. He must have been upset by something, because he wasn't a drinking man. He must have looked up from his glass and glimpsed Teale asettin' there with his rifle."

Hesketh had been quick. The instant his eyes fell on Teale, he knew what Teale was there for. He turned around. "Jacob Teale! Just the man I need! How would you like to make ten thousand dollars?"

"When I was a youngster," Teale said, "a snake got into our rabbit hutch where I had baby rabbits. You're like that snake."

"Ten thousand dollars!" Hesketh said. "I might even raise the ante a little because you're the kind of man I can use."

Jacob Teale lifted his rifle. At that distance there was no need to aim. Hesketh saw it, choked with horror and fear; he saw the long rifle pointed at him, right at his belly. "*No!*" he pleaded. "Not me! You don't understand! You can't—"

Teale shot him.

The blow of the heavy lead bullet slammed him back into the sideboard. Some glasses fell and a bottle uncorked by Hesketh rolled to the floor, spilling some of its contents.

"No! Please! You don't . . . don't . . ." He started forward and fell against the table, sliding off it to the floor. He started to crawl toward Teale. "This is wrong!" he whispered hoarsely. "It's *wrong!* Not *me!*"

He started to get up, his waistcoat saturated with blood. He pushed himself up from the floor, and Teale shot him again.

He was sitting there like that when the door burst open, and people rushed into the room. Hesketh was dead, lying at Teale's feet.

SIXTY

Only John Santley stood at the graveside when Albert Hesketh was laid to rest.

"I never liked him," he told Ledbetter, "but he was my employer."

"What about his piece of the Solomon?"

"He left no will. I don't believe he ever expected to die. Once I mentioned a will to him, and he just gave me a blank, unbelieving kind of stare.

"He had parents, I believe, but he did not write to them. With a search they might be found, and of course, they must be. There will be dividends."

Trevallion was waiting at the foot of the stairs as Margrita descended. He held out his hand to her. "You are like a princess," he said, "you have the grand manner."

She smiled. "Of course. Don't forget, Mr. Trevallion, that I am an actress. An actress or an actor is taught to play roles, and do it in a very convincing manner. But because a man plays a king superbly well does not mean that he would make a good king. The chances are he would make a very bad one.

"We all have learned to smile on cue, to be sincere when it is necessary, and to be most convincing at whatever we do. We are a lot of children playing games for grown-ups."

He drew back her chair for her, then sat down opposite. "I really don't believe that of you," he said.

"To tell you the truth, I'm not much of an actress either, although I believe acting comes more naturally to women than to men. Most little girls begin acting as soon as they are aware of anything at all."

"Well, you've a new role. You own a mine, and a very rich one. It needs to be managed."

"I know nothing of mining. I never so much as saw a mine until we went to the Solomon, and that's something I'd rather forget."

"You're doing very well with your theatrical company, and you can do just as well with the mine. The secret is to hire the right people, and learn enough to know what they're talking about.

"Will Crockett paid me to do a quick study of his mine, and I drew up a tentative plan for its development which I never got a chance to discuss with him. You can have that plan, and if you wish I'll help you find a good man to operate it, somebody who knows men as well as ore."

"Val? If you can find the time, would you do it for me? I've problems enough with my company. Maguire has finished building his opera house, and it's simply beautiful. I'd love to work there, and I must discuss it with him."

She glanced toward the door. "Here comes Bill Stewart."

Trevallion gestured to a chair. "Join us, Bill. What's happening? You've met Margrita?"

"Yes, I have." He grinned. "But I met her too late."

He was a tall, strongly made young man. With a quick glance around, he said, "Trev, I need your help."

He ordered a drink, and when the waiter had gone, he said, "I've never forgotten how you came to court when Sam Brown came to make trouble."

"You certainly needed no help."

"The point is that you were there, and I might have. I might have."

"That's past. The point is that I need your help now. We're making a move toward statehood, and we have to get out the vote. I want it to be a smashing victory to impress Washington. There's a lot of people back there who say we don't have enough people for a state. They say we're just a mountain at the edge of a desert with a handful of people. So we've got to make this election as impressive as we can."

"You'll have no trouble. Everybody I know wants statehood. Then we can have some decently regulated courts and some representation in Washington."

"Not everybody, Trev. There's quite a strong group, some of them representing powerful mining interests, that do not want statehood at all. They've teamed with some of those who are afraid of our vote on the Emancipation issue.

"Frankly, Trev, I am working with the President on this. He needs the vote Nevada can give him. He needs our support."

"What do you want from me?"

"You can be a very real help. We've two fiercely partisan groups here, and we all know how they will vote. There are also a lot of newcomers and fence-sitters. The fence-sitters haven't made up their minds, and the newcomers don't understand the issues.

"Whether you realize it or not, Trev, you've the reputation for being a solid character. You're one of the best mining men around, and you are liked and respected. They respect your opinion."

He chuckled. "Now, Bill, the fact that I know something about mining doesn't make me a judge of anything but ore and the lay of the land. However, if you just want me to say what I think, I'll do it."

"That's what I want. Just say it often and in as many places as possible."

He paused. "There's one other thing. One of these days very soon I'll be riding to the telegraph station. It is going to take me quite awhile to get the message off, it's a long one, and there may be some who would like to stop me. So I'd like you to come along, packing a gun."

He stood up. "Thanks, Trev. I'll not bother you any more to-night." He bowed to Margrita and left.

"Will there be trouble, Val? I was hoping that was all over."

"I think he's just being careful, that's all, and I'm glad to help. Sometimes a show of force can prevent trouble."

There was a low murmur of conversation from about the room, the tinkle of silver and the rustle of garments of the people passing. Yet it was quiet, and it was pleasant.

"I like this," he said, after a minute, "and I don't want it to end, not ever."

"It needn't, Val."

"What about the company?"

"We've two shows scheduled, and we've done them both, many times. *The Betrothal* and *The Colleen Bawn*. After that we will close down."

"What about your people?"

"Manfred is staying here. He and Mary are getting married. It has been coming for a long time."

"He's a good man. Why don't you hire him to take Santley's place?"

"He could. He's been handling most of the details for me ever since he joined the company. He's a good bookkeeper, and I know he's honest."

"The others?"

"They'll have no trouble. Dane likes it here and he may stay."

Behind them somewhere there was music, coming softly from one of the other rooms. They spoke quietly of matter-of-fact things, the little details of their lives falling into place to leave way for what was to come.

"There are things I must do," he said. "There's a timber claim I have in the Sierras. There's a need for heavy timber now since all the mines are using square-sets. I must open it and put a man in charge."

He stood up. "Grita, come on! Let's go over to the bakery. I want you to meet Melissa, and maybe Jim will be there.

"There's something I want to tell him, but I want you to be there."

"You've already told me, Val. You've told me all I need to know."

"This is something else."

The crowds were thinning out, the big ore wagons had delivered their loads, the night was growing more still. Up the street a drunk leaned against a post and tried to sing an Irish ballad.

Trevallion turned to her suddenly. "I can tell Jim when we get there. What I wanted to say is, I struck it today. I'm into bonanza."

"Bonanza?"

"A while back I started to run a short drift to the outside, just to get a better circulation of air, and to have another way out if it was needed. Well, I cut into a vein of almost solid silver. Not the richest on the Comstock, but rich.

"Tomorrow they will be saying I'm the canniest mining man on the lode, but believe me, it was pure luck. I put in a round and spit the fuses and left it, and when I went in this morning there was silver everywhere. The vein is so wide I can't see top or bottom of it, and it dips right down toward the richest part of the Comstock. I'm a rich man."

They stopped at the bakery. "I've got to tell them." He peered within. Jim was there, at Melissa's table. Christian Tapley was there also. He opened the door for Margrita.

"Trevallion?"

He knew by the sound what the voice meant. He saw passersby stop suddenly, and stare. Margrita's lips parted and she started to speak.

"Go inside, honey," he said gently, "it seems there's always something left undone."

It was the Ax.

He was standing there, feet apart, flamboyant as always, poised and ready.

"Why, hello, Ax," Trevallion said gently. "Are you getting lonely, Ax?"

"Lonely?" He was surprised by the unexpected question.

"Why, yes, Ax. They're all on Boot Hill. Are you wanting to join them, Ax?"

This was not happening as Ax had planned. All the speeches he had ready that were to be repeated afterward no longer fitted. It was his turn to reply and he was on the defensive.

"They're all gone, Ax, all that cozy little bunch of river-rats and scoundrels who were your friends. A pretty shoddy bunch, Ax, just like you.

"Nothing daring, nothing heroic, just a bunch of murdering scum. Just like you, Ax."

Ax was furious. The coolness on which he prided himself didn't seem to be there.

"Come on, Ax. They call you the Clean-Cutter. Now that's a pretty name. What did you ever do that was clean, Ax? When you killed two women back there on the Missouri? Or when four of you murdered my father and came hunting me, when I was a boy?

"I'm not a boy any longer, Ax. They tell me you're very good with that gun. That you're fast with it."

The Ax was trembling. He was so crazy with anger that he was literally trembling with fury. His hand was poised, ready.

He wanted to kill. Never in his life had he wanted to kill anyone so much.

"You know what I've got here, Ax? It's your gun. The gun you lost when you were running away. *Running*, Ax. All you bold, daring thieves, you were running and you dropped your gun.

"See? It has your name on it. I'll show you."

He drew and fired, beating the Ax by a hair.

The Ax took a slow backward step, his gun going off into the dust of the street.

Trevallion took a step closer, ready for a second shot. "Being fast, Ax, is not always enough, is it? I'm sorry, Ax. I didn't come looking for you. I could have tracked you down, Ax, but you came to me."

The gun slipped from the Ax's fingers. He started to speak, turned away, and fell.

There was a faint acrid smell of powder smoke, the lights of buildings shining out on the dark street, and on the darker, sprawled body of the Clean-Cutter, Mr. A.X. Elder.

Somewhere a woman laughed and a piano started a jangling tune. There was the distant pound of stamp-mills and compressors.

Trevallion turned and walked into the bakery. Grita caught his arm. "Val? Are you all right?"

"I'm all right," he said as he reached to hold her. "I'm all right now."